CRITICAL CONCEPTS

an introduction to politics fourth edition

edited by Janine Brodie and Sandra Rein
University of Alberta   University of Alberta

PEARSON

Prentice
Hall

Toronto

For our students

Library and Archives Canada Cataloguing in Publication

Critical concepts : an introduction to politics / edited by Janine Brodie and Sandra Rein. — 4th ed.

Includes bibliographical references and index.
ISBN 978-0-13-223766-6

1. Political science—Textbooks. I. Brodie, M. Janine, 1952– II. Rein, Sandra, 1971–

JA66.C75 2008   320   C2007-905990-2

ISBN-13: 978-0-13-223766-6
ISBN-10: 0-13-223766-0

Vice-President, Editorial Director: Gary Bennett
Senior Acquisitions Editor: Laura Forbes
Executive Marketing Manager: Judith Allen
Associate Editor: Brian Simons
Production Editor: Söğüt Y. Güleç
Copy Editor: Martin Townsend
Proofreaders: Colleen Ste. Marie, Betty Robinson
Production Coordinator: Avinash Chandra
Composition: Laserwords
Art Director: Julia Hall
Cover Design: Anthony Leung
Cover Image: Corbis Canada

Cartoons used with permission of Malcolm Mayes of the *Edmonton Journal.*

Statistics Canada information is used with the permission of the Minister of Industry, as Minister responsible for Statistics Canada. Information on the availability of the wide range of data from Statistics Canada can be obtained from Statistics Canada's Regional Offices, its World Wide Web site at http://www.statcan.ca, and its toll-free access number 1-800-263-1136.

2 3 4 5   12 11 10 09 08

Printed and bound in USA.

Brief Contents

A Great Way to Learn and Instruct Online

The Pearson Education Canada Companion Website is easy to navigate and is organized to correspond to the chapters in this textbook. Whether you are a student in the classroom or a distance learner you will discover helpful resources for in-depth study and research that empower you in your quest for greater knowledge and maximize your potential for success in the course.

Companion
Website

[www.pearsoned.ca/brodie]
Enter

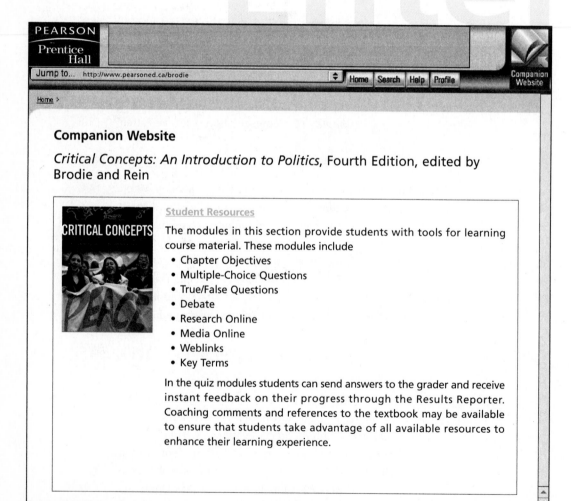

PEARSON
Prentice
Hall

Jump to...   http://www.pearsoned.ca/brodie   ▼   Home   Search   Help   Profile   Companion Website

Home >

Companion Website

Critical Concepts: An Introduction to Politics, Fourth Edition, edited by Brodie and Rein

CRITICAL CONCEPTS
PEACE

Student Resources

The modules in this section provide students with tools for learning course material. These modules include

- Chapter Objectives
- Multiple-Choice Questions
- True/False Questions
- Debate
- Research Online
- Media Online
- Weblinks
- Key Terms

In the quiz modules students can send answers to the grader and receive instant feedback on their progress through the Results Reporter. Coaching comments and references to the textbook may be available to ensure that students take advantage of all available resources to enhance their learning experience.

Contents

Part II FOUNDATIONS OF GOVERNANCE   73

Preface

This text explores key and contested political concepts arising from the Western tradition of political thought, the evolution of political regimes and institutions, civil society, and international and global systems. This fourth edition has a number of innovations. We have redesigned the introductory section on political thought to include traditions of political thought as well as the enduring themes of modern political life: liberalism, democracy, and radical politics. We have also expanded the final section on global perspectives to address "the West and the Rest," regionalization, global cities, and global political economy. In addition to reorganizing the major themes of the text and significantly revising chapter content, we have added new chapters on the politics of diversity, Indigenous peoples, and the environment. Our objective in this fourth edition, however, remains the same as in the first: to introduce students to the fundamentals of political science, to engage them with key and enduring debates, and to explore conceptual shifts in a world marked by growing insecurity, political upheaval, and global tensions. Most important, the chapters in this text are designed to challenge students with the political issues and ethical dilemmas that they confront daily. Each chapter attempts to frame these issues as part of the disciplinary heritage of political science and to make them accessible to first-year students.

Introductory courses are often a challenge for political science instructors because of differing philosophies about how best to acquaint students with the complex world of politics. Some are convinced that an introductory course should concentrate on the foundations of political analysis, most notably the canons of Western political thought. These instructors emphasize the study of great thinkers. Others prefer a course that serves as an intensive institutional primer, reasoning that students require a working knowledge of the mechanics of political life before they can explore more advanced subject matter. These instructors focus on key political institutions, such as regimes, bureaucracies, and constitutions. Still others suggest that foundations and mechanics will come with time and that the primary goal of an introductory course should be to offer students a sampling of the many intriguing perspectives on the political world that political science offers. Each of these perspectives has merit, considering the multiple and complex dimensions of political life.

There is no equivalent in political science to the laws of supply and demand in economics or the laws of motion in physics. Neither is there a neutral doorway into the political world. Any entry to the study of politics is already saturated by, among other things, history, political ideas, institutional constraints, prejudices, and power inequalities among political actors. Moreover, students come to their first course in political science already influenced by and engaged in the political world around them. Political science offers few road maps to move from the simple to the complex, in part because politics is always complex, especially for students who study politics in the contemporary era. The early twenty-first century has witnessed the erosion of key assumptions and institutions that helped us "make sense" of the politics of the past century. Added to this, the planet itself is increasingly under threat, not from military or political forces, but instead from our everyday lifestyle decisions, which have accelerated global warming. Increasingly, global citizens are challenged by "natural" as well as political threats to well-being.

A Chinese proverb goes something like this: "May you live in interesting times." In many respects, students of politics have always lived in interesting times. The most enduring work in political science has taken up the challenges of "its time," both to make sense of political life and to change and improve it. Political scientists have studied the ravages of war, of industrialization, of colonialism, and of genocide. They also have advanced the causes of human rights, good governance, individual well-being, and peaceful co-existence within and among states. Today's students of politics will go on to face many similar challenges, but they will also confront new ones in this new century. More than ever before, citizens are asked to consider the implications of their everyday decisions, not only for the future of their neighbourhood and country, but also for the planet.

This introductory text is designed to address both the fundamentals of political science and many of the current challenges to governance in the twenty-first century. It examines the critical concepts that we believe students should master during their first encounter with political science. Each chapter introduces a critical political concept, describes its importance in the study of politics, and outlines the debates that the concept has engendered in political life and for the discipline of political science. Each chapter also explores how the contemporary political environment challenges the meaning and relevance of these concepts. The text acquaints students with traditional debates in political science as well as those recently introduced to the discipline by, for example, feminists, ecologists, and post-modernists.

The text is divided into four sections, examining (1) the politics of ideas, (2) foundations of governance, (3) arenas of politics, and (4) global perspectives. The contents of each section are described below.

Part I, *The Politics of Ideas,* explores a broad range of conceptual and theoretical issues that lie at the core of the study of politics. Chapter 1 ("Power and Politics") introduces many of the critical concepts, such as power, authority, and sovereignty, that are developed in later chapters. Chapter 2 explores the enduring legacy of classical political thought, especially with respect to the questions of political leadership. Chapters 3 through 5 (devoted to liberalism, democracy, and radical politics) explore the foundations of Western political traditions and institutions and their critics.

Part II, *Foundations of Governance,* begins with a detailed account of the evolution of the liberal democratic state and its three principle forms: *laissez-faire,* welfare, and neo-liberal. Chapter 7 then explains the elementary relationships between the state, society, the market, and global interactions that lead to specific regime formations. The remaining chapters provide detailed accounts of challenges to core practices of modern governance, including constitutions and the rule of law (Chapter 8), public bureaucracy (Chapter 9), and representation (Chapter 10).

Part III, *Arenas of Politics,* explores less formal influences on political outcomes, including the most basic units of liberal democratic politics at the level of state, community, group, individual and, increasingly, the environment. This section begins with two key formal areas of political life: parties and elections (Chapter 11) and citizenship (Chapter 12). This section goes on to explore a series of social and cultural forces that increasingly shape both the context and practice of contemporary politics. These include community (Chapter 13), gender (Chapter 14), culture (Chapter 15), diversity (Chapter 16), indigeneity (Chapter 17), and the environment (Chapter 18).

Part IV, *Global Perspectives,* shifts our focus to the international and global domains. This section surveys familiar domains of international politics, including the international system (Chapter 21), international relations (Chapter 22), international organizations (Chapter 23), and global political economy (Chapter 24). This section also highlights critical tensions and new political forms that increasingly shape the global political environment, among them political violence (Chapter 19), global cultural clashes (Chapter 20), global political economy (Chapter 24), global cities (Chapter 25), regionalization (Chapter 26), and the persistent question of global poverty (Chapter 27).

This textbook has been designed to enhance the first-year student's encounter with political science. Each chapter provides study questions, suggested further readings, and websites for further research on the topic. Key terms are identified within the text and defined in a glossary at the end of the book.

Supplements

No matter how comprehensive a textbook is, today's instructors and students require a complete teaching package. *Critical Concepts: An Introduction to Politics,* Fourth Edition, is accompanied by the following supplements:

Instructor's Resource Manual. *The Instructor's Resource Manual* features a variety of teaching resources, including chapter objectives, chapter summaries, and lecture suggestions.

PowerPoint Presentations. A set of PowerPoint slides offers additional lecture aids for each chapter in the text.

Test Item File. This test bank contains multiple-choice, true/false, and short answer/essay questions for every chapter. The *Test Item File* is available in both Word and My Test formats. My Test is compatible with both Windows and Macintosh software.

Instructor's Resource CD-ROM. The instructor supplements listed above are conveniently available on one Instructor's Resource CD-ROM.

Companion Website (www.pearsoned.ca/brodie). An interactive website is available for instructors and students who use *Critical Concepts: An Introduction to Politics,* Fourth Edition. Visitors will find a range of interactive resources, including self-assessment quizzes, available in every chapter that can be emailed to instructors or teaching assistants.

Acknowledgments

Many people deserve our thanks and appreciation for their contributions to this ongoing project. First, the authors wish to thank Christine Cozens, Laura Forbes, Brian Simons, Katie Hearn, and Söğüt Y. Güleç at Pearson Education Canada, as well as Martin Townsend, Colleen Ste. Marie, and Betty Robinson for their editorial magic.

We also want to extend our thanks to Malcolm Mayes, editorial cartoonist at the *Edmonton Journal*, whose obvious talents, political insights and, above all, his sense of humour demonstrate that cartoons can indeed be a "weapon of mass destruction." Selecting the cartoons for each chapter is one of the greatest pleasures of editing this book. A library of his work can be found at **www.artizans.com**.

Last, but certainly not least, we thank Sandeep and Malinda for spending another year with *Critical Concepts* and providing their love and support.

Janine Brodie and Sandra Rein
Edmonton, Fall 2007

About the Editors

Janine Brodie

Janine Brodie is a professor of political science and Canada Research Chair in Political Economy and Social Governance at the University of Alberta. Dr. Brodie was elected as a Fellow of the Royal Society of Canada in 2002. Before joining the University of Alberta in 1996, she was also the first Director of the York Centre for Feminist Research, the John Robarts Chair in Canadian Studies at York University, and the University of Western Ontario Visiting Chair in Public Policy. She has published widely in the areas of Canadian politics, gender and politics, and globalization and governance.

Sandra Rein

Sandra Rein is an assistant professor of Political Studies at the University of Alberta. Dr. Rein's primary fields of interest include international political economy, international relations, and social theory. She is currently completing a manuscript on the early philosophical works of Raya Dunayevskaya.

About the Cartoonist

Malcolm Mayes

Malcolm Mayes was born in Edmonton, Alberta, in 1962. A love of cartooning and interest in newspapers steered him naturally toward political comment. He studied design art for two years at Grant MacEwan College in Edmonton and freelanced for a dozen Alberta weeklies before landing a full-time position at the *Edmonton Journal* in June 1986.

Mayes is one of Canada's most widely read political cartoonists; his work has been published in over 150 Canadian publications, including *Maclean's*, the *Toronto Star*, the *Montreal Gazette*, and the *Ottawa Citizen*. He's won numerous internal Southam awards and was nominated twice for a National Newspaper Award. In 1996 he published a cartoon collection entitled *Political Asylum*.

Mayes is also the founder of Artizans.com—a comprehensive online service that delivers digital artwork to publications around the world.

WEAPONS OF MASS DESTRUCTION.

The Politics of Ideas

There is rarely a simple answer for why political events unfold as they do. Political outcomes are the combined product of many forces that often clash and pull in opposite directions. Some of these factors are immediate and observable, while others are more distant and concealed, lodged in historical legacies and political traditions. There is, however, one inescapable constant in political analyses. Everything political is embedded in ideas—in the way we understand the political world around us. All political and social interactions, both harmonious and conflict-ridden, are informed and directed by ideas. The five chapters in this section of the text provide an introduction to the key concepts and different streams of political thinking that have structured politics in the West for millennia. The chapters in this section link particular ideas about politics to historical contexts; however, they are organized around the critical and enduring concepts of power, sovereignty, authority, leadership, democracy, liberalism, and radicalism. We will discover that the questions of how we ought to live together and govern ourselves have always animated political thought and debate. We will also find that the issues of fairness, inclusion, freedom, and equality rest at the very heart of political choice and action. Political life, however constrained by historical and structural factors, is fundamentally about the choices that we make and about the consequences of those choices.

APPARENTLY, I'M ON THE NO-FLY LIST...

CHAPTER 1

POWER AND POLITICS

JANINE
BRODIE

Objectives

We often encounter the flat assertion that "power and politics are everywhere." And so they are, but this truism reveals few guideposts that point to where and how to begin studying political power. The world of politics is multi-layered, multi-dimensional, and multi-centred. The study of politics can lead us to the most diverse places, ranging from the home and the workplace to political party organizations, international bureaucracies, and the realm of ideas. But to enter the complex world of politics, we must first equip ourselves with some basic conceptual tools.

This chapter introduces many of the critical concepts that will be explored throughout this text. In particular, we discuss the relationship between politics and power. We then explore a few of the many faces of political power, among them "power to," "power over," knowledge and power, sovereignty, and authority. The chapter next introduces some of the dominant approaches to the study of politics—institutional, pluralist, elitist, and class approaches. Finally, we touch on some of the ways that the current era of globalization challenges both the study and practice of contemporary politics.

Introduction

Aristotle, contemplating political life over 2000 years ago, made an enduring observation about the human condition. "Man," he said, "is by nature a political animal." Aristotle quite literally meant *man*—indeed, only the men of ancient Greece's ruling class. Contemporary political theorists now understand Aristotle's man as a representation of all people and politics as an ever-present force in all societies. Whenever two or more people come together, there is invariably some form of politics at play. Politics, whether we recognize it or not, informs how we think about others and ourselves. It flows through all social relationships. It is the glue that holds these relationships together. It also is the friction that erupts in disagreement and conflict, sometimes tearing apart friendships, neighbourhoods, nations, and the international community. Politics is all around us, not unlike the air we breathe. And, like air, it is often difficult to see, to capture, and to study. Politics, whether experienced at the level of the individual, the community, the country, or the globe, is constantly shifting. The push and pull of conflict and consensus mean that political life is always moving in directions that we can never fully predict.

The instabilities of contemporary politics provide an obvious example. No one could have predicted the terrorist attacks of September 11, 2001, although many explanations have been offered about why they occurred. Neither could we have predicted the ongoing ramifications of that fateful day in global politics or in our daily lives. Beyond the personal tragedies of the victims, September 11 prompted concerted military reprisals that have cost of thousands of innocent lives and fuelled a proliferation of terrorist activity across the globe. The ill-planned occupation of Iraq by a "coalition of the willing" and the execution of its brutal dictator, Saddam Hussein, moreover, have failed to usher in a new era of democratization in this war-torn country. Instead, Iraq continues to be ravaged by sectarian violence, an almost complete breakdown in the rule of law, and levels of insecurity unknown under the previous regime. In a few short years, the optimism that rang out at the beginning of the new millennium has dramatically given way to the destructive unilateralism of an angry superpower, strained international alliances, intensified surveillance, increased racial profiling, assaulted individual liberties, and, of course, endless queues at airports. In the contemporary era, security has become the overarching priority of governments around the world, but, paradoxically, we all feel less secure in the face of mounting tensions between clashing world views, global warming, and relentless economic competition.

Uncertainty and unpredictability were, for Karl Mannheim, writing over 70 years ago, at the very heart of the definition of politics. He drew a fundamental distinction between administration and politics. The administration of our daily lives was routinized, rule-based, and predictable—what he called the "routine affairs of the state." Politics, in contrast, was the play of irrational forces, social competition, and struggle. Mannheim identified two main sources of uncertainty that still fuel political struggles around the globe—uncontrolled competition and domination by force. Both conditions, he argued, "constitute the realm of social life which is still unorganized and where politics becomes necessary" (1936, 115–116).

Despite ongoing and emergent challenges, politics is an "essential human activity of deciding how to live together in communities" (Tansey, 2004, xv) of all kinds—local, national, and global. How, then, are we to understand, let alone study, something that is so fundamental to our daily lives and yet so fluid and so unpredictable? Some argue that an all-embracing approach to the study of politics, one that sees its operations and consequences everywhere, is not very useful. How are we to distinguish a political relationship from other kinds of relationships? If politics is everywhere, they point out, then it is nowhere.

The discipline of political science rests on the basic premise that politics does have a number of defining characteristics that make it amenable to study. While there is considerable debate about what these characteristics are, political scientists agree on at least one point of departure. Politics is about power, and political science is devoted to the study of its various distributions, uses, and outcomes. Who has political power, and why? How does it flow through institutions and societies, and to what end? Can it be used ethically to build a better society?

Politics and Power

UNDERSTANDING THE FUNDAMENTAL LINKS BETWEEN ETHICS, POLITICS, AND POWER has been a perennial issue for students of politics. Niccolò Machiavelli (1469–1527) is sometimes called the first modern political scientist because he distinguished between the "is" and the "ought" of politics. While religious and ethical codes may prescribe to us what action ideally we ought to take, the grim realities of politics are more often concerned with what is possible, although not always fair or desirable. Almost 500 years ago, Machiavelli, in his famous book, *The Prince*, advised the ruling elite of Italy to give up any notion of governing according to ethical ideals and, instead, to use the power of both force and persuasion to disarm opponents. He believed that ethical codes and the demands of political survival often conflicted and that princes sometimes had to act unethically to hold onto political power. The end—staying in power—could justify unethical and brutal means.

For Machiavelli, politics was mostly about the effective exercise and consolidation of political power and position. Early in the twentieth century, the great Russian revolutionary Vladimir Lenin defined politics in a similar way as "who does what to whom" (quoted in Guy, 1995, 5). Perhaps the most often quoted definition of politics, however, comes from Harold Lasswell, a distinguished American political scientist writing in the 1930s. For him, the study of politics was about "who gets what, when, and how" (1936).

Yet to say that politics is about the exercise of power only raises the obvious question—what is **power**? Most political scientists agree about the ubiquity of power. As Amos Hawley explains, "every act is an exercise of power, every social relationship is a power equation, and every social group or system is an organization of power" (1963, 433). Think about how often in our daily conversations or in the media we hear the word "power." This person has power, that person is seduced by power, another person is "on a power trip," while Ford trucks have more power and Sidney Crosby has perfected the power play. Do these various usages convey the same or different meanings?

In fact, we find little consensus in political science about the meaning of power. Like politics, it has many faces. There are literally dozens of definitions of power. At the most basic level, power is understood as "bringing about consequences." Power, in other words, makes something happen that probably would not happen in its absence. But, beyond that, there is widespread disagreement about the fundamentals of power. For example, how is power acquired? Is it through wealth, knowledge, cunning, good looks, force, race, or something else? How do we experience power? Is it through ideas, influence, coercion, violence, or some other mechanism? Are we even aware when power is weighing down on us? Who benefits—individuals, select groups, or the community as a whole? Who decides how power will be used (Philp, 1985, 635)?

"Power to" and "Power over"

Political scientists have generally treated power in one of two ways: either as power *to do* something or as power *over* something. "**Power to**" connotes the capacity to realize personal or collective goals or, in today's parlance, "being empowered" (Kourvetaris, 1997, 41). The popular notion that, in democratic systems, power ultimately rests in the hands of citizens conveys the idea of "power to" realize social consensus and collective goals through democratic institutions, such as fair elections and representative legislative assemblies. Through democratic practices, citizens are supposed to be able to decide how best to live together in national communities, to hold their political leaders accountable for their actions, and, if need be, to throw them out of office.

For political cynics, this idea of "power to" is, at best, naive and, at worst, an outright sham. They argue that people are encouraged to believe that they can change political outcomes or govern themselves democratically when, in fact, the present and the future are already determined by the capitalist class, political elites, faceless bureaucrats, the military-industrial complex, the world's only superpower . . . the list of potential conspirators is endless. Clearly, political power is unevenly divided even in the most equalitarian of societies as well as among the international community of national states. But any suggestion that we are powerless to shape the kind of society in which we want to live also does not square with history. One need only think of the whistle-blower at Enron, the lone student staring down a tank in Tiananmen Square, the droves of Yugoslavians who packed the streets until Slobodan Milosevic left office, the Lebanese that stood vigil until Syria withdrew from their country, or Rosa Parks, who refused to go to the back of the bus in a racist American South to realize that people, both individually and collectively, have the power to bring about political change. The fight for political change may be protracted and bring only partial victories. Political action also exacts costs, whether it is the small investment of time to attend a political rally or write a letter to a public official or the ultimate price of one's life. If the graveyard of history is filled with political elites, even larger graveyards are filled with those who opposed them.

The notion of **power over** focuses our attention on inequalities in the distribution of power, as well as the forces that hold regimes of inequality in place. It tells us that politics is often the result of the interplay between empowerment and disempowerment. The idea of power over reminds us that there are forces outside our direct control that constrain and direct our actions, making us do things that we would not otherwise do and that might be contrary to our interests and well-being. Robert Dahl's definition of power is a good example of the idea of "power over." For Dahl, "*A* has power to the extent that *A* makes *B* do something that *B* would not otherwise do" (1961, 203). Dahl's thinking about power is often associated with the **behavioural approach** to politics that dominated Canadian and American political science thinking in the 1960s and 1970s. Behaviouralists advocated the scientific study of politics, focusing especially on the behaviour of individuals. They assumed that, in much the same way as natural scientists were able to discover the building blocks of nature, political scientists could discover the laws of politics and thus predict the occurrence of such things as electoral outcomes, wars, and revolutions.

Political scientists, unfortunately, have proven time and again that politics defies regularity and prediction. We were not able to predict the collapse of Soviet-style communism in 1989 or the attacks of September 11, although, arguably, these are the two most significant political events underlying contemporary politics. To be fair, economists, wedded to the science of the market, have not done much better, being unable to predict with precision the onset of the nine deep recessions that have hit capitalist economies since the Great Depression of the 1930s. The problem, it would seem, is not the discipline of study but, instead, the questionable assumption that the complexity of human relations can be reduced to timeless scientific generalities.

Ahistorical and individualized approaches to power contrast greatly with societal approaches, such as **class analysis**, which locate the sources of politics and conflict in the historical organization, the structures, of different kinds of societies. Consider, for example, the depiction of "power over" provided by Karl Marx and Friedrich Engels in the *Communist Manifesto*. "The history of all hitherto existing society," they write, "is the history of class struggles. Freeman and slave, patrician and plebeian, lord and serf, guildmaster and journeyman, in a word, oppressor and oppressed, stood in opposition to one another" (Marx and Engels, 1998, 34). Marx and Engels, and many after them, were trying to convey an important point: people are political animals; they are also born into specific historical contexts and patterns of politics before they take their first breath of air.

Class analysis focuses almost exclusively on the systemic inequalities arising from the organization of economies according to the principles of capitalism. At different times and in different places, however, to be born black, indigenous, female, gay, or a member of a religious or ethnic minority, to name a few examples, was already to be in a position of being subjected to "power over" within the broader historical contexts of racism, sexism, and colonialism. These and other foundations for systemic oppression, grounded in social structures, invariably meet resistance and often survive only through the exercise of force. To paraphrase Marx, people engage with a political world that is marked by profound imbalances in political resources—in other words, under conditions not of their own choosing.

Power and Knowledge

Post-modern political theorists, such as Michel Foucault, reject the idea that power is simply a thing to possess or to hold over other people. Foucault argued that thinking about power as something outside us, to be gained, lost, or used to empower or to disempower is not the only or perhaps the most appropriate way to understand the operation of power in contemporary societies. Instead, he suggested that the "real power" of power is productive. For Foucault, we never stand outside power but instead are created (produced) by it. Power runs through all social relations and, indeed, through our bodies like capillaries. These capillaries of power can be so innocuous, even commonsensical, as to be undetectable. They nonetheless have a defining influence on the way we think and behave, not only in politics but in every waking moment.

Foucault argued that the nature and exercise of power shifted with the transition from feudalism to modernity. In earlier times, monarchs exercised ultimate or sovereign power over their subjects, as suggested in the phrase "off with their heads!" Foucault explains that in modern societies, however, non-sovereign forms of power have become far more important than the non-negotiable and often brutal exercise of the power of the sovereign. Non-sovereign power is embedded in the way we think about things, in knowledge systems that tell us what exists, who we are, what is true. He used the term "discourse" to convey the idea of the inseparability of power and knowledge. For Foucault, discourses embody "an accumulation of concepts, practices, statements and beliefs" that "necessarily extend beyond language" (2003, 40, xix). By advancing particular ways of thinking and acting as unchallenged realities—the truth—discourses produce societies and social relations in their own image. By way of example, think about the kinds of power relations that emanate from two opposing truth claims: (1) our future is pre-determined by forces outside our comprehension or control; (2) our future is determined by our own actions.

Foucault expanded modern thinking about power to include the ideas of **disciplinary power** and **dividing practices**. Disciplinary power exacts appropriate behaviours, not through force but by defining what is normal. Dividing practices stigmatize those who do not fit the mould by naming them scientifically as being different or abnormal. People exercise productive power over themselves and others quite unconsciously. For example, when a scientific discourse defines what is normal, we discipline ourselves to fit this definition in order to avoid social rejection and, in turn, reject those who, through dividing practices, do not conform. Long before we act, we have power inscribed on us through these disciplinary and dividing practices. As Foucault explains, power and knowledge directly imply one another. This means that there can be no knowledge "out there" that is free of power relations to be used for good or evil. Claims to knowledge are also claims to power. Fields of knowledge categorize, discipline, and divide people for the purposes of social control. Modern governments, Foucault argued, use these various categories to manage populations.

Foucault's work focused on the dividing and disciplinary practices that came out of the scientific naming of homosexuals, the mentally ill, and criminals. More generally, Foucault argued that the accepted truths of knowledge and their resulting disciplinary practices are like a panopticon. The panopticon was a model prison designed such that the prisoners could always be watched but could never see the guard. The beauty of the design was that prisoners would eventually come to behave as if they were being watched even when they were not (Fink-Eitel, 1992, 50). Foucault used the analogy of the panopticon to convey the idea that knowledge systems work in the same way, producing appropriate behaviours without coercing them.

Foucault's approach to power has been criticized for being too all-encompassing and for effectively foreclosing the possibility of individual action, political contestation, and political change. Foucault, however, rejected this interpretation of his work. He argued that disciplinary power always evokes some form of political resistance to its form of truth-telling. He also recognized, however, that there were situations where opportunities for political opposition were limited, but he called these examples of domination, rather than power. Foucault argued that some states of domination can be so complete that there is no room for resistance. "Slavery," for example, "is not a power relationship when man is in chains" (quoted in Simons, 1995, 82).

Foucault insisted that the exercise of power always presupposes resistance in some form or another, but he never had the opportunity to fully respond to his critics. He died of AIDS in the mid-1980s. His work remains important because it underlines the critical notion that claims to knowledge and truth embody power relations, which, in turn, generate particular forms of political resistance and conflict. His conception of power, moreover, challenges us to take responsibility for the power relations embedded in the way we think about the world and ourselves.

Authority

There is another stream of study that locates power in institutions and value systems. This approach emphasizes the idea of power as **authority**, rather than as force, although the two are usually mutually reinforcing. In cases of authority, governments secure obedience from the governed, without resorting to bribes or coercion, because the governed accept that it is legitimate for certain institutions and individuals in society to have more power than others. Consider the following two scenarios. In the first scenario, you are driving down the street and a police officer demands that you stop your car. You are likely to comply. In the second scenario, a naked person demands that you stop your car. In this case, you may stop but are probably more likely to lock your doors and speed down the street. What is the difference? It is the authority vested in a policeofficer's uniform. Authority is "socially approved power" that entails both legitimacy and impartiality (Kourvetaris, 1997, 51). Someone is accorded power and legitimacy less for who they are than for the institution that they represent, whether that be the police, the judiciary, or elected office. This legitimacy is often backed by the threat of sanction or punishment. Most of us obey the law both because we believe in the rule of law—that is, that everyone should be subject to the same laws—and because we realize that failure to comply with the law might very well result in a fine or jail sentence.

Max Weber (1864–1920), one of the fathers of modern social science, argued that societies have been governed by three different kinds of authority: traditional, charismatic, and legal-rational. He identifies **traditional authority** as the social glue that held together pre-industrial societies. Power was vested in certain individuals because of custom or heredity. The tribal chief or the king was obeyed because that was how it was intended or how it had always been. While traditional authorities might take advice from others, including a god, their authority was personal and incontestable. **Charismatic authority** is similarly vested in individuals. It, however, is grounded in the personal qualities of the charismatic leader, rather than in tradition or in birth. Weber argued that charismatic leaders tend to gain authority during periods of profound crisis and social upheaval. Their authority, he argued, grows out of "a certain quality of an individual personality by virtue of which he is set apart from ordinary men and treated as endowed with supernatural, superhuman, or at least specifically exceptional powers and qualities" (quoted in Bendix, 1960, 88). The social upheavals of the Great Depression in the 1930s, which saw the rise of fascist dictators, such as Hitler in Germany and Mussolini in Italy, provide obvious examples of what Weber meant by charismatic authority.

Weber saw both traditional and charismatic authority as waning in modern societies, which were increasingly governed by **legal-rationalism**. This kind of authority is based in the rule of law and in the bureaucratic and impersonal procedures of modern institutions, such as the courts, constitutions, bureaucracy, and legislatures. Legal-rational authority is accorded to leaders who hold positions in, administer, and abide by the rules of these institutions. They, in turn, are considered legitimate by the public only to the extent that they uphold established rules and procedures. In a legal-rational system, claims to authority, even by charismatic leaders, are unlikely to be considered legitimate unless they are framed within a system of legal-rationality. To put the point more clearly, no matter how charismatic an individual or how royal a bloodline, a person could not make claims to political leadership and authority in a legal-rational culture unless accorded legitimacy through, for example, a democratic election. Similarly, those in positions of power lose their legitimacy if they fail to adhere to institutional norms and expectations. Examples would include a policeofficer "on the take" or a political leader caught in an influence-peddling scheme.

Although these different kinds of authority tend to characterize different kinds of society, from the simple to the complex, all can be found in contemporary culture. A religious leader or one's parents or teachers make claims to traditional authority, although many traditionalists lament that these authority figures no longer command the obedience that they once did. Any day of the week, you can find someone on television linking the problems of the world to lax discipline in schools, a decline in religious deference, and the collapse of family values. Charisma also remains a formidable force in political life. The international political stage still affords a role to charismatic leaders. The somewhat perplexing leader Kim Jong-il governs North Korea through a cult of personality, both his and that of his father, the "Great Leader" Kim Il Sung. Yet in a world dominated by legal-rational authority, such leaders are condemned as throwbacks to another time and as anomalies that stand as obstacles to good governance and development.

State and Sovereignty

The rise of legal-rationalism is intimately tied to the ideas of sovereignty and the birth of the modern state. Traditional leaders, especially the rulers of feudal Europe, claimed sovereignty in their person. **Sovereignty** means supreme power. There is no question or debate about the right to exercise power where sovereignty has been established. In feudal societies, power and authority were dispersed and divisible, often shared and struggled for among the nobility, the monarch, and the Church. Gradually, from the fifteenth to the seventeenth centuries, coinciding with the demise of feudalism and the ascendancy of capitalism, political power began to consolidate both territorially and practically within the early predecessors of the modern state. These predecessors took on two dominant personalities—the "absolute" monarchies of France, Prussia, Austria, Spain, and Russia and the "constitutional" monarchies and republics, based on representative government, which were beginning to take form in England and Holland (Held, 1996, 66).

Under absolute monarchies, the sovereignty of traditional hereditary monarchs, such as King Louis XV of France, who ruled from 1715 to 1774, was effectively imposed on the state through the person of the king. Louis XV, for example, pronounced that "*l'état, c'est moi.*" Absolute monarchs maintained that their power was God-given, and thus to disobey the monarch was to disobey God, which was the greatest offence in these times. Absolute monarchies eventually crumbled in the face of democratization, class conflict, and the idea of popular sovereignty—that is, the idea that political power ultimately rested in the hands of all citizens instead of leaders alone. Absolute monarchies, nonetheless, provided the institutional underpinnings of the modern state, especially the centralization of political, military, and administrative powers within defined territorial boundaries (Held, 1996, 68).

During the past four centuries, the modern state has taken on a number of different forms, ranging from representative democracies to fascist dictatorships to communist regimes. Regardless of form, states share one defining characteristic—the non-negotiable claim to sovereignty. All modern states claim the supreme and indivisible power to rule over a national territory. This non-negotiable monopoly of state sovereignty was recognized formally in the Peace of Westphalia in 1648, which cast the world community as consisting of "sovereign states." These states controlled their own territories and could legitimately use force to repel threats to national security and sovereignty arising either from domestic politics or external threats (Held, 1996, 69). This idea of the fusion of power, sovereignty, authority, and legitimacy, which structures current thinking about politics, is clearly conveyed by Weber's often-cited definition of the **state**. He called it "a human community that successfully claims monopoly of the legitimate use of physical force within a given territory" (quoted in Gerth and Mills, 1958, 78). In recent years, a number of countries have been identified as "failed states," among them, Sierra Leone, Sudan, and Iraq. This term is used when states lose their monopoly over the legitimate use of violence within their territories, usually because state armies have been displaced by war lords, private militias, tribal leaders, and other non-state actors who exercise violence and control over domestic populations.

To sum up, the study of politics revolves around a number of critical concepts, among them power, authority, legitimacy, sovereignty, and the state. But political scientists have adopted quite distinct perspectives on how politics works within and among national territories. Next, we will briefly review four broad approaches, each of which serves as a guidepost to explore the complex world of politics. Institutionalism, pluralism, elite analysis, and class are only four among the many perspectives that political scientists have adopted to compare and explain the political world around us. Approaches are simply perspectives. They highlight one part of the complex matrix of political life, often to the exclusion of other aspects. Approaches to politics are neither true nor false, but they can be more or less useful in helping us understand political events. However, when we elect to use one approach rather than another, we also accept a number of other assumptions about the nature of political actors, the basic structures of social organization, and the appropriate ways to achieve political change. Theories of politics are also theories of society, providing answers to such questions as what the basic units of political society are and how power is distributed.

Approaches to the Study of Politics

Institutionalism

Early political scientists largely understood their task as explaining those things obviously contained within the political sphere, especially laws and political institutions and formal political processes, such as elections. Institutionalism provided descriptive and comparative analyses of different kinds of political systems and institutional infrastructures and, for the most part, applauded the superiority of the liberal democratic state. Texts focused on such questions as the differences between parliamentary and congressional systems, federal and unitary systems, a separa-tion of power versus a fusion of power, and written versus unwritten constitutions. A.V. Dicey's book, *An Introduction to the Study of the Law of the Constitution*, first published in 1908 and reprinted many times and in many languages since then, is a classic example of the legal-institutional approach.

The events leading up to World War II, however, created doubts that institutional-ism could explain how politics really worked. For example, the horrors of Nazi Germany could not be predicted or explained by studying its constitution. How could the politics of a modern industrial country with a history of constitutionalism take such a turn? Could something similar be prevented in the future? The institutional approach could not provide answers to these questions.

Advances in scientific polling after World War II also created doubts about whether liberal democracies actually worked in the ways that institutionalists contended. Institutionalists assumed that citizens behaved according to the prescriptions of dem-ocratic theory. In theory, at least, citizens were active and informed, could identify and prioritize the political choices offered to them at election time, and voted accordingly. Early public opinion polls, however, showed that most citizens did not pay attention to politics, that even fewer were active in political parties and other political organi-zations, that most had trouble distinguishing between the political right and the polit-ical left, and that most did not understand the implications of particular policy choices. This mismatch between political theory and political behaviour encouraged political scientists, overwhelmingly located in the United States, to rethink the rela-tionship between society and the state.

The questions posed by institutional analysis, however, remain important to political scientists today. In fact, introductory textbooks, such as this one, devote a great deal of effort to clarifying the distinctions between different kinds of political institutions and political systems. In past decades, there also has been a renewed interest in the impact of institutional design on public policies. Neo-institutional studies demonstrate that political institutions can affect policy outcomes quite independently of other political factors, such as national histories, political ideologies, and political actors. For example, recent studies show that the way we organize elections can have indirect impacts on pol-icy outcomes. Cuts to social programs have been less pronounced in countries with pro-portional representation electoral systems, for instance, than in those with plurality systems. Neo-institutionalists also point to the importance of ideas and policy frame-works that operate inside political institutions. Policy communities—that is, academics and bureaucrats sharing similar perspectives on policy problems—often have a far greater influence on the eventual shape of public policies than elected officials do.

Pluralism

After World War II, political science took on the task of developing an approach to politics that would explain the realities of modern politics and, at the same time, preserve the idea of the superiority of a democratic system. Strongly influenced by liberalism, the **pluralist theory** argued that, although the individual remained the key actor in democratic politics, the sheer size and complexity of modern society had long ago ruled out a democratic politics revolving around the informed and active democratic citizen. Instead, pluralists saw politics as the play for preferred policy outcomes among an endless variety of competing groups in civil society.

Pluralists argue that the governance of modern society is far too complex and the society too large to nurture the direct political participation of everyone in the political process. Instead, individuals join groups that promote their interests. Since modern citizens have many interests, they may hold memberships in many different kinds of groups, ranging from a parent–teacher organization to an association to abolish capital punishment, an anti-racist coalition, a gun collectors' club, or a lesbian and gay choir. Many of the groups to which citizens belong have a direct interface with the public sphere, but most do not. According to the pluralists, groups become politically active around political issues that affect the interests and values of their members. They make coalitions and compete with other groups for preferred policy outcomes. No one group is a permanent player in pluralist politics. Neither does one group always win. Different groups with different resources move in and out of the political sphere when their interests are affected. Politics is a constant play of groups that both advance the interests of their respective memberships and check the power of other groups. Everyone gets to play, and there are no winners assumed at the onset of a political debate. As prominent pluralist theorist Robert Dahl contended, "all active and legitimate groups in the population can make themselves heard at some critical stage in the process of decision making" (1956, 137).

The pluralist approach was very much committed to promoting the idea that both the democratic citizen and the democratic system, although somewhat modified, were alive and well in post-war America. The message of this approach was that democratic pluralism was a system of governance that could and should be emulated in countries emerging from the rubble of fascism and World War II, as well as in new countries recently released from the bonds of European colonialism in the 1950s and 1960s. Citizens were free to join groups, to advance their interests, and to choose group leaders, and, indeed, to become leaders themselves to represent their interests in the policy process. Just as important, the state was not predisposed to favour one group over another. The game of politics, in other words, was not stacked for or against anyone. Pluralists viewed the state as neutral, serving to mediate among competing groups and to strike compromise and consensus in public policy. From a pluralist perspective, the state processed group demands, or inputs, and converted them to public policies, or outputs. Officials inside the state did not adopt policies that were self-serving, and the institutions of government did not manipulate democratic processes to favour some groups over others. The strength of democracy on the ground, as it were, in clubs, groups, and communities, in turn, was a powerful preventive to the rise of authoritarian or corrupt regimes.

Elitism

At the same time that the pluralist school was advancing its celebration of democratic pluralism, the approach found powerful critics both inside and outside the United States. E.E. Schattschneider, an American political scientist and liberal thinker, criticized the pluralist school for misrepresenting the extent and nature of group membership in the United States. Most group members were decidedly middle-class, and most groups rarely engaged directly with politics. Schattschneider mused that if there were a pluralist heaven, then "the heavenly chorus sings with a strong upper-class accent." Schattschneider also argued that political institutions were not neutral but, instead, set in motion what he termed a "mobilization of bias" (1960, 29). By this he meant that most political institutions systemically favour some groups, such as the wealthy, the educated, and dominant racial or religious groups. Other critics of the pluralist approach point out that its singular focus on the outcomes of the political decision-making process obscures the fact that power is also exercised, perhaps even more strongly, when issues never make it to the public agenda and when no decision is made. In these cases, inaction would obscure and preserve an unequal and power-saturated status quo (Bachrach and Baratz, 1970).

The most sustained criticism of the pluralist approach in the United States, however, came from the new proponents of **elite theory**. They revived a long tradition of elite theorizing about the possibility of sustaining a meaningful democracy in modern societies. Elite theorists, for different reasons, argued that a select few, in all societies, manipulate the levers of government for their own advantage. President Dwight Eisenhower, just before departing from office in 1960, warned the American public of the growing power of what he termed the "military-industrial complex." Himself a former general and war hero, Eisenhower argued that a triad of military leaders, arms manufacturers, and sympathetic public officials posed a threat to American democracy. Elite theorist C. Wright Mills fleshed out the "military-industrial complex" in his famous book, *The Power Elite*, which appeared on bookshelves beside Robert Dahl's pluralist primer, *Preface to Democracy*, in 1956. Elite theory has a long tradition in political theory and in the evolution of political science. It is based on a very different view of society from the one advanced in the pluralist model. While pluralism focused on individuals in groups, elitism proposed a stark divide between the few and the many. The few, the elite, occupy the most powerful positions in the central institutions of society—the military, religion, economy, politics, and culture. The few hold the power, while the many do not.

There is little debate about the fact that there are leaders and followers in all societies. The questions posed by elite theory are twofold. First, is this a good or a bad thing? Second, do elites threaten democracy? Plato advanced the idea that good governance was best achieved when an elite of "philosopher kings," endowed with wisdom, virtue, and prudence, were given the exclusive power to rule. At the turn of the twentieth century, Italian sociologists Vilfredo Pareto (1848–1923) and Gaetano

Mosca (1858–1941) claimed that elite rule was an inevitable fact of human existence. For these elite theorists, all societies were characterized by a fundamental truth: the few (elites) rule the many (masses). Pareto advanced this dichotomous model of society quite starkly. "Whatever certain theorists may like to think," he wrote, "human society in fact is not a homogeneous thing, and different individuals are physically, morally, and intellectually different" (1978, 247). A few excel but the great majority do not.

Mosca presents a similar depiction of social organization. "In all societies," he contends, "two classes of people appear—a class that rules and a class that is ruled." The first class performs "all political functions, monopolizes power, and enjoys the advantages that power brings" while controlling the second class, which partakes in none of these things (quoted in Knuttila, 1987, 50). Pareto and Mosca advanced the case that elite rule is a basic fact of human existence and is inevitable. A meaningful democratic politics, therefore, was neither possible nor desirable. It is perhaps for this reason that European fascists of the 1930s embraced these theorists, especially Mosca, and their anti-democratic thought. Students of contemporary politics do well to remember that it is a short leap from the repugnant claim that some people are naturally superior and destined to hold power over others to all kinds of political pathologies and regimes of discrimination and injustice.

Roberto Michels (1876–1936), perhaps the most often-cited elite theorist, also argued that elite rule was inevitable, although not necessarily desirable. Michels was active in social-democratic politics and observed how elites captured the party organization, even though party ideology was committed to democracy. According to Michels, modern society was governed by what he called "the iron law of the oligarchy" (rule by a few) (1962). Modern societies require large and complex organizations that are characterized by specialization and division of labour. The latter creates a hierarchy in which a few, because of their organizational position and skills, gain experience, expertise, power, and control. As the elite's skill set grows and its grasp on power becomes more complete, it becomes increasingly distant from the rank-and-file side of the organization, which, in turn, grows apathetic and disempowered. It is through this process, according to Michels, that democracy inevitably leads to oligarchy, or elite rule (Knuttila, 1987, 52–53). Michels' point was that elites gain their power because of their strategic position within modern organizations and not because of human nature.

Most elite studies now identify powerful institutions and key figures within them as the starting point of their analyses. These studies often find that the elite of a variety of sectors, including politics, the military, the media, and business, are overwhelmingly white, wealthy, and male. They share similar backgrounds, attend the same elite schools, frequently interact socially and through marriage, and share similar values and opinions. But these similarities do not necessarily demonstrate that we are governed by oligarchy or that the study of elites tells us all that we need to know about power and politics.

Pareto once mused that "history is the graveyard of elites" (1976, 249), and in some ways it is. It is hard to imagine examples in politics where there are no leaders and followers. The starting point of elite theory, that society is composed of two groups—the elite and the masses—seems obvious and, thus, for many, elite theory is an appealing approach to the study of politics. Few would argue that the study of leaders and leadership is not important, but this does not mean we can explain politics through the narrow lens of elite analysis and its intellectual cousin—conspiracy theory.

Critics of elite theory argue that it overemphasizes the cohesion of elites. As we know, there is considerable conflict and competition among the powerful. What factors determine the winners and losers in struggles among the elite? Others suggest that elite theory ignores the institutional constraints that make it impossible for elites to ignore the masses. Elected officials, after all, still have to get elected by the people. Finally, others, especially Marxist critics, suggest that elite analysis is simply a poorly theorized class analysis, which fails to locate elites in the broader historical–economic context and ignores the ever-present tensions arising from class conflict.

Class Analysis

Class analysis is one stream of structural analysis, which envisions society as being divided into hierarchical strata or ranks that have unequal access to power, authority, and influence. Sociologists call this the study of social stratification. All societies, past and present, are divided by systems of advantage and disadvantage, grounded in, for example, racism, the sexual division of labour, and **colonialism**, which are produced and reproduced in political institutions, social organizations, and common value systems. Class analysis has been the most prominent form of structural analysis in political science, although its dominance is now challenged by feminist, anti-racist, and post-colonial theorists, to name a few. In class analysis, political scientists and political activists, following from the work of Karl Marx, see social classes antagonistically grounded in the organization of the economy, while followers of Max Weber see status groups that can be ranked on the basis of wealth and prestige. Karl Marx's theory of the capitalist organization of politics and society is explained in more detail later in this volume. Here, we will concentrate on the concept of social class and its implications for the study of politics.

Although social stratification has always been recognized in political theory, Marx was the first to develop a comprehensive theory of social class. Marx, as we saw earlier in this chapter, believed that all societies were divided along class lines and that, moreover, classes were necessarily and always in conflict over the distribution of material resources in society. Marx provided an overarching explanation of politics grounded in the historical organization of the economy. He argued that economic structures invariably provided the foundation for society's legal structure and politics. Although Marx argued that a focus on the way economies are organized and the class divisions that result explained the politics of all societies, the bulk of his writings on social class pertain to the emergence of capitalism and industrialization in Europe. He contended that democratic government was the result of a political revolution of a new class—commercial and industrial capitalists or, as Marx called them, the **bourgeoisie**.

At the same time, the emergence of capitalism created another new class—the working class or the **proletariat**—whose members sold their labour to capitalists and were exploited by them. Marx's careful analysis of the logic of capitalism led him to conclude that, in time, the middle class would be absorbed into the working class and the living conditions of the working class would become more and more desperate. The politics of capitalist societies would then revolve around a struggle between capitalists and workers. The working classes of the world, through revolution, would ultimately win and establish a communist society. Capitalism, unlike previous systems, Marx concluded, had a distinctive identifying feature. As he and Engels put it in the *Communist Manifesto*, capitalism "has simplified the class antagonisms. Society as a whole is more and more splitting up into two great hostile camps, into two great classes directly facing each other, bourgeoisie and proletariat" (1998, 34).

Marx's work on social class and the inevitability of class conflict significantly influenced political science as well as the politics of the twentieth century. The Cold War (1945–1989) between the capitalist and communist world is one example of this politics. Many of the political developments of the twentieth century also suggested that Marx's analysis was too extreme and failed to account for many of the subsequent changes in the stratification of society. His work has been criticized for its *economic determinism*—that is, for reducing the explanation of all social phenomena to a single factor, the organization of the economy. Others argue that, contrary to Marx's prediction, the middle class did not disappear as capitalism matured but, instead, grew to be an important political force. White-collar workers and professionals do not fit easily into Marx's scheme of class conflict because they are neither capitalists nor working class in a traditional Marxist definition of these terms. Finally, others, following from the work of Max Weber, argue that social stratification occurs along many dimensions due to a variety of factors, not solely due to one's position in the organization of economic relations.

When Weber contemplated the ways that societies were stratified, he saw quite a different world from the one Marx did. The starkly oppressive conditions of emerging industrialization had been somewhat improved, the working class had organized into unions and socialist political parties, democracy had expanded, and, as Weber saw it, society was increasingly governed by legal-rational authority and large bureaucracies. He argued that social stratification could no longer be studied as a product of social class alone. For Weber, social class remained an important determinant of power, but it was not the only factor. Modern society was divided into many status groups whose positions on the social hierarchy were also determined by prestige and by political power. Prestige could involve things as intangible as tastes and patterns of consumption that are socially valued, such as driving a Mercedes or being a celebrated athlete, a hip-hop artist, or the winner of *Canadian Idol*. This kind of social power, while not entirely unrelated to social class, is not reducible to economic relations alone.

Weber's work on status groups encouraged political scientists and sociologists to explain social divisions in influence and power on the basis of a variety of factors, including patterns of consumption, the social prestige assigned to some professions, such as medicine or law, and such factors as ethnicity, gender, race, and religion. Weber's work also encouraged political scientists in the United States, where the Marxist tradition was not strong, to talk about class divisions in non-antagonistic ways. Social class was analyzed along a continuum—upper class, middle class, and lower class—without any notion of exploitation or conflict among these groups. Weber's work, nonetheless, underlined the many ways that power and influence are unequally distributed in society, quite often on the basis of characteristics we are assigned at birth, such as gender and race.

To sum up, the institutional, pluralist, elite, and class approaches to the study of politics are only four among many ways to view the political world. They do, nonetheless, highlight many of the critical concepts in political science. Institutionalism emphasizes the importance of formal political institutions and how constitutions structure the rules of the political game and, thus, often, the outcome. Pluralists, in contrast, emphasize the informal ingredients of power, individual political actors, and the competition among groups for their preferred policy outcomes. They emphasize the play of politics from the bottom up, from the citizen to the state, while elitism focuses on the opposite flow, from leadership down. Although the elite approach probably exaggerates the isolation and independence of elites from the vast majority, it does point to the ways that ordinary citizens are often distanced from the political world and lack the expertise and information to engage in effective political participation. Finally, the class approach points to the ways in which power and influence are unevenly distributed in societies on the basis of social structure, position, and identity. Whether we agree with Marx or with Weber about the singular or multiple causes of social stratification, the class/status approach tells us that we can never study the individual political actor outside the context of history or the broader social divisions of power and influence. Having traced many of the key perspectives of the political world, this chapter concludes with a discussion of some of the new challenges facing political science in the twenty-first century.

Politics in the Twenty-First Century

IN RECENT YEARS, THE TRADITIONAL APPROACHES AND CONCERNS OF THE DISCIPLINE of political science have been challenged by, among others, feminist, post-colonial, and post-modern perspectives. The current era of intensifying globalization, however, poses perhaps the most far-reaching challenges to both the study and the practice of politics in the twenty-first century. As the chapters in this book explain, globalization has eroded familiar political institutions and patterns of politics without signalling what will or should take their place. Contemporary politics are marked by uncertainty and insecurity.

Although increasingly present in our daily vocabularies, globalization is very much a contested concept. At the very least, globalization can be understood as an unfolding political drama involving a number of transformative processes, some reinforcing and others contradictory. These processes stretch social, political, and economic activities across political frontiers and the formal boundaries of the national state. In so doing, they intensify interdependencies, accelerate social exchanges, and blur the boundaries among the local, the national, and the global (Held and McGrew, 1999, 484). As these epochal shifts become inescapable facts in our daily calculations, it is important to unpack globalization into its component parts, especially to distinguish between transformations in our social world and the governance of these changes. Beck calls the first **globality** and the second **globalism** (2000).

Globality refers to epochal shifts in social and political organization that have irreversibly altered the political world and our daily lives. Globality focuses our attention on new technologies, social and political issues that transcend territorial boundaries, and the possible emergence of the planet as the relevant space for political action. Beck argues that globality is an unavoidable and irreversible fact of twenty-first-century politics with "all interventions, victories, and catastrophes" occurring on a local–global axis (2000, 11, 15). September 11 and its ongoing reverberations everywhere illustrate this point forcefully.

Globalism, in contrast, refers to the transnational embrace of a common world view and institutions of governance. As many of the chapters that follow explain, the embrace, in varying degrees, of neo-liberalism by most national governments and by international organizations approaches this idea of a common world view. Many commentators on globalization, both for and against, fail to distinguish between globality and globalism. Recognizing the difference between these two concepts, however, is an important key to understanding contemporary politics. The distinction allows us to recognize the profound changes that define this globalizing era while leaving open to analysis and activism the essential questions of how these changes will translate into public policies and political institutions. The progressive shaping of the planet into an interdependent whole may be inevitable, but contrary to the pronouncements of the promoters of neo-liberal globalism, there is nothing inevitable about the way this process should be governed. Indeed, as Foucault reminds us, discourses such as neo-liberalism engender resistances of all kinds, whether in the form of the alter-globalization movement, renewed emphasis on local politics and production, environmentalism or, indeed, various religious fundamentalisms that resist what they see as the globalization of Western values and institutions.

Summary

This book focuses on critical concepts in political science. A concept is generally understood as an idea—a representation of a class of things or practices. The adjective "critical" is meant to convey three meanings that are elaborated in the chapters that follow. The first is that the concepts we identify are critical to our understanding of power and politics. Such concepts as democracy, the state, community, and international relations, to name a few, have been the bread and butter of political science since its conception. Second, "critical" is meant to convey the idea that these concepts are contested—subject to ongoing debate and struggle about their very meaning and practice. Finally, these concepts are critical because the stakes of politics—of who wins, loses, or is simply ignored—generally hinge on how foundational political concepts are commonly understood and embedded in our political institutions.

There is an old cliché that says, "We cannot understand where we are going unless we understand where we have been." This cliché resonates in contemporary political affairs. As we debate today's political issues, it is important to realize that similar questions vexed other societies and that, through politics, they arrived at either reasonable or horrible solutions. The kinds of politics we will have in the twenty-first century, as well as the solutions we find to global co-existence, are still ours to create, although, as Marx would remind us, not necessarily under conditions of our own choosing. Globalization challenges old assumptions and creates new political problems. It does not, however, release us from the responsibility of constantly revisiting the fundamental political questions of what is and, more important, what ought to be.

Discussion Questions

1. Think about your day. How often did you encounter politics? What kind of politics did you encounter? Were there some encounters that entailed more power than others? Why? In what ways could you have resisted that power?
2. Compare and contrast the approaches to politics discussed in this chapter.
3. What ought our politics to look like in the twenty-first century? Why?
4. Identify and discuss the bases for systemic discrimination in contemporary Canadian politics.

References

Bachrach, Peter and Morton Baratz. 1970. *Power and Poverty: Theory and Practice.* New York: Oxford University Press.

Beck, Ulrich. 2000. *What Is Globalization?* Translated by Patrick Camiller. London: Polity Press.

Bendix, Reinhard. 1960. *Max Weber: An Intellectual Portrait.* Garden City, NY: Doubleday.

Cromarte, Allan. 2003. "Legitimacy" in Richard Bellamy and Andrew Maser, eds., *Political Concepts.* Manchester: Manchester University Press.

Dahl, Robert. 1956. *Preface to Democratic Theory.* Chicago: University of Chicago Press.

———. 1961. *Who Governs?* New Haven, CT: Yale University Press.

Dicey, A.V. 1908. *An Introduction to the Study of the Law of the Constitution,* 7th edition. London: Macmillan.

Fink-Eitel, Hinrich. 1992. *Foucault: An Introduction.* Philadelphia: Pennbridge Books.

Foucault, Michel. 1977. *Power/Knowledge.* New York: Pantheon.

———. 2003. *Society Must Be Defended.* Translated by David Macey. New York: Picador.

Gerth, H.H. and C.W. Mills, eds. 1958. *From Max Weber: Essays in Sociology.* New York: Oxford University Press.

Guy, James John. 1995. *People, Politics, Government: Political Science: A Canadian Perspective.* Scarborough, ON: Prentice Hall.

Hawley, Amos. 1963. "Community Power and Urban Renewal Success." *American Journal of Sociology,* Vol. 68 (January).

Held, David. 1996. "The Development of the Modern State" in Stuart Hall, David Held, Don Hubert, and Kenneth Thompson, eds., *Modernity: An Introduction to the Modern Social Sciences.* London: Blackwell.

Held, David and Anthony McGrew. 1999. "Globalization." *Global Governance,* 5, no. 4.

Knuttila, Murray. 1987. *State Theories.* Toronto: Garamond.

Kourvetaris, George. 1997. *Political Sociology: Structure and Process.* Boston: Allyn and Bacon.

Lasswell, Harold. 1936. *Politics: Who Gets What, When and How.* New York: McGraw-Hill.

Mannheim, Karl. 1936. *Ideology and Utopia.* New York: Harvest Books.

Marx, Karl and Friedrich Engels, 1998. *The Communist Manifesto: A Modern Edition.* London: Verso.

Michels, Roberto. 1962. *Political Parties.* New York: The Free Press.

Mills, C. Wright. 1956. *The Power Elite.* New York: Oxford Press.

Pareto, Vilfredo. 1978. *Sociological Writings.* Oxford: Basil Blackwell.

Philp, Mark. 1985. "Power" in Adam Kuper and Jessica Kuper, eds., *The Social Science Encyclopedia.* New York: Routledge.

Schattschneider, E.E. 1960. *The Semi-Sovereign People: A Realist's View of Democracy.* New York: Holt, Reinhart and Winston.

Simons, Jon. 1995. *Foucault and the Political.* New York: Routledge.

Tansey, Stephen. 2004. *The Basics,* 3rd edition. London: Routledge.

Further Readings

Bellamy, Richard and Andrew Mason. 2003. *Political Concepts*. Manchester: Manchester University Press.

Bottomore, Tom. 1979. *Political Sociology*. London: Harper and Row Publishers.

Hall, Stuart, David Held, Don Hubert, and Kenneth Thompson, eds. 1996. *Modernity: An Introduction to the Social Sciences*. London: Blackwell.

Weblinks

American Political Science Association
www.apsanet.org

Canadian Political Science Association
www.sfu.ca/igs/CPSA.html

Department of Political Science, University of Alberta
www.ualberta.ca/~polisci/index.html

International Studies Association
www.isanet.org

PLENTY OF REGIONAL WARS, RIVAL FACTIONS AND SUICIDE BOMBERS... BUT ALAS, A CRITICAL SHORTAGE OF WISE MEN.

CHAPTER 2

TRADITIONS OF POLITICAL THOUGHT

Objectives

This chapter has two purposes. One is to introduce political philosophy as a special kind of inquiry—a great conversation about ideas, which extends in time. The chapter begins with a broad distinction between ancient Greek, or "classical," and modern Western political philosophy, dating back to the early sixteenth century. Its first purpose is to introduce a number of individual philosophers. There are not many fields of study in the university where books that were written 2500 or 500 or 150 years ago are still read as if they have contemporary relevance and where some familiarity with their ideas is the mark of a well-prepared graduate. Politics is one. The chapter's second purpose is to weave through its introduction a particular interest in political leadership or rule. In this respect, the distinction between ancient and modern is a useful one. Preoccupations do change. Modern political philosophy, for reasons that will be discussed, has had little to say about questions that once preoccupied the ancient Greek philosophers: Who should rule? What virtues or other qualities are required of those who rule? Since leaders now monopolize media coverage of politics and since recent examples, such as Nelson Mandela in South Africa, suggest that

ROGER
EPP

quality of leadership can matter a great deal in complex circumstances, such important questions are still worth asking.

Introduction

Political philosophy is systematic thinking about the nature and *public* requirements of the good life. It is the realm of fundamental concepts such as freedom, justice, equality, rights, order, and authority. It is also the realm of such big questions as these: What does each of those concepts mean? What are their limits, and what is their source—God, nature, force, reason, the logic of history, or none of these? Is there a universal and timeless *human* nature, which must be harnessed because, left to ourselves, like the characters of *Lord of the Flies*, we are self-destructively self-interested and fearful of others? Or, alternatively, must our human nature be unleashed through the right kind of social and political arrangements, since we are a creative and capable species? Are cultural differences important? How can people who are not alike—whether in culture and ethnicity, physical characteristics, wealth, or basic beliefs—live together in a single **polity**?

Introduced in this way, political philosophy can seem intimidating and almost irrelevant to the action that draws most students to the study of politics: such things as elections, law-making, street demonstrations, international diplomacy, and armed conflict. It is misleading, however, to characterize political philosophy as a mere intellectual exercise. One reason to resist this temptation is that the very words that people use to participate in politics, the conflicting claims they make, and the assumptions embedded in those claims about the good life and human beings, are precisely the stuff of political philosophy. It is no coincidence that we have inherited from the ancient Greeks not just the word "politics"—the root *polis* referring to a city state and the active life among citizens in that place—but also the first systematic political texts by such thinkers as Plato (c. 427–347 B.C.E.) and Aristotle (384–322 B.C.E.).

The fact that these texts continue to be read suggests that political philosophy represents a different kind of inquiry than is found in, say, the natural sciences. When students in physics are introduced to the history of human attempts to make sense of the universe—from Aristotle to Newton to Einstein—the subject is taught as the history of error and correction. In keeping with the scientific method, a radical new discovery sweeps existing theory aside. Students in political philosophy, on the other hand, are introduced to a "canon" of texts, which have emerged from a variety of epochs and historical contexts and reflect a diversity of literary genres. Most are formal treatises, while others take the form of dialogues, plays, letters, or manifestos issued in the heat of the moment. The selection of books that belong to the "Western canon" is itself a matter of argument. Old works are rediscovered and newer ones are added because preoccupations change. But some prominent texts and thinkers endure. None of them is necessarily dispatched to the museum by the sudden arrival of an entirely new way of political thinking. Instead, new editions are promoted in publishers' catalogues alongside ancient texts, which find new advocates, interpreters, and critics and continue to shed light on political practice. In this sense, political philosophy should be understood, less intimidatingly, as an *extended conversation* involving different voices, traditions, and texts, as well as shifting topics of interest. This conversation is more than a shouting match. Its participants, past and present, tend to change their positions over time, in response to events and other ideas around them, and they cannot necessarily control the radically different ways in which others may hear them or put their words to use. In any case their positions are seldom reducible to simple study notes, short excerpts, or cookie-cutter ideological labels. They are best read as whole texts, with some knowledge of the historical context in which they are written.

Looking for a Leader

IN ONE OF HIS POLITICAL ROCK ANTHEMS ON THE CD *LIVING WITH WAR* (2006), NEIL Young sings that he is "looking for a leader to bring our country home/reunite the red, white, and blue before it turns to stone/lookin' for somebody young enough to take it on/clean up the corruption and make the country strong." There is nothing complicated about the message. On the same CD Young proclaims, "Let's impeach the president for lying." Meanwhile, neo-conservative writers in the United States have rediscovered Theodore Roosevelt, rugged outdoorsman and war hero, as a model of muscular presidency for our own time. His famous motto, "Speak softly and carry a big stick," carried U.S. public opinion into its first imperial commitments in the Caribbean and the Philippines. Obviously, political leadership matters. So does the quality of that leadership; it can be better or worse. This focus on leaders might seem exaggerated, a product of the media shorthand that reduces politics to celebrity personalities, which in turn encourages politicians to focus on image-making. But I do not think it is helpful to assume that leaders are pretty-faced figureheads or mere puppets of hidden forces. Leaders have real power. Good or bad, leaders command podiums from which to shape the language of public life. They make consequential judgments. Sometimes they are in a position to make decisions that alter the course of national or world history or, more plainly, determine who lives and who eats. Think, for example, of Saddam Hussein, George Bush, and Tony Blair; Ronald Reagan, Mikhail Gorbachev, Helmut Kohl, and Margaret Thatcher; Augusto Pinochet and now Michelle Bachelet in Chile; Sir John A. Macdonald, Louis Riel, and Cree chief Big Bear; Tommy Douglas; Pierre Trudeau; Ralph Klein. Our involvement in and our appreciation of political life often is shaped by the leaders of the day.

Political leaders, inside and outside formal office, can articulate aspirations and mobilize people in complex circumstances of historic injustice and anger. Political leaders judge when to confront, when to negotiate, and when to withdraw. In rare circumstances, leaders also can initiate courageous acts of public reconciliation and "give their societies permission to say the unsayable" about the past, so that the "spiral of intergenerational vengeance" can be broken (Ignatieff, 1998, 188–189).

In short, political leadership matters. Nation-states, oppositional movements, and civil society organizations all require individual and collective leadership to act in effective and principled ways. And yet—readers will need to take my word on this—what is striking about modern political philosophy is that it is mostly silent on the subject. Instead, as if only corporations needed leaders, the field is left to the writers of best-selling management books, the kind displayed prominently in airport shops, with number-touting titles like *The Five Temptations of a CEO* (Lencioni, 1998), *The Seven Habits of Highly Effective People* (Covey, 1989), and *The 21 Indispensable Qualities of a Leader* (Maxwell, 1999).

Classical Political Thought

IF POLITICAL PHILOSOPHY IS AN EXTENDED CONVERSATION, THEN TO PICK UP THE metaphor, it is one that is sometimes marked by ruptures and silences. Or else it happens in different rooms—one group in the kitchen, another in the basement, each occasionally in hearing distance of the other when one gets loud or the other quiet. Perhaps the most common distinction in political philosophy is between ancients and moderns, or between the classical tradition, which began with the Greeks, and the strands of modern Western thought that date back to the emergence of the territorial "sovereign" state and market economy. This distinction makes intuitive sense. The ancient Mediterranean world is distant in time and space. At the same time, for that very reason, the historical study of political philosophy opens up the possibility of alternative perspectives held up against our own time. The ancient Greek texts will seem strange to those who have been immersed from birth in the "common sense" of liberal political ideas about the primacy of individuals, the limited state, **representative democracy**, and the **rule of law**. In classical philosophy, politics is often presented as a moral activity, oriented to the common good and the enabling of the good life—the content of which is more than a matter of personal opinion. Classical philosophy also considers goodness and justice as attributes of both individuals and cities. The virtue of the individual and the quality of the regime are deeply interconnected, so that it would have been impossible to imagine a good life in a corrupt polity. Immanuel Kant (1724–1804), by contrast, is decidedly a modern when he writes that a constitutional state could be established by "even a nation of devils"—so long as they could calculate the conditions most amenable to pursuing their own interests with minimal interference (Kant, 1970, 112–113). For Kant and other modernist thinkers, it mattered little if individuals were good or bad. In classical thought, as well, freedom was a matter of public life rather than the non-political domain of private choices and individual rights. Freedom meant acting together with one's equals. Glory—a place in the stories that would be told by future generations—was valued more highly than security for cities and individuals. Finally, ancient Greek texts are distinguished by their intense interest in questions about who should rule (one, a few, or many) and in what manner. What kind of wisdom, what character, and what training are required? What about the problem of the tyrant?

Greek political philosophy is hardly the product of an era of quiet contemplation. Instead, it emerges from two kinds of experience. One is the rough practice of politics in untried citizen-assemblies. The second is prolonged conflict among and within Greek city states, culminating in the collapse of the Athenian empire after a restless, foolish attempt to conquer inhospitable Sicily. In the account of the war written by the historian Thucydides, the leader Pericles convinces the Athenian assembly to support war in the first place against rival city state Sparta. He praises the dead with a speech after the first campaign and urges the city to stay the course even as the shock of defeat, disease, and hunger hit home. Not long after, Pericles' death leaves room for the private ambition, demagoguery, and poor judgment of his successors. None of them could match his intelligence and integrity, his grasp of the city's character, and his ability to speak the right words—angry or encouraging—to balance its mood (Thucydides, 1972, 164). This view of Pericles, however, is not universally held. In Plato's dialogue *The Gorgias*, the character Socrates engages a teacher of rhetoric, a prized skill for participants in the assembly. Distinguishing oratory from truth, Socrates proposes that while Athens has experienced many persuasive speakers, who knew how to pander to popular opinion, it has had no good statesmen in its history—Pericles included. How could a leader be praised when, like a bad animal trainer, he left the city "fiercer than he found it" (Plato, 1971, 516/130)?

The paradox that Plato, the first political philosopher, was deeply skeptical of politics is partly explained by the fact that the Athenian democracy had put the real Socrates, his teacher, to death. Throughout Plato's writings, the question of whether truth and political power could ever be joined, or whether the philosopher who cares for truth should shun public life, is a continuing theme. It animates his best-known work, *The Republic*. This long, meandering dialogue begins as a late-night argument involving the character Socrates. The argument moves through a series of questions: whether justice is merely the advantage of the stronger; whether rulers—one, the few, or the many—invariably make laws in their own interests; and whether it is realistic to acknowledge that those who succeed at injustice on a grand scale, conquering cities, are to be admired most in life. Socrates proposes that people of good character would rule neither for honour nor for money, but unwillingly, only out of fear of being ruled by someone worse (Plato, 1974, 347b). He is dismissed as naive. Trying again, he develops an analogy. In the well-ordered soul, he proposes, the parts of *appetite* and *spirit* are subjected to *reason,* and each of these three parts is directed to its particular "excellence": moderation, courage, and wisdom (the ability to see beyond the surface of things). In the well-ordered city, there is a sharp division of labour. Those who love money and things provide materially for the city; those who love honour protect it; and those few who love wisdom—philosophers—rule. These three kinds of people are sheep, watchdogs, and shepherds, respectively (416a).

The position that Plato has Socrates present in the dialogue reflects both a fear of discord and the conviction that most people are not fit to rule. The interlocutors debate the practical difficulties of building this ideal city. How would it be established? How would philosopher-rulers be identified, trained, and persuaded to rule, and then reproduced? Who would watch the watchdogs? In the end Socrates is pessimistic. Even if the city could be established, it could not be preserved generation after generation, against a predictable cycle of decay whose final steps are unbridled liberty, the rise of a people's champion, and then tyranny. He has an intriguing response, however, for those who first propose that the ruler who can act with impunity is most admirable. This tyrant, he says, is least happy. Lacking moderation, he is enslaved to his own material desires; he must continue to steal from others to satisfy those desires. While those in his immediate circle flatter and obey him, he lives without friends. He and his city are imprisoned by fear. He cannot even abandon his position without worrying that he will face the punishment he has inflicted on others. He is suspicious of others. He is confined to his home "like a woman" (579b). He cannot move freely about the city or visit another. Plato's psychological portrait recalls Saddam Hussein (Al-Khalil, 1990) and, in his last decade, Pinochet (Dorfman, 2002).

Aristotle, though he was Plato's student, did not denigrate politics or trade in out-of-reach ideal constitutions. He worked from observation, not abstract logic. He accepted that political arrangements vary according to the character of particular cities. Aristotle began from the premise that the polis is the highest form of human association since it gives citizens a setting in which to pursue the good life and to develop fully their nature as "political animals." In other words, the polis provided a space where citizens, through the experience of debating and deciding in the assembly, could develop their capacity for reasoned speech about what is just and unjust. Aristotle placed political virtues within human reach: citizens must know how to rule and be ruled, hold office, defend the city, make laws, and respect them. They should each take a turn at ruling, he proposed, out of obligation to the city and their friends.

The attribute that Aristotle's citizens required most of all was practical judgment, which could be developed only through experience and the emulation of those who displayed it. The Greek word for practical judgment is *phronesis*. Aristotle meant by this the ability to make decisions that are informed by general principles of justice but also sensitive to the particularities of a situation. At the same time, Aristotle was no egalitarian, at least in the way we understand the term. He did not think that *phronesis* is equally distributed. He did not want just anyone managing the treasury or leading in battle. He was suspicious of the young, whom he found lacking in experience and prone to impetuous action. Consistent with his culture, he assumed that slaves would do the work of the household, freeing citizens to participate in the assembly. As most commentators read him, he also assumed that women lack the rational capacity or at least the opportunity to develop *phronesis* (Aristotle, 1980; 1985).

All that said, when Aristotle considered who should rule, his qualified answer was "the many." A singularly wise king might be best, but what about succession? In most cases, Aristotle argued, the collective wisdom is more reliable in the end. He compared its advantages to those of a potluck meal over a single dish, however delicious. The collective wisdom could draw on diverse perspectives, while a king had only one pair of eyes and ears—and no equals, so no true friends and no sense of mutual obligations. The many, Aristotle reasoned, are also less likely than one individual to be corrupted or mercurial in temperament. But the rule of the many, he noted, still requires the cultivation of virtue and good judgment, since the many are as capable of losing sight of the common good as one or a few.

Modern Political Thought

"Knowing how not to be virtuous"

THE LEAP FROM ANCIENT GREECE TO EARLY-MODERN EUROPE IS A COMMON ONE IN introductory surveys of political philosophy, though obviously it passes over some important historical developments. In the West, there was the rise of Christianity, the withering of the Roman Empire into a fragmented agrarian feudalism, the struggle for pre-eminence between the two authorities—princes and popes—and the complex relationship with the Islamic world, which stretched as far as Spain. It was actually the great library at Alexandria, Egypt, and Islamic scholarship that preserved the texts of the ancient Mediterranean so that they could eventually be read again in Europe. Medieval philosophy readily absorbed at least some of Aristotle, including his stress on character; but it lacked anything like a polis in which the idea of citizenship and an active public life could even make sense, with the exception of the city states that emerged in northern Italy. Commonly, the *body politic* of medieval Europe was imagined as an organic whole, in which people were joined to each other in a web of personal obligations, hierarchical but mutually dependent, with the ruler as the head, and others, the hands, feet, and stomach. Rulers in particular became the subject of a new genre of writing—"mirror of princes"—that advised them how to govern virtuously: keep promises, punish without cruelty, defend the weak, find security in the love of one's subjects, and so on. The political spectrum ranged along a single axis from good kings to tyrants.

This medieval world was dealt a double intellectual blow in the early sixteenth century. First, the Protestant reformer Martin Luther (1483–1546), among others, challenged the authority of the Church in "secular" matters. His position gave new legitimacy to the territorial princes but also limited their authority. They were divinely ordained to keep public order but not to make people good or fit them for eternal salvation; they were able to punish the body but could not touch people's thoughts (Luther, 1974). Second, Niccolò Machiavelli (1469–1527), a civic official and diplomat in the Italian city state of Florence, who was exiled to the countryside by a change in regime, wrote a controversial manuscript called *The Prince*. The book's purpose has been debated ever since. Was it a satire, a job application, a call to unify Italy and throw out the foreigners, or simply a counsel of evil? Machiavelli pulled no punches. His intention was to draw up "an original set of rules" based on political reality rather than the naive imaginations of the mirror-of-princes authors: "The fact is that a man who wants to act virtuously in every way necessarily comes to grief among so many who are not virtuous. Therefore if a prince wants to maintain his rule he must learn how not to be virtuous, and to make use of this or not according to need" (1981, Ch. XV, 91).

Machiavelli was a transitional thinker. He accepted the classical interest in the character of rule while turning the old virtues upside-down. He advised the prince to learn from history, imitate great rulers, and never be timid. In seizing a state, for example, the ruler must "determine all the injuries that he will need to inflict" and "inflict them once for all" (Ch. VIII, 66). Machiavelli did not advise that the prince be a thug; instead he should use violence sparingly to maximum effect. The prince's real *virtu*— the root word of virtuosity—was his ability to anticipate change and act accordingly. *Virtu* helped him to appear compassionate, truthful, and pious, and to be those things but also to "know how to do evil" when necessary. Machiavelli's maxims might seem ready-made for the spin doctors of the television age: "everyone is in a position to watch . . . few experience what you really are. . . . The common people are always impressed by appearances and results" (Ch. XVIII, 101). He reminds us that politics is part theatre and that those who participate in the public realm are, in some sense, actors.

The Liberal Turn

WITH THE EMERGENCE OF LIBERAL IDEAS, ESPECIALLY IN ENGLAND, THE AXIS OF political philosophy tilted again toward a suspicion of politics. The intent of leading liberal philosophers, such as Thomas Hobbes (1588–1679) and John Locke (1632–1704), was, respectively, to pacify politics after a time of civil war and to fence in the political realm. Hobbes' *Leviathan* painted in words a world stripped of institutions. His **state of nature** is populated by individuals who have been left to their own devices and are fearful of their own survival. As a result, life in this state is, in Hobbes' famous phrase, "solitary, poor, nasty, brutish, and short" (1994, Ch. 13, 76). Such a world, he argued, would be so universally intolerable that people, if they thought about it, would all readily surrender their natural right to do whatever they wished and establish a government strong enough to "keep them in awe" and afford them proper protection. Hobbes' radical turn was to locate authority in the **consent** of the governed. While he offered some prudent suggestions on how to rule a stable state, he was not writing primarily for or about rulers. It is the rest of us who must reason, day after day, that security is our highest priority and that it is better to consent to government—*any government*—than to risk sliding back toward the imagined state of nature. This kind of calculation might seem extreme to us, but perhaps less so to someone living in a place like post-Saddam Iraq. For Hobbes, the character of rule faded in importance next to the calculated consent that authorized it.

Locke also employed the device of a state of nature to build a case for authority by consent. He questioned why free people would establish a government with authority over them. His answer was that there is only one purpose for government: the "mutual preservation of their lives, liberties, and estates" (1980, Ch. 9, 124), which requires laws, impartial judges, and a capacity to enforce justice. Otherwise, people would be left to be judges and executioners in their own case. The immediate target for Locke and the tradition of liberal-constitutional political philosophy was the arbitrary rule of European monarchs, who assembled power and legitimized their authority by reference to divine right or fatherly analogies. For Locke, there was only consent, and only for limited purposes. A ruler who broke trust put himself above the law and, in effect, declared war on his society; rebellion was then a matter of duty. For Locke, the primary work of citizens was vigilance against encroachments on property and personal convictions. Politics, in other words, was a kind of necessary evil, not the realm in which humans live freely, but the protector of it as well as a constant threat to it.

This reversal of the priority of public and private became increasingly characteristic of liberal philosophy and societies over time. In *Democracy in America*, the French politician-writer and traveller Alexis de Tocqueville (1805–1859) observed that in the U.S. the brightest individuals were scarcely found in political office (1945, Vol. 1, 207). Convinced he had seen the future and was describing it back to Europeans, he was equally fascinated by the robust American society he had witnessed and worried about what would happen if the cultural checks on its worst tendencies were to disappear. On one hand, absolute sovereignty of the people again raised the spectre of tyranny, but a **tyranny of the majority**, whose subtle power had already produced more conformity in ideas than existed even in the conservative monarchies of Europe (Vol. 1, 273). On the other, and more troublesome, hand was what Tocqueville called "soft despotism." In this new condition, people's withdrawal from public life into the privacy of their homes and personal pleasures, together with the centralization and expansion of the state as a means of ensuring people's security, equality, and happiness, created an "immense and tutelary power"—however mild—that sapped their ability to exercise freedom in an ancient Greek sense (Vol. 2, 334–348). The need for it no longer existed. Confined to periodic elections, the scope of individual and collective political action was diminished.

Tocqueville's critique telegraphed later concerns about the rise of bureaucracy. If the effect of liberal ideas was to diminish the political and focus on the line between public and private, government and individual, the modern state also impersonalizes rule in successive historical stages. Hannah Arendt (1958, 40) described bureaucracy as "rule by nobody"—not that there is no rule, but there is no longer anyone in whom responsibility visibly rests, no one who sees the whole, and seemingly no one to whom an appeal might be made. The new despotism had no face. The state was transformed by consolidation into larger territorial units, and the need for a more complex organization to manage its taxes, wars, and population counts, convey orders and, later, implement educational and social reforms. In this new hierarchical organization, authority became attached to offices, occupied by career staff hired for their expert knowledge. They dealt with cases, not individual people, on the basis of general rules. We generally still approve of this. We want scientists to ensure our water is safe, and we are scandalized when someone gets special treatment because of personal friendship or a family relationship. But the sociologist Max Weber (1864–1920) described this kind of legal-rational authority of rule as an iron cage: there is no escaping the process of bureaucratization in modern societies. The power of Weber's dark insight may lie in the fact that those successful revolutionaries in Russia abolished the old regime only by building a more comprehensive bureaucracy.

Weber also provided one of the few sustained examples of modern political thinking on the subject of who should rule in the face of the new realities he described. His essay "Politics as a Vocation" (1919) described a set of grim qualities—rare ones—that make individuals fit for leadership. The political actor, he writes, must possess (1) the passion and sense of purpose that a specialist bureaucracy cannot provide; (2) the ability to calculate the consequences of both action and inaction; (3) a "trained relentlessness [to] face up to the realities of life"; and (4) a "willingness to pay the price of using morally dubious means or at least dangerous ones" (1946, 119–126). Weber called this the **ethic of responsibility**. It is entirely about defending the state, its interests, and its people, and it requires the fortitude to order the use of violence—the "decisive means" of politics. Weber's conception of political leadership also was resignedly elitist. Only the capable few could bear the burden of responsibility. Private individuals, meanwhile, were free to indulge in the luxury of ethical purity, but they could not judge a political leader's actions without putting themselves in his or her shoes. Put another way, Weber's strict separation of the few and the many let citizens put aside the demands of politics and be critical, or not, from the sidelines.

Weber's ethic of responsibility was framed for the extreme situation, such as post–World War I Germany, and may seem an odd, unsatisfying place to end. It does not tell us much about the everyday leadership needed in a democratic society. It does not help us think about what kind of political leadership might be needed at all levels—say, to tackle serious and looming ecological threats—engaging citizens and experts alike. It gives little recognition to the place of words and the art of persuasion. What it does is, first, fix a silence between rulers and ruled and, second, feed the temptations toward contempt on one side and deference mixed with contempt on the other. As Mark Kingwell (2001) writes, one danger of focusing only on political leadership is losing sight of its relational character to citizens or "the people," who have a role in creating leaders. Another is forgetting that it is not only leaders in a democracy who have public and private lives and roles to which we may apply somewhat different standards; citizens do, too. They include political virtues of scrutiny, participation, tough-mindedness, and civility. In some ways that brings us back to Aristotle. Even if his expectations about active citizenship seem overly demanding or find no easy place in our world, it is partly what he meant by knowing how to rule and be ruled.

Summary

This brief chapter has obvious limitations. It skates lightly over only a few complex texts and a long history. It says nothing about non-Western traditions. Certainly, its interpretation can be challenged. What it offers is a reading that is itself part of the conversation of political philosophy. The chapter shows how ancient Greek thought treated the question of who should rule, and how. It then proposes that modern political philosophy, at least after Machiavelli, has lost interest in that question for several reasons. One is the liberal tradition's devaluation of politics and its greater interest in the line between public and private, state and individual. Another is the democratic twist given to liberalism's doctrine of authority by consent: so long as an election is properly conducted, we get the leaders for whom we vote, and we reserve the right to turf them out next time. A third is the increasingly impersonal character of government. But the quality of political leadership matters. In some ways it is inseparable from the quality of citizenship.

Discussion Questions

1. Identify a political leader you admire and one you decidedly do not. What characteristics do you associate with them? Is a good leader the same as a successful one? Ask the same questions for a leader you dislike.
2. While we are all officially democrats now, wasn't Plato right in asserting that (a) most people are unfit to rule and (b) the best regime is one ruled by those who are wise?
3. What kind of leadership does a democracy require, whether at the national or the local level?
4. Political leadership in most countries is still overwhelmingly a male domain. While it is sometimes debated whether the few women leaders, such as Britain's Margaret Thatcher, have represented an approach that is different from or better than that of their male counterparts, what conclusions might a feminist analysis reach about political leadership? What interest would it have in the question of who rules, and how?
5. How does the advent of television and new media change the nature of political leadership and the relationship between leaders and citizens, or leaders and movements?

References

Al-Khalil, Samir. 1990. *The Republic of Fear: Inside Saddam's Iraq.* New York: Pantheon.

Arendt, Hanah. 1958. *The Human Condition.* Chicago: University of Chicago Press.

Aristotle. 1985. *Nichomachean Ethics.* Translated by T. Irwin. Indianapolis: Hackett.

———. 1980. *The Politics.* Translated by T. Sinclair. Harmondsworth: Penguin.

Dorfman, Ariel. 2002. *Exorcising Terror.* New York: Seven Stories Press.

Hobbes, Thomas. 1994 (1651). *Leviathan* (E. Curley, ed.). Indianapolis: Hackett.

Ignatieff, Michael. 1998. *The Warrior's Honour: Ethnic War and the Modern Conscience.* Toronto: Viking Penguin.

Kant, Immanuel. 1970 (1795). "Perpetual Peace" in H. Reiss, ed., *Kant's Political Writing*. Translated by H. Nisbet. Cambridge: Cambridge University Press.

Kingwell, Mark. 2001. *The World We Want: Virtue, Vice and the Good Citizen*. Toronto: Penguin.

Locke, John. 1980 (1690). *Second Treatise of Government* (C. Macpherson, ed.). Indianapolis: Hackett.

Luther, Martin. 1974. *Selected Political Writings* (J. Porter, ed.). Philadelphia: Fortress Press.

Machiavelli, Niccolo. 1981 (c. 1514). *The Prince*. Translated by G. Bull. London: Penguin.

Plato. 1971. *The Gorgias*. Translated by W. Hamilton. Harmondsworth: Penguin.

———. 1974. *The Republic*. Translated by G. Grube. Indianapolis: Hackett.

Thucydides. 1972. *The Peloponnesian War*. Translated by R. Warner. Harmondsworth: Penguin.

Tocqueville, Alexis de. 1945 (1835, 1840). *Democracy in America*, 2 vols. Translated by P. Bradley. New York: Alfred A. Knopf.

Weber, Max. 1946 (1919). "Politics as a Vocation" in H. Girth and C. Mills, eds., *From Max Weber*. New York: Oxford University Press.

Further Readings

Boucher, David and Paul Kelly, eds. 2003. *Political Thinkers from Socrates to the Present*. Oxford: Oxford University Press.

Elshtain, Jean. 1993. *Public Man, Private Woman: Women in Social and Political Thought*. Princeton: Princeton University Press.

Havel, Vaclav. 1993. *Summer Meditations*. Translated by P. Wilson. Toronto: Vintage.

Taylor, Charles. 2004. *Modern Social Imaginaries*. Durham, NC: Duke University Press.

Weblinks

Filosofica Politica
http://lgxserver.uniba.it/lei/filpol/filpole/homefpe.htm

The Keele (University) Guide to Political Thought and Ideology on the Internet
www.keele.ac.uk/depts/por/ptbase.htm

The University of Michigan Library Documents Center, Political Science Resources, Political Theory
www.lib.umich.edu/govdocs/pstheory.html

CHAPTER 3

LIBERALISM

Objectives

This chapter explores liberalism with attention to its historical development and main commitments. Liberalism tovday is committed to two central values—freedom and equality—which it protects as rights. Over time, however, these commitments have developed in different ways. Where liberalism was once somewhat narrow and individualistic, it has developed today into a range of broader and more social commitments. We begin by considering this historical development with reference to three major liberal thinkers: Locke, Mill, and Rawls. We then examine the ideas of freedom and equality, with particular attention to the different ways they have been understood. We conclude by showing what is involved in protecting these values as rights.

DON CARMICHAEL

Introduction

Liberalism is centrally committed to the **freedom** and **equality** of individuals. But there have been considerable shifts in the way these commitments have been understood. In traditional liberalism, freedom and equality were valued rather narrowly and legalistically. Freedom was understood primarily as liberty, or the absence of legal interferences from the state, while equality was seen mainly as equality before the law. These commitments are important in liberalism today, but they have come to be understood more broadly and from a more social perspective as the equal freedom of individuals to live on terms of their own choosing.

In these commitments, liberalism focuses on the individual. That is, liberalism understands the political community as an association of separate individuals, each with different and sometimes conflicting interests. Liberalism holds that no one individual is more important than any other. All individuals and their interests must be respected equally. This is strongly tied to an insistence on the freedom of individuals to live as they choose. But this freedom is problematic. It is a wonderful thing in the abstract, but what happens when some individuals want to live in ways that others dislike? And what happens when these others are powerful enough to compel conformity among the less powerful and marginalized? Consider the case of gay men and lesbian women living in a homophobic community. Their attempts to live freely will almost certainly be obstructed by others. For example, they may find it difficult to secure employment, housing, respect from their neighbours, or a welcoming church. On this account, their freedom and equality require some form of special protection in law.

Politically, therefore, liberalism is committed to political measures that protect and support the freedom and equality of individuals. For the most part, these measures protect activities or areas of life by establishing protective walls around them, typically in the form of **rights**. Within these protective walls, each individual is free to do as she or he chooses. There are different kinds of rights. In some cases, whole aspects of life are walled off from regulation by the state. Traditional liberals typically regarded the economy in these terms, and religious practice is still seen this way today. For example, liberal constitutions typically guarantee "freedom of religion." Sometimes these "walls" are described as private versus public areas of life, where "private" indicates areas where individuals should be free from legal controls as opposed to the "public" areas that are legitimately subject to regulation. Perhaps the most familiar example of this approach today is the *Canadian Charter of Rights and Freedoms*. The Charter stipulates that a law may be declared invalid if it violates certain basic rights and freedoms, even if the law is enacted democratically and supported by the majority.

But a word of caution is important here. We noted that the understanding of freedom and equality has changed in liberalism, moving from a narrow and somewhat legal conception to a broader and more social conception of the equal freedom of individuals to live on terms of their own choosing. With this shift in the understanding of the values of freedom and equality, there has been a corresponding shift in the measures needed to protect and support them. In addition to protecting individuals from interference, liberalism now aims to support individuals in important areas of life in more positive ways by providing them with the resources they need to live as they choose. This shift in liberalism is tentative and ongoing, and, as such, it occasions controversy, uncertainty, and reversals. In this chapter, accordingly, we will explore liberalism today with attention to these changing understandings of its central commitments. Three critical concepts will be examined: *freedom* and *equality*, as the two value commitments of liberalism, and the idea of protecting these values as *rights*.

Historical Development: Some Major Thinkers

Hobbes

The roots of liberalism reach back to the Enlightenment, with its celebration of the rational individual and the struggles of individuals and new classes to free themselves from the hierarchies of medieval state and society. But it took time for liberal ideas to emerge clearly. For example, Thomas Hobbes (1588–1679) argued that all persons are by nature equal, and that political authority must be based in their consent. Hobbes, however, was no liberal, for he insisted that state authority should be absolute; without such authority, he argued, society would collapse into war, and life would become "solitary, poor, nasty, brutish, and short" (1968, 186).

Locke

Hobbes' formula for government was challenged in short order by John Locke (1632–1704). In Locke's view, all persons are endowed by God with natural rights to life, liberty, and property. These rights cannot be given up—they are "inalienable." Locke reasoned that any law that violates these rights is illegitimate, and, in the extreme, any government that enacts such laws may be legitimately overthrown. Thus Locke agreed with Hobbes that by nature all persons have equal rights and that political authority requires their consent, but he also insisted that such authority is further limited by their inalienable natural rights to life, liberty, and property.

The central terms here are "government" and "the individual." Locke recognized that government must protect individuals from one another and from external invasions, but looking back at this conception, we can see that it protected one range of interests at the expense of others. It protects individuals against government with a thick wall of rights, but this wall limits the ability of government to protect individuals against other forms of power in the society. In the same manner, the thick wall of individual rights severely limits the ability of the community to promote common interests. Wherever a community interest runs up against an individual's right, the individual wins. In general, any interest that can be covered by a natural right becomes "private" rather than "public": an area of protected individual choice that cannot be regulated by the community. Religion and property were particularly important to Locke in this respect. Locke was concerned to protect individual choice in matters of religion, although interestingly not if the individual was Catholic or atheist. In protecting religious choice as a natural right and therefore as "private," Locke established the principle that the state may not support or require any form of religious practice in the public domain—for example, prayer in schools. Similarly, in covering property as a natural right, Locke established a thick wall against government interference (regulation) in the economy. In short, Lockean liberalism is distinctive in that it protects individual choice through natural rights—as thick walls that isolate individuals against one another and severely limit their ability to promote (or even understand) common interests. This perspective strongly influenced the development of liberalism in the British and American contexts. European liberalism developed differently, placing less emphasis on Lockean individualism and natural rights.

Mill

Writing two centuries later, John Stuart Mill (1806–1873) justified liberty on a different basis. In his great work *On Liberty* (1859), Mill rejected the idea of liberty as a natural right. Instead, he argued that liberty is valuable because it facilitates the fullest possible development of individuals. Thus the best society for Mill was one that allowed for maximum individual liberty. But in which aspects of life should people be free? Mill answered this question by what has come to be known as the **harm principle**. Mill reasoned that if a person's conduct directly harms others, society has the right to control it. But where a person's conduct does not directly harm others, society has no right to control it and the person should be completely free from interference.

Mill's greatest concern was providing a theoretical rationale for complete freedom of thought and belief. He noted that ideas can be expressed in ways that are harmful and, as such, can be restricted. Shouting "Fire!" as a joke in a crowded theatre is an example. Also, when ideas are expressed in ways that cause harm, this particular manner of expression may be restricted. But Mill believed that ideas themselves never cause harm, at least in the long run, and so he argued that there should be absolute freedom of thought and belief. Mill thought that censorship could never be justified because it always hinders truth. Even if an opinion seems completely mistaken, Mill argued, it might still turn out to be true or to contain a part of the truth.

In other areas of life, Mill supported the idea that conduct can be regulated where it directly harms others. But here also Mill insisted on complete freedom unless direct harm to other persons was a result. This means that individuals should be free even where their conduct is offensive or considered morally wrong. For example, sexual practices among consenting adults cannot legitimately be prohibited, even where others in the society consider these practices offensive and immoral. By the same token, individuals should be free to act in ways that may harm themselves. If no one else is directly harmed, society has no right to interfere. Thus, individuals cannot legitimately be forced to use safety equipment, such as safety belts in cars. But what if a person's conduct harms other persons indirectly? This situation is a common feature of complex societies because, arguably, just about everything we do affects others indirectly (even breathing contributes to global warming!). Thus, if we limit liberty to prevent indirect harms, in the end there might be no liberty left. On this account Mill held that indirect harms should be controlled only at the point that the harm becomes direct. For example, alcohol makes some people belligerent, leading to fights. Alcohol causes harm indirectly, but should we ban drinking entirely? Mill's view is that we should ban the direct harm—the fighting—but leave people free to drink if they choose.

In short, Mill's liberalism permits state action only where it is strictly necessary to protect other persons from direct harm. This vision projects a minimalist state, confined to functions of police protection and military defence. Mill and Locke, in fact, advocated quite similar views about the proper role of the state, but they did so in different ways and for different reasons. Where Locke uses liberties to protect important areas of individual life, such as religion and property, Mill seeks to protect individual *choice* and the ability of individuals to live on their own terms, whether these terms are seen by others as "important" or not. And where Locke protects liberties behind a thick wall of individualistic natural rights, Mill advocates liberty instead because it enables us to become the best human beings we can be. This difference has important consequences. Where Locke sees the state as the threat to liberty, Mill believes that society can also be a threat. The state threatens liberty through its legal power to compel obedience, but society also threatens liberty through its ability to pressure individuals into social conformity. Recall that Mill advocated liberty because he believed that it makes possible the development of the best kind of person, which was, for Mill, a free-spirited and responsible person. This free-spiritedness, in Mill's view, could be squelched by both legal restrictions and pressures from friends and family and society at large.

This point leads to a further difference between Locke and Mill. Over the course of his lifetime Mill came to advocate a wider role for the state—in protecting individuals from other forms of power in society, providing basic social services, and guaranteeing the needs of life for those in need. These state functions go well beyond the minimal state and thick natural rights of Lockean liberalism, but for Mill these state functions were necessary to protect the ability of individuals to live effectively on their own terms. Thus Mill's liberalism is open—in a way that Locke's is not—to a wider role for the state in providing for the needs of individuals.

After Mill's death, "social liberalism" advocated an increasing role for the state on this basis. In the twentieth century, the Western liberal democracies moved from being minimal states to being regulatory welfare states with these features:

- extensive regulatory controls to protect workers and consumers from abuses of power in the marketplace;
- measures for the provision of public goods (education, transportation, and sometimes health); and
- increasing protections for human rights.

With these developments, the role of the state has expanded considerably. These new state activities have generally been justified by liberals as necessary to protect the ability of individuals to live freely, but they have also created a need to reconsider the nature of liberalism in the context of the large state. John Rawls (1921–2002) is generally thought to have provided the most influential version of liberalism, especially in the United States, which may be considered the leading liberal state today.

Rawls

Rawls held that a just state must meet two requirements. First, it must guarantee maximum liberty and equality of opportunity. Second, the state must minimize inequalities of power, wealth, and income. Such inequalities can be justified only if they make everyone in the society better off over time. Rawls believed in incentives—that allowing unequal incomes can sometimes encourage people to work harder or take risks that result in economic growth. For Rawls, however, such inequalities can only be justified if they benefit everyone in the society, including those in the worst-off positions. Rawls held that these two requirements generally capture the sense of justice in our society today. But he also held that they could be shown to be justified as the principles of justice that each of us would choose for our society if, in the name of fairness, we had to do so without knowing how the choice would affect us personally. On this account, Rawls' theory came to be known as "justice as fairness."

Out of this general theory Rawls developed a specific principle of public justification: that discussions of public law and policy are required to respect the freedom and equality of all persons in the community. This seems reasonable enough, but for Rawls it requires that such discussions be stated in terms that all others can accept or, at least, cannot reasonably reject. This means specifically that no one can advance or justify a public policy that rests on the outlook or beliefs of just one part of the community, even if this "part" is the majority. For example, it is fine to propose that we have public holidays, but if my choice for a public holiday is one that already has special significance for some members of the community, for example, December 25, then in effect I am requiring that days that are significant for some persons (but not others) should be public holidays for everyone. In Rawls' view, this would violate the equality that I owe others as fellow citizens.

Liberalism Today

LIBERALISM HAS DEVELOPED THROUGH SOME QUITE DIFFERENT FORMS OVER time. These variations continue today, so that "liberalism" has become a composite position covering several quite different and sometimes conflicting views. These variations generally have a common matrix: they are all committed to freedom and equality as central values, and to protecting these values as rights. But they differ in the ways that understand these values.

Liberty/Freedom

Locke and Mill understood **liberty** primarily in negative terms, as the absence of interference in an individual's life. This liberty was somewhat legal and institutional, and it suggested a minimal role for the state. Accordingly, the state has an important role in protecting individuals from interference by others, but it also must minimize its own interference in doing so. Today, **freedom** is understood in more positive terms, as the ability of people to live on their own terms. This freedom (sometimes called "autonomy" or "self-rule") is broader and more social than the legal-institutional "liberty" of traditional liberalism. Freedom can be limited through interference, of course, but also through ignorance, dependence, disability, or not having access to the resources needed to live the life one has chosen. This broader view of freedom opens the door to a wider and more positive role for the state. It is not just a question of protecting people from interference but of more actively making available to them the resources and supports they need to lead their lives.

This perspective has led to a different understanding of the relationship between freedom and equality. For many traditional liberals, these values were opposed to each other. Efforts by the state to reduce inequality or to make valued goods, such as education or health care, available on a more equal basis invariably involve measures of regulation that interfere, to some degree, with people's choices. Where liberty is understood as the absence of interference, these equalizing measures will be seen as restrictions of liberty. However, this opposition between liberty and equality disappears when liberty is understood more broadly as freedom. Today, when the community publicly provides education or health care, these provisions may be justified in the name of both equality and freedom. Public education is understood as promoting equality and the ability to live on one's own terms.

The upshot is that discussions of freedom today can be quite complex. Freedom is no longer just a matter of minimizing interferences in people's lives but of supporting their ability to live on their own terms. Making this support available frequently involves some restriction of choice, but this restriction may be justified, especially compared with the larger freedom it facilitates. Even safety legislation can be justified this way. The requirement to use a safety belt in a car or a helmet on a motorcycle is an interference in people's lives, but the interference may be considered negligible in relation to the freedoms it protects.

In liberalism today, then, discussions of freedom generally operate within the following parameters. First, freedom of thought and belief is treated as an absolute value. Liberals insist that ideas, and access to ideas, should never be restricted, although they recognize that the particular manner of expressing an idea may be regulated to prevent harm. Second, there is firm support in liberalism for the freedom of people to live as they choose, so long as their choices do not harm others. Third, it is recognized that the community, expressed through the state, has an important role in supporting this freedom and that, as a result, it is sometimes necessary to restrict some freedoms in order to promote others that are more important.

Equality

As with liberty/freedom, equality has been understood in different ways. Traditional liberalism stressed the equality of basic citizenship rights, such as equality before the law. This equality is formal and legal and does not require that people be equal in their ability to exercise these rights. For example, we all have an equal right to be represented by a lawyer when charged under the law. But there is no right to equality in paying the legal costs. We each pay what we can afford, and the result is that those who are better off may secure better legal representation and thus have a better chance of being acquitted.

On this account, many liberals today hold that equality of citizenship rights also requires some equality in the ability to exercise these rights. The aim here is not to make people equal but to minimize any inequalities that might prevent them from exercising their rights adequately. In our legal example, this would take the form of legal aid, which, in principle, ensures that all citizens, whatever their means, are adequately represented by legal counsel, though perhaps not the most expensive counsel.

A third and more controversial sense of equality is equality in the resources needed to live a good life. In this view, equality is taken to mean that the resources of the community should be used to create the conditions and opportunities of a good life for all persons, considered equally as members of the community. The goal, however, is not to make people completely equal, but merely to reduce the inequalities that most severely limit the ability to live a good life. Even for egalitarian liberals, then, "equality" is not a positive goal in its own right but rather a means to increasing effective individual freedom.

With reference to these three types of equality, liberals have always accepted the first (equality of rights), and most liberals today accept some measures of the second (equality in the ability to exercise basic rights). The third—removing significant inequalities in the resources needed for a good life—is controversial, and some liberals reject it. At the extreme point, **libertarianism** holds that we should go back to the basic liberal rights and minimal state of classical liberalism. Its first cousin, **neo-liberalism**, also referred to as "economic liberalism" or "Market Liberalism," similarly advocates a minimal state, specifically in relation to the economy. As such, neo-liberalism promotes free trade, deregulation and privatization, and minimal taxation.

Thus, liberalism today covers many different positions—unified by a common commitment to freedom and equality as central values, but distinguished by differing and contesting views about what these values mean and require. It is important to note this because the word "liberal" is sometimes used today in a negative way. Because liberalism covers so many contesting positions, it is not uncommon to find people using the term "liberal" pejoratively—when what they mean to do is to disparage just one kind of liberalism, whether that be social liberalism or neo-liberalism. It is important in such cases to clarify what is at issue.

Because of its diversity, liberalism can sometimes seem to be the only political position today—as if all political debates were arguments between different versions of liberalism. But we need to take care here. The central values of liberalism—liberty/freedom and equality—are important values for almost everyone in our community. In this sense we are all committed to liberal values. But this does not make us all "liberals." Strictly, a "liberal" is one for whom freedom and equality are *the* fundamental values of political life, and the only such values. And this is distinctive because many of us, while committed to these values, are committed to other fundamental values as well, such as thicker notions of equality and the public good. Liberalism recognizes these other values but treats them as secondary—that is, subordinate to its central values of individual freedom and equality. Consider, for example, the debate over free university tuition. This can be seen as an in-house liberal debate, with free tuition being advocated by "left" (or egalitarian) liberals and opposed by neo-liberals, with everyone else in between. In this version of the debate, the left liberals support free tuition because they believe that access to higher education is essential if people are to live on terms of their own choosing. Neo-liberals, in contrast, oppose it as a violation of individual and market choice. But the issue need not be seen or cast in these terms. Free tuition might be proposed for other reasons, such as strong equality (quality education should be equal for all), or on grounds of community values and the public good (we want to live in a community in which all are educated to their abilities, and community resources should be deployed to this end). These can be important values in their own right. They do not have to be seen just as instruments of individual freedom, which is a distinctively "liberal" view.

Rights

A right is the ability to require the performance of a specific duty. More exactly, the claim that a person has a **right** means, first, that other persons or agencies have some definite duty and, second, that the person with the right can require the performance of this duty. For example, your right to free speech means (1) that other persons have duties not to interfere with you when you are giving a speech and (2) that if they do interfere, you can require that they stop.

This means that the nature of any right depends on the duties it imposes on others. Earlier, in the discussion of equality, we saw that the right to a lawyer could take two different forms. It could be just the right to hire a lawyer if you can afford one. Here, the right imposes on the state the duty not to stop you from doing so. But the right could take a stronger form, as in the right to hire a lawyer if you can afford one and the right to have a lawyer paid by the state if you cannot afford one. Here, the right imposes a different set of duties on the state. Thus, the same expression—"the right to a lawyer"—can designate different kinds of rights, and the difference lies in the duties that the right requires.

One way to classify rights, accordingly, is in terms of what they protect. Some rights protect liberties (or choices), and they do so by imposing duties of non-interference on the part of others. Other rights protect claims to particular benefits (such as education), and they do so by imposing the duty to provide the benefit to specific persons or agencies.

Legal rights are rights that are protected by law. Here, the law protects rights by providing a mechanism (through the courts) for their authoritative adjudication and enforcement. For some theorists, this enforceability is essential to the idea of a right. But there is a broader sense in which we may talk of **moral rights**. If Mary agrees to meet John for coffee, it can reasonably be said that she has a duty to turn up and that John has a right to expect this, even though he has no legal power to require it. A rich variety of these moral rights and duties exists in our social practices today, and these rights can be very important. There was a time, just one generation ago, when the law made it very difficult for women to obtain abortions. Those who opposed the law typically asserted, "Women have a right to abortion." Sometimes, this meant that women *should* have a right to abortion and that the law should be changed to allow it. But sometimes the claim meant, more strongly, that women do have a right to abortion because they have the right to control their own bodies, and that the law violates these rights by making it difficult for them to obtain abortions.

Historically, these moral rights have sometimes been presented as **natural rights**. These are rights that, it is said, people possess "by nature" as human beings, and not just as members of particular societies. As we have seen, John Locke held that people have natural rights to life, liberty, and property and that any laws that violated these rights would be illegitimate. Today, rights of this kind are more commonly called **human rights**. These are asserted as standards that must be respected by all societies because, it is held, they are the rights of people as human beings. In most cases, they are "moral," rather than legal, rights because there are few legal mechanisms for their adjudication and enforcement. But they are still "rights" because they assert duties whose performance can reasonably be demanded even if they cannot legally be enforced. The United Nations Declaration of Human Rights is a prime example of unenforceable human rights.

It is troubling that human rights cannot ordinarily be enforced and that, as a result, basic human rights are often violated with impunity. It may seem on this account that human rights are not "really" rights at all. However, such a view is mistaken. It is true that if a right is non-enforceable, then it cannot be a legal right. But this is because legal rights, by definition, are enforced by the courts. If the courts do not recognize a right, it cannot be a legal right. But it may still be asserted as a moral right. It may still be true that certain persons or agencies have specifiable duties in relation to the right and that the right-bearer is justified in demanding that these duties be performed. Where these conditions apply, the right exists. If it is not enforceable, it is still a right, just one that is not, or not yet, legally enforceable.

Summary

This chapter has outlined three key concepts of current liberalism: liberty/freedom, equality, and rights. In the case of liberty/freedom, we noted that there has been a shift away from the traditional and narrow understanding of liberty as the absence of interference toward a broader and more social understanding of freedom as the ability to live on one's own terms. This newer understanding is more easily consistent with the value of equality, although we also found that the idea of equality can be understood in three different ways, each reflecting quite different conceptions of citizenship. These two concepts—freedom and equality—are the central value commitments of liberalism today. The chapter concluded by showing how these values may be protected by establishing them as rights.

Discussion Questions

1. Where there is a conflict between the freedom of individuals and the desires of the community, which do you think should prevail? Suppose a few people want to do something that does not directly harm anyone but greatly offends the majority. Should the majority be able to forbid them? Can you think of issues that would put you on one side of this question and other issues that would put you on the other side?

2. Would you allow clearly racist books to be freely published and distributed? Should they be available through publicly funded libraries?

3. In your opinion, is citizenship better understood as a set of rights that people have as individuals (such as the right to vote) or, instead, as a range of responsibilities and freedoms that people have as members of their community?

References

Hobbes, Thomas. 1968. *Leviathan*. London: Penguin Books.

Mill, John Stuart. 1859. *On Liberty*. In A.D. Lindsay, ed., *Utilitarianism, Liberty, Representative Government* (pp. 61–170). London: Everyman's Library.

Further Readings

Macpherson, C.B. 1978. *The Life and Times of Liberal Democracy*. Oxford: Oxford University Press.

Rawls, John. 2001. *Justice as Fairness: A Restatement*. Cambridge, MA: Harvard University Press.

Taylor, Charles. 1992. *The Ethics of Authenticity*. Cambridge, MA: Harvard University Press.

Weblinks

Stanford Encyclopedia of Philosophy: Liberalism
http://plato.stanford.edu/entries/liberalism

Stanford Encyclopedia of Philosophy: John Locke
http://plato.stanford.edu/entries/locke

Stanford Encyclopedia of Philosophy: John Stuart Mill
http://plato.stanford.edu/entries/mill

Policy Library: John Rawls
www.policylibrary.com/rawls

CHAPTER 4

DEMOCRACY

Objectives

Democracy is a critical concept because it highlights the question of the "public." The distinction between what is public and what is private has been extremely important to the study of politics. This chapter begins by showing how the concept of democracy involves the question of the public. Then it provides a brief history of democratic thought, from the philosophers of the polis of ancient Greece to today's theorists of radical democracy. We find that dramatic shifts in thinking about democracy often occur in periods of social change, when societies are forced to reflect on themselves and on their assumptions about the fundamentals of social organization and governance. The current era of globalization is just such a period of reflection. Key assumptions about governing, such as the nature of the capitalist market and its relationship with the state, are now being revisited and reformulated. Moreover, some contemporary theorists of democracy are questioning the distinction between public and private. In this sense, contemporary democracy is said to be "in crisis." As a way of trying to understand this current crisis, the chapter concludes by introducing ongoing debates in contemporary democratic thought.

CATHERINE KELLOGG

Introduction

The word "democracy" comes from the Greek *demos* (people) and *kratos* (rule). In the classical literature we refer to, democracy means the "rule of the many," which is generally contrasted with the "rule of the few" (aristocracy) or the "rule of one" (monarchy). More recently, however, "democracy" is used to refer to its literal translation as "the rule of the people." Simply put, democracy is any form of government in which the rules of society are decided by the people who will be bound by them. This is how the concept of democracy implicates the public: it suggests that public affairs—the rules of society—should be decided by the public itself.

What is distinctive about theories of democracy is their common insistence that the authority of the state begins and ends with the public. At the root of the practice of democracy lies a faith in the capacity of people to decide key issues of governance for themselves. While this belief is the central tenet of democratic theory, it is not limited to classical democratic theorists, such as Jean-Jacques Rousseau or John Stuart Mill. It is also found in the editorial pages of our newspapers. Indeed, the view that governments should operate only through the "will" of the people is so widespread that the only regimes in the modern world considered legitimate are those based on popular consent.

Despite the widespread appeal of democracy, anyone who looks closely at this concept is bound to notice that it means many different things to different people. Indeed, Robert Dahl explains that a "term that means anything means nothing. And so it has become with 'democracy,' which nowadays is not so much a term of restricted and specific meaning, as a vague endorsement of a popular idea" (Dahl, 1989, 2). Not only does the word itself imply the "populus" or the public, but also democracy as an ideal receives seemingly unanimous support the world over. The word is often used simply as a synonym for "good" and hailed as the master principle of our age.

Theory and Crisis

DEMOCRATIC THEORY IS THE DOMINANT FRAME OR THEORY THROUGH WHICH we organize and make meaningful the world of politics. In fact, constructing theories is nothing more than the process through which we organize and make our lives meaningful. Even when we are performing a mundane task, we are doing so within a set of assumptions, which have rendered that activity meaningful in some way. All social life is founded on theory—a compilation of ideas that tell a coherent story about a given human practice. Theory is an activity that goes on all the time, even when we are unaware of it. But at certain moments the theories making our lives meaningful no longer seem to fit our experience or make sense of the world. These are times of *crisis*.

Political theories are interpretations—coherent stories that order and make sense of the world—about politics. In fact, the history of political thought can be understood as the history of waves of *crisis* that have forced human beings to reflect upon practices of human governance—democratic and otherwise. The current crisis in democratic theory stems from a variety of factors, including a crisis in contemporary practices of democracy. For instance, "democracy" has generally been taken to mean something as simple as the representation of citizens in legislatures where we are recognized as "formally" equal. But certain thinkers have begun to question whether formal equality can mean anything very profound when we are so demonstrably unequal to each other with respect to our access to other kinds of power. The power at work in the areas of our lives previously considered "private," such as our workplaces, our families, or the "private sector," is as important politically as are the formal processes of political decision making. Can we consider truly democratic a set of political and social arrangements that render us formally equal to each other when the way that we actually live our lives is increasingly unequal? What are the real requirements of democratic citizenship? To begin making sense of these questions, we will look at three historical "models" of democratic thought.

A History of Democratic Theory

CANADIAN POLITICAL THEORIST C.B. MACPHERSON TELLS US THAT,

> in looking at models of democracy . . . we should keep a sharp lookout for two things: [the theory's] assumptions about the whole society in which the democratic political system is to operate, and its assumptions about the essential nature of the people who are to make the system work (which for a democratic system means the people in general, not just a ruling or leading class). (MacPherson, 1977, 5)

The following section offers a brief history of democratic theories. It pays particular attention to the assumptions those theories make about the essential nature of both society and the people who inhabit it.

Ancient Greek Democracy

The development of democracy in Athens during its "golden age"—which lasted for about 50 years in the fifth century B.C.E—has been the source of inspiration for much modern democratic political thought. The modern ideals of equality before the law, liberty, and respect are often traced to the ancient Greek polis. This small, self-contained institutional form nurtured intense communal life. The polis formed the ethical model for subsequent thinkers as diverse as Thomas Hobbes, John Locke, Alexis de Tocqueville, Jean-Jacques Rousseau, and G.W.F. Hegel.

The Greek word "polis" is the root for a range of English words, including "politics," "politician," "political," and "police." While there is no exact English equivalent, polis is commonly translated as both "state" and "city" because it possesses the attributes of both. The Athenian polis was small; some 300 000 people lived in Athens at its height, and only 40 000 were citizens. The rest of the population—women, children, foreign residents, and slaves—were excluded from the ranks of the citizens and from formal participation in political life. The "public" realm, then, was actually made up of a very small percentage of the inhabitants of the Greek city state. The small size of the polis allowed citizens to partake of a distinctive communal way of life. Spheres of life we now consider non-political—religion, art, sport, and commerce—were all considered within the purview of politics. They were, therefore, subject to democratic deliberation. The small size of the polis also provided its citizens with a sense of active engagement in public affairs that has not been widely duplicated at any other time. Greek direct democracy was probably the most *participatory* form of politics that Western civilization has ever seen.

Approximately 50 years into the life of this regime, ancient Athens and its allies entered into a conflict with oligarchies that sided with Sparta. This conflict, known as the Peloponnesian Wars, ended with the complete defeat and occupation of democratic Athens. Precisely because the Greek city state or polis was in crisis, Plato and Aristotle were impelled to think about politics in a new way and to write their important works. For instance, the trial and execution of Socrates inspired Plato to question the validity of rule by those who were ignorant of the most pressing questions of the purpose of life. He suggested that Greek citizens were not truly able to rule themselves but required the leadership of those specifically trained in the art of state-craft and soul-craft. Despite the democratic nature of the ancient Greek state, then, the political thinkers we most associate with ancient Greece—Plato, Aristotle, and Thucydides—were uniformly hostile to the direct democracy represented by the Greek polis. Their objections had to do with the essential unruliness of what we might now call a "mob."

Notwithstanding this hostility to democracy, both Plato and Aristotle were profoundly influenced by the participatory nature of the Greek city state. Significantly, Aristotle argued, "Man is a political animal." By this he meant that human beings could attain their full potential only by living in political association with each other. It is only through active involvement in the life of one's political community that citizens can know what is truly important. Thus, we can see that for the ancient Greeks, a good citizen was someone actively involved in the day-to-day running of the government.

The Middle Ages and Italian Republicanism

There is a strange silence in the history of democratic thought that begins shortly after the demise of Athenian democracy and ends with the early Renaissance. This period overlaps significantly with what we call the medieval period, or the Middle Ages, which are meant to mark the "middle" period between the collapse of the Roman Empire in the fifth century and the beginning of the Renaissance in the fourteenth. This silence in the history of political thought is a complex matter to explain, but in its simplest terms, the ascendancy of the Christian faith in the Western world, as well as the rise of feudal forms of social organization, meant that the "good" citizen of the ancient Greek polis was replaced by the "true believer." The idea that humans could organize their common futures democratically was replaced by the idea that everyone's fate was pre-determined by God.

By the middle part of the medieval period, Europe was also dominated by **feudalism**. This form of social and economic organization was characterized by a strict hierarchy between the property-owning aristocracy and the landless peasants. This way of life emphasized the deeply held belief that people were fundamentally unequal; those who held power did so because they were essentially "better" than those whom they ruled. Feudalism was set against the backdrop of the Holy Roman Empire—a complex web of kings and rulers who were understood to rule by "divine right." The authority of these rulers was said to come directly from God. In short, throughout the Middle Ages, European politics was heavily influenced by three great supranational institutions: the Church, the Holy Roman Empire, and feudalism.

By the beginning of the sixteenth century, a number of political communities had established some form of popular control, especially in northern Italy. What eventually became the new "city states" or city republics were run by elected councillors. Councillors were ultimately accountable to male householders with taxable property. This notion of accountability represented an important challenge to the prevailing understanding that rule was God-given. An outcome of this new social order was a return to the idea of **civic republicanism**, first articulated by Aristotle: that is, the idea of active involvement in the state as a "good." Central to this is the notion of a political community with a shared history and a shared destiny. Thus, the Renaissance (literally, rebirth) was so named because it recalled many of the ideas of ancient Greek democracy.

Capitalism and the Liberal Revolution

While the Reformation was a revolution against the traditional church and the Renaissance was the revalorization of some of the ideas from Greek democracy, the Enlightenment was a revolution against traditional philosophy and science. It was a "movement" that sought to understand the world and humanity on a new basis. This period was accompanied by the growing belief that all people were equal because, no matter what their social position, each possessed the capacity for reason. The presumption of equality was revolutionary because it led people to challenge the validity of political institutions that distributed power and wealth unequally among citizens. Legitimate political power was seen to emanate from the people themselves; the people were seen to be the source of ultimate political and legal authority.

The Reformation and the Enlightenment were accompanied (and in some senses precipitated) by the end of feudal forms of life and by the rise of capitalism and market economies. While feudal society did have market activity—there were individual transactions of labour goods and services—it was not a market economy. In feudalism, most economic activity was for the purposes of immediate consumption, rather than for exchange. What was distinctive about capitalism was the newly emerging notion of "private property" and the accompanying right of an individual (or corporate entity) to exclude others from the use or benefit of it. Significantly, human labour itself also became a commodity that could be bought and traded on the market. The transformation from feudal forms of life (characterized by the predominance of the Church, absolutist sovereigns, and a landless peasantry) to a market of "free" producers and buyers was a complex one that had profound social, political, and cultural consequences.

The Reformation, the Enlightenment, and the emergence of capitalism reinforced each other and together formed the *liberal revolution*, which marked the passing from feudal society to what we now recognize as capitalist modernity. An organic, hierarchical, traditional society was rapidly being replaced by an individualistic, fluid, and pluralist society in which reason replaced custom as a standard by which to judge policy and institutions. Perhaps the most graphic representations of this liberal revolution were the American Revolution of 1776 and the French Revolution of 1789. Both revolutions were dramatic uprisings against traditional, hierarchical forms of rule, and both were infused with the energy and enthusiasm of the liberal slogan, "Liberty, equality, and solidarity."

Early Liberal Democratic Theory

The dramatic changes in political rule in Europe and North America brought with them the most important variant of democratic thought: **liberal democratic theory**. This view was first articulated by such theorists as Thomas Hobbes, John Locke, and John Stuart Mill. The most important aspect of liberal democratic theory, and what distinguishes it from the models of democratic thought reviewed so far, was the belief in the importance of political, moral, and economic *liberty*. This variant of democratic theory clearly distinguished the public—understood as the institutions of the state—from the private, which was significantly different from the civic republicanism and the Greek ethos of the polis that preceded it. For both the previous models, the *public* included some dimensions of human life that were consigned to the private sphere in the modern model.

The notion of freedom was very important to these liberal thinkers, but it was a specific kind of freedom: the freedom to pursue private property. Moreover, liberal democrats had a distinct view of what constitutes human nature—i.e., that individuals are rational maximizers of self-interest, who rationally choose what is in their own best interests, even when those interests are not necessarily those that grant them the most immediate satisfaction. For example, individuals will choose to live under a government that restricts some of their destructive activities because it will also restrict the destructive activities of others.

One of the most passionate defenders of this perspective was Thomas Hobbes. While he was no advocate of democracy in principle, his justification of government was that state authority, rather than monarchs or God, was created by individuals acting out of self-interest.

People created the authority of the state to protect themselves from each other. Hobbes believed that individuals ought willingly to surrender their rights of self-government to a powerful single authority. Democracy, in this view, was the mechanism by which citizens could check the powers of the state against arbitrarily punishing its citizens.

John Locke revised Hobbes' argument with the view that "government" should be conceived as an instrument for the defence of "life, liberty and estate" (Locke, 1965). One important difference between Hobbes and Locke is that, whereas Hobbes emphasized democracy as a mechanism for protecting *individuals* from the state, Locke understood democracy as a mechanism for protecting the *market* from the state. And here is the second important assumption shared by classical liberal democrats: the society in which the democratic political system operates is understood to be a capitalist one. This is why, in Locke's view, the state should leave the "private" economic transactions of individuals entirely unregulated.

In the nineteenth century, John Stuart Mill developed his important objection to the purely formal dimensions of the position laid down by earlier liberal democrats. Mill went far beyond previous liberal democrats with respect to *moral* freedom. Mill formulated his theory with a view to protecting iconoclasts or "free thinkers" from the imposition of conventional or traditional morality. In this sense, Mill was passionately dedicated to the protection of minorities within a majoritarian system.

Classical liberal democrats, then, constructed a relatively coherent theory of democracy. In it, the institutions of the modern state were understood to be public and, therefore, subject to collective control. The modern distinction between the public realm of the state and the private, unregulated, and apolitical realms of the family and the economy was vital to this theoretical framework.

Contemporary Challenges

THE CONTEMPORARY PERIOD IS DOMINATED BY THE SO-CALLED "TRIUMPH" of democracy worldwide. The conversation about what constitutes democracy is, however, far from over. While the majority of contemporary democratic theorists continue to be preoccupied with the major questions of liberalism, they have shifted their focus from freedom to equality. As well, there are some radical democratic critiques of the public–private distinction laid down by liberalism that require important scrutiny. In the following section, we look at the debates among contemporary liberal democrats, who are divided over the question of what vision of "the good" should drive contemporary liberal democracies.

Contemporary Liberal Democratic Theory

The transition from pre-modern absolutist states and traditional societies to modern liberal democratic representative democracies has been largely achieved in the Western world. Not surprisingly, therefore, liberal democrats are currently less concerned with the freedom of individuals from the arbitrary powers of the state than they are with the nature of the equality that democracies can deliver to their citizens. The most important debate among contemporary liberal democrats—known as the *liberal–communitarian debate*—takes the liberal notion of equality as its central focus.

John Rawls, for example, suggests that the only "good" of democracies lies in their ability to formally recognize the equality of each citizen. More precisely, Rawls argues that the only idea of "the good" that we can agree upon is a thinly conceived notion of political *tolerance*. Any other concept would be in some way threatening to the multicultural, diverse political culture in which we live. In other words, we can never agree that we *should* worship one particular kind of God, or even that we should worship at all; that we *should* hold certain kinds of values when raising our children; or that we *should* mate in these and not other ways. The only *should* we can agree upon is to be tolerant of a variety of ways in which to worship, instill values, make families and structures of kinship, and so on.

Noted communitarians, such as Charles Taylor and Alasdair MacIntyre, take issue with Rawls' vision of the "good." They say that this conception of democracy has no "end." It is not directed toward making us better patriots or even better people. The idea of tolerance, they argue, is nothing more than a *procedure* that suggests that we deal fairly and equally with each other. Recalling the civic republicanism first articulated by Aristotle, Taylor and MacIntyre maintain that political life involves much more than representation in democratic institutions; liberal democracies are forms of civic association in which we discover who we really are. In fact, they say that we do not discover our "identities" (as Canadians, as Muslims, or as lesbians) in isolation. We discover them in dialogue with each other—in the give and take of a "public" conversation. Communitarians take their point of departure from people's real sense of alienation from the formal public institutions that represent them.

Rawls and other liberals respond that this is precisely the price that citizens must pay for living in a society that treats us all as equals, regardless of our particular ethnic, racial, religious, sexual, or other identities. It is the very neutrality of the public sphere that protects our freedom as citizens. Rawls thus proposes that the principle of equality is complete in itself and that the differences between us are, in the final analysis, politically irrelevant. In contrast, Charles Taylor understands, in his unique situation as an anglophone living in Quebec, that the demand for public recognition (by such institutions as the state or schools) by a people is more than simply a psychological quirk. It is a constitutive feature of liberal democracies. Taylor and other communitarians recall the civic republican tradition first articulated by Aristotle when they suggest that something more than empty "equality" ought to govern the public sphere and that we might be better served to return to traditional religious or cultural values.

However, both these contemporary liberal democratic positions share the division between public and private laid down by the earlier liberal democrats. While communitarians like Taylor want to infuse public institutions, such as the judiciary or

Parliament, with a sensitivity to cultural differences among us, the question of the market, the family, or the very real political and economic differences between people are conceived only as "cultural." The question of economic equality—rather than political equality—does not appear as a variable in this dispute.

Marxist and Radical Democratic Critiques

The focus on economic equality is another way of talking about the compatibility of liberal democracy with capitalism. Marxist and radical democratic critics have questioned this compatibility with most insistence. Marx argued that historically and logically, capitalism is tied to the private ownership of the means of production—the right of individuals or corporate entities to the exclusive use of land, money, and labour power. This private ownership encourages wealth to accumulate predominantly in one class. It is, thus, surely not accidental, Marx argued, that the "rights of private property" are at the foundation of the whole constitutional and juridical superstructure we have come to know as *liberal democracy*. Marx felt that capitalism could tolerate "democracy" because in the final analysis, real power is not to be found in democratic institutions but instead rests with those who control the means of production.

Specifically, capitalists control the working class, not by means of exclusive political rights but by means of exclusive property. This means that even in its best and most democratic forms, capitalism can, and must, confine equality to a separate "political" sphere that does not, and must not, intrude into the economic sphere or subvert economic *in*equality. People in capitalist societies spend most of their waking hours in activities and relationships where there is no democratic accountability at all. This is true not only in the workplace, where they are likely to be under the direct control of others, but also in all spheres of life that are subject to "market" imperatives. In liberal democracies such as Canada, large areas of human life lie entirely outside the reach of democratic processes. Following from this fact, radical democracy theorists argue that traditional democracy has failed to deliver on its promise of real equality and civic participation. Radical democrats claim that a thoroughgoing understanding of democracy necessarily entails extending the principles of democracy—freedom, equality, and solidarity—into every area of daily life: work, education, leisure, and home.

Unlike traditional Marxists, radical democrats insist that class is not the only source of inequality in contemporary society. They argue that we are unequal in ways that go beyond the economic. For instance, the great disparity in real economic and political power between men and women, between white and non-white people, and between those who live in the "North" and those who live in the "South" reflects the inability of our "democratic" institutions to deliver any kind of substantive equality. Radical democrats claim that if the principles of liberal democracy are to be taken seriously, the limited scope of what constitutes "the public," who might come to appear in that public, as well as a limited sense of what constitutes "political activity" offered by contemporary liberal democracies must be changed.

For much of liberal democratic theory, the way that "the people" rule themselves is through the formal process of electing representatives to sit in legislatures where laws are debated and drafted. The only question under dispute on this view is what constitutes "the people." For example, for some, ruling can be considered democratic if it involves decisions made by institutions that balance the competing interests of a wide variety of groups. For some others, ruling can be understood to be democratic if it means "the people" were able to choose their leaders in elections, whereas for others, ruling can't really be understood to be democratic unless many citizens participate in the debate about the issues that will be resolved in legislatures and enforced by judiciaries, police, and the military. All of these disagreements, however, are about who rules and by what principles they do that ruling. They are not about whether politics involves anything other than law-making.

A newer strain of "radical democratic" theory suggests that we should remember that rule by something as undetermined as "the people" is always going to be very close to *un*ruly. Some radical democrats have recently argued that this idea of "unruliness" is an essential part of democratic politics, which is "inherently unstable, inclined towards anarchy, and identified with revolution" (Wolin, 1994, 37). What Wolin is getting at is the idea that calls for increased democratization are almost always ways of challenging the established form of rule.

Perhaps the easiest way to think about this is to look to a scene we are confronted with daily: women, immigrants, visible minorities, Aboriginal people, lesbians and gays, the disabled, the poor, the disenfranchised, or the overlooked continue to insist that they have not been adequately represented by our public institutions or public discourses. Each of these "groups" of people came into existence by speaking in the public about the ways that their interests, or ways of life, have not been attended to in the public domain. Struggles on the part of these voices for representation are calls for "democratization" in the sense that they are claims that seemingly universal categories, such as "the people," or citizenship, are not yet inclusive enough. What some radical democrats have argued is that this "not-inclusive-enough-ness" is in fact the radical and emancipatory thrust of democracy, and that the point of democratic politics is not to make universal categories—like citizen—inclusive "enough" but rather to always leave room for whatever, and whoever, can't be anticipated. For some radical democrats, then, the practice of democracy is precisely the process of trying make a universal term like "the people" actually live up to its promise (of including everyone) while also trying to keep that term permanently open (because who "everyone" might be cannot be anticipated in advance) (Laclau, 1996). A contemporary French thinker, Jacques Rancière, makes this point when he says that democracy is what happens when those who have been understood to have no part within a regime suddenly appear and speak in public without authorization (Rancière, 2001). In this sense, the practice of democracy, in its most radical sense, can always involve unauthorized voices exposing the injustice—the failure to be truly "democratic"—at the heart of all forms of ruling that consider themselves democratic.

This new strain of political critique also responds to the challenge of **globalization**, which, it is widely argued, has reduced the capacities of the state to curb stark inequalities in social, political, and economic power, both nationally and internationally. In this sense, the current era is witnessing a contraction in the realm of what we can meaningfully talk about as public. Increasingly, the values of the capitalist market dominate questions of public policy. Nations are required to be increasingly efficient and competitive (the dominant values of the market), while the accountability of the state to its citizens is increasingly restricted. This new era of so-called "global competitiveness" or globalization represents the crisis forcing democratic theorists to rethink the distinction between public and private at the heart of liberal conceptions of democracy. If the nation-state becomes less and less able to act as an arbiter of social life, this rethinking may involve the creation of a global democracy beyond the level of the nation-state.

Summary

This chapter has surveyed the way that democratic practices and theories have consistently raised the question of the relationship between what is "public" and what is "private." Beginning with a brief history of democratic thought, we found that dramatic shifts in thinking about democracy often occurred during periods of fundamental social change. We then investigated the direct and participatory nature of Greek democracy, the revitalization of that tradition in civic republicanism, and the re-articulation of democratic ideals of freedom and equality in early and contemporary liberal democratic thought. The fundamental premise of liberal democratic theory is the importance of individual, political, moral, and economic *freedom*. This democratic theory draws lines between the public and the private in terms that we might currently recognize. Specifically, the family and the market are carved off from what was understood as "public" and placed in the category "private." They are, thus, outside the purview of those issues that traditionally concerned democratic politics.

More recently, liberal, Marxist, and radical democratic theorists, especially in Western democracies, have shifted the emphasis from freedom to equality in questioning how all citizens of a democratic society can participate equally. They have asked whether the formal political equality of the contemporary liberal democratic state is truly adequate to satisfy the important differences between us. Does democracy require *economic* or simply *political* equality? Does democracy imply the end of social discrimination? In the shift in emphasis from freedom to equality, many contemporary democratic theorists are challenging the validity of the claim that the market or the family is private and, therefore, outside the bounds of democratic deliberation. Despite the apparent success of democracy as the dominant ideal and practice of governing worldwide, it remains an unfinished project.

Discussion Questions

1. Do you agree with the modern liberal perspective that it is only the neutrality of the public sphere that protects our freedom as citizens?

2. Do you think that democracy should imply economic as well as political equality in the way that Marxist and radical democrats suggest?

3. As argued in this chapter, theory is something that becomes evident when the human practices it orders and makes meaningful come into crisis. Can you think of a set of human practices less complex than the democratic processes of governing, to which this idea might apply?

4. Democracy is the dominant value of our age. What values are or should be embedded within this term?

References

Aristotle. 1948. *Politics.* Translated by Ernest Barker. Oxford: Oxford University Press.

Bernal, Martin. 1987. *Black Athena: The Afroasiatic Roots of Classical Civilization.* New Brunswick: Rutgers University Press.

Connolly, William. 1991. *Identity/Difference: Democratic Negotiation of Political Paradox.* Ithaca: Cornell University Press.

Dahl, Robert. 1989. *Democracy and Its Critics.* New Haven: Yale University Press.

Dworkin, Ronald. 1977. *Taking Rights Seriously.* Cambridge: Harvard University Press.

Held, David. 1987. *Models of Democracy.* Cambridge: Polity Press.

Hobbes, Thomas. 1977. *Leviathan.* Hammondsworth: Penguin.

Kymlicha, Will. 1995. *Multicultural Citizenship.* Oxford: Oxford University Press.

Laclau, Ernesto. 1996. "Deconstruction, Pragmatism, Hegemony" in Chantal Mouffe, ed., *Deconstruction and Pragmatism.* New York: Routledge.

Locke, John. 1965. *Second Treatise on Government.* New York: Mentor Press.

MacPherson, C.B. 1965. *The Real World of Democracy.* Toronto: CBC Publications.

———. 1977. *The Life and Times of Liberal Democracy.* Oxford: Oxford University Press.

Marx, Karl and Friedrich Engels. 1968. "The Communist Manifesto" in *Selected Works.* London: Lawrence and Wishart.

McIntryre, Alasdaire. 1981. *After Virtue.* Notre Dame: University of Notre Dame Press.

Mouffe, Chantal. 1994. *The Return to the Political.* London: Verso.

Philips, Anne. 1991. *Engendering Democracy.* Cambridge: Polity Press.

Rawls, John. 1971. *A Theory of Justice.* Cambridge: Harvard University Press.

Rousseau, Jean-Jacques. 1964. *A Discourse on the Origins of Inequality.* New York: St. Martin's Press.

Sandel, Michael. 1984. *Liberalism and Its Critics.* Oxford: Clarendon Press.

Taylor, Charles. 1992. *Multiculturalism and the Politics of Recognition.* Princeton: Princeton University Press.

Trend, David, ed. 1996. *Radical Democracy: Identity, Citizenship and the State.* London: Routledge.

Wolin, Sheldon. 1996. "Norm and Form: The Constitutionalization of Democracy" in *Athenian Political Thought and the Reconstruction of American Democracy.* Princeton: Princeton University Press.

Further Readings

Aristotle. 1948. *Politics.* Translated by Ernest Barker. Oxford: Oxford University Press.

Held, David. 1987. *Models of Democracy.* Cambridge: Polity Press.

————. 1995. *Democracy and the Global Order.* Oxford: Polity Press.

MacPherson, C.B. 1973. *Democratic Theory: Essays in Retrieval.* Oxford: Oxford University Press.

Tocqueville, Alexis de. 1946. *Democracy in America.* New York: Knopf.

Wolin, Sheldon. "Fugitive Democracy" in Seyla Benhabib, ed., *Democracy and Difference: Contesting the Boundaries of the Political.* Princeton: Princeton University Press.

Wood, Ellen Meiksins. 1995. *Democracy Against Capitalism.* Cambridge: Cambridge University Press.

Weblinks

Amnesty International
www.amnesty.org/ailib/intcam/femgen/fgm1.htm

Canadians for Direct Democracy
www.npsnet.com/cdd

Canadian Centre for Policy Alternatives
www.policyalternatives.ca

Democracy Watch
www.dwatch.ca

CHAPTER 5

RADICAL POLITICS

SANDRA REIN

Objectives

Just the mention of the terms "radical" and "ideological" will raise eyebrows and cause the exchange of knowing looks. After all, in today's political parlance, to be radical is to be ideological and suspect—at least in the eyes of the main-stream media and those offering political commentary. Rather than exercise this same tendency to discredit "radicals" and "ideologues," this chapter will introduce **ideology** as a critical concept in political science and discuss key radical political ideologies of the past two centuries. Finally, the chapter will conclude with an overview of the ways in which these radical ideas continue to influence politics today.

Introduction

The concept of *ideology* has been a constant theme in the study of social and political life. Terry Eagleton's survey of a legion of definitions reveals that more than 16 different uses are commonly invoked by scholars. So, how is a student to understand ideology? Generally, we must understand that the history of ideology as a concept is essentially the competition between negative and more neutral connotations of the term. Negative representations define ideology as myth, illusion, or false consciousness. More neutral approaches see ideology as the study of the role of ideas in social and political life. Terry Eagleton argues that we can straddle these two approaches by viewing ideology as both "lived relations" and an "organizing social force" (Eagleton, 1990, 2, 30, 222). We can think about ideology as key sets of both those beliefs and values that serve to legitimate a certain social order, the so-called dominant ideology, and those values and beliefs that may be said to oppose or challenge that dominant ideology. There are several important implications that result from using such an approach to ideology. First, it is people who promote and contest dominant ideologies. Second, Eagleton's definition accepts that ideologies have interested parties who stand to benefit from the adoption of their ideas and that the individuals adopting these ideas may be misled. Finally, this definition of ideology focuses attention on the contestable nature of social ideas. Although we recognize that ideologies play an important role in organizing social stability, they are also the primary midwives of social change. The combination of these implications means that ideology—the study of ideas as they inform society and construct the conditions for social change—are at the core of how we practise politics.

Modern Radical Political Ideologies

TRADITIONALLY, POLITICAL SCIENCE HAS TREATED MAJOR THEORIES THAT CHALLLENGE the status quo as radical political ideologies. Of course, what is judged as radical will change in accordance with the specific social context of the time. Specifically, we will review Marxism, socialism, anarchism, and communism. Each can be considered a radical political ideology and a political movement. Each offers an analysis of the ideas that organize social relations as well as a program of change. In Eagleton's words, each political ideology under discussion here has something to say about "lived relations" and "organizing social forces." However, before proceeding to a discussion of Marxism, a word or two needs to be said about why these particular ideologies are termed "radical."

Much like "ideology," the term "radical" often suffers from a pejorative connotation. The very use of the word signals to one's audience that whatever follows is extreme and should, in the name of reasonableness, be discounted. However, "radical" has a more nuanced meaning. Rather than beginning our analysis by prejudging radical ideologies as extreme, we are better served by looking at radical thought as critical social theory. The Latin origin of "radical" is *radic*, meaning root. Radical critiques, thus, are those that propose to go to the root of the problem. All four ideologies under consideration offer fundamental and thorough critiques of various forms of social organization. In this sense, to be radical means to significantly challenge the status quo. Social scientists today who draw their analyses from radical political thought, particularly from the Marxist tradition, tend to avoid the pejorative title "radical" and instead opt for the general name "critical theory." Nevertheless, the key consideration is always a critique of the status quo or, in the words of Marx, "a ruthless criticism of everything existing" (Marx, 1978, 12–15).

Marxism

Marxism is often one of the most difficult "schools of political thought" to reduce to an essential core. The association of Marxism with the failed Soviet Union often causes confusion—what is Marxism? For our purposes, Marxism is drawn primarily from the works of Karl Marx (1818–1883), such as his famous treatise *Das Kapital*. Marx's writings include both a theoretical analysis of capitalism and a commitment to radical political change. As he noted in his well-known eleventh thesis on Feuerbach, "The philosophers have only *interpreted* the world, in various ways; the point, however, is to *change* it" (Marx, 1978, 145). Although Marx's own writings are expansive (*Das Kapital* alone spans three volumes and thousands of pages), his major contributions can be seen as the development of a materialist conception of history, a critique of capitalist social relations, and the identification of workers as the agents of revolutionary change.

Method   For Marx, human history can be understood by looking at the way production is organized. In other words, the ways in which land, labour, and resources—what he named the **means of production**—come together to make things create unique forms of social organization. Marx called these the **mode of production** and identified several historical modes as a result: slavery, feudalism, and capitalism. Each of these historical modes, or epochs, in human history is defined by a specific social antagonism or conflict. Slavery sees the struggle between owner and slave, feudalism sees the conflict between lord and serf, and capitalism is defined primarily by the struggle between the **bourgeoisie** (capitalists or owners of the means of production) and the **proletariat** (the workers). It is the capitalist period of human history that Marx is most interested in, and he names the conflict between the bourgeoisie and the proletariat **class struggle**. By using a materialist approach—that is, by looking at how societies organize themselves to produce things—Marx reveals the essential elements of class society as defined by the capitalist mode of production.

Before examining Marx's critique of capitalism, it is important to stress that Marx's analysis focuses on antagonistic relations caused by a particular mode of production, but this focus should not be read as an indication that history itself must unfold in predetermined ways. His method, known as dialectics, instead revealed that history is about real struggles taking place within real historical societies with real historical consequences. However, as we have already noted, Marx believed philosophy needed to go beyond understanding history to changing history. In his analysis of capitalism, Marx's end goal was to outline the conditions under which the proletariat might overcome the bourgeoisie and end class struggle through the formation of communist (what he calls human) society. Let us turn now to an examination of Marx's critique of capitalism.

A Critique of Capitalism   Marx's life's work was focused on understanding the capitalist system "as a whole"—that is, the type of social relations a capitalist mode of production creates. Marx argued that the transformation from feudal and merchant societies to capitalist society created a new relationship between the labouring class (the proletariat) and those who owned the productive means of capital (the bourgeoisie). Capitalism established the conditions in which the only way for the labourer to survive was by selling her labour power (for a wage) to the bourgeoisie. This **wage–capital relationship** created two important social outcomes for the worker. First, the proletariat was **alienated** from the items being produced because of the factory division of labour. Second, the proletariat was vulnerable to **exploitation** by the owner because she relied on a paid wage to procure the necessities of life.

Although Marx was viewing the early days of the development of industrial capitalism dominated by the new factory system, his basic analysis of the working class's reliance on wage labour continues to hold true. One need only reflect on Michael Moore's well-known documentaries, such as *Roger and Me* or *The Big One*, to know that workers continue to be vulnerable to plant closures, economic recessions, and capital relocation. However, it is not simply Marx's point that workers *can be* exploited under capitalism; rather, it is his point that worker exploitation is the *raison d'être* for capitalism. Why? Because by exploiting the worker (lowering wages, increasing working hours, and/or maintaining a "reserve army of labour" or "casual labour pool"), capitalists are able to realize what Marx termed **surplus value**, the value over and above the costs associated with production. Although it is slightly more complicated, we can think of surplus value as the ability of the bourgeoisie to realize a profit and to reinvest in further production (Marx referred to this as capitalist accumulation).

One may be inclined to ask, what is wrong with profit? For Marx, two key problems arise from concentrating capital under the ownership of a single entity (be it an individual, state, or corporation) and pursuing surplus value. First, workers are treated like any other piece of machinery or commodity. They are exploited and often treated as expendable. Marx says that even in situations where standards of living and wages improve for the workers, they continue to be exploited because they are always vulnerable to the whims of the owners. Second, the owners are able to use their wealth and social position to ensure that they maintain political power in capitalist societies. Today, we are familiar with the sayings "money talks" and "money makes the world go around." These truisms embody the essence of Marx's assessment of capitalist social relations: those responsible for actual production (the workers) are disenfranchised both in the workplace and in the political arena by those possessing wealth (the owners).

For Marx, the great irony of capitalism was that it held the potential to eradicate human want. Poverty, hunger, and scarcity could be ended through the technological innovations and efficiencies in production that present themselves in capitalism. Because of increasing concentration of capital (and the tendency toward monopoly), however, these technological innovations that could end scarcity merely serve to further impoverish the worker. A fair and equitable distribution of wealth, Marx argued, would first require the working class to become conscious of their exploitation.

Revolutionary Change A fundamental question for us to put to Marx, then, is how do workers become conscious of their class position under capitalism? His answer was that modern capitalism produces fundamental contradictions in the lives of the working class that lead the worker to realize and ultimately contest her exploitation. The first contradiction workers experience is that the pursuit of surplus value leads to the ongoing attempt to decrease labour costs (through decreasing wages and imposing automation). So, even when capitalists are making huge profits and realizing surplus value, they are inclined to cut their labour forces or institute automation technology to replace human labourers. The second contradiction experienced by workers (and capitalists), according to Marx's analysis, is that the capitalist system is inherently unstable, frequently following periods of high growth rates (booms) with deep recessions (busts). These cycles of crises leave wage-dependent workers increasingly vulnerable to the dictates of a social system that they do not control.

Workers become conscious of their exploitation by their lived experiences under the capitalist system. The factory model, in particular, brings workers together and increases the possibility for their collective political organization. Moreover, Marx believed that there is no simple reform that could be initiated to improve capitalism. Instead, he argued that, to create a new society, these organized workers must overthrow the system through revolution. Thus, the end to the alienation and exploitation of the working class is through a revolutionary movement, led by the proletariat, that first establishes socialism and then communism. Communist society would embody the principle that "the free development of each is the condition for the free development of all" (Marx, 1978, 491).

Socialism

Historically, socialism as a political ideology predates Marxism, although it is impossible to deny that Marx's writings irrevocably changed socialism. The intellectual heritage of the key ideas of socialism are traced to Rousseau's critique of differences in property ownership, the concept of organic society, and the belief that individuals can aspire to the greater good (Baradat, 1988, 170). Rousseau's ideas were felt throughout revolutionary France. Another important early socialist who found inspiration in the French Revolution was Francis Babeuf (1760–1797). Babeuf advocated an extreme socialism that called for revolutionary transformation and the existence of an elite corps to lead the masses to revolution (Baradat, 1988, 171). Typically, we can delineate utopian, scientific, and social democratic forms of socialism.

Utopian Socialism Breaking from its revolutionary roots, socialism coalesced into a coherent set of ideas in the form of what has been termed utopian socialism. This form of socialist thought advocated the public ownership of the means of production, democratic social organizations, and the eradication of all want in society. Robert Owen (1771–1858) is identified as the "father" of utopian socialism. Ironically, Owen was a successful industrial capitalist who embarked on realizing his utopian vision after retiring from business. He was convinced that his factories had been productive because of his ethical treatment of employees. To prove his point, Owen participated in setting up communes on the principles of economic self-sufficiency and democratic decision making. The New Harmony commune, established in 1825 in Indiana, is recognized as one of Owen's most successful attempts at communal living. New Harmony, like all of the communal experiments of the time, ultimately failed because of an inability to be economically independent and to sustain democratic group decision making.

Scientific Socialism Following utopian socialism, socialist thought was dominated by Marx's influence. Marx proposed that his form of socialism was scientific—drawing on Enlightenment notions of rationality and science. Marx argued that socialism is merely a stage of economic and social development following the demise of capitalism. Although scientific socialism had tremendous impact on the organizational forms of the working class (most notably in the case of the formation of the International Workingmen's Association, known as the First International), Marx's theories quickly became subject to debate leading to significant revision by subsequent socialist thinkers. Two areas of Marxist thought were most hotly contested: (1) the commitment to change through revolution only, and (2) what was perceived as the over-emphasis on economic relationships (economic determinism). The resulting revisionist movement argued that social change could be achieved through evolution, rather than revolution. The revisionists also stressed the moral/social values of socialism, rather than economics. This was the position taken by Canada's most influential social democratic party—the Co-operative Commonwealth Federation (CCF)—which emerged from the depths of the Great Depression of the 1930s.

Social Democracy Today, socialism remains a vibrant political ideology. While some movements still maintain a link to historical scientific socialism, the more prevalent legacy is apparent among the social democratic parties found in Western Europe. Social democracy is characterized by a commitment to universal social programs for citizens, a mixed economy of public and private enterprise, and public taxation to decrease income disparities. In the European Union, social democratic parties continue to have a significant presence on Europe's political landscape. The success of these parties has sustained interest in social democracy, and socialist thinking more generally, proving the ongoing relevance of this ideology.

Anarchism

Defined most simply, anarchism is the rejection of hierarchical forms of governance. Yet this definition fails to capture the rich history of anarchist thought. Anarchism as a political ideology became popular in the early nineteenth century in response to the Industrial Revolution. Since that time, subscribers to anarchist thought have organized in most industrialized countries and have had a significant impact on developing political regimes, particularly in Africa. Generally, anarchist thinking can be divided into two distinct categories: social or collectivist versus individualist anarchism. We will examine each in turn.

Social Anarchism Pierre Joseph Proudhon (1809–1865) was the first political thinker to call himself an anarchist. Proudhon is best remembered for his answer to the question, "What is property?" He replied, "Property is theft." Proudhon outlined the key elements of anarchism that would see the eradication of the state and the free and harmonious association of individuals. Specifically, Proudhon advocated the organization of workers into syndicates that would collectively make all decisions about production and collectively share ownership. Proudhon's form of anarchism is often referred to as anarcho-syndicalism. Anarchist syndicate experiments did enjoy some short-lived success in Spain between 1936 and 1939. However, these syndicates obtained worker control through violent means, in contrast to Proudhon's non-violent prescription.

One of the best-known anarchists, Mikhail Bakunin (1814–1876), believed that violence was necessary to achieve an anarchist society. Closely associated with social (or communist) anarchism, Bakunin argued that revolution would be achieved by arming the most undesirable elements of the population. Clearly one of the most radical anarchists, Bakunin left a legacy of his strong belief in the necessary role of violence in effecting social change. Another well-known anarchist who subscribed to Bakunin's radicalism is Emma Goldman (1869–1940), who carried her anarchist message throughout the United States, the Soviet Union, and Canada. A tireless radical, Goldman was also outspoken on issues concerning women's rights and was particularly active in working for the legalization of contraception for women.

In her later years, however, Goldman became less committed to violent overthrow, largely because of the influence of Peter Kropotkin (1842–1921). Kropotkin argued that society was more likely to progress through cooperation than aggression. Also a communist anarchist, Kropotkin believed that the modern state was "the personification of injustice, oppression, and monopoly." Kropotkin's vision of anarchist society was one of harmony and cooperation, rejecting the idea that revolutions were the best way to change social organization. He believed that industrial progress and technology would eventually eradicate human want. Once this level of technological advancement had occurred, Kropotkin believed, society would evolve to communism.

Individualist Anarchism Both anarcho-syndicalism and communist anarchism share a belief that government prevents the free association among individuals and, therefore, limits personal autonomy and the possibility of cooperative and harmonious social organization. However, there is another strain of anarchist thinking that asserts that individuals should be completely free of social responsibility. Lyman Sargent notes that "[t]he individualist anarchist recognizes nothing above his ego and rebels against all discipline and all authority" (Sargent, 1996, 177). Individualist anarchist thought is historically associated with Max Stirner (1806–1856), who nicely summarized his political ideology with the slogan "The people are dead. Up with me!"

Stirner represents individualist anarchism at its most extreme. Libertarianism, in many ways, represents a softer variant of Stirner's philosophy and continues to have a significant impact on contemporary politics, especially in the United States. Libertarianism is closely associated with the work of Robert Nozick, who asserts the "pre-eminent right" of private property. Libertarians reject government intervention in areas of social life and economic markets, although conceding the need for a very limited government. Threads of libertarian thought run through the rhetoric of political movements and political parties that promise to "downsize government" and to guarantee the "free market." For example, during the 2000 American presidential campaign, George W. Bush frequently asserted that he believed in "the people" and not "government." Indeed, a handful of libertarians typically compete in Canadian federal elections to deliver this message.

Communism

Communism, of all the ideologies discussed here, is the most difficult to define. We all have a sense that we know what communism is. We have seen it in its application in the former Soviet Union, China, Cuba, and the former Yugoslavia. With the demise of many of these communist regimes, we are also left with the sense that communism is a failed experiment, a political ideology that was "good in theory" but did not work in practice. However, this is a far too simplistic dismissal of the question of what communist ideology consists of and means in application. The "failure" of avowedly communist regimes and the more recent movement toward "democratization" and market liberalization does not speak to the theoretical and ideological concepts that underpin communist theory. In fact, many traditional Marxists were highly critical of the Soviet experiment. As with all political ideologies, there is often a large gap between political ideas and their concrete expression in political actions and institutions.

Marx argued that communism could only be achieved after capitalism and socialism, but he actually wrote very little about what communist society would look like. Some ideas, however, are found in his theoretical work. Communist society would involve the social ownership of the means of production (factories and so on), absolute social equality (that is, a classless society), and the "withering away" of the state. For Marx, the communist ethic was embodied in the statement "from each according to his abilities, to each according to his needs." From Marx's original work on the question of communist society, other Marxists began to develop a more defined picture of communism. Most notable among these thinkers is Vladimir Lenin (1870–1924). Lenin's concern was to take the theories that Marx espoused and to put them into action. As one of the key leaders of the Russian Revolution, Lenin was in a unique position to further develop communist political thought. Lenin was consumed by two concerns: how capitalism worked internationally, and how to organize a successful revolution. With regard to the latter concern, Lenin developed the notion of the party vanguard. Lenin argued that to successfully organize a revolution, it would be necessary to have a well-trained cadre of dedicated individuals who would work tirelessly for the success of the revolution. Following the revolution, this vanguard would ensure the nationalization of industry and the dictatorship of the proletariat.

Following Lenin's death in 1924, Joseph Stalin came to power in the Soviet Union. Stalin consolidated his personal authority in the Union of Soviet Socialist Republics (USSR) through bloody purges and political intrigue, and challenged one of the fundamental precepts of Marxist thought. Marx believed that socialism had to be an international project. Stalin, in contrast, contended that "socialism in one country" was not only possible but also desirable. To this end, Stalin implemented intense industrialization and centralized planning. Some argue that his policies led inevitably to the demise of the Soviet economy in the 1990s. However, Stalin was not alone in attempting to offer significant revision to Marx's work. In China, Mao Tse-tung (1893–1976), leader of the Chinese revolution, argued that mobilization of the peasants, not workers, was the key to revolutionary success. This also represented a significant shift away from Marxist reliance on the working class as the focal point of revolution. Mao's communist reforms focused on the collectivization of farming as opposed to the Soviet model of speedy industrial development.

This very brief overview of communism leads us to two general conclusions. The first is that communist ideology need not be tied to the projects of the formerly communist countries. In fact, the basic tenets of communism—classless society and social production—can be separated from those movements that have named themselves communist. Second, a political ideology can espouse a view of social organization in theory that is quite different from what is achieved in the application. The Soviet Union, Yugoslavia, China, and Cuba each had to adapt and change their political ideologies to face changing domestic and international circumstances.

The Intellectual Heritage of Radical Politics

AS YOU WERE READING THESE OVERVIEWS OF RADICAL POLITICAL MOVEMENTS AND theories, it is likely that you could think of current organizations that still espouse these ideas. For example, the Communist Party of Canada (Marxist-Leninist) still exists and even contests elections. However, the intellectual heritage of these ideas should be identified much more broadly than by looking for the names to reappear in modern political parties. This section will briefly trace the ongoing legacy of radical politics, particularly as these critiques reassert their salience in an era of globalization.

The Birth of the New Left

In May 1968, students in Paris organized a sustained revolt that was supported by industrial workers who went on strike across the French provinces. Although there are many interpretations of the events and the conditions that fostered them, what is clear is that the student protestors were drawing on critiques of capitalist society and calling for revolutionary change. These protests were not exclusive to France and, in fact, took place worldwide. In the United States, opposition to the Vietnam War was a major catalyst for organizing protest groups, which engaged in critiquing American society and challenging American imperialism around the globe. These movements took hold of the intellectual ideas presented in critical academic publications, such as the *New Left Review*, that published works strongly influenced by such radical thinkers as Karl Marx, Friedrich Engels, and Vladimir Lenin. Rather than succumbing to anti-communist Cold War propaganda, these types of scholarly publications attempted to preserve the critical nature of Marxism, Leninism, and socialist thought more generally. What is particularly significant is that these modern radical movements and the political critiques they espoused, like those radicals that preceded them in history, were calling for an overthrow of the dominant power structures under which they lived in favour of a new vision of society. To sustain their radical critique, these varied movements drew on Marx's critique of capitalist society and the anarchist tendency toward open, non-hierarchical forms of social organization. The commune movement within "hippie culture" was itself an attempt to practise a form of communist social organization. In short, the radical politics of the nineteenth century had been adapted to the emerging critical practices of the mid-twentieth century.

Anti-Colonialism and National Liberation Movements

Radicalized politics were not restricted to North America or Western Europe. The 1960s were also a period of radicalization for colonized peoples, particularly those on the African continent. Often drawing on such ideas as Lenin's analysis of capitalist imperialism and "uneven development," as well as notions of justice and democracy, resistance groups formed and eventually won their independence in such places as Algeria, Gambia, and Tanzania. Although the movements, experiences, and outcomes of independence movements varied across the continent of Africa, the leaders, activists, and outside supporters did draw on the analysis and critiques, as well as organizational forms, presented in earlier radical movements. Outside Africa, we can also see the social democratic legacy in Nehru's India or the socialist lineage of Salvador Allende's rise to power in Chile (1970).

Anti-Globalization and Anti-War

Lest we should begin to think that radical political ideas disappeared after the 1970s, it is important to recognize that the intellectual heritage is preserved and further enhanced in today's "anti-globalization" and "anti-war" movements. For example, the tens of thousands of protestors who converged during a World Trade Organization meeting in Seattle in 1999 were not unified by a single political program. They were, however, drawing on critiques of capitalism and questioning the logic of economic globalization that privileges corporations and trade over people. Present at the protests were anarchists, socialists, communists, environmentalists, anti-racism groups, feminists, trade union and labour activists, students, academics, farmers, and "average" citizens—to name just a few.

What drew together these disparate groups was the sense that we need a radical critique of the nature of the global distribution of political and economic power. More recently, the global wave of protests that followed the U.S. invasion of Iraq in 2003 and the ongoing anti-war movement have also drawn on various critiques of global inequality and the exercise of what is often termed "American imperialism."

Whether one is looking at the "people of '68" or "anti-colonial movements" or "anti-globalization protestors" or even the "anti-war" movement, it is possible to see the common thread of radicalism that draws each of these together in a historical relationship. Each of these groups may have had a different political platform or series of demands, but all were drawing on Marx's call to ruthlessly critique "all that is existing." For the "people of '68" the focus was necessarily on the ways in which "the Establishment" oppressed groups of people, either domestically or through imperialist practices globally. For the anti-colonial movements, radical ideas offered the promise of a self-determined, better future. And for today's anti-globalization movements, the very act of challenging the logic of global capitalism and its institutions draws on older, radical traditions. Each of these movements has taken the radical political ideologies covered in this chapter, added their own adaptations and lessons, and offered us the opportunity to continue the practice of radical criticism in ever-changing conditions.

Summary

Recently, some academics and political commentators have been trumpeting the "end of ideology," and by implication, the end of radical politics. They confidently declare that this has been achieved by the worldwide acceptance (or at least striving toward acceptance) and realization of American-style liberal democracy. However, we should be suspicious of this argument on at least two counts. In the first place, it implies that democratic governments, such as those found in Canada or the United States, are non-ideological, which, if we recall Eagleton's definition of ideology, is simply impossible. And in the second place, it denies the continuing influence of radical ideologies on political movements around the globe. As we have already noted, Western Europe seems to be witnessing a resurgence in socialist-influenced politics, and countries in parts of the developing world, such as Africa and South America, continue to draw on the insights and programs of previous ideological movements.

Moreover, the end-of-ideology view tends to overlook the importance of new and emerging critical movements. Critical political projects, such as the varied anti-globalization movements, will continue to draw their organizational forms and critiques from the legacy of radical ideologies. Returning to Eagleton for a moment, ideology's role of making sense of our lived experiences and helping us envision new forms of social organization is going to be a consistent feature of our social existence. To argue that ideology is no longer a relevant concept and that radical politics is dead is to deny our ability as human beings to contest current social conditions and to create alternative ways of living.

Discussion Questions

1. Do you find that your thinking about some issues could be considered ideological? In what ways? Do you engage in radical politics? How so?

2. Are radical political ideologies desirable? Why, or why not?

3. What do you think is the future of socialist or communist movements today?

References

Baradat, Leon. 1988. *Political Ideologies: Their Origins and Impact.* Scarborough, ON: Prentice Hall.

Eagleton, Terry. 1991. *Ideology: An Introduction.* New York: Verso.

Marx, Karl. 1978. *The Marx-Engels Reader* (Robert C. Tucker, ed.). New York: Norton.

Sargent, Lyman Tower. 1996. *Contemporary Political Ideologies: A Comparative Analysis.* New York: ITP.

Further Readings

Anderson, Kevin. 1995. *Lenin, Hegel, and Western Marxism: A Critical Study.* Chicago: University of Illinois Press.

Dunayevskaya, Raya. 1991. *Women's Liberation, and Marx's Philosophy of Revolution,* 2nd edition. Chicago: University of Illinois Press.

Goldman, Emma. 1969. *Anarchism and Other Essays.* New York: Dover Publications.

Kliman, Andrew. 2006. *Reclaiming Marx's "Capital": A Refutation of the Myth of Inconsistency.* New York: Lexington Books.

Weblinks

The Socialist International
www.socialistinternational.org

Institute for Anarchist Studies
www.anarchist-studies.org

World Socialist Web Site
www.wsws.org

The Communist Party of Canada
www.communist-party.ca

Marxists.org Internet Archive
www.marxists.org

World Social Forum India
www.wsfindia.org

Foundations of Governance

PART II

"Governance," simply defined, refers to the ways in which we organize our common affairs. Although the exercise of political power and authority is often informal, all modern societies are governed by formal rules and practices exercised through political institutions. In political science, institutions are defined as deliberate, formalized, and expected patterns of behaviour. Political institutions are the embodiment of a state's history of conflict and compromise as well as sites of ongoing political struggles. In this section of the text, we will discover that different countries at different times have had different configurations of political institutions or regime types, ranging from monarchies to dictatorships to liberal democracies. Yet central to all is the state, an amalgam of political institutions that claims sovereignty over a defined territory. All states tend to share common political institutions—perhaps, most fundamentally, a constitution. Constitutions are the basic blueprint for the daily operation of the state, dividing powers among levels of government, across institutions, and among leaders, elected legislators, public administrators, and the bureaucracy, which is empowered to enforce state laws and regulations. The core institutions of the modern state contain and manage political conflict, make and enforce public policies, and realize political ideas and visions. The final chapter in this section, however, raises the critical issue of whether these core institutions are adequately representing our values and interests by creating what some have referred to as the democratic deficit.

CHAPTER 6

THE MODERN STATE

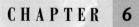

Objectives

The state is the core concept in political science that identifies where the formal and institutional terrain of politics begins and ends. There have been many different kinds of states in recorded history, ranging from the early Greek city state to the modern liberal democratic state. All states, however, perform similar tasks, such as making and implementing political decisions and protecting communities from internal and external threats. This chapter explores the role of the modern state, which traces its origin to sixteenth-century Western Europe. We will discuss the primary roles performed by the modern state as well as three different variations of the liberal-democratic state that have prevailed in Western societies for the past two centuries. Finally, we will explore the future of the national state in the contemporary global era.

LOIS HARDER

Introduction

All societies, from the most simple to the most complex, have organized some way to govern themselves. History has witnessed many experiments in government and many different kinds of states. Some have been efficient and enduring, while others have been decided disasters. States have been a pervasive fact of our collective political history. Their sheer number and variety, however, make a simple definition of the term elusive. The famous political sociologist Max Weber described the state as a distinct entity that can "successfully claim the monopoly of the legitimate use of physical force within a given territory" (1947, 154). Others make the rather circular argument that the state is the other side of civil society. Liberals tend to define the state as the public sector and contrast it to the private realm of the economy and the family. The state is, thus, contrasted to those areas of social life—the domestic world, the economic sphere, and cultural activities—organized by private and voluntary arrangements, individuals, and groups (Held, 1996, 57).

Sometimes, the terms "state" and "government" are used interchangeably, but it is important to draw a distinction between the two. One way to think about the difference between state and government is to imagine a car and its driver. The car is analogous to the state, while the driver is analogous to government. All cars have certain components that are required for them to run and that distinguish them from other modes of transportation. These components may be organized in a variety of ways and may be more or less powerful depending on the car's design. Similarly, all states perform certain basic functions, such as maintaining the rules through which people interact, though some states may do this more actively than others. Obviously, a driver is essential if the car is to move, but there is no requirement that the driver always be the same. Different drivers may treat the car differently and may choose to steer the vehicle down different paths. They may be more active or passive, but there are limits as to what the machine itself will bear.

Consider the replacement of one political party by another within a modern liberal democracy. A **liberal democracy** is the system of government in which citizens elect representatives in periodic elections. When a new party is elected to form the government, voters have chosen to alter the leadership or policy orientation of the government by selecting a party that will drive the state differently. The offices of the state remain largely the same. The positions of president or prime minister remain, as do general institutions and constitutions. In other words, the offices of the state persist despite the change in government, although the policies pursued by these departments may be altered.

Political scientists generally trace the origins of the modern state to the Treaty of Westphalia of 1648. The treaty brought an end to almost 150 years of religious and territorial conflicts and settled the Thirty Years' War, the first pan-European war. In one sense, the Treaty of Westphalia was simply an agreement to cease hostilities and impose specific terms of settlement. But it also laid the foundations for the elaboration of what we now understand as the modern state, as well as articulating the rules that govern interstate relations, even to the present day (Valaskis, 2001, 49–55).

Contributions of the Treaty of Westphalia to the modern state system are as follows:

- recognition of the primacy of sovereignty—each state exercises absolute authority over the fixed geographic territory it governs, and the national state is recognized as the ultimate power in international relations;

- emergence of international law based on treaties between sovereign countries—all states are regarded as equal before the law (Held, 1996, 70);
- retention of war as a recognized instrument of international relations and the ultimate expression of sovereignty (Valaskis, 2001).

What States Do

AFTER RECOGNIZING THE MODERN STATE'S TERRITORIALITY AND SOVEREIGNTY, political scientists typically study the state in terms of what it does. The most important among the state's functions are its legislative, executive, administrative, and judicial ones. It is important to recognize that while all states perform these roles, the specific mechanisms or institutions that perform them vary from one country to another and across time. In the liberal democratic systems that are the focus of this chapter, for example, institutional configurations vary most sharply between presidential and parliamentary systems.

Generally speaking, the *legislative function* of the state is concerned with the making of laws. Who makes the laws, what areas of social life are open to law-making, and how the process of law-making will occur are all dimensions of the legislative function. The legislative function is undertaken by people formally elected as legislators, although the executive and the bureaucracy also play an influential role in law-making. For the purposes of this discussion, however, we are concerned with two broad approaches to the role of legislatures. In a congressional model of government, such as that of the United States, the power of the legislature (or Congress) is separated from that of the executive (the president and the cabinet). In such a system, the legislature plays an active role in the legislative process. By contrast, in parliamentary systems of government, such as those of Canada, the United Kingdom, Australia, and New Zealand, there is a fusion of legislative and executive powers. Hence, the initiation and formulation of legislation is largely undertaken by the executive (the prime minister and the cabinet), while the legislature serves an overseeing and approval function.

The active role of legislatures in congressional systems results from the strict separation of power that characterizes this system. The architects of the American Constitution—the originators of the congressional model—were particularly concerned with limiting the powers of the state generally and also ensuring that no single branch of the state would dominate the others. As a result, they implemented a system of checks and balances through which the legislature (the House of Representatives and the Senate) and the executive (the president), while having unique responsibilities, also have the power to review each other's decisions. For example, executive choices for judges to sit on the U.S. Supreme Court are subject to confirmation by the Senate. Bills passed by Congress must receive the assent of the president before they become law. In both situations, the opportunity exists to overturn the desired action of the president or Congress, respectively.

Fixed terms of office (the American president serves four years, members of the House of Representatives two years, and Senators six years) and separate electoral contests for these branches of government further reinforce the separation, tension, and distinct powers of the legislature and executive. Although citizens of parliamentary democracies sometimes envy the degree of legislative autonomy built into the congressional model, it does have its drawbacks. The legislative process can be very drawn out and unwieldy, with no guarantee that the platform of either the president or the majority party in either house of Congress will be realized. Indeed, if any legislative action is to occur, cooperation between the branches of government is essential. When the executive and legislature are controlled by different political parties, a situation that characterized most of Bill Clinton's presidency (Democrat president and Republican House and Senate) and the last two years of George W. Bush's presidency (Republican president and Democrat House and Senate), the process of law-making can be especially challenging. Bush's desire to maintain U.S. troops in Iraq and to bomb Iranian nuclear plants, for example, faces strong Congressional resistance.

In contrast to the separation of powers in the congressional system, parliamentary systems of government are characterized by the fusion of the legislative and executive branches. Rather than holding separate elections for these branches, a single electoral process is undertaken. The leader of the party that gains the most seats in that election is then named as prime minister (PM). The PM then chooses the members of his or her cabinet (also known as ministers of government departments), generally from among the elected members of the PM's party. The PM and the cabinet then constitute the executive, also known as the government. The remaining elected representatives serve as legislators.

Fixed terms of office are not a feature of the parliamentary system, although there is a maximum time limit that a government can remain in office before an election must be called. This creates a situation in which the government must maintain the confidence of the legislature to remain in office—a feature of parliamentary systems known as responsible government. If the executive is unable to maintain this confidence (that is, majority support of the elected members), the government must resign and, usually, an election will ensue. It has become accepted practice, however, that governments are only obliged to resign when they are defeated on a money bill—generally the budget.

Because of this uncertain tenure, party discipline is a key feature of parliamentary governments. It is only through the reliable support of all government party members, be they members of the executive (cabinet) or the legislature (backbenchers), that the government can be assured of its ongoing survival. Of course, this situation does not require that all members of the various opposition parties vote along party lines. Nonetheless, if they are to represent themselves as a potential alternative to the current government, a coherent voice of opposition is the logical stance to assume.

While legislatures form the heart of democratic representation and policy-making, in recent years the growing complexity of law-making has shifted the active process away from legislatures and toward the bureaucracy and the executive. The result has been a decline in the role and power of Parliament, with elected legislators serving an overseeing role and rubber-stamping initiatives taken elsewhere.

In both presidential and parliamentary systems, the formal role of a state's executive is to implement the laws passed by legislators. Presidents and prime ministers, assisted by members of the cabinet, oversee the implementation process within specific areas of jurisdiction. They set the policy agenda, determining which issues will command the most attention. This function has been referred to as steering (Osborne, 1992).

Obviously, it is the head of government—that is, the president or prime minister—who is the most prominent member of the executive. But these positions are not synonymous, given the rather distinctive systems of government in which they operate. As we noted previously, for the president's agenda and decisions to be accepted, a high degree of cooperation with the legislature is required. As a result, a considerable portion of the president's staff and executive offices are engaged in this process of negotiation. The president does have a cabinet, but its members are selected by the president from the country at large, rather than from among the elected representatives. Cabinet members serve at the discretion of the president and are not responsible to either congress or voters.

The prime minister, as both the leader of the largest party in Parliament and the head of the cabinet, has a great deal more control over the policy agenda than his presidential counterpart. Nonetheless, the prime minister does not simply proclaim her wishes to cabinet members and proceed to pass legislation through parliament. Instead, the cabinet members work together to formulate the general principles of the government's legislative program, and cabinet members stand together to support this program.

An additional distinction that must be drawn between the roles of the chief executives in presidential and parliamentary systems is the designation "head of state." The term "head of state" refers to the symbolic representation of a country's identity both to its own citizens and to the world. In the United States this symbolism is embodied in the person of the president, who also serves as the head of government. In Canada, the head of state is the Queen or, more practically, her representative, the Governor General, while the prime minister serves as the head of government. In functional terms, however, the president and the prime minister both serve as the highest-ranking decision-maker for his or her country in international forums. Advocates of the separation of these executive functions observe that, under circumstances in which a government's reputation is sullied by scandal, the broader reputation of the country remains unblemished when it is represented by someone who is detached from the gritty world of politics. The example of the Watergate scandal that eventually forced President Nixon from the White House is generally offered as evidence for the benefits of a split executive.

Non-elected officials, however, undertake the majority of executive functions. In this regard, we might think of the offices and agencies we typically recognize as the bureaucracy. Unlike the elected politicians or political appointees who make up the cabinet and are expected to steer, the role of the bureaucracy is to row (Osborne, 1992). Their job is not to set the overall policy direction but to provide the means by which that policy direction can be achieved.

In simple terms, the act of administering is one of making distinct entities work toward a set of common goals. Coordination is central to successful administration. The governance of society is a highly complex administrative task, in terms of the relationships both among the state, citizens, organizations, and corporate entities and within the myriad offices of the state itself. It should not be surprising, then, that administration is a key function of the state. It is made more complex in a democratic society by the demand for accountability. As citizens, we want to know how decisions are made and why things are done as they are. This demand for knowledge requires that the trail of decision making be easily followed.

As Western democracies have attempted to reduce the size of the state in recent years, many governments have shifted some administrative functions to the private sphere. The delivery of some social services, for example, has been taken over by community groups, private agencies are contracted to undertake accounting functions, and public utilities have been sold to private interests. Although selling off public services or contracting to private providers may reduce the size of the government's budget, the ability to ensure that these private entities work in the service of the public good is circumscribed, and hence the trail of decision making can be obscured. Further, the opportunity for governments to reward supporters through the granting of contracts can counter the cost-saving rationale of privatization and undermine the government's credibility. In Canada, a scandal surrounding fraudulent payments and/or over-payments to Quebec-based public relations firms with ties to the governing party led to the electoral defeat of the longstanding Liberal government in 2006.

The fourth function integral to the state is the judicial function. Laws are not always precise, and hence there may be differing views as to whether and how they should be enforced. It is the state's role to undertake this process of determining whether actions fit within the purview of the law. The largest share of this function is undertaken by a country's court system, but judicial functions also may be undertaken in less formal settings with less punitive outcomes. The state is responsible for ensuring that the "rule of law" is upheld. Effectively, the rule of law refers to the conditions that must exist for a law to be justified. Certain procedures must be followed in the development of law for it to be considered valid; the punishment for breaking a law must be the same for all people; and laws must apply to everyone equally, regardless of their position within society.

Since the implementation of the *Canadian Charter of Rights*, concerns have arisen regarding the degree to which the courts have extended their powers beyond adjudication and into the realm of making law. Some critics of the Charter argue that in usurping Parliament as the ultimate law-making authority, the Supreme Court enables social movements (dubbed "the Court Party" by their detractors) to bypass the democratic process of political debate and obliges society to recognize identities and practices that they would otherwise not support (Morton and Knopff, 2000). Gay and lesbian marriages are an example. On the other side of this debate, social movements argue that legal challenges are only one strategy in their struggle for recognition and that being granted a right is often more symbolic than substantive.

So far, we have outlined the basic functions of the state. However, knowing that all states fulfill legislative, executive, administrative, and judicial functions does not tell us much about how power operates within states or about how that operation of power may be altered over time. To begin exploring these questions, we can examine some of the different forms assumed by the liberal democratic state.

Variations on the Liberal Democratic State

EARLIER IN THIS CHAPTER, WE EXPLORED THE ANALOGY BETWEEN CAR AND state and between driver and government. Within the context of that discussion, it was asserted that drivers may change but the structure of the car remains more or less the same. Over time, however, the vehicle's structure is subject to innovation and redesign in response to new demands, new technologies, and changed conditions in which it must operate. Similarly, the form of the state has also undergone transformations. Revolutions represent the most dramatic method of altering the form of the state, shifting dictatorships to democracies, as in the case of the former Soviet republics, and democracies to dictatorships, as occurred in Guatemala in 1956 and Chile in 1973. Less radically, modern liberal democratic states also evolve and transform. These changes in state form are significant because they reflect a reordering or rebalancing of power within society and, as such, indicate the parameters framing citizen participation in their own governance. For the purposes of this introduction we will examine three liberal democratic state forms that have been implemented in Western liberal democracies in the past two centuries. These include the *night watchman* or *minimalist* state, which saw its most profound incarnation in Britain's industrial revolution in the nineteenth and early twentieth centuries; the welfare state, which prevailed, in varying degrees within all Western liberal democracies in the period between the 1930s and the early 1970s; and the neo-liberal state, which is now ascendant, again with numerous variations, on a global scale.

The Night Watchman State

It is not surprising that Marx, writing in the mid-nineteenth century during Britain's industrial revolution, would assert that the state was nothing more than "an executive committee of the whole bourgeoisie." He was arguing that the state operated solely in the interests of capital. During this period, participation in elections and the holding of public office were limited to property owners, who had little compulsion to consider the interests of the majority of the population. Because of the unprecedented level of technological development that was occurring during this period, the production of goods increased at an astounding rate and industrialists were enriched accordingly. Agents of the state and elected representatives, most of whom were part-time politicians and full-time businessmen, saw their role as facilitating economic growth, primarily by allowing the market to function in as unencumbered a fashion as possible. In practice, this meant intervening as little as possible in the economy while upholding the laws of property, contract, weight and measurement, and the criminal code.

On the surface, the night watchman state, also termed the *laissez-faire* and minimalist state, appears passive, but its effects on the majority of people were profound. In the absence of any regulation of the conditions of work and the length of the working day, business owners required their employees to labour for long periods of time in dangerous environments. Further, the Poor Laws were implemented, which, rather than providing a means of subsistence, subjected the jobless to increased misery and forced labour. The rationale behind this treatment was to make the condition of unemployment so terrible that people would be willing to labour under undesirable circumstances to avoid the even more horrendous conditions of the poorhouse. By refusing to play a role in regulating the workplace, the state appeared to be acting passively. However, for the majority of the population, this passivity had significant consequences in terms of their health and their independence. While business owners enjoyed an impressive level of personal liberty, such was not the case for the workers, who were the vast majority of the population.

This minimalist approach to the regulation of business—the distance between the rhetoric of equality, liberty, and solidarity that imbued the liberal democratic tradition and the real conditions of life for the majority of people—could not be maintained indefinitely. It became increasingly apparent that the long-term success of capitalism was not being well served through employment practices that regularly left workers debilitated and, hence, unable to provide for themselves. To persist with such practices would mean either that factories would run out of workers or that workers would become so disillusioned or angered by their ill-treatment that they would organize to overthrow their employers and perhaps the state as well. Moreover, as governments were increasingly pressured to broaden the electorate on the basis of the contribution that non–property-holders were making to the growth of the economy, politicians were compelled to address the demands of workers as well as owners to secure their re-election. It would take the Great Depression of the 1930s, however, before sufficient support for a more interventionist role for the liberal democratic state was achieved.

The Welfare State

The economic crisis that gripped the world in the aftermath of the American stock market crash in October 1929 represented a dramatic challenge to the existing economic and political order. The breadth of the collapse cast so many workers into the ranks of the unemployed that it was no longer possible to blame individuals and their moral weaknesses for their inability to find work. It was clear that some action on the part of the state would have to be undertaken to prevent people from perishing and to salvage failing capitalist economies. It was during this period that social welfare and unemployment insurance programs began to be implemented and legislation facilitating workplace organization by trade unions was put into place. It should be noted, however, that these initiatives, particularly in Canada and the United States, were rather tentative in their initial stages. In fact, it was only after World War II that most of the policies and programs of the welfare state were elaborated.

The war's devastating effect on the economies of Europe and Japan and the sacrifice of so many soldiers' and civilians' lives were powerful catalysts for a rethinking of the role of the state within society. It was clear that an active state would be necessary to rebuild war-torn countries. Further, the enfranchisement of virtually the entire adult population of most Western countries meant that the interests of a broad range of the population would have to be incorporated within the decision-making process. It was under these conditions that the welfare state realized its fullest expression.

Wanting to prevent further economic dislocations of such magnitude, governments in Western industrialized countries attempted to regulate their economies through the taxing and spending—or fiscal—policies that were first advocated by the British economist John Maynard Keynes. Keynes and the governments that took up his ideas wanted to balance out the boom-and-bust cycles that are characteristic of capitalist economies. Rather than leaving the market to sort itself out on its own, Keynesianism promoted state intervention through fiscal and monetary policy instruments. In times of economic downturn, governments would use their capacity to borrow as well as the revenues generated during times of growth to inject funds into the economy. Make-work projects, such as bridge and road construction and other public works initiatives, as well as unemployment insurance and social assistance payments, would ensure that people had money to purchase goods, maintain demand, and fuel production. To offset the deficits created during these periods of economic downturn, the state would extract surplus funds during periods of economic growth, thereby creating a balanced budget over the long term.

The welfare state also is associated with a variety of universal social programs, including public education, health care, child care, and wage replacement programs such as unemployment insurance, old age pensions, maternity benefits, and social assistance. Of course, not every country offered the same range of services. Neither were services equally generous across national borders. In the Anglo-American democracies of Canada, Great Britain, the United States, and Australia, for example, many social programs were not universally available to all citizens. Those with adequate incomes might be required to purchase services through the market, rather than relying on the state. Other services, particularly public education, would be available to all citizens regardless of income. With regard to services provided on an income, or means-tested, basis, citizens who could not afford to purchase services in the market were subject to the surveillance and regulations of state officials to prove their need and establish their worthiness. Moreover, because women were more likely to seek social assistance, they often were evaluated by social assistance workers with respect to their worthiness as "good women" or "good mothers." Often, this relationship between citizen and social worker could be quite paternalistic. It is not surprising, then, that as the economic interventionism of the welfare state came into question, so too did the interventionism of state agents in the lives of citizens.

Perhaps the greatest promise of the welfare state lay in its presumption that all citizens should be able to maintain a minimum standard of living—that there should be some rough equality, if not in terms of outcome, then certainly in terms of opportunity. Initially, this equality was to be realized among members of the working class. White male industrial workers and their families, in particular, were the objects of these ambitions. Yet, many other groups were also interested in taking advantage of the opportunities promised by the welfare state. Hence, the post-war period is marked by the struggles of various groups. The Civil Rights movement, Aboriginal peoples, women, the disabled, and youth demanded that the state include their concerns and perspectives within the policy-making process. These growing demands on state resources by groups previously marginalized by the economy and the political process were perceived as a threat by the established order, whose members had long benefited from those exclusionary practices. In addition to the economic crisis and the criticism of the welfare state's methods of service provision, then, the welfare state was subject to criticism from groups that viewed the broadening of the welfare state's constituency as an unwarranted drain on increasingly limited resources, leading to demand overload and a crisis in governability. Others viewed these welfare-related controversies as a distraction from the more fundamental role of the state in ensuring the smooth functioning of the market.

As these criticisms intensified and various Western industrialized countries elected governments inclined to rethink the welfare state, it underwent a profound crisis. Although certain elements of the welfare state persist in the state form prevalent in liberal democracies today, it would appear that a new arrangement between state and society is in the process of being consolidated. This new state form has been named the neo-liberal state.

The Neo-Liberal State

The central concern of the agencies of the neo-liberal state is to expand the terrain of the free market through cutbacks in social spending, the deregulation of industry, and the privatization of public services (Yeatman, 1994). This objective is reminiscent of that of the night watchman state of nineteenth-century Britain. The current neo-liberal state, however, emerges amid the increased complexity of contemporary societies, the historical experience of the welfare state, and popular expectations regarding the accountability of democratically elected governments. The welfare state both made the promise of equality and incorporated an ever-broadening circle of legitimate claims-makers within the purview of policy-making. In the process, it created expectations of openness among those who wished to challenge the new state form. The neo-liberal state's emphasis on the primacy of the market, however, has closed many familiar avenues for groups to challenge its policy objectives. The political interventions of disadvantaged groups often are simply dismissed as reflecting "special interests" or as unwarranted impositions of "political correctness." It has become increasingly unpopular to make demands on the state. Instead, we, as individuals, are expected to look out for ourselves (Brodie, 1995).

The emergence of the neo-liberal state form reflects the belief that the power of the state has extended too far, with deleterious consequences for the market and for individual freedom. According to its proponents, power would be better organized on the basis of the informal networks of the family, community, and market, with the state limiting its role to ensuring suitable conditions for economic growth. It is important to note here that the work of governing continues in these various arenas, as success in the market necessitates certain behaviours, while societal expectations dictate how people comport themselves if they are to be included in the broader community. Moreover, state policies may support this indirect form of governance through the state's purposeful withdrawal. For example, neo-liberals assert that the national state should divest itself of those functions that impede the market's operation, particularly those that consume the greatest share of tax revenue, as well as state functions that attract political controversy. Even within the formal institutional realm, the neo-liberal vision includes shifting state power so that regional and local states and governments can take on greater responsibility. Subnational governments are viewed as more appropriate sites for political struggle, since the impact of such disputes can be confined within a limited geographic region (Kristol in Devigne, 1994).

Another significant motivation behind the push for the neo-liberal state is the desire to accommodate the global mobility of capital, particularly financial capital. In the attempt to address the problem of over-production and declining profitability that contributed to the demise of the welfare state, large corporations began to shift their operations beyond their home countries. Subsequently, a global marketplace has been created, in which states compete with each other to attract and maintain increasingly mobile capital. To succeed in this process, many governments have chosen to re-orient the state structures they administer so as to create an appealing environment for investors. While such an environment may be created through a highly educated and skilled workforce, a healthy population, a safe physical environment, and an efficient and effective infrastructure, such an approach requires high levels of public expenditure. Rather than making these investments, many governments have chosen, instead, to promote a low-wage workforce, minimum levels of regulation, and low taxes, especially for the corporate sector. Not surprisingly, levels of public service provision have been reduced accordingly. The degree of citizen participation in governance has also dropped. International trade agreements, such as the North American Free Trade Agreement and the trade agreements of the World Trade Organization (WTO), limit the range of policies available to governments. Proposals that might be perceived as infringing on profitability or protecting the domestic economy are open to challenge from other countries. The elevation of the economy and of trade liberalization as a primary organizing principle in public policy, in turn, gives financial managers and business interests inordinate influence in the policy-making process. The capacity of citizens to influence their national governments has been reduced, both in terms of opportunities and avenues of appeal and in terms of the social acceptability of organized dissent.

The State in a Globalizing Era

AS THE CONTEMPORARY PROCESS OF GLOBALIZATION HAS ADVANCED, scholars have engaged in lively debates concerning the ongoing relevance of the state. Reductions in barriers to the flow of goods, services, and finance capital and the promotion of production for global, rather than national, markets have created a situation in which economies no longer correspond to nation-states. In this context, it is asserted that the national state has been "hollowed out." Power has moved upward to international institutions, such as the WTO, outward to the market, and downward to sub-national levels of government, the family, and the individual (Jessop, 1993).

But as the effects of globalization become increasingly apparent, the voices of moderation are becoming louder. Even the most fervent supporters of the global market, from the World Bank to the World Economic Forum (WEF), now concede the need for a reinvigorated state and a renewed focus on the need for social cohesion and political stability. As well, growing international concern surrounding the effects of global warming has intensified demands for increased state regulation of high polluting industries and the implementation of programs designed to reduce greenhouse gas emissions.

The reassertion of a role for the national state is also evident in responses to the increased security concerns that have emerged after September 11, 2001. A raft of legislation has been passed in liberal democracies, enabling national governments to infringe on democratic rights, including free speech, freedom of association, and the right to privacy. As these rights were enacted to protect citizens from the arbitrary use of state power, their diminishment is a clear representation of a perceived need for a strong state in the face of ambiguous but certain threats. The exercise of nation-state power in areas including security, disease, surveillance, immigration, and border controls aptly demonstrates that the nation-state continues to command considerable power.

Jamie Peck and Adam Tickell have assessed the contemporary debate surrounding the state in terms of a contrast between "roll-back" and "roll-out" neo-liberalism. They argue that the period of dramatic and overtly ideological dismantling of the welfare state can be described as roll-back neo-liberalism (2002, 388). Beginning in the mid-1990s, however, politicians came under pressure to mediate the worst effects of the roll-back policies, although they continued to uphold neo-liberal principles of smaller government and larger roles for the market and the family. These more recent initiatives are described as "roll-out" neo-liberalism, also sometimes termed "the Third Way" (Giddens, 1998) or the "social investment state" (Dobrowolsky, 2002). In its "roll-out" iteration, neo-liberalism becomes a way of "doing government." It is a logic that permeates the policy-making process, making deregulation a central activity of economic management and communicating norms of labour force participation and "appropriate" family life through social policy design. This logic serves to transform neo-liberalism into a generalized "common sense," helping to internalize the global forces that perpetuated neo-liberalism in the first place (Peck and Tickell, 2002, 389). Thus, as Peck and Tickell assert, roll-out neo-liberalism responds to the failings of roll-back neo-liberalism—doing so within the overarching frame of neo-liberal globalism, while underscoring both the frailty and the deepening of the neo-liberal project (389–390).

Summary

This chapter demonstrates that the state is both constant in its enforcement and reflection of the power dynamics at work within a given society and adaptable to the historical circumstances in which it is situated. Although the state is often perceived as monolithic and impenetrable, a long-term view reveals that the institutions and functions of the state change considerably over time.

This introduction to the state has attempted to provide a sense of the breadth of this topic, an overview of the key functions of the state, a brief account of the various forms of the liberal democratic state, and some consideration of contemporary challenges facing the state. To undertake this task, it was necessary to trace the origin of the concept of the state and clarify the distinction between state and government. All states—regardless of whether they are liberal democracies, dictatorships, or capitalist, command, or barter economies—must fulfill legislative, executive, administrative, and judicial functions. How these functions are fulfilled, however, depends on the specific political system and the character of a particular government.

Context also is central to the consideration of state forms. The transformation of the liberal democratic state from night watchman through welfare to a neo-liberal form demonstrates the dynamic character of the relationship between the state and the society it governs. The state is not fixed in time but is reformed through political struggle and altered circumstances. The study of the state should be viewed as a rich field of inquiry and one that, in all its complexity, is an essential component of the study of politics.

Discussion Questions

1. What are the primary functions of the state, and how do they relate to each other?

2. Assess the strengths and weaknesses of the congressional and parliamentary models of government.

3. Is it fair to say that Canada's national state is undergoing a change in its form? What evidence can you produce to support your claim?

4. What is the likelihood that international institutions will replace nation-states as the primary mechanisms for governance?

References

Brodie, Janine. 1995. *Politics at the Margins: Restructuring and the Canadian Women's Movement.* Halifax: Fernwood.

Devigne, Robert. 1994. *Recasting Conservatism: Oakeshott, Strauss and the Response to Postmodernism.* New Haven: Yale University Press.

Dobrowolsky, Alexandra. 2002. "Rhetoric Versus Reality: The Figure of the Child and New Labour's Strategic 'Social Investment State.'" *Studies in Political Economy,* 69 (Autumn): 43–73.

Giddens, Anthony. 1998. *The Third Way: The Renewal of Social Democracy.* Cambridge: Polity Press.

Held, David. 1996. "The Development of the Modern State" in Stuart Hall, David Held, Don Hubert, and Kenneth Thompson, eds., *Modernity.* London: Blackwell.

Jessop, Bob. 1993. "Towards a Schumpeterian Workfare State? Preliminary Remarks on a Post-Fordist Political Economy." *Studies in Political Economy,* 40: 7–39.

Morton, F.L. and Rainer Knopff. 2000. *The Charter Revolution and the Court Party.* Peterborough: Broadview Press.

Osborne, David. 1992. *Reinventing Government: How the Entrepreneurial Spirit Is Transforming the Public Sector.* Reading, MA: Addison-Wesley Publishing.

Peck, Jamie and Adam Tickell. 2002. "Neoliberalizing Space." *Antipode,* 34 (3): 380–404.

Valaskakis, Kimon. 2001. "Long-term Trends in Global Governance: From 'Westphalia' to 'Seattle'" in Organisation for Economic Co-operation and Development, *Governance in the 21st Century.* Paris: OECD, 45–66.

Weber, Max. 1947. *The Theory of Social and Economic Organization.* New York: Free Press.

Yeatman, Anna. 1994. *Postmodern Revisionings of the Political.* London: Routledge.

Further Readings

Held, David. 1989. *Political Theory and the Modern State: Essays on State, Power and Democracy.* Stanford: Stanford University Press.

Lovenduski, Joni, ed. 2005. *State Feminism and Political Representation.* Cambridge: Cambridge University Press.

McBride, Stephen. 2001. *Paradigm Shift: Globalization and the Canadian State.* Halifax: Fernwood Publishing.

Pierson, Christopher. 2004. *The Modern State,* 2nd edition. London: Routledge.

Weblinks

Political Resources on the Net
www.intute.ac.uk/socialsciences

www.psa.ac.uk/cps

Government of Canada
www.gc.ca

United States Government
www.usa.gov

CHAPTER 7

REGIMES

FRED JUDSON and SANDRA REIN

Throughout human history, we find groups that have developed different organizational forms to secure the means to life, ensure survival, and create and transmit culture. Within all of these organizational forms there is an identifiable pattern of authority that governs decisions regarding fundamental activities. The study of those patterns is the essence of political science. Power is the capacity to make decisions and **governance** is the organized exercise of that capacity. In other words, governance is the way we organize our common affairs. Political science studies power, often focusing on government as a key institution that embodies power. From the focus on governments, political scientists can study the many ways in which human beings have organized their societies. The term "regime" is applied to the comparative study of different social formations. This chapter defines the concept of regime and examines three dominant types of political regimes. First, we will briefly explore the historical development of regime typologies and the comparative study of government. Next, the composition of regimes is examined by defining four spheres of study: state, society, market, and globe. Finally, the chapter describes three common regime-types that are present in modern history—authoritarian, democratic, and revolutionary—and speculates about the nature of regimes in the future.

Introduction

There is a long history of human beings developing ways to compare and contrast different types of social organization. Aristotle, one of the first political scientists, vested much of his intellectual efforts in creating categories to facilitate the study of the natural and social world. It is in his writings that we find the first systematic attempt to develop categories to define and study political organization. In fact, we find many of Aristotle's categories are still with us in the modern study of comparative government. Aristotle's typology was quite straightforward. He classified political forms based on the way authority was exercised in a given polity. His typology is summarized in Table 7.1.

It is apparent from Aristotle's typology that the interests of the rulers is a key concern for deciding if a government is "good." Some students may be surprised to see that Aristotle includes democracy as a less than desirable form of government; however, Aristotle's concern was with a kind of "mob-rule" mentality that would take over and displace the pursuit of the common good.

Since Aristotle's time, others, such as Machiavelli and Hobbes, have built on Aristotle's typology to study patterns of authority and to determine the best form of regime to instill stability and order among human communities. Karl Marx (1818–1883), writing in the nineteenth century, argued that regimes (derived from the mode of production) were dynamic and ever-changing and that change was the most constant element of human society; however, studying change means finding the defining features of any particular social organization. Following Marx, German social scientist Max Weber (1864–1920) coined the term "ideal-type" as a way to categorize and understand politics and society. The ideal-type is a way to abstract key characteristics of an object of study in order to create categories for study and comparison. Ideal-types are not intended to fully represent the diversity and complexity of real governments or societies but, instead, to provide a way to understand the core functions and mechanisms that make up actual regimes.

Weber delineated three broad types of authority that characterize power and governance: traditional, charismatic, and bureaucratic. Traditional authority was vested

TABLE 7.1 *Aristotle's Classification of Political Forms*

	BEST REGIMES (RULE FOR THE COMMON GOOD)	WORST REGIMES (RULE FOR SELF-INTEREST)
Rule by One	Monarchy	Autarchy
Rule by Few	Aristocracy	Oligarchy
Rule by Many	Polity	Democracy

SOURCES: Adapted from Aristotle, *Politics*, Book III, Chapter 7, and *The Internet Encyclopaedia of Philosophy*, www.iep.utm.edu/a/aris-pol.htm.

in kinship and/or some external source of authority. The most common example from history is the belief in the divine right of kings to rule. Charismatic authority, on the other hand, is derived from the personal leadership qualities of an individual or group. Weber associated bureaucratic authority with modern governance. In this case, authority is derived from laws and rules and is vested in government offices and related institutions (such as the police). Even this brief explanation of Weber's ideal-types will cause many students to say, "Wait a minute . . . traditional authority was often charismatic as well, and in many cases governed by laws and related institutions." Exactly. Real-world examples may contain all aspects of Weber's ideal-types. As students of politics, we want to identify the most important characteristic of a regime so that we can begin to categorize and understand the way one regime governs in comparison with others. As Weber himself insisted, specific experiences of governance would never precisely conform to such ideal-types. By defining key components that make up a regime, it is possible to analyze and compare different governments. In the next section we will outline the four spheres we can examine to define modern regimes.

Defining Regimes Today

How can "regime" be defined? The Latin stem reg- refers to "rule," and so the basic meaning of "regime" is "form of rule" over given aspects of human activity. The concept of regime as "organized governance experience" contains four spheres: namely, **state**, **society**, **market**, and **global insertion**. Each sphere is very complex and relates to the other three and to the whole that they form together—in other words, each sphere's dynamics affect and are affected by the others. We break down regimes into these components so that we can identify similarities and differences across a variety of regimes.

State

The term "state" conveys the idea that a society is organized economically, socially, and politically, and develops coherence over time. The word "country" is closest to "state" at such a general level and corresponds to geographical divisions. Today, the world is divided into 192 countries. When we think of countries, we are thinking of states as sovereign units in the international political system. This means that, at least in theory, no external authority is able to prevail over domestic authority. No matter what regime type characterizes that sovereign domestic authority, all states share the attribute of **sovereignty**. However, the ways in which sovereign power are exercised in various national settings can differ significantly. For example, states may have parliamentary or presidential systems of government. In the case of parliamentary systems, such as Canada's, the legislative and executive branches of government are "fused" in one institution, Parliament. Presidential systems, such as that of the United States, function on a basis of a "separation of powers" so that executive and legislative branches are distinct. Obviously, these differences will help define the nature of the regime.

Society

W eber held that a society's composition would determine the character of the state and its structures of authority, and influence political institutions. In other words, society shapes its state. Using this approach, political scientists and sociologists theorized that societies dominated by "traditional values" would often result in monarchies, such as that found in pre-1917 Russia. Similarly, they theorized that societies in transition to modern capitalism would most likely challenge state forms inherited from feudal, traditional, and aristocratic periods in massive social revolutions; these challenges typically resulted in the development of liberal democracies or industrializing authoritarian states.

Relating the nature and composition of a society to the ruling regime is at best an imprecise science. Studying society necessarily puts us in the realm of culture, values, and beliefs. Moreover, we know that societies are dynamic and ever-changing. While cultural or religious attachments do not necessarily correspond to the adoption of a specific type of regime, the link is strong enough to force us to be attentive to the complex relationship between these elements and politics. In his own studies, Weber attempted to draw conclusions based on the "Protestant work ethic," for example, while contemporary political scientists like Samuel Huntington rely on culture and social values as defining features of the politics of specific countries and regions of the world.

Market

A fter more than two centuries of capitalist economic development, with its prodigious increases in production and consumption, the importance of the economic dimension for understanding the modern state, society, and regimes is unquestioned. The triumph of capitalism over socialist experiments of the twentieth century and the acceleration of globalization also underline the centrality of economic relations. Weberian and Marxist approaches find common ground in our third sphere, the *market*. Considered broadly, the market sphere includes production, exchange, and distribution. Taking a cue from Marx, it includes relations of property and production, particularly who controls the means of production, finances the processes, and controls the profits. Today, we can characterize most of the world's societies as "market societies." In such societies, the social worth of individuals and groups is determined, to a great degree, by "market principles," such as property ownership, price, income, costs, and supply and demand.

Both Marxists and Weberians link wealth and political power to the market sphere. The market is where production and accumulation of wealth occur, where the social contours of modern societies take shape, and where power focuses its attention. The market is the sphere in which a society's economic "mode of accumulation" operates, and from which states, like social classes, draw material resources for the exercise and retention of power. Some political scientists use the phrase "regimes of accumulation" to capture these social, economic, and political aspects of the market sphere. The phrase conveys the sense that market decisions regarding such things as investment, production, and currency values are as important in influencing political decisions as are parliamentary, legislative, executive, and party activities or elections.

Global Insertion

It is a short leap from observations about the market to the fourth sphere necessary for a critical conception of regime: *global insertion*. All countries—their respective societies, states, and markets—occupy certain positions in larger international or global contexts. One context is the international state system. Another is the international economic system, comprising trade and financial transactions among states and firms, comparative economic development experiences, patterns of production and distribution, and, increasingly, globalization. These two contexts, the modern state system and the international economy, have constituted a "world system" since the sixteenth century.

Historically, the state system has been shaped by a small number of "great powers" whose interests and exercise of power determine the "rules." The system has been conflictual; war, preparation for war, and national security concerns are constant elements. It is a hierarchical system, reflected in the twentieth century's experience of colonies, great and regional powers, client states, and superpowers with their alliance systems. The economic dimension of the world system also has been hierarchical, often marked by domination and exploitation. Capitalist development also was accompanied by European colonial acquisition of much of the world. Simplifying greatly, capitalist economies in the core countries determined the patterns of economic development and under-development in the rest of the world, in a system often called **imperialism**. The crucial political and economic decisions affecting the world's peoples were made by small numbers of people in the ruling classes of core countries.

How a regime is "inserted" into these contexts can help us understand and study its political nature. For example, historically, we consider the United States to be a liberal democracy. It has also exercised dominance over other states through both military and economic means. Such a history poses a problem for political scientists. On the one hand we have a democracy "within" a specific country that, on the other hand, is marked by behaviours that are often decidedly undemocratic "outside" its borders. What is it about the U.S. regime that produces and perpetuates this type of global insertion? Is it specific to certain regimes? Other states, such as North Korea,

Figure 7.1   *All regimes contain four spheres.*

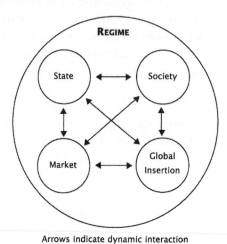

Arrows indicate dynamic interaction

appear to only be "inserted" into global considerations when it comes to nuclear weapons or regional security in East Asia. Again, political scientists attempt to understand how the regime of Kim Jong-il reflects and creates the global position of North Korea.

In sum, the four spheres allow us to define "regime." A **regime** is a mode of governance over the organized activity of a social formation within and across its particular configuration of society, state, market, and global insertion (see Figure 7.1). As organized units of governance across the four spheres, regimes are "modes of accumulation" for a social formation. Society's form and cohesion are produced, enforced, and changed. The state is provided with its institutions and practices and is shaped, staffed, and managed. The market sphere maintains its means and relations of production, property, and distribution, provided that the conditions it needs to thrive are met. A social formation's global insertion defines and governs its economic and political relationships beyond and within its borders. A regime coordinates processes of accumulation within, between, and among the four spheres; in that sense a regime is a system-controller for a social formation.

Twentieth-Century Regimes

TWENTIETH-CENTURY REGIMES FALL UNDER THREE BROAD CATEGORIES: authoritarian, democratic, and revolutionary. They should be understood as ideal-types *and* as specific collective experiences. **Authoritarian regimes** are thought of as "rule by the few" or even the one, where force or the threat of force to maintain "order" is implicit or explicit. **Democratic regimes** are considered to be "rule by the many," where force is rarely necessary because the majority accept and support the particular "order" of the society, especially its economic and political arrangements. **Revolutionary regimes** are those where certain elites, groups, and/or the majority have overthrown the given socio-economic and political order and undertaken a radical transformation, usually in the name of a dominated and exploited majority.

Authoritarian Regimes

By definition, absolutist monarchies are authoritarian, but few now persist. Examples include Saudi Arabia and Brunei, but most existing monarchies are constitutional, with greater or lesser degrees of authority and symbolic importance— they do not "rule." There is a stronger association between authoritarian regimes and "late" industrialization. Following Weber, analysts sought to explain ultra-authoritarian regimes, usually called *totalitarian,* in both capitalist and socialist countries, as deriving from the stresses of "late" and rapid industrial development. The two main cases are Nazi Germany and the Soviet Union under Joseph Stalin. Japan, another "late-industrializing" country, also experienced a militarist authoritarian regime in the 1930s and 1940s. Some have deemed the People's Republic of China totalitarian, at least for various periods since its establishment in 1949. Also included in this category are North Korea and Cambodia under the Khmer Rouge.

In the twentieth century a number of core countries had fully authoritarian or semi-authoritarian regimes, usually called *dictatorships.* Semi-peripheral countries such as Portugal, Spain, Greece, and Turkey endured dictatorships of varying longevity in the twentieth century. Authoritarian socialist regimes ruled virtually all of Eastern and Central Europe from the 1940s until the 1990s. A number of authoritarian regimes in Latin America, in West, Central, South, East, and Southeast Asia, in Africa, and in the Middle East/Persian Gulf played roles in the global political, military, and economic strategy of the United States and other core states during the twentieth century. In many cases, American (and "allied") policy had a direct hand in the establishment and maintenance of "client" military-dominated authoritarian regimes. The term "bureaucratic-authoritarian" designates several such Latin American regimes of the 1960s to 1980s. But it is not sufficient to reduce these regimes to "sub-fascist client states" or "tools of multinational corporations," just as European and Third World authoritarian socialist regimes should not simply be considered Soviet "satellites." Authoritarian regimes are shaped not only by their global insertion but also by their respective spheres of state, society, and market.

Decolonization after World War II transformed most of Africa, the Middle East, and much of Asia. Authoritarian regimes have abounded in these post-colonial social formations, though democratic and revolutionary regimes also have been prominent. Various explanations are offered for the high incidence of authoritarian regimes in post-colonial countries. For example, they have been considered "artificial" creations of colonial powers or elites created under colonialism as well as products of ethnic, cultural, and religious divisions, which often are more pronounced and less manageable than in core countries. It also is argued that the political culture of democracy either does not exist, or is under-developed, or cannot compete with tradition, religion, ethnic politics, or ideology. Some suggest that authoritarianism is convenient for former colonial powers or international capitalism. For others, capitalism in the periphery is incomplete, distorted, and externally oriented and thus cannot support civil society and liberal democracy as they have developed in the West. Finally, it is argued that authoritarian regimes are a predictable stage in the modernization process leading eventually to democratic regimes.

As in most broad explanations, each of the above has some applicability. A deeper understanding of Third World authoritarian regimes results from considering each regime's specificity of state, society, market, and global insertion. What we can assert is that just as patterns of economic dependency and U.S. power are necessary but not sufficient bases for understanding Latin American authoritarian regimes, the historical experiences of colonialism, insertion into the state system, and international division of labour in the twentieth century are necessary but not sufficient for understanding post-colonial regimes in Africa, the Middle East, and Asia. We also can suggest that post-colonial regimes manifest more "traditional" affinities, values, and identities than do core countries. But we must be careful here not to fall into "othering" and patronizing because the same can be found in core countries as well. Aboriginal peoples, women, ethnic minorities, and disadvantaged social classes have experienced as much (or more) marginalization and repression under Western liberal democracies as have their counterparts under Third World authoritarian regimes.

Many post-colonial social formations lack a capitalist "ruling class" with the material substance and social cohesion of its counterparts in the core and semi-periphery. Various factions contend for control of the state apparatus more from a patrimonial perspective—that is, from a historical sense of entitlement, rather than from an inclusive national "regime of accumulation" perspective. Such post-colonial elites have been vulnerable to military coups, external intervention, or revolutionary social forces. In cases where oil or another commodity is important to the international economy or where the country has strategic traditional, nationalist, or military importance, authoritarian elites have had regime alliances with multinational corporations and/or core states.

The variety of post-colonial authoritarian regimes is striking. In Africa, personalist semi-authoritarian regimes often followed initial experiments with democracy. Charismatic figures of the independence movement headed presidential and single-party regimes. There were instances in Asia and the Middle East as well. In some African countries experiencing wars of national liberation won by revolutionary movements, the regimes have had personalist, single-party, and authoritarian elements. Other personalist regimes were more identified with foreign patrons, corruption, an opulent lifestyle, and varying degrees of repression. In cases lacking a charismatic figure, a series of military leaders or groups managed varieties of authoritarian regimes in some of Africa's richest and poorest countries.

In the Middle East, several forceful leaders (Nasser, Qaddafi, Assad) in the 1950s and 1960s articulated a mix of populist, nationalist, pan-Arab anti-imperialist, and anti-Israeli messages while promoting economic development and state social responsibility. Their regimes were semi-authoritarian, with varying degrees of repression, culminating in a fully authoritarian Iraq. Most Gulf states were semi-authoritarian monarchies or oligarchies dominating the oil wealth. At present, several countries have self-denominated Islamic regimes (Iran, Saudi Arabia, Sudan); their authoritarianism varies (it should be said that Islam is not inherently authoritarian).

Authoritarian regimes also have appeared in South and Southeast Asia, though not exclusively. More than half of Pakistan's political history and much of Bangladesh's has been dominated by military rule. Even democratic India has experienced periods of semi-authoritarian governance. Indonesia has emerged from decades of personalist, military-backed semi-authoritarianism, while the military has played central roles in Myanmar and Thailand. The Cold War's global dynamics greatly influenced regime formation in much of the region, ranging from the semi-authoritarian Marcos regime in the Philippines and the pro-U.S. dictatorships of Indochina to the authoritarian socialist regimes that followed, reaching the tragic extreme of the Khmer Rouge in Cambodia.

Democratic Regimes

Just as a continuum of authoritarian regime types reflects diverse experiences across the four spheres, there also is considerable variation among democratic regimes. Generally, a liberal democracy is characterized by near universal franchise among citizens, the opportunity for citizens to stand for election, and the fair and frequent conduct of elections. States that are in the process of implementing these elements are often referred to as transitional democracies, while countries like Canada and the United States can be said to have "consolidated" or well-established democracies. In practice, liberal democratic regimes are more representative than participatory, with elected officials and with appointed and merit-based bureaucracies. Together, these bodies manage the state and exercise actual governance, embodying power in and over civil and market society. The inclusiveness and pluralism of such societies is ostensibly reflected in these regimes.

Liberal democratic regimes in transitional and consolidated forms are currently the dominant regime type. As many formerly authoritarian regimes are in transition to liberal democracies, political scientists often refer to the current period as "the globalization of democracy." A premise of this celebration is that capitalism and democracy are natural and necessary partners. Authoritarian regimes, however, have co-existed with capitalism in every part of the world. As a harsh judgment puts it, "for capitalism, democracy if possible, but not necessarily." This polemic highlights a basic tension in liberal democracies. There may be formal political democracy and citizen equality in such regimes, but there is not an equivalent economic democracy and market equality. Market societies are characterized by the concentration and centralization of property and wealth in private hands, and their regimes tend to prioritize "ruling class" interests. Historically, this tension has been managed either by force or by the state's appropriation and redistribution of some of the wealth generated by the "operation of the free market." Thus, many liberal democracies have taken a social democratic form. The state acts to bring the citizenry's social and economic status closer to the political equality all formally enjoy.

Critics consider liberal democracies of wealthy countries to be fundamentally "ruling class regimes," and they are skeptical regarding newly democratizing regimes in former "authoritarian capitalist" countries in the Third World and "post-socialist" countries in the Second World. Usually, critics associate neo-liberal policy and globalization, which favour core economies and periphery or semi-periphery elites, with those post-authoritarian regimes. They argue that formal democracy is accompanied by "savage capitalism" and a deterioration in living standards. Some argue that terms like "oligarchic," "limited," or "dependent democracy" better describe these regimes. They insist that working-class, peasant, and leftist movements were crushed or severely weakened by decades of repression and now have no significant role in competitive electoral politics, making post-authoritarian regimes less democratic. Some view the political conditionality of international financial institutions' debt-restructuring policies as an imposition of vacuous democratic processes and institutions. As with authoritarian regimes, however, we should consider "democracies-in-transition" across all four spheres of the regime, acknowledging multiple sources of democratic impulses.

An illustration of this latter point is the rapid transformation of authoritarian socialist regimes into liberal democracies. It was not only "flawed" global insertion that brought about the demise of authoritarian socialist regimes; the other three spheres need explanatory inclusion. Transitional regimes are characterized according to emphasis on one or another sphere. For example, some term Russia's successive economic crises and the impoverishment of the majority its "Third Worldization." Others focus on patterns of capital accumulation and certain business successes as "primitive capitalist accumulation" or "gangster capitalism." In the formal political realm, the assessment of democracy seems to follow the electoral fortunes of particular individuals, such as Yeltsin and Putin, as much as it does "efficiency" in governance or public opinion poll results. Fears are expressed about a "return to socialism," virulent nationalism, Russian imperial designs, instability, and even fascism.

Revolutionary Regimes

Transitions under way in post-socialist regimes resemble the transformational dynamics of revolutionary regimes. A number of core countries have had democratic (state sphere), bourgeois or middle-class (society sphere), and capitalist (market sphere) revolutions, though not socialist revolutions. Some early twentieth-century revolutions (Mexico in 1910, China in 1949) combined nationalism with a partial socialism. But generally we associate twentieth-century revolutions with Marxism, centrally planned economies, the suppression of capitalism, Communist Party monopoly, and commitment to the interests of the working class over others.

Failed socialist revolutionary efforts significantly outnumber actual revolutionary regimes, but two sets of circumstances seem to favour the latter—international wars and national liberation struggles. The Bolshevik (Russian) and Chinese revolutions emerged from World Wars I and II, respectively. From the 1930s to the 1970s, anti-colonial and anti-imperialist struggles in Asia and Africa assumed a Marxist revolutionary character. Dozens of attempts to replicate the Cuban Revolution of 1959 took place throughout Latin America, all considering themselves anti-imperialist and anti-capitalist. Only one achieved state power—the 1979 Sandinista Revolution in Nicaragua. Few revolutionary movements have been able to gain power through formal democratic means. A rare example is the Popular Unity coalition that elected Salvador Allende in Chile in 1970, only to be overthrown by an American-backed military coup in 1973.

Given that most revolutionary regimes are born in violence, it is not surprising that many have had strong militaristic, security, and disciplinary elements. Defending the revolution, confronting capitalist and other domestic and international opposition, launching massive projects of "socialist economic accumulation," especially socialization of commerce, collectivization of agriculture, and rapid industrialization—all these tasks seemed to require authoritarian regimes. Democratic processes were considered dangerous opportunities for the class enemy, unaffordable luxuries that impeded central planning and the creation of socialist values—or to be postponed until socialism matured into communism.

World War II's destructive impact on state, society, and economy, along with strategic dispositions at its end, combined with the Cold War in Europe and Asia to cast countries into opposing regime types. Liberal democracies were established in Germany and Japan. Dual authoritarian regimes divided Korea, while totalitarian regimes prevailed in Eastern Europe, generally under the control of the USSR. The economy and market engagement of these states generally followed the command economy model; however, as Soviet power waned in the 1980s, European states became much more responsive to market principles, permitting small private enterprise, large worker-controlled cooperatives, and engagement with fully capitalist economies through trade and investment. Today, the majority of transitional democracies are found among the former Soviet states of Eastern Europe.

Marxist political strategy, centrally planned industrialization, and agricultural collectivization held strong appeal for many independence movements in Asia and Africa. The Soviet Union's rapid industrialization provided an example. After its 1949 revolution, China also provided an example, especially because of its official anti-colonial and anti-imperialist ideology. Both communist countries, thus, became "natural allies" for national liberation movements. A number of those movements came to power and affiliated with the "socialist community," with trade and aid, arms, and advisers becoming integral to their regimes.

While Marxist revolutionary ideology certainly emphasized internationalism and solidarity, most Third World revolutionary regimes concentrated on the spheres of state, society, and market. Replacing the previous regime, trying to transform social and class relations, and creating a national identity and a viable socialist economy absorbed the energy of people undertaking those tasks. These transitions would not have been easy in the best of global circumstances. Yet the achievements—measured by increased equality, reduced exploitation, and marked improvements in quality-of-life indices for many Third World revolutionary regimes—cannot be discounted.

Future Trends

THE HISTORICAL PREPONDERANCE OF AUTHORITARIAN REGIMES IS NOW strongly contrasted by consolidated and transitional liberal democratic regimes. Neither type is guaranteed, though revolutions are more likely to issue from authoritarian than from democratic regimes. All four spheres should be considered in determining whether transitional regimes in both the Third and the Second Worlds become consolidated democracies. People are more likely to adopt a revolutionary stance against a repressive authoritarian regime than a democratic one, even if the democracy is limited or corrupt. The expected stresses of democratic transitions, when exacerbated by the unevenness of globalizing capitalist accumulation, are more likely to lead to renewed authoritarian forms than to revolution. But the circumstances become more volatile, even for liberal democracies, when economic recession or depression increases marginalization and impoverishment, especially when there is an obvious and wide gap between the rich and other members of society.

War, of course, introduces other factors prompting regime change. Both Marxists and Weberians would agree on that point, but we are already witnessing other outcomes. In parts of Western Africa and in Somalia, it is possible to speak of failed states, vacated states, or non-regimes. In some situations of humanitarian disasters, such as war, genocide, and famine, there have been temporary but functional United Nations peacekeeping regimes, non-governmental organization aid regimes, or proxy regimes operated by a militarily intervening neighbour. Since the events of September 11, 2001, there are American occupation regimes in Afghanistan and Iraq. In a certain sense, these are all forms of transnationalized regimes.

The manifold processes we call economic globalization also hold regime implications. Whether in **export processing zones (EPZs)** or in countries where global corporations are the most important economic and political actors, there is a semblance of corporate feudalism, much like the "banana republics" of the early twentieth century, which operated as fruit company fiefdoms. And with the evident power of finance capital, currency markets, banks, and international financial institutions to affect governments' borrowing, debt-restructuring, and budgets, we have in effect yet another realm of transnationalized governance.

None of these transnationalized forms amounts to a full regime across the four spheres, yet clearly sovereignty is affected. In many instances, we could speak of "layered" regimes, some exercising governance over single spheres, some operating at local, regional, and national levels, and others transnationalized. Layered experiences, in fact, are not limited to poor, peripheral, or transitional regimes. Richer or larger countries, however, are generally better able to resist the transnationalization and layering of governance across their four spheres.

Summary

This chapter provided a definition of "regime" for comparative studies of governance. The four spheres that regimes control and coordinate are state, society, market, and global insertion. In surveying regimes of the twentieth century, it is clear that attributes of one regime type are often found in another. Democratic aspects of authoritarian regimes, for example, should not be ignored. Similarly, many democratic regimes have manifested authoritarian features. It is helpful to think of concrete regimes as composites or hybrids, both unique and comparable within a typology. We have seen, for example, that both authoritarian and liberal democratic regimes in capitalist countries employ corporatist arrangements to manage business or labour relations and public policy. We have also seen some convergence of social democracy and democratic socialism, though perhaps more in theory than in practice. And some revolutionary regimes have engaged with democratic pluralism and experimented with "market socialism." As the processes of globalization accelerate, variations in contemporary political regimes are both expanding and contracting. In this century as in the last, we should expect regime diversity and more regime composites.

Discussion Questions

1. What do you think will be the impact of globalization on our current typology of regimes?
2. Why were authoritarian regimes so common in the twentieth century?
3. Where are revolutions possible in the twenty-first century? Why?
4. What kind of regime or combination of regimes best suits the problems of governance in the current era of intensifying globalization?

Further Readings

Hobsbawm, E.J. 1994. *The Age of Extremes: A History of the World, 1914–1991.* New York: Pantheon Books.

Marx, Karl. 1967. *The Communist Manifesto,* with an introduction and notes by A.J.P. Taylor. Harmondsworth: Penguin Books.

Weber, Max. 1949. *Max Weber on the Methodology of the Social Sciences.* Translated and edited by Edward A. Shils and Henry A. Finch; foreword by Edward A. Shils. Glencoe: Free Press.

Weblinks

Comparative Politics Online: Internet Resources
http://classweb.gmu.edu/chauss/cponline/links.htm

Comparative Politics Resources
www.psr.keele.ac.uk/area.htm

U.S. State Department Background Notes
www.state.gov/www/background_notes/index.html

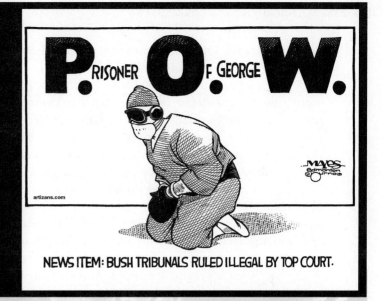

NEWS ITEM: BUSH TRIBUNALS RULED ILLEGAL BY TOP COURT.

CHAPTER 8

CONSTITUTIONS AND THE RULE OF LAW

Objectives

Constitutions provide the blueprints for modern government. In this chapter we examine the importance of the rule of law to governing in liberal democracies. We also consider what constitutional provisions and change tell us about a country's politics. We explore the difference between political systems governed by written and unwritten constitutions, as well as the critical importance of constitutional conventions or customs. We discuss how constitutions may or may not divide sovereignty between national and regional governments, how constitutions are changed, and several features distinguishing parliamentary from presidential systems. We end by looking critically at the idea that written constitutions are crucial to the protection of the rights of citizens.

IAN URQUHART

Introduction

The conviction of Saddam Hussein for crimes against humanity, former U.S. president Bill Clinton's sexual indiscretions, the imprisonment of so-called "enemy combatants" by the United States in Guantanamo Bay, Cuba—other than high drama, what might these events share? How are they related to constitutions? The **rule of law**, a fundamental concept in democratic politics, joins these stories together and, through them, to constitutions. I only appreciated the importance of the rule of law to democratic politics late in my student life, as a graduate student, when I read the Supreme Court of Canada's decision in *Reference re Manitoba Language Rights*. There, the Court said the rule of law demanded at least two things. First, it required "that the law is supreme over officials of the government as well as private individuals, and thereby preclusive of the influence of arbitrary power." In Washington, those who dogged President Clinton for allegedly lying under oath and obstructing justice used this rationale to respond to the President's claim to possess absolute immunity from the ordinary criminal law process while in office. To his foes, Clinton's argument violated a fundamental premise of the rule of law: all citizens are subordinate to the law, regardless of wealth, social status, or political position.

Saddam Hussein's conviction in Iraq for executing 148 Shia men and boys in Dujail in 1982 is linked to the second condition demanded by the Supreme Court. Here, the rule of law "requires the creation and maintenance of an actual order of positive laws which preserves and embodies the more general principle of normative order. Law and order are indispensable elements of civilized life." Ensuring a fair trial for Saddam Hussein was regarded as essential to American efforts to establish the legitimacy of overthrowing Saddam and to enhance the prospects for democratizing Iraq. The trial, however, was bedeviled by the same chaos that has plagued Iraq since Saddam was deposed—three defence lawyers were murdered, judges were under intense political pressure from the Iraqi government to deliver a quick conviction, and more than two dozen witnesses were too intimidated to testify. Respected international legal experts felt Saddam was not given the essential right to present a full defence against the charges. That the best that may be said was that the trial was "reasonably fair" is unlikely to convince many Sunni insurgents to see the value of Western democracy and abandon their efforts to destabilize the Iraqi government.

A somewhat similar situation may be seen with respect to Guantanamo Bay, the American naval base on the southeastern coast of Cuba, where more than 450 "detainees" in the American-led anti-terrorism campaign were being held in the fall of 2006. These prisoners are the subject of a tug of war between the Bush administration, Congress, the courts, and civil liberties organizations over whether the prisoners must benefit from the guarantees customarily associated with the rule of law. In decisions from 2004 and 2006 the United States Supreme Court ruled that aliens had the right to challenge the legality of their detention before the federal courts and that the Bush administration could not try detainees because its military commissions were unauthorized by Congress and violated international law. Whether these shortcomings were rectified by the *Military Commissions Act* of 2006—a law endorsing the presidency's refusal to grant detainees the rights to ask a judge to determine if their imprisonment is legal, to examine all of the evidence against them, and to prohibit the use of testimony allegedly obtained by coercion—undoubtedly will be tested before the American courts.

The principle of the rule of law, as Canada's Supreme Court argued, is implicit in the very nature of a constitution. The constitution stands out as the most important source of legal authority. Its overarching importance arises from the fact that constitutional provisions regulate the fundamental operations of the political system and the relationships between the system's key political institutions. Constitutions offer us basic information about the rules of the political game, who may play, and who is likely to play starring and supporting roles.

The American constitution illustrates this point well. Its first three articles clearly delineate the separation of powers among the legislature, the executive, and the judiciary. The first article locates legislative power in the House of Representatives and the Senate. It next outlines the structure and powers of these institutions, the qualifications needed to run for electoral office, and the timing of elections. What powers does the president have? Who can run for president? Such questions are answered in the second article's discussion of the executive powers of the presidency. Information about the responsibilities of the federal courts rests in the third article.

Not all written constitutions, however, offer good guidance as to how a political system operates or the values it respects. In Zimbabwe, for example, government-orchestrated political violence and human rights abuses thrive despite the constitution's impressive written commitment to rights. In liberal democracies, too, political practice may stray—but far less severely and regularly—from constitutional expectations. Sometimes, as discussed later in this chapter, constitutional conventions are responsible for such departures. On other occasions, these departures are best seen not as absolute rejections of core constitutional values (for example, freedom of speech or equality), but rather as expressions of debates about what limits on the exercise of a right, if any, are consistent with respecting that bedrock value.

Constitutions as Barometers of Political Conflict

CONSTITUTIONS SHOULD BE STUDIED FOR REASONS OTHER THAN WHAT THEY tell us about how the political process operates. Constitutions bear examination for what they reveal about the nature of political conflict and the balance of political power in the countries we study. The evolution of constitutional documents and debates also tells us a great deal about the sorts of changes occurring in a society.

Canada's *Constitution Act* of 1867 provides a snapshot of the significant political conflicts that shaped Canada's formation. A number of its provisions may be traced to the importance of English–French tensions in the colonial politics of British North America. The political importance of "les Canadiens," the French-speaking population centred in Quebec, forced reluctant English-speaking politicians to accept a federal rather than a unitary political system. Powers such as education, property rights, and civil rights were regarded as essential to the preservation of Catholicism and the French language and culture in Quebec. Consequently, they were entrusted to the provincial governments. Features of the Canadian parliamentary structure also testify to the importance of the French–English cleavage in the struggle to unite the British North American colonies into one country. For example, Quebec was guaranteed 65 seats in the House of Commons, the same number of seats it claimed in the pre-Confederation legislative assembly. If Quebec's population fell, the province's political representation in the Commons would not fall below this minimum number.

The evolution of constitutions, like their creation, is also a valuable indicator of underlying political currents in societies. Amendments to the United States Constitution testify to how emerging political conflicts modified the political consensus forged in the original document. The American *Bill of Rights* of 1791—the first ten amendments to the Constitution—harked back to the American Revolution's emphasis on individual liberty. The Constitution drafted at the Constitutional Convention of 1787 lacked an explicit commitment to protect individual freedoms. Those who feared that a strengthened national government would be emboldened enough to try on the robes of the English king demanded the addition of a list of guaranteed freedoms.

Some subsequent amendments to the Constitution testify to the importance of battles over the importance and meaning of political equality in American politics. One of the consequences of the conflicts leading to the Civil War of the 1860s appeared as three constitutional amendments, the Thirteenth to the Fifteenth, amendments promoting black political equality. For example, part of the Fourteenth Amendment protected freed slaves. All persons born or naturalized in the United States—former slaves included—were citizens of the United States and the state they lived in. States were prohibited from abridging the privileges or immunities of citizens of the United States, from depriving any person of life, liberty, or property without due process and from denying people the equal protection of the laws. Expanding the boundaries of political equality also inspired several twentieth-century amendments, the most significant being the Seventeenth (popular election of Senators), the Nineteenth (extending the right to vote to women), and the Twenty-sixth (reducing the voting age to 18).

None of this is to say that constitutions will ensure that the political differences responsible for conflict will be accommodated successfully. Democratic constitutional government demands certain attitudinal commitments—for example, to accommodation, tolerance, and a willingness to live together. Without these attitudes constitutions may be written in ways that punish some citizens while privileging others. The communal civil war raging throughout Iraq in early 2007 may underline this scenario tragically. Just three months after the overthrow of Saddam Hussein's Baathist government in April 2003, the United States established the 25-member Iraqi Governing Council to help draft a new constitution. Little more than two years later, the National Assembly of this "immature polity with little history of compromise" was presented with a draft constitution acceptable to two of

Iraq's key sectarian/ethnic groups—the Shiites and Kurds—but not to the Sunnis, who had profited handsomely during Saddam's rule (Biddell, 2006). Sunni negotiators rejected the draft, fearing, with considerable justification, that the majority Shiite population and the Kurdish minority wanted the new constitutional arrangements to punish the minority Sunnis for the largesse they had enjoyed at the hands of Saddam.

The most controversial Iraqi constitutional issue was federalism: the division of powers between the national and provincial/regional governments. The Iraqi constitution gave the Kurds a largely autonomous region in the north and the Shiites the possibility of creating their own "Shiastan" region composed of the nine, predominantly Shiite, southern provinces. For the Sunnis such decentralization was an "anathema" (Iraq Study Group, 19, 2006). The Sunnis oppose such a decentralized federation because first, Iraq's oil resources are located in Shiite and Kurdish territories, not in central and western Iraq, where the Sunnis are concentrated. Given this geographical and demographic distribution of oil in Iraq, none of the Sunni-controlled provinces were deemed "economically feasible" (Iraq Study Group, 19, 2006). Article 110 of the Iraqi constitution likely will make this situation even worse for the Sunnis. While revenues from *current* oil and gas production are to be shared nationally according to Iraq's sectarian and ethnic divisions (Shiites, 55 percent; Kurds, 25 percent; Sunnis, 20 percent), the revenues from *new* reserves will go exclusively to the regions. These constitutional provisions led the Iraq Study Group, a group established to recommend U.S. policy options in Iraq, to conclude "that key Shia and Kurdish leaders have little commitment to national reconciliation" (Iraq Study Group, 19, 2006). Iraq's constitutional order, inasmuch as it, justly or not, punishes Sunnis for the crimes of the Saddam era, may certainly be seen as fuel for the Sunni–Shiite sectarian violence plaguing Iraq.

Written or Unwritten Constitutions and the Importance of Conventions

A key distinction made in the study of constitutions is between *written* and *unwritten* constitutions. The United States Constitution is the classic example of a written constitution. In that one document you will find most of the information needed to understand the basic structure of political institutions and the logic of the American political process—in particular, the division of power among the three branches of government. A second defining feature of the written constitution, the type of constitution that most nations have adopted, is that it is an extraordinary legal document. It carries much more interpretive importance and weight than ordinary laws passed by a legislature. Article VI of the U.S. Constitution outlines the document's overarching importance. There, the Constitution is identified as "the supreme law of the land." As such, it takes precedence over any state constitution or state law. All American law, federal or state, must correspond to the provisions and principles of the American Constitution.

When the written portion of the Canadian Constitution was enlarged in 1982, an even more explicit statement of the Constitution's importance was included. After following the American example by identifying the Constitution as "the supreme law of Canada," Section 52 of the *Constitution Act* (1982) went on to point out that "any law that is inconsistent with the provisions of the Constitution is, to the extent of the inconsistency, of no force or effect."

Britain is generally regarded as the classic example of a country guided by an unwritten constitution. But the label "unwritten" is quite misleading. It really means that the British Constitution, unlike its American counterpart, cannot be found primarily within the confines of one document called "The Constitution." In fact, the unwritten British Constitution is made up, in part, of many written laws. Some were authored by monarchs before the dawn of parliamentary supremacy. The Magna Carta, signed by King John in 1215 and modified by Parliament in 1297, is one of the written pillars of Britain's unwritten Constitution. This constitutional document responded to a rebellion by English noblemen who believed King John was abusing his powers, especially by taxing them too severely. The Magna Carta limited the monarch's power and protected the English lords from royal authority. Its contemporary relevance to life in modern Anglo-American democracies may be found in sections such as the one guaranteeing that people may not lose their liberty or property without a trial by their peers.

The insistence on calling the British constitution "unwritten," rather than, say, uncodified, is best defended by pointing out that many of its most significant and well-accepted elements do not rest in written laws at all. They exist as constitutional conventions. **Constitutional conventions** may be regarded as extra-legal constitutional rules, rules without a foundation in the law. Because they lack a basis in law they cannot be enforced by the courts. But their extra-legal nature does not make them, as one might think, less important. In 1981, for example, the Supreme Court of Canada was asked whether the Canadian government could ignore the constitutional convention that the approval of the national government and a substantial number of provinces was needed to amend the constitution. A majority of the Supreme Court answered that "some conventions may be more important than some laws. Their importance depends on that of the value or principle which they are meant to safeguard."

The most important conventions are ones that effectively transfer *de facto* power from one authority or one actor to another. In Britain, for example, the Queen has the legal prerogative to refuse to give Royal Assent to any legislation passed by her Parliament. Without Royal Assent, the bills passed by Parliament cannot become laws. Use your imagination for a moment. Suppose that the Queen had objected to the Labour government's *Scotland Act*, the law that gave some of the British Parliament's powers to a Scottish Parliament. She had the legal power to refuse to give the assent needed for this bill to become law. But her refusal would have violated the British political convention that monarchs must sign legislation passed by a parliamentary majority. What we have here is the type of clash identified above by the Supreme Court of Canada—a clash revolving around the importance of the value of representative democracy. In a country where the legitimacy of electoral politics is unshakable, it is unthinkable that a monarch who sits on the throne because of an accident of birth would frustrate an elected and publicly accountable Parliament. Because of its democratic pedigree, the convention that the Queen always grants her assent when it is requested trumps the legal possibility that Royal assent may be withheld. While the Queen continues to hold this *de jure* power, the *de facto* power to say yea or nay to legislation has been passed to the prime minister and a parliamentary majority.[1]

Constitutional Change

SHOULD YOU CARE ABOUT THIS DISTINCTION BETWEEN WRITTEN AND UNWRITTEN Constitutions? One reason this distinction is valuable concerns the possibility of constitutional change. Written constitutions are notoriously difficult to amend. Since written constitutions are supposed to reflect the fundamental and enduring values of their host societies, constitutional amendments usually require extraordinary majorities. If a constitution is to be amended, the proposed change must be welcomed by a broad consensus in the society.

Canada's *Constitution Act* (1982) illustrates this point about extraordinary majorities. Changes to some institutions, such as the composition of the Supreme Court or the amending formula itself, require the unanimous consent of the national legislature and all of the provincial legislatures. According to the general amending formula, a formula that applies to subjects such as the powers of the Senate and the method of selecting senators, a constitutional amendment requires the agreement of the national Parliament and the legislatures of at least two-thirds of the provinces (seven of ten) that have at least 50 percent of the total provincial population. The failure to incorporate the Meech Lake Accord into the Canadian constitution demonstrates the substantial hurdles raised by the extraordinary majority requirement.

The situation with respect to an unwritten constitution is significantly different. Since the constitution does not live in one document, a formal amending formula does not exist. Without this formula, advocates of constitutional change face a far more flexible environment. For decades, this flexibility was "academic" in the pejorative sense of the word—it did not seem to have much bearing on daily life. However, the path taken by the Blair government in Britain changed that. Devolution, the

---

[1] The same relationship exists in Canada between the prime minister, Parliament, and the Governor General. Another important convention in Britain and Canada is that the leader of the party winning the most seats in an election is asked to form a government.

Human Rights Act, and the reform of the House of Lords led *The Times* of London to conclude: "Constitutional reform is changing the way Britain is governed in much more radical ways than is generally appreciated" (*The Times*, 1998). The flexibility of the unwritten constitution is key here. Without it, these radical changes would be much more difficult—perhaps impossible—to realize.

But should Canadians *want* that kind of flexibility? In the first place, since the Blair changes all took place through individual pieces of legislation, some worry that this approach to constitutional change is not as comprehensive or as well thought out as it should be. In other words, should constitutional change be a piecemeal process or a coherent and encompassing one? The flexibility afforded by unwritten constitutions also raises important democratic issues. If constitutions should reflect a political consensus in society, is it wise or desirable for the constitution to be changed only by the party that holds a parliamentary majority? In 2005 Blair's Labour government, for example, only received 36 percent of the popular vote. Should fundamental changes to a constitution not be subject to a wide-ranging public debate—a more inclusive debate than these issues saw when they were debated in the British Parliament?

Unitary or Federal?

ANOTHER IMPORTANT ASPECT OF CONSTITUTIONS IS HOW THEY DIVIDE POWER, IF AT all, between national and sub-national governments. In other words, the constitution sets out the rules for both unitary and federal systems. What do we mean when we say that a constitution is federal? The term "federal" refers to how sovereignty or ultimate governing authority is arranged between the different governments ruling over a shared territory. A **federal constitution** divides sovereignty between a national government and sub-national governments (American states, Canadian provinces). In some policy areas, the national government will have the constitutional authority to act or to exercise sovereignty; in other areas, this sovereignty will rest with regional governments.

The idea of sovereignty offers a useful means to distinguish between federal and unitary constitutional systems. In a **unitary** system, all governmental sovereignty rests in the national government. Although sub-national governments may exist in a unitary state, they are empowered to govern by the national government. Their authority comes from the national government and is not constitutionally entrenched and protected. When the Scottish Parliament was elected in 1999, it was empowered to legislate on matters such as education, health, and local government. It was also allowed to vary the income tax Scots pay by a very small amount—a so-called "Tartan Tax." These powers were given to the Scottish Parliament by the British Parliament, not by the constitution. To the dismay of Scottish nationalists, the British Parliament retains the power to modify the Scottish Parliament's basket of powers in any way it wishes.

Separation or Union of Powers? Legislative/Executive Relationships in Canada and the United States

We noted earlier how the American constitution outlines the separation of powers between the legislative, executive, and judicial branches of government. To a significant extent, this choice underlined the Americans' rejection of the British system they had suffered under, a system featuring the union of executive and legislative power. In Canada, emulation, not rejection, was the perspective taken toward the British model of parliamentary government. Consequently, Canada was established under "a Constitution similar in principle to that of the United Kingdom" (Preamble, *Constitution Act, 1867*).

These constitutional choices have important consequences for the power and responsibilities of the two nations' legislatures and executives. The union of powers in Canada's parliamentary system enables the political executive (the prime minister and Cabinet) to dominate the legislature when the governing party holds the majority of seats in the House of Commons. Prime ministerial domination, enforced through strict **party discipline**, neuters individual members of Parliament when it comes to making laws. Presidents, crucial political leaders that they are, nonetheless cannot dominate Congress in the same way. Members of Congress are powerful legislative players. Budgets, the lifeblood of governments, illustrate this difference well. No Canadian newspaper would describe the introduction of a prime minister's budget to Parliament in the way the *Washington Post* described the budget President Bush introduced to Congress in 2002—as "a recommendation." The *Post*'s language testifies to the crucial importance of Congress in the legislative process, reflected here in its power to challenge and amend presidential spending priorities and plans (Goldstein and Allen, 2002). The public questioning of their spending priorities that presidents regularly endure from Congressional members of their own parties is unheard of in Canadian politics. Parliamentary careers, governed as they are by the prime minister's wishes, would be ruined rather than made through this type of behaviour.

Rights and Constitutions

JUST AS FEDERAL CONSTITUTIONS LIMIT THE LEGAL AUTHORITY OF GOVERNMENTS vis-à-vis each other, constitutions may also limit the legal authority of governments vis-à-vis their citizens. This function is both important and controversial. The power of the American government over its citizens is limited by the *Bill of Rights* and other constitutional amendments. Canada's *Charter of Rights and Freedoms* plays the same role. Part of the drive to incorporate the Charter into Canada's constitution developed out of a major shortcoming of the *Canadian Bill of Rights* (1960)—as an ordinary piece of federal legislation it did not apply to provincial actions.

Viewers of NBC TV's *Law and Order* series are familiar with the Miranda warning that American police must give to arrested suspects. The requirement to warn suspects that they have the right to remain silent and to consult a lawyer arose from the case of *Miranda v. Arizona.* There the Supreme Court overturned the conviction of a confessed kidnapper and rapist because the police violated Miranda's Fifth Amendment right not to be compelled to make self-incriminating statements. This Fifth Amendment protection exemplifies **negative rights**—rights individuals have against being interfered with by other actors such as government. In the context of the government–citizen relationship, negative rights protect people from government interference.

Written constitutions also may guarantee **positive rights**—rights that require government intervention to be realized. The minority-language educational rights outlined in Section 23 of the *Canadian Charter of Rights and Freedoms* illustrate this alternative form of rights guarantee. This section stipulates that, where the numbers of children warrant, Canadian citizens have the right to have minority language (English or French) education and educational facilities provided and paid for by the government.

Constitutional guarantees of rights are controversial for many reasons. The Miranda case raised one of the controversies associated with legal rights. Respecting individual rights occasionally may mean that the guilty escape punishment because their rights were violated. For some people, constitutional rights are controversial because interpreting constitutional meaning is turned over to the courts. Some critics of **judicial review** in Canada and the United States worry that judges will hijack the constitution and fill its language with meanings never intended by the framers.

Courts and Legislatures

IMPORTANT AS THESE CONTROVERSIES ARE, I WOULD LIKE TO WARN AGAINST what may be a developing mythology, particularly significant in Canada, about constitutional rights. The core of the mythology is that judges, through judicial review, further rights while politicians and public servants, through their laws and actions, restrict rights. This is a dangerous caricature. It exaggerates the rights-protecting nature of the judiciary and undervalues the extent to which legislatures also may champion the rights and well-being of citizens.

There are several important fallacies in the conventional outlook on rights, courts, and legislatures. One fallacy lies in the message that the Charter simply protects the rights of individuals against the state. While this is sometimes true, it is also true that, when the courts interpret the Charter, they may instead protect the rights of some individuals at the expense of another category of individuals. In other words, individuals or groups of similar individuals both win and lose in some Charter decisions. Judicial review of the Charter may involve considerably more than upholding the rights of the individual against the government.

This general point that Charter cases may deal with inter-group conflict was illustrated dramatically in *R. v. Seaboyer*, a case that struck down Canada's rape-shield law. This federal law sought to abolish some old common-law rules that permitted evidence of a rape victim's sexual conduct to be heard by a jury, irrespective of whether or not the evidence was relevant to the case at hand. The judge in Seaboyer's trial followed the letter of the law; he refused to let the defence question the complainant about her sexual history. Seaboyer's attorney argued this decision denied Seaboyer his Section 11(d) Charter right to a fair trial. Justice Beverly McLachlin, writing for a majority of the Supreme Court, agreed. She concluded the law created "the real risk that an innocent person may be convicted." At one level, this decision fits the individual versus the state framework well. Government law treated Seaboyer harshly; the Supreme Court vindicated his rights. However, at another level we can also see that the state's law existed to protect the rights or the interests of vulnerable victims of sexual assault. Here the decision protected the interests of one category of individuals (the accused) at the expense of the interests of others (the alleged victims). Court battles over whether laws violate the Charter may well be battles between classes of individuals and not simply battles between individuals and the state.

The Seaboyer case also allows us to argue that the core of the constitutional rights mythology, that courts protect rights and legislatures restrict rights, is fallacious. The example of Seaboyer shows the reality to be far more complicated. Government legislation actually may protect or further the rights or interests of particular, not necessarily majority constituencies. Through legislation such as the rape-shield law, governments may improve the position in our society of vulnerable or disadvantaged groups. This possibility also casts a more favourable light on the often criticized **notwithstanding clause**. This clause, Section 33 of the *Canadian Charter of Rights and Freedoms*, enables the federal and provincial governments to reinstate laws found to be unreasonable violations of the rights guaranteed under Sections 2 (fundamental freedoms) and 7 to 15 (legal and equality rights).

More recently, judicial review of Canada's anti-terrorism legislation illustrates just how complicated the relationship may be between legislatures, courts, and the protection of rights. In October 2006 Justice Rutherford of the Superior Court of Ontario found that the so-called motive clause in Canada's *Anti-Terrorism Act* violated the Charter's fundamental freedoms. He concluded that the law, by defining terrorist activity as any act or omission committed "in whole or in part for a political, religious or ideological purpose, objective or cause," invited ethnic and/or racial profiling. But some argue that Parliament, by including the motive clause to its anti-terrorism legislation, actually sought to limit the reach of the law, thereby protecting the civil rights of some groups (such as trade unions) whose activities might otherwise be at risk under another, broader definition of terrorism. Irwin Cotler, a former federal Justice Minister, noted scholar, and champion of international human rights, argued that the motivation clause actually increased the burden of proof on government when it came to proving terrorist activity. "It's ironic," said Cotler, "that it's defence counsel that is moving to impugn that provision, when in fact the prosecution may find that it will facilitate prosecutions without that provision" (Dabrota and Galloway, 2006). In light of this conclusion it becomes more difficult to judge where the greatest threat to rights may rest—in Parliament's law or in Justice Rutherford's interpretation of the law.

Summary

In this chapter we have sketched out several roles constitutions play in liberal democracies. They establish the essential rules of political competition. They define the relationships among a country's key political actors. In this respect, they may or may not divide sovereignty between different levels of government and stipulate the sorts of protections and duties citizens can expect from their governments. We have also argued that constitutions are focal points for political conflict. For centuries, political actors have regarded constitutional provisions as key political resources—an outlook that is bound to flourish in the twenty-first century.

Discussion Questions

1. If you were given the job of drafting a constitution for a new country, would you require extraordinary majorities in the constitutional amendment formula?
2. Would making the Canadian Parliament operate more like the United States Congress improve the Canadian system of government? What factors might complicate such a change?
3. "The notwithstanding clause is a valuable addition to Canada's constitution." Would you agree with this statement? Why?
4. What lessons may we learn from the process of drafting the first post–Saddam Hussein constitution in Iraq?

References

Biddle, Stephen. 2006. "Seeing Baghdad, Thinking Saigon." *Foreign Affairs*, March/April.

Dobrota, Alex and Gloria Galloway. 2006. "Portion of Law on Terror Struck Down; Convictions Will Be Easier, Experts Say." *The Globe and Mail*, October 25.

Goldstein, Amy and Mike Allen. 2002. "Bush Proposes Defense Boost, Cuts Elsewhere; 'New Realities' Drive Plan, President Says." *The Washington Post*, February 5.

Iraq Study Group. 2006. *The Iraq Study Group Report.* United States Institute of Peace.

The Times (London). 1998. "The Oracle of Westminster." July 27.

Further Readings

Cairns, Alan C. 1995. *Reconfigurations: Canadian Citizenship and Constitutional Change.* Toronto: McClelland and Stewart.

Hiebert, Janet L. 2002. *Charter Conflicts: What Is Parliament's Role?* Toronto: McGill-Queen's University Press.

Hogg, Peter. 2006. *Constitutional Law of Canada,* 2006 Student Edition. Toronto: Carswell.

Weblinks

Centre for Constitutional Studies
www.law.ualberta.ca/centres/ccs

Judith Bowers Law Lists
www.cugini.net/law/canada.htm

Political Database of the Americas—Georgetown University
http://pdba.georgetown.edu

United States Institute of Peace: "Constitution-Making Web Links" and "Library and Links" (Jeannette Rankin Library Program)
www.usip.org/library/topics/constitution.html

CHAPTER 9

PUBLIC BUREAUCRACY

Objectives

This chapter offers an introduction to the administrative state. It introduces students to the public bureaucracy and examines the character of that bureaucracy. Readers will be encouraged to reflect on the ways in which politics and administration intersect within the public bureaucracy. There will also be an examination of the many different organizational forms that are found within the state. The overriding objective of the chapter is to encourage students to think critically and ask the tough questions about public bureaucracy: To what extent is the work of the bureaucracy actually "political"? To what extent can we, as citizens, be confident that there are mechanisms for limiting the power of the public bureaucracy? How should we assess the recent preference for adopting private-sector management techniques within the public bureaucracy?

MARCIA NELSON and STEVE PATTEN

Introduction

The bureaucratic structures of the state touch our lives in innumerable ways. As citizens, we pay taxes, work in regulated industries, utilize public services, and receive public benefits. All of our lives will, at some point, be affected by the character of the public bureaucracy. For this reason, each of us has a stake in its ongoing transformation. Over the past two decades, a neo-liberal governing paradigm has been embraced as the successor to the twentieth-century welfare state. While neo-liberalism was ascendant, a new paradigm of administration known as the "new public management" was altering the character of administrative institutions and processes. New public management (NPM) and its impact on the character of public bureaucracy in Canada will be discussed later in this chapter. The chapter begins, however, by exploring the nature of public bureaucracy and the character of the various organizational forms found within it. Attention subsequently turns to an examination of the various checks and balances that are intended to ensure that the power of the administrative state is wielded in the public interest. The chapter concludes with a discussion of the ways in which the new public management departs from traditional notions of public administration.

Public Bureaucracy
Administration and Politics

THE PUBLIC BUREAUCRACY IS THE SET OF INSTITUTIONS AND ACTORS THAT form the administrative machinery of the state. Sometimes called the civil service, the public bureaucracy is the coterie of administrative officials who take responsibility for policy implementation. They transform government policy into the concrete programs that enable elected governments to deliver on their political promises and agendas.

The fact that state bureaucrats are often called "civil servants" suggests that the administrative officials of the public bureaucracy exist to serve their elected political masters. By tradition, the civil service has been portrayed as the neutral implementers of politically determined policy directions, as if administration was purely technical and value-free. Policy-making, by contrast, is understood to be an inherently political and value-laden process requiring politicians to make choices among competing interests. Thus, policy-making and administration have been viewed as distinct roles, with a clear division of labour between the political work of our elected governments and the apolitical work of appointed civil servants. This notion of the separation between politics and administration is known as the **politics–administration dichotomy**. It was first popularized in the late nineteenth century, when students of government were concerned about excessive patronage and extensive political manipulation of what was, by today's standards, only a very small public bureaucracy (Mellon, 1999).

While it was an American, Woodrow Wilson, who popularized the idea that the modern state's bureaucratic apparatus could rise above politics to provide apolitical administration, it was a German scholar, Max Weber, who outlined the ideas underpinning the notion of bureaucracy as the epitome of the rationalization of modern society. Weber's conception of bureaucracy as a form of human organization based on clearly specified jobs, merit-based hiring, hierarchical supervision, unity of command, and rules-based governance combined with the Wilsonian depiction of the politics–administration dichotomy to form the basis of the majority of twentieth-century scholarship in public administration.

Today, few observers consider the politics–administration dichotomy to be a realistic portrayal of the relationship between policy-making and public administration (Whitaker, 2004). Almost everyone would agree that the public bureaucracy should remain strictly non-partisan; civil servants, in other words, should not be motivated by the interests associated with party politics. But few observers would accept the view that all aspects of public administration are entirely apolitical. For civil servants to serve their political masters, they must act in accordance with the government's agenda, and they must give advice that involves making choices among competing interests. Making this sort of choice is an inherently "political" activity in the sense that it influences the content of public policy and helps to determine the distribution of resources and benefits that are allocated by the state.

While we have long expected public bureaucrats to be non-partisan, it is usually recognized that the various tasks of civil servants are arrayed along a continuum, from relatively apolitical to obviously political. The most senior bureaucrats, in particular, are expected to give politically sensitive policy advice to their political masters (Sutherland, 1993, 86). But the political nature of administration does not stop with giving this sort of politically sensitive policy advice. Even program administrators who have no contact with politicians are often required to use their discretion as they carry out their tasks and serve the clients of government programs. These discretionary decisions have policy consequences that are clearly political—they determine the manner in which programs are delivered. From decisions taken by civil servants reviewing contracts for highway repairs to the judgments of case workers reviewing social assistance applications, administrative discretion shapes the way that policies and programs are played out in real-life situations. There is little doubt, then, that granting administrative discretion to civil servants involves bureaucrats in making policy decisions with political implications.

Recognizing the political nature of administrative discretion and policy advice, newly elected governments often worry about the extent to which they can trust and rely on the civil servants who served the previous party in government. On the one hand, it could be argued that elected politicians need not worry who is staffing the public bureaucracy because highly professional bureaucrats are truly non-partisan "servants" ready to serve whichever party is in power. On the other hand, governments are elected with a mandate to act on their campaign pledges. Thus, if the senior strata of the public bureaucracy are instrumental to the successful implementation of a government's policy mandate, it could be argued that senior civil servants (such as the deputy ministers who head government departments in the Canadian system) should hold their positions at the pleasure of the elected government of the day. Indeed, that is the situation in Canada. The most senior civil servants are appointed by the prime minister and Cabinet, and they serve only so long as they maintain the confidence of the political executive. Similarly, Canada's most senior bureaucrat, the clerk of the Privy Council, will remain in that office only so as long as she or he has the trust and confidence of the prime minister.

In the United States, the notion that the administration serves at the discretion of the president reaches further into the public bureaucracy. A large number of important administrative posts and politically sensitive positions are held by presidential appointees. In the twenty-first century, there has been much less of the partisan political manipulation of hiring of mere functionaries that troubled nineteenth-century advocates of the politics–administration dichotomy. Still, the power of political appointment at more senior levels remains extensive, and it is justified by the fact that some dimensions of administration are political.

Organizational Forms
of the Public Bureaucracy

IT IS EASY TO THINK ABOUT THE PUBLIC BUREAUCRACY AS A LARGE AND undifferentiated monolith—"the government bureaucracy." The bureaucracy processes our income tax, bureaucrats license our child-care programs, administrative officials ensure restaurants meet public health standards, civil servants issue our marriage licences, and so on. However, to understand public bureaucracy, we must recognize that there are, in fact, a number of organizational forms that have been used to accomplish the tasks associated with delivering programs and pursuing policy objectives. The language used to identify various organizational forms of public bureaucracy varies from country to country. The discussion in this section will highlight some of the more common labels in current use, with a particular focus on the Canadian experience.

Central agencies and operating departments are the core of Canada's civil service. Central agencies are the "big picture" agencies that sit at the top of the bureaucratic hierarchy. These agencies—which include the Privy Council Office, the Treasury Board Secretariat, and the Department of Finance—work closely with the prime minister and the Cabinet to coordinate the government's agenda (Thomas, 1999). They have considerable administrative, fiscal, and policy power. Their role is to test policy proposals for compatibility with the overall government agenda and analyze the potential costs, economic impacts, and legal and constitutional implications of various policy options. The Privy Council Office (PCO) is an agency designed to serve the prime minister and the Cabinet. The most senior official in the PCO, the clerk of the Privy Council, is deeply involved with providing non-partisan policy advice to the prime minister, as well as with appointing and supervising the deputy ministers who serve as the senior civil servants in government departments. With a staff of several hundred, the PCO helps the government set, control, and manage its policy agenda across the various departments. The Treasury Board acts as the manager and employer for government, setting the rules and administrative practices for departments in such areas as staff recruitment, budgeting, and reporting. Organizationally, the Department of Finance appears to be a regular department of government, but the powers the department has to carry out economic assessments of government initiatives, shape fiscal policy through the annual budget, and influence monetary policy are, in combination, enough to elevate the Department of Finance to the status of a central agency. In recent years, the coordinative power of central agencies, such as the PCO and the Department of Finance, has increased quite significantly, not only in Canada, but throughout the world (Savoie, 1999).

In the first instance, the administrative state is organized around a number of operating departments with functional program and policy responsibilities. In Canada, for example, citizens would be familiar with such departments as Environment Canada, Human Resources and Social Development, the Department of Justice, and Agriculture and Agri-Food Canada. Government departments such as these are directly controlled by Cabinet ministers who provide political direction to civil servants who are responsible for delivering government programs and services, such as Employment Insurance or the Canada Student Loans Program. Of course, the role of departmental bureaucrats is not confined to service delivery. Ministers also rely on civil servants to provide policy advice on a wide array of issues. As the administrative state has grown in size and complexity, public bureaucrats have begun to serve as key points of contact for interest groups and public stakeholders who are working to influence policy development or program delivery. Indeed, Cabinet ministers now expect their senior civil servants to play a role in managing relations within the various policy communities that impinge on the responsibilities of their departments.

The many other organizational forms constituting the public bureaucracy have been created to replace traditional operating departments when governments have, for one reason or another, preferred "arm's-length" service delivery or the removal of critical policy decisions from the realm of partisan politics. This is the case with regulatory agencies, state-owned corporations, and independent advisory bodies (Thomas and Zajcew, 1993). Regulatory agencies, such as Canada's National Energy Board or the Canadian Radio-television and Telecommunications Commission (CRTC), were created to administer and enforce policies and regulations set by Parliament. These policies could be administered by an operating department, but a decision has been made to delegate considerable administrative and policy discretion to an agency that, being independent of the minister, is free from partisan influence. Similarly, the advice given by advisory bodies, such as the Royal Commission of Aboriginal Peoples or the former Law Reform Commission of Canada, could have been generated within an operating department under the supervision of a Cabinet minister. But a decision was made to create a non-departmental entity that would be considerably more independent.

State-owned, or "Crown," corporations are enterprises that take a corporate form but exist for public purposes. Some, such as Petro-Canada and the Canada Development Corporation, were created to compete in the marketplace with the goal of influencing developments in particular economic sectors. Others, such as Ontario Hydro, were created to deliver goods that were not being delivered satisfactorily through private enterprises. Still others, such as Canada Post Corporation, exist to deliver a government service but do so on a private-sector model. These public enterprises represent examples of the government's competing in the private sector. But, interestingly, they are also examples of private-sector organizational forms being adopted by the public bureaucracy.

In recent years, the organizational forms of the public bureaucracy have undergone a number of innovations. One fairly recent development has been the creation of special operating agencies, such as the Canadian Passport Office, that exist as separate "business units" within operating departments. While ultimate control and accountability continues to rest with the minister, these agencies are exempted from many of the administrative rules that ordinarily curtail management flexibility. Indeed, in the 1990s, an agency known as Consulting and Audit Canada was authorized to compete with the private sector for contracts as a way of funding the services it provided to government. Another recent innovation has been for government to establish and endow independent foundations, such as the Canadian Foundation for Innovation and the Canadian Millennium Scholarship Foundation. These foundations are independent, non-profit corporate entities with multi-billion-dollar endowments to invest, manage, and allocate. While the mandates of these foundations are established in the legislation that brought them into existence, they function as independent granting agencies outside traditional bureaucratic accountability networks.

Being aware of the various organizational forms of the public bureaucracy allows for a more sophisticated understanding of government administration. It is important, for example, to understand the unique power of central agencies, such as the Department of Finance and the PCO. Citizens also should be aware that the trend toward creating and assigning responsibility to non-departmental organizations—such as foundations, special operating agencies, and regulatory agencies—means, for both good and bad, less direct ministerial control of certain administrative functions of the state. Now that non-departmental organizational forms are increasingly common, students of public bureaucracy should give some serious attention to the issue of which organizational forms are most appropriate for which purposes.

Checks, Balances, and Accountability

A CENTRAL AND ONGOING ISSUE FOR MODERN GOVERNMENT IS THE QUESTION of whether adequate checks and balances exist to ensure that the power of the administrative state is wielded in the public interest. In the context of the British parliamentary system that has been adopted in Canada, there are four broad categories of checks on the power of the public bureaucracy (Inwood, 2004, 344–361). These are the principles of ministerial responsibility and responsible government, statutory and constitutional protections of citizenship rights, formal administrative audit procedures, and informal "political audits" that are carried out on an ongoing basis by members of the policy community.

In Canada, the principle of **responsible government** confers upon the prime minister and Cabinet—sometimes called the government of the day—the power to establish the legislative and governing agenda and oversee the administrative machinery of government, but only so long as they maintain the support and confidence of the House of Commons. In other words, while the prime minister and Cabinet are empowered to govern, they are responsible to Parliament for the way in which they govern. Cabinet ministers, in the parliamentary system, are the direct political masters of operating departments and ultimately responsible for the functioning of any arm's-length agencies for which they have legislative responsibility.

The principle of **ministerial responsibility** has, at least traditionally, demanded that ministers answer to Parliament for the activities and omissions of officials within the public bureaucracy. As an operating principle, ministerial responsibility was meant to shield civil servants from public blame and to simultaneously establish clear lines of accountability through the responsible minister. While Canadian governments continue to pay lip service to the principles of responsible government and ministerial responsibility, these principles have, in practice, been watered down. For some time now, observers of parliamentary government have argued that while government ministers are "answerable" to Parliament, it is increasingly rare for the government of the day to take full and meaningful "responsibility" for the actions and omissions of the public bureaucracy. Ministerial resignations (or firings) precipitated by the indiscretions of public servants are almost unheard of in Canada (Sutherland, 1991).

The passage of the Harper government's 2006 *Accountability Act*, which the new government enacted in the wake of the previous government's sponsorship scandal, raises further doubt about the relevance of the principle of ministerial responsibility. The *Accountability Act* designates the most senior bureaucrats in government departments—the deputy ministers—as "accounting officers" who are accountable before appropriate committees of Parliament. While the Act is careful to state that this formal bureaucratic accountability to Parliament exists "within the framework of ministerial responsibility," it is not entirely clear how the two principles can work in concert. For example, when opposition parties moved, in the winter of 2007, to challenge a minister over problems with a controversial $500 million contract, the responsible minister was able to avoid public responsibility by having his deputy minister inform a parliamentary committee that he must assume blame as the department's "accounting officer." While there is truth to the claim that senior bureaucrats play a more direct role in the actual decisions that are under question, the fact that Parliament cannot take the type of action against bureaucrats that they can against ministers raises some doubt as to whether establishing deputy ministers as accounting officers is a step toward, or away from, greater accountability.

Most liberal democracies now have legal and constitutional protections of citizens' rights that act as a check on the power of the public bureaucracy. In Canada, for example, the *Privacy Act*, the *Access to Information Act*, and the constitutionally entrenched *Charter of Rights and Freedoms* all serve to curtail bureaucratic power by defining the rights that the state must respect. The *Charter of Rights* is the most far-reaching. It details a wide range of rights and freedoms, and empowers the courts to protect citizens from violations of rights by the state. The *Privacy Act* outlines clear limits on the collection, use, and disclosure of personal information by government departments and agencies, and gives a Privacy Commissioner the power to investigate complaints and carry out periodic privacy audits. The *Access to Information Act* ensures that individual citizens, advocacy groups, and journalists can request and secure the information necessary to hold civil servants to account. The Harper government's *Accountability Act* extended the coverage of the *Access to Information Act* to include a wider range of organizations, including Crown corporations and foundations. The Act also established a Public Sector Integrity Commissioner with responsibility for, among other things, enforcing the protection of "whistle-blowers"—those who publicly disclose wrongdoing within the public bureaucracy.

The regular reports from the office of the auditor general are perhaps the best-known formal internal administrative audits of the Canadian public bureaucracy. The auditor general reports to the public directly through Parliament and, as such, is independent of control by the Cabinet ministers who serve as the political masters of the public bureaucracy. While initially established to carry out traditional audits of the government's financial statements, the auditor general now engages in broad reviews of decision making and management in the public bureaucracy, assessing management and accountability structures, the utilization of human, physical, and financial resources, and compliance of government programs with the legislation and regulations establishing such programs. The auditor general's reports have become a primary tool for opposition politicians, journalists, and citizens intent on identifying and addressing misuses of bureaucratic power. There are, however, other offices—such as the office of the procurement auditor—that perform a surveillance role within the public service. The 2006 *Accountability Act* also established a new Parliamentary Budget Office within the Library of Parliament to assist members and committees of the House of Commons in their ongoing analysis of the Canadian government's finances.

A final, informal, but often powerful check on the power of the public bureaucracy is the ongoing political audit carried out by members of relevant policy communities. A **policy community** includes all the public and private actors with an active interest in an issue or area of public policy. These informal communities take their shape as interest groups, lobbyists, private think tanks, and social movement organizations; citizen stakeholders work to influence the character of public policies and programs. While the first order of business of members of a policy community may be influencing policy-making, many of those affected by policies, programs, and regulations have a desire to ensure that bureaucratic power is exercised fairly and within the limits specified by established policies. When there is a lack of progress on key government initiatives or when unexpected or unfair negative results occur, members of the policy community act as pubic watchdogs, bringing their concerns to the attention of appropriate civil servants, politicians, and the media.

There was a time when political scientists suggested that the bureaucracy could be held fully accountable through the operation of responsible government and ministerial responsibility. Today, less faith is placed in these formal operating principles of Parliament. While parliamentary principles ensure the opposition parties are able to put political pressure on the government to address bureaucratic indiscretions, citizens, activists, and politicians can now use statutory and constitutional protections of rights, reports of the auditor general, and pressure politics to help ensure that the power of the administrative state is wielded in the public interest.

From Public Administration to Public Management

PUBLIC BUREAUCRACIES ARE NOT STATIC INSTITUTIONS. THEIR FORM, STRUCTURE, and functioning evolve with national political cultures, economic conditions, and broader trends in governing paradigms. Over the past quarter-century, for example, public bureaucracies throughout the liberal democratic world have been transformed by a new set of ideas and values regarding the organization and management of public service bureaucracies. This new paradigm has been labelled the **new public management** (NPM). For most of the twentieth century, particularly during the era of the Keynesian welfare state, the values of traditional public administration guided public bureaucracies. In recent years, however, as neo-liberal approaches to governance have been reshaping the accepted goals and purposes of the state, NPM values have reshaped the structure and culture of the civil service. The contrast between traditional public administration and the NPM provides a unique vantage point from which to consider the changing character of public bureaucracy.

Traditional Public Administration

Careful academic examinations of the character of public bureaucracy and the administrative functions of the state began in the late nineteenth century. This was the era of the minimalist state. Government intervention in the economy and society was extremely limited. The civil service was small, with only the most basic administrative structures. The embryonic character of the public service limited the organizational distance between politicians and front-line public servants and increased the likelihood of hands-on political control and patronage.

In Canada, Cabinet ministers micro-managed departmental affairs and regularly intervened in funding and hiring decisions to reward their political allies. This led to considerable public distaste of politicians meddling in and "politicizing" the bureaucracy. Influenced by a public sector reform movement that began in the United States in the late nineteenth century, Canada moved to reform its civil service in the early twentieth century. Embracing the ideals associated with the politics–administration dichotomy, the government established a Civil Service Commission, formalized the merit principle in federal government hiring, and adopted what are now considered traditional public administration principles.

The principles of traditional public administration can be summed up as follows. First, professionalism in civil service employment is best demonstrated by a dedication to administrative prudence and a commitment to achieving equity and fairness through impartial and standardized approaches to the provision of public services. Second, administration is distinct from politics because the integrity of civil servants flows from their impartiality and non-partisanship. Third, public bureaucracies are, quite properly, rule-governed and process-oriented hierarchies. Centralized bureaucratic command and upward accountability are embraced, both as the essence of rational management and as a means of facilitating the functioning of ministerial responsibility.

In Canada and the United States, these principles were embraced early in the twentieth century and subsequently guided the rapid expansion of public bureaucracies in the context of the post-war welfare state. In contrast to the minimalist state, the welfare state was an activist state, prepared to intervene in the economy and society. Indeed, in the context of the post-war governing paradigm, it was commonplace to assume that state interventions were the solution to emerging social and economic problems. As such, the number and range of government regulations and programs expanded, the public bureaucracy grew ever larger, and process-oriented bureaucratic hierarchies became increasingly complex. By the early 1970s, the welfare state was at its zenith, as a massive corps of civil servants administered and enforced an unprecedented number of programs and regulations.

New Public Management

When the conditions that had maintained the post-war economic boom began to unravel in the 1970s, economists, politicians, bureaucrats and, finally, the public lost much of their faith in the governing paradigm of the welfare state. Increasingly, state intervention was rejected as inherently ineffective; market-oriented ideologies that championed non-government solutions to social and economic problems gained ascendancy. The ideas with the most political currency were ideologically neo-liberal: that is, they placed faith in markets and rejected the activist state as a source of problems, not solutions. In this ideological context, the values and principles of traditional public administration also came under attack. Critics argued that the traditional paradigm had misunderstood the character of human organizations, placed too much emphasis on standardization, hierarchy of command, and due process. Public bureaucracies were criticized by neo-liberals for chasing abstract notions of the broad public interest while ignoring individual client satisfaction. In time, this anti-bureaucratic critique of the welfare state spawned a new paradigm of public bureaucracy that insisted that government should be run more like a business; this was the new public management (Charih and Rouillard, 1997).

Over the past quarter-century, the core principles of the NPM have increasingly displaced those associated with traditional public administration. First, innovation and risk taking are promoted over administrative prudence. Public bureaucracies are now expected to be flexible and creative institutions that place emphasis on individual "customer" satisfaction over the old values of impartiality and standardization. Second, there is a renewed commitment to the politics–administration dichotomy. Cabinet ministers and their most senior bureaucratic advisers are expected to focus on policy-making, not administration—or, in the NPM lexicon, on "steering, not rowing." They are expected to "let the managers manage." This has resulted in the dismantling of the hierarchical processes that facilitate direct political oversight. Instead, the trend is toward establishing organizational forms that give public bureaucrats more independence from ministerial control. Third, the NPM demands a commitment to more flexible organizational structures in which hierarchical process-oriented accountability is replaced by performance measures and accountability by results.

The NPM paradigm has been accompanied by a measurable trend toward the use of **alternative service delivery (ASD)**, which involves the transfer of responsibility for program and service delivery to private-sector providers, non-profit organizations, or new public-sector organizational forms, such as special operating agencies or foundations. Another important example of ASD has been the use of public–private partnerships in which contractual arrangements are established to allow the government and the private sector—either voluntary sector organizations or private corporations—to share authority and responsibility for the delivery of particular programs or the achievement of specific public policy objectives. As an extension of the neo-liberal critique of public bureaucracy, ASD moves responsibility for public administration from traditional operating departments to non-traditional organizational forms and the private sector.

At the same time, inside traditional operating departments, the rise of the NPM has meant the importation of private-sector management techniques. For example, government departments now establish annual "business plans" to guide departmental operations, and performance measures are established and monitored to hold senior managers accountable for specific results and outcomes. These private-sector management tools are a major departure from the traditional public administration's reliance on hierarchical rule structures and process accountability.

The benefits and drawbacks of the NPM are the subject of much debate (Savoie, 1995; Borins, 1995). Proponents of the NPM tend to be critical of the size, cost, and rigid character of the administrative machinery of the post-war welfare state. As such, their watchwords are efficiency, responsiveness, and flexibility. Indeed, they claim that program efficiencies achieved in the context of the NPM are partially responsible for the decreasing size of government and the trend away from the practice of deficit financing. They argue, further, that NPM management techniques have unleashed the innovative capacity of staff, that operating departments have achieved a new clarity of purpose through the process of developing and implementing "business plans," and that client satisfaction has risen as program administrators embrace the NPM emphasis on service and responsiveness.

Of course, advocates of the traditional public administration paradigm remain critical of the NPM. Canada's Task Force on Public Service Values and Ethics summarized the traditional critique of NPM, noting that "[the new] public management pays too little attention to the democratic, parliamentary, political and public context, treats public goods as if they were private, ignores the complexities and trade-offs that characterize the public sphere, and downplays the importance of due process, vertical accountability, and the ultimate importance of the public interest or the common good" (cited in Gow and Hodgetts, 2003, 193).

Part of the critique of NPM is ideological. Many observers note that the NPM is associated with the rise of neo-liberal governance. They are concerned that it is really just an attack on government and public bureaucracy—nothing more than a management paradigm designed to reduce departmental staff, lower operating costs, and privatize services once located in the public sector. Those who are concerned about the neo-liberal privatization agenda point out that the NPM's enthusiasm for ASD often removes government activities from traditional methods of accountability, such as investigations by the auditor general and parliamentary oversight. While a new emphasis may be placed on responsiveness to individual "customers" of government programs, there is concern that this atomistic approach, when combined with outsourcing and ASD, actually undermines the traditional public administration's holistic approach to democratic accountability and transparency. There is, then, an ongoing debate, not only regarding the wisdom of assuming that public bureaucracies can be managed like businesses, but also concerning the core values and approach to governance that are associated with the NPM.

Summary

The purpose of this chapter has been to introduce students to public bureaucracy and review some issues that are relevant to citizens whose lives are touched by the programs, regulations, and policies public servants administer. The chapter began with a discussion of the character of public bureaucracy, including the extent to which the work of public servants is, in fact, political. A discussion followed of the different organizational forms of the public bureaucracy. But the issues of greatest political importance came in the latter half of the chapter. How effective are the existing mechanisms for limiting the power of the public bureaucracy? How should citizens react to the new public management and its preference for adopting private-sector management techniques within the public bureaucracy? These are issues that go to the heart of democratic governance. They deserve our attention.

Discussion Questions

1. What does it mean to argue that the work of civil servants is actually "political"?

2. What are the core differences between traditional public administration and the new public management?

3. How would advocates of traditional public administration respond to the suggestion that the shortcomings of modern public bureaucracies can be overcome by demanding that the civil service be run more like a business?

4. Outline the existing checks on the power of the public bureaucracy, and comment on how confident Canadians can be that bureaucratic power is wielded in the public interest.

5. What are the public bureaucracy's "central agencies," and why do some observers consider them the most powerful of bureaucratic organizations?

References

Borins, Sandford. 1995. "The New Public Management Is Here to Stay." *Canadian Public Administration* 38(1), 122–132.

Charih, Mohamed and Lucie Rouillard. 1997. "The New Public Management" in Mahomed Charih and Arthur Daniels, eds., *New Public Management and Public Administration in Canada.* Toronto: The Institute of Public Administration of Canada.

Gow, J.I. and J.E. Hodgetts. 2003. "Where Are We Coming From? Are There Any Useful Lessons from Our Administrative History?" *Canadian Public Administration* 46(2), 178–201.

Inwood, Gregory J. 2004. *Understanding Canadian Public Administration: An Introduction to Theory and Practice,* 2nd edition. Toronto: Prentice Hall.

Mellon, Hugh. 1999. "Politics and Administration: Separate, Connected, or Integrated? Looking at Possibilities" in Martin W. Westmacott and Hugh P. Mellon, eds., *Public Administration and Policy: Governing in Challenging Times.* Toronto: Prentice Hall.

Savoie, Donald J. 1995. "What Is Wrong with the New Public Management?" *Canadian Public Administration* 38(1), 112–121.

———. 1999. *Governing from the Centre: The Concentration of Power in Canadian Politics.* Toronto: University of Toronto Press.

Sutherland, S.L. 1991. "Responsible Government and Ministerial Responsibility: Every Reform Is Its Own Problem." *Canadian Journal of Political Science,* XXIV: 1, 91–120.

Sutherland, Sharon L. 1993. "The Public Service and Policy Development" in Michael M. Atkinson, ed., *Governing Canada: Institutions and Public Policy.* Toronto: Harcourt Brace Jovanovich Canada Inc.

Thomas, Paul G. 1999. "The Role of Central Agencies: Making a Mesh of Things" in James Bickerton and Alain-G. Gagnon, eds., *Canadian Politics,* 3rd edition. Peterborough: Broadview Press.

Thomas, Paul G. and Orest W. Zajcew. 1993. "Structural Heretics: Crown Corporations and Regulatory Agencies" in Michael M. Atkinson, ed., *Governing Canada: Institutions and Public Policy.* Toronto: Harcourt Brace Jovanovich Canada Inc.

Whitaker, Reg. 2004. "Politics Versus Administration: Politicians and Bureaucrats" in Michael Whittington and Glen Williams, eds., *Canadian Politics in the 21st Century,* 6th edition. Toronto: Nelson Canada.

Further Readings

Dun, Christopher. 2002. *The Handbook of Canadian Public Administration.* Toronto: Oxford University Press.

Dwivedi, O.P. and James Iain Gow. 1999. *From Bureaucracy to Public Management: The Administrative Culture of Canada.* Peterborough: Broadview Press.

Johnson, David. 2002. *Thinking Government: Public Sector Management in Canada.* Peterborough: Broadview Press.

Shields, John and B. Mitchell Evans. 1998. *Shrinking the State: Globalization and Public Administration "Reform."* Halifax: Fernwood Publishing.

Weblinks

Canadian School of Public Service
www.ccmd-ccg.gc.ca

The Institute of Public Administration of Canada (IPAC)
www.ipaciapc.ca

Public Policy Forum
www.ppforum.ca

Treasury Board of Canada Secretariat
www.tbs-sct.gc.ca/index_e.asp

CHAPTER **10**

REPRESENTATION

Political representation is at the core of modern democratic politics. Indeed, representation is so taken for granted in political life that few people ever pause to explore what it means. As such, the initial objective of this chapter is to encourage the sort of critical reflection that is necessary to ensure students appreciate the complexity of political representation. A second objective is to illuminate the ways in which the institutional biases of various institutions of political representation—including electoral systems, legislatures, political parties, interest groups, and social movements—shape the nature of political representation. Finally, students will be pressed to consider the claim that representation is an active and formative relationship that shapes our political identities and the character and content of politics. At every stage, the chapter's overriding intent is to facilitate consideration of the relationship between the nature of political representation and the character and quality of democracy.

STEVE PATTEN

Introduction

Liberal democratic political regimes, such as the governments of the United States, Canada, and the United Kingdom, are—by design—representative democracies. The people, it is said, govern themselves through their elected representatives. In fact, one of the chambers of the United States Congress is called the House of Representatives. In Canada and other parliamentary systems, the House of Commons is considered a representative chamber, and members of Parliament are expected to serve as representatives of their constituents. But what does it mean to identify an elected governing body as representative? What is meant by the concept of political representation? What are the possible relationships between representation and democracy? These apparently simple questions do not have simple answers. Political representation is a multi-faceted and evolving concept. Even among the academic experts there is only limited agreement on what constitutes political representation. This chapter begins with an introduction to the concept of political representation. Attention then turns to an examination of the core institutions, mechanisms, and processes of political representation. This is followed by a discussion of the ways in which the processes of representation serve to constitute our political identities and shape the character of politics. Finally, the chapter concludes with some observations regarding the relationship between political representation and the quality of democracy.

The Concept of Political Representation

POLITICAL REPRESENTATION IS A CONCEPT OF THE MODERN AGE. IN THE medieval era, the concept of representation had but one meaning; to represent was to symbolize or be the concrete embodiment of that which was represented. Thus, to say that the medieval monarch "represented the realm" was to suggest that the queen or king embodied, in her or his very person, the essence of the realm. Obviously, this notion of representation as **symbolic representation** was depoliticized and pre-democratic; there was no notion that consent had to be established through political arrangements, such as electoral democracy. In the era of the absolutist monarchs, it was commonly thought that sovereignty—or supreme and final governing authority—rested with the monarch by divine right, not political authority.

In Britain, France, and America, the liberal revolutions of the seventeenth and eighteenth centuries established parliamentary and republican systems of representative government, and the modern concept of political representation was born. With the establishment of freer and fairer elections and the extension of the vote during the nineteenth and early twentieth centuries, these governing systems were progressively democratized. This spawned considerable debate about the defining characteristics of political representation in a representative democracy. Leading liberal thinkers of the time offered a perspective that has come to be known as **descriptive representation**. From this perspective, the condition of representation—and, it could be argued, democracy—is met only to the extent that our legislatures are a representative microcosm of the broader society. But conservative thinkers insisted on more formalistic notions of representation that were rooted in the assumption that representation and democracy merely require that legislative bodies are authorized and/or held accountable by regular elections. As long as our law-making bodies are elected, the condition of **formalistic representation** is fully met.

Today, both descriptive and formalistic notions of political representation fail to capture popular thinking because it is now more common to conceive of representation as a process or activity, rather than a state of affairs. Since the 1960s, the most influential academic interpretation of political representation has been Hannah Pitkin's claim that representation involves representatives "acting in the interest of the represented in a manner that is responsive to them" (Pitkin, 1967, 209). By construing representation as an active, or instrumental, relationship, our attention shifts from the adjective "representative" to the verb "to represent"—and democracy hinges on responsiveness. This marks a shift to what is known as **instrumental representation**. The defining feature of instrumental representation is the commitment to take action and speak for the represented.

But the concept's evolution does not stop there. Since the 1980s, a growing number of scholars have begun to argue that the essence of political representation can never be fully captured by instrumental notions of representatives acting for the represented (Dobrowolsky, 1998). Arguing that it is a mistake to assume that there are clear and already existing interests waiting to be represented, students of representation now argue that representation is never merely a matter of acting for a particular interest or community. Instead, representation is, by its nature, a formative relationship that actually serves to define the character of the political identities and interests that are being represented.

The point being made here is somewhat abstract, but it can be reformulated in fairly straightforward terms. Think, for a moment, of the notion of representation as a portrayal of something. Now, consider the fact that because individual citizens and communities are complex and multi-faceted, there can be many different portrayals of the political interests of a particular citizen or community. It should be clear that, in instrumental terms, representing a community of interest—such as agricultural workers, Atlantic Canadians, hard-working taxpayers, or New Yorkers—is, as Pitkin argues, acting for this community of interest. But the action of representing cannot be undertaken without making assumptions about the proper portrayal of that community's core identity and political interests. Moreover, to make and then act on such assumptions is to offer a portrayal that actually serves to define the community in our collective imagination. In other words, the act of representing feeds back on the represented, defining who they are and what their political interests are. Representation, then, is a "formative relationship"; it "forms," "constitutes," or "gives meaning to" the identities and interests that are represented.

There are, then, two dimensions to contemporary political representation. The instrumental dimension involves acting for a particular segment of the population or political interest. The constitutive dimension involves giving meaning to that interest by defining who it is that is being represented—this is known as **constitutive representation**. To understand political representation, it is necessary to explore both its instrumental and its constitutive dimensions (Jenson, 1992).

Instrumental Representation in Contemporary Liberal Democracy

PITKIN'S READING OF THE MEANING OF POLITICAL REPRESENTATION ACTUally signifies an attempt to steer a course between two views on the proper role and responsibilities of modern political representatives. The debate Pitkin attempts to navigate pits delegate against trustee models of instrumental representation. At bottom, the **delegate model of representation** stresses the importance of responsiveness, of mirroring as well as possible the interests of the represented. The delegate model's first premise is that representative democracy is a necessary but highly imperfect substitute for direct democracy. The goal, therefore, should be to maximize responsiveness in an effort to approximate the outcomes that would result from direct democracy. The actions of representatives should not be found to be at odds with the wishes of the represented.

The more conservative **trustee model of representation** rejects the suggestion that good political representation is merely responsive representation. Representative democracy, according to the trustee model, is not merely a second-rate alternative to direct democracy. Instead, the virtue of representative democracy is that it provides a unique opportunity for a select group of trustees of the public interest to meet and thoughtfully discuss issues of governance in the deliberative chambers of Congress or Parliament. The trustees do not necessarily mirror specific community interests but, instead, work together to find policy solutions for the common good. Representative democracy is, in other words, an opportunity to make wise decisions that are not constrained by the short term—and perhaps ill-considered—wishes of the population. The eighteenth-century political theorist Edmund Burke, himself a member of the British Parliament, was known for his advocacy of the trustee model of political representation. In a famous public speech, Burke argued that political representatives should never be bound by the inclinations of those they represent. Parliament, he stressed, is a deliberative assembly, and the first obligation of members of Parliament is to employ their reason and judgment in deliberations regarding the national interest.

Today, the Burkean trustee model of political representation is inconsistent with the trend toward emphasizing responsiveness. Indeed, enthusiasm for the principles of direct democracy has informed both the popularization of the delegate model of representation and, more recently, calls for a form of **plebiscitarian democracy**. Plebiscitarianism combines a delegate model of representation with the regular use of the tools of direct democracy, such as referenda—the people voting directly on key policy issues—and mechanisms of recall that allow citizens to, in essence, fire their elected representative if that representative is unresponsive and fails to accurately reflect public opinion.

At first glance, most students will assume that the delegate model and plebiscitarianism are preferable because they appear to have a greater claim to the mantle of democracy. Indeed, the democratic principle of majority rule is often invoked to defend the use of referenda and justify binding representatives to act as delegates of the dominant opinion within the community they represent. But the supporters of a trustee model argue that the overuse of referenda and treating representatives as mere delegates will not allow for the protection of minority interests. Nor will it ensure that representatives have the freedom to use their judgment to rise above parochial local interests in favour of the national interest. Perhaps that is why Pitkin advocated an understanding of political representation that demands that representatives use their judgment to act in the broad interests of citizens, but to do so in a manner that is responsive to them. The freedom afforded by the trustee model has the virtue of allowing representatives to consider when national or minority interests might be threatened by simply responding to public opinion, while the delegate model's demand of responsiveness is an important check on the inherently elitist notion that elected politicians know better than ordinary citizens what is in the public interest. In considering the design and functioning of our political institutions, there is good reason to follow Pitkin in trying to find a balance between the delegate and trustee models of instrumental representation. Students will note, however, that in Canada our political institutions are actually biased in favour of the trustee model.

Institutions and Processes of Instrumental Representation

WHEN EVALUATING THE PROCESSES OF INSTRUMENTAL REPRESENTATION AND the quality of democracy in liberal democratic political regimes, political scientists have tended to focus on the role played by political parties and the elected members of legislative bodies, such as members of the United States Congress and the House of Commons in the United Kingdom and Canada. It is useful to extend our gaze slightly to also consider the role of the electoral system and some less formal institutions of political representation, specifically interest groups and social movement organizations.

Electoral Systems

The electoral system is the framework for translating citizens' votes into legislative seats. What is often not apparent to the casual observer is that electoral systems are not politically neutral; they have significant consequences for the content and character of political representation and, therefore, for the quality of democracy. For example, the **single-member plurality (SMP)** electoral system found in Canada, the United Kingdom, and the United States has the effect of limiting the number and range of truly competitive political parties and increasing the likelihood of politicians' adopting a stance consistent with the trustee model of political representation. The reasons for this are not complex. In a single-member plurality electoral system, the voters in each constituency elect just one member, and that election is determined by a simple plurality—that is, the candidate with the most votes wins. This is a winner-take-all system that disadvantages smaller political parties because parties that cannot win the most votes win nothing at all. Larger parties are, in effect, over-represented, while small parties without unique regional concentrations of support are under-represented. This system of translating votes into seats discourages the maturation of small parties that are committed to a delegate model of representation and advocating on behalf of particular societal interests. So long as electoral success depends on broad popular appeal, politicians will be inclined to campaign on inoffensive and ideologically vague themes that do little more than position their party as competent trustees of the broad public interest. In other words, the rule structure of the electoral system promotes a Burkean trustee model of representation and middle-of-the-road political parties that focus more on enhancing their capacity to form a majority government than achieving particular policy objectives.

By contrast, adopting a multiple-member **proportional representation (PR)** electoral system—which allocates legislative seats in proportion to the percentage of votes a party wins—will tend to encourage smaller parties with more focused platforms. Abandoning the existing winner-take-all scenario would allow voters and partisan activists to throw their support behind small parties with confidence that their votes and efforts will pay off. Politicians may also alter their behaviour because it is apparent that smaller political parties are able to achieve a degree of success while embracing a delegate model of representation and taking clearer stances in favour of the representation of particular societal interests. In other words, the institutional biases of different types of electoral systems have consequences for the character of political representation and democracy.

Legislatures

As the branch of government responsible for law-making, the legislature—the Parliament in Canada, the Congress in the United States—is a primary institution in the process of political representation. The first principles of the parliamentary system are the **fusion of power** and **responsible government**. These doctrines put the political executive—the prime minister and the Cabinet—in charge of both the executive function of state administration and law implementation and guiding the legislative function of law-making. The executive dominates law-making but is responsible to Parliament in the sense that the Cabinet's agenda must be approved by the majority of members of the House of Commons. Of course, given that almost all members of the House of Commons were elected as candidates who offered themselves under particular party banners, the thrust and parry of parliamentary politics is shaped by the informal rules of the parliamentary party system. Paramount among these is **party discipline**—that is, the injunction that MPs support their party's line on all important issues. Members of Parliament are, in other words, expected to accept the trustee model of representation and the Burkean notion that when their sense of the local interests they represent conflicts with the party's view on what is in the broader public interest, they shall espouse the party line.

In the United States, by contrast, the **separation of powers** eliminates the possibility of direct executive dominance and weakens party discipline. Under the American congressional system, there is a clear separation of the Congress, with its legislative powers, from the presidency, with its executive powers. The president works hard to influence the legislative process in Congress and has some levers to influence Congress—including the threat of a presidential legislative veto—but the power to initiate and approve legislation rests, in the end, with Congress. Moreover, while members of Congress tend to vote along party lines, the notion of party discipline is considerably weaker in the congressional system. American legislators are much more likely than their Canadian counterparts to embrace a perspective on political representation that is in keeping with the principles of a delegate model of representation. In Congress, legislative politics is as much about accommodating conflicting regional and local concerns as it is about broader party interests. As such, the institutional bias in the congressional system is toward the delegate model of representation.

Political Parties

Electoral politics and political parties are central to the processes of political representation in modern liberal democracies. In fact, political scientists often assume political parties should be the primary representative institution in a democracy. In the early 1990s, for example, a major royal commission examining electoral reform issues—the Royal Commission on Electoral Reform and Party Financing—concluded that parties are the key to effective political representation because "only political parties can reconcile and accommodate diverse and competing interests to reach agreement on public policy" (cited in Dobrowolsky and Jenson, 1993, 65).

Particularly interesting, from the perspective of theories of representation, were the commission's implicit assumptions about the preferred character of political parties. The commission implied that parties are, ideally, large integrative institutions that work to accommodate diverse and competing interests. Parties of this sort are known as **brokerage parties** or, sometimes, catch-all parties. Rather than committing themselves to the representation of particular societal interests, brokerage parties present themselves as champions of the broader public interest. They privilege pragmatism over policy consistency, often allowing their commitment to act as trustees of the public interest to overshadow unique or bold policy platforms. Brokerage parties strive to make a virtue out of being non-doctrinaire. Typically, these parties will have a particular base of support to which they feel some obligations, and like all modern political parties, brokerage parties do promise to be responsive. But in terms of models of representation, they are quite Burkean; they promise, first and foremost, to be accommodative trustees of the national interest.

Not everyone accepts the suggestion that the ideal political party acts as a broker of competing social demands. One consequence of the accommodative politics of brokering is that many voices, particularly those associated with minority interests, are not heard. That is why supporters of a delegate model of representation often prefer more programmatic **doctrinal parties** that commit themselves to steadfastly articulating the views of particular ideological currents or political interests within society. Of course, in Canada, this alternative viewpoint on parties and political representation runs counter to the views of the political elite, as well as to the institutional biases of the single-member plurality electoral system.

Groups and Movements

While political parties operating through the electoral system and within legislatures are understood to be at the core of representative democracy, interest groups and social movement organizations are also important mechanisms of political representation. Interest groups are organizations that act to influence the content and direction of public policy by representing particular interests directly to government, while not seeking to hold political office. Broad social movements, such as feminism and environmentalism, are informal networks of individuals and groups primarily interested in bringing about societal change by influencing our ideas and behaviour (Phillips, 1996). Of course, many social movement organizations direct a portion of their energies into influencing government policy and, by doing so, play a role similar to interest groups.

Advocates of a trustee model of representation often criticize groups and movements as "special interests" that subvert the representational processes of electoral democracy. But from the perspective of a delegate model, interest groups and social movement organizations provide valuable representational opportunities and alternative avenues for political representation. As representatives of particular interests, they ensure that more voices are heard and a wider range of issues is addressed. In the end, however, the question of whether group and movement politics enhances or detracts from representative democracy may hinge on the types of voices that are heard through group politics. Historically, interest group politics was characterized as the realm of covert backroom politics—or elite accommodation—in which the social and economic elite interacted with the political and bureaucratic elite to shape public policy in their own self-interest (Presthus, 1973). Obviously, the representational processes of elite accommodation do little to enhance democracy. But since the 1960s, the range of groups and movements involved in interest group politics has increased. There are now many highly visible citizens' action groups advocating for policies in the interest of non-elite segments of society. As such, many advocates of a delegate model of representation see real potential for the representational activities of groups and movements to enhance democracy.

Constitutive Representation: Defining the Content and Character of Politics

As suggested earlier in this chapter, focusing exclusively on the institutions, mechanisms, and processes of instrumental representation can hide the fact that representation is about more than advocating on behalf of pre-existing political interests. It is important, therefore, to consider the constitutive dimension of political representation. The starting point for understanding constitutive representation is the observation that political identities and interests are socially constructed and, moreover, that the discursive processes of political representation play a role in their social construction.

But what does it mean to say that political identities are socially constructed? Essentially, it means that our political identities do not flow naturally from some objective facts about ourselves or the communities in which we live. Instead, there are social processes of debate, dialogue, and the exchange of ideas that give meaning to things. These are called discursive processes because they involve the sharing of language, or discourse, that is imbued with meaning. When we reflect upon our own personal characteristics and our place in various social structures, it is clear that there are many factors with the potential to be important to how we understand our political identities and interests. These factors include our gender, employment status, wealth, race, ethnic background, sexual orientation, religion, region of residence, and status as taxpayers or, perhaps, recipients of government social assistance. The discursive processes of constitutive representation play a role in determining which of these factors will be most politically salient and, therefore, central to our political identities and interests. Is it politically significant, for example, that you are white, gay, or a taxpayer? Historically, in Canada, regional and national political identities have been most salient. But there is nothing inevitable about this, and that is why Stuart Hall has stressed that representation "has to be understood as an active and formative relationship" that forges and gives meaning to interests by discursively defining *who* it is that is being represented (Hall, 1983, 26).

To argue that the constitutive dimension of political representation is, at bottom, a process of identity formation is to make a point of considerable political consequence. Political identities serve to orient political action. We are all called into the world of politics on the basis of our political identities. We find political allies, understand and navigate salient political cleavages, and define the norms and values of politics from the perspective of our political identities. It can be said, therefore, that the politics of representation helps shape who we are and what politics is all about. How important is the politics of race? Are our interests defined by our class position or our status as taxpayers? The representational activities of groups, movements, and parties shape the range of identities and interests that are considered politically relevant. Political representation, from this vantage, is an exercise of profound power; it defines the content and character of politics (Jenson, 1999, 44).

In discussions of constitutive representation and the discursive processes of identity formation, students may come across the idea of *identity politics*, which is a term reserved for the conscious pursuit of group-based identities by movements of, for example, women, Aboriginal peoples, or gays and lesbians. Since the 1960s, numerous progressive social movements have struggled to transform oppressive social relations. In the process, they have altered the landscape of salient political interests and identities in ways that have allowed new types of politics to emerge. As Barry Adam argued in his study of the gay and lesbian rights movement, it was only by embracing and articulating a collective political identity that homosexuals could be organized as a movement capable of representing and defending its interests (Adam, 1987, 107–108). Gay-positive political advocacy groups actively represent the political interests of gay men and lesbians in Canada. At the same time, however, they legitimize queer political identities and alter the landscape of political cleavages that define Canadian politics. This type of identity politics is just one possible manifestation of constitutive representation.

Political Representation and the Quality of Democracy

Given the normative character of the issues at hand, there is no correct—or best—specification of what would constitute truly democratic representation. Nor can we specify the ideal formulation and mix of institutions and processes of representation for enhancing the quality of democracy. There are, however, some observations about instrumental and constitutive representation that are worthy of close attention as we explore the politics of democratic representation. First, the trustee model of instrumental representation allows our representatives the freedom that is necessary to consider competing viewpoints and reflect on when national or minority interests might be threatened by a decision to simply follow majority opinion on a particular issue. To the extent that protecting minority rights is democratic principle and representative democracy is meant to allow for the effective use of wise deliberation, there is good reason to believe that institutions and processes that take advantage of the positive aspects of the trustee model are essential to protecting and enhancing democracy.

At the same time, it is very important that we recognize the extent to which the delegate model of representation is meant to serve as a check on the potentially elitist notion that elected representatives are better equipped than ordinary citizens when it comes to deciding on issues of the day. The trustee model values expert opinion and wise deliberation. The delegate model balances this with an emphasis on respect for the situated knowledge and opinion of average citizens. Representatives, from this perspective, are expected to act on the majority opinion of the represented. In essence, the delegate model demands that institutions and processes of political representation ensure that representatives are responsive to the opinions of ordinary people. Of course, the crux of the democratic challenge is balancing the imperatives of the trustee and delegate models of representation—while also fostering a degree of direct democracy by creating appropriate spaces for the direct involvement and active participation of citizens.

But the challenges do not stop there. So long as we are aware of the constitutive nature of political representation, we must avoid representational processes that impose particular identities on communities of interest. It is essential that strong democrats turn their minds to creating opportunities for the uncoerced self-representation of political identities and interests. Democratic institutions must protect the right of groups to self-define their political identities, and political processes must create spaces for the political voices and self-representation of communities of interest. In other words, whether acting in the context of a trustee or delegate model of political representation, political representatives must adjust their representational stance in response to organically defined political identities and interests.

Summary

The preceding discussion has been quite wide-ranging. The chapter began with an exploration of the concept of political representation that identified its instrumental and constitutive dimensions. This was followed by an outline of the delegate and trustee models of the proper role and responsibilities of political representatives. An examination of the core institutions, mechanisms, and processes of political representation—electoral systems, legislatures, political parties, interest groups, and social movements—revealed the extent to which institutional biases favour particular models of representation. In Canada, despite a popular trend toward embracing the delegate model, the existing institutions of political representation are biased in favour of the trustee model. Finally, after a detailed examination of instrumental representation, the chapter concluded with a brief discussion of constitutive representation that aimed to show how the discursive politics of representation shapes our political identities and the character of politics.

Discussion Questions

1. How would you characterize the relationship between democracy and representation?

2. Have you ever been a member of a political party? Why or why not? Would you consider being a member in the future? Why or why not?

3. Do you feel you have a particular political identity? How would you characterize the relationship between identity and political representation?

4. Which representation model do you believe is most effective? On what grounds do you make this assessment?

5. Are there some interests that are better represented in politics? Why or why not?

References

Adam, Barry D. 1987. *The Rise of a Gay and Lesbian Movement.* Boston: Twayne Publishers.

Dobrowolsky, Alexandra. 1998. "Of 'Special Interest': Interest, Identity and Feminist Constitutional Activism in Canada." *Canadian Journal of Political Science* XXXI: 4, 707–742.

Dobrowolsky, Alexandra and Jane Jenson. 1993. "Reforming the Parties: Prescriptions for Democracy" in Susan D. Phillips, ed., *How Ottawa Spends 1993–1994: A More Democratic Canada … ?* Ottawa: Carleton University Press.

Jenson, Jane. 1992. "A Political Economy Approach to Interest Representation" in Alain-G. Gagnon and A. Brian Tanguay, eds., *Democracy with Justice/La juste démocratie: Essays in Honour of Khayyam Zev Paltiel.* Ottawa: Carleton University Press.

———. 1999. "Understanding Politics: Concepts of Identity in Political Science" in James Bickerton and Alain-G. Gagnon, eds., *Canadian Politics*, 3rd edition. Peterborough: Broadview Press.

Phillips, Susan D. 1996. "Competing, Connecting, and Complementing: Parties, Interest Groups, and New Social Movements" in A. Brian Tanguay and Alain-G. Gagnon, eds., *Canadian Parties in Transition*, 2nd edition. Toronto: Nelson Canada.

Pitkin, Hannah. 1967. *The Concept of Representation.* Berkeley: The University of California Press.

Presthus, Robert. 1973. *Elite Accommodation in Canadian Politics.* Cambridge, U.K.: Cambridge University Press.

Further Readings

Carroll, William K., ed. 1997. Organizing Dissent: *Contemporary Social Movements in Theory and Practice: Studies in the Politics of Counter-Hegemony*, 2nd edition. Toronto: Garamond Press.

Pross, A. Paul. 1992. *Group Politics and Public Policy*, 2nd edition. Toronto: Oxford University Press.

Thorburn, Hugh G. and Alan Whitehorn, ed. 2001. *Party Politics in Canada*, 8th edition. Scarborough: Prentice Hall.

Weblinks

Council of Canadians
www.canadians.org

Democracy Watch
www.dwatch.ca

Elections Canada
www.elections.ca

Arenas of Politics

PART III

This section examines some of the most important spaces and actors in political life. The play of power and influence is ubiquitous, occurring both inside and outside the formal boundaries of the state and taking on many different forms. Perhaps the most familiar arenas of politics involve the formation and representation of political identities and interests, and the linking of these to democratic institutions and the policy process. Political parties and elections are two of the most prominent arenas in contemporary politics. Nevertheless, political identities and interests are also forged in a variety of settings, including citizenship practices, diverse communities, indigenous struggles, engendered spaces, and the environment. Each of these arenas demonstrates that the informal and the personal are often very political.

CHAPTER 11

POLITICAL PARTIES AND ELECTIONS

Objectives

Political parties and elections play a central role in shaping the type of representation that we have in democratic states. **Political parties** help to determine who will run for office, the ideas—or *platform*—on which they will run, and who will form the government following an election. **Party systems** are distinguished by the number of political parties that compete for legislative seats during elections, the intensity of competition during elections, and often the types of political parties that compete for power. The types of political parties and party systems are often related to the electoral system used within a country. **Electoral systems** establish the rules that prescribe who can vote and run for office, how citizens actually cast their votes, and the ways that votes are counted and translated into seats. These three aspects of democratic governance—political parties, party systems, and electoral systems—are discussed in this chapter, including alternative systems and their relative strengths and weaknesses. Overall, this chapter aims to introduce students to how political parties and elections work, and to provide certain criteria for evaluating different systems, particularly those in place in Canada.

SHAUNA WILTON

Introduction

As citizens in a democratic country, we hold many rights. However, along with these rights come responsibilities. One of the central political rights and responsibilities of citizens in any democratic state is to vote—to cast a ballot for a candidate or party in an election. Ideally, voting is a critical way of ensuring that our voices are represented and that our legislatures reflect the diversity of values, beliefs, and opinions found in the population. But there are endless variations in the complexion of political parties, party systems, and electoral systems, raising central questions about, among other things, how votes are cast and counted, and whether political parties are representative of the population and offer meaningful choices to voters at election time. As we gain an understanding of political parties, party systems, and electoral systems, we can begin to answer these questions and develop criteria for evaluating how well they work in any specific country.

Political Parties

POLITICAL PARTIES ARE ORGANIZATIONS, USUALLY CONSISTING OF VOLUNTEERS and paid staff that nominate candidates and compete in elections. Political parties are seen as a vital part of representative democracy because they provide an important link between citizens, civil society, and government. It is difficult to imagine how democratic governments would work and how states would fulfill their functions without political parties to help provide them with structure and a direct link to the people.

In some cases, political parties exist primarily to win elections. Shortly before he retired, former prime minister Jean Chrétien was asked by a journalist what made a good politician. He said that a good politician is one who wins. Presumably, by this he meant that good politicians can win elections and seats for their party because it is primarily through electoral success that politicians are able to influence policy. At the same time, however, many political parties continue to compete in elections with little hope of taking enough seats to win an election and form the government. For example, the federal New Democratic Party (NDP) has never formed the national government in Canada. During the federal election of 2006, Jack Layton, the leader of the NDP, encouraged Canadians to vote for his party not so that they could form the government, but so that they could influence the winning party and government in a minority parliament. Another example in Canada is the Green Party, which has competed in federal elections since 1984. Even though it has not yet won a seat in the House of Commons, it has been instrumental in pushing environmental concerns to the top of the public agenda, while its growing popularity has pushed other federal parties to introduce decidedly more "green" policies into their electoral platforms.

Political parties fulfill many important functions within democratic political systems, including these:

- helping to structure and organize elections through the nomination of candidates and/or the preparation of party lists;
- actively recruiting and training future political leaders;
- helping to structure legislatures and organize government by providing a way to determine who has won the election (generally the party with the most seats);
- bringing together different interests in society and providing a collective voice for them within the political arena; and
- shaping the policy outcomes of our representative institutions.

As such, political parties have both representative and governmental functions, both of which provide structure to the political process. How well political parties fulfill these functions, however, depends on the specific political parties involved, as well as the party and electoral systems within which they operate.

Types of Political Parties

Political parties began to appear in Western democracies in the seventeenth century. It is only in the past 100 years, however, that political parties began to take on the form we recognize today. The development of political parties was linked to the emergence of democratic governance. As more people gained the franchise, or right to vote, and as ideas of popular sovereignty gained popularity, the role and organization of political parties increased. Richard Gunther and Larry Diamond (2003) have developed a comprehensive typology of modern political parties, reflecting the diversity of political party formations that have emerged worldwide. In doing so, they looked specifically at the following criteria: the nature of the party's organization, the role of ideology in the party, the level of tolerance for diversity exhibited by the party, and whether the party aims to work within the system or change it. As a result, they divide political parties into five broad categories—elite-based, mass-based, ethnicity-based, electoralist, and movement—all of which are discussed below.

The first type of political party to emerge along with the limited, male franchise was the **elite-based political party**. Founded around traditional elites or notables, elite-based political parties have historically exercised considerable influence over the local, primarily rural, and uneducated peasants. The organization of these political parties tends to be minimal and based on established elite networks. They are not ideological but, rather, aim to distribute benefits to their "clients." Examples of elite-based political parties include earlier forms of the British and French conservative parties (Gunther and Diamond, 2003, 175–176).

In the nineteenth century, with the expansion of the franchise to working men, the labour movement mobilized the working classes of Europe, leading to the formation of worker and then socialist political parties. Due to their organization, ongoing political program, and broad membership, these parties are called **mass-based political parties** and are characterized by a large base of dues-paying members who are active within the party structure. They tend to have an ideological program for the transformation of society and are often allied with related institutions, such as trade unions, or religious or social organizations. Depending on the ideology embraced by the party, this group can be further divided into socialist political parties (for example, the Social Democrats in Germany and the Socialists in France), nationalist political parties (such as Basque Partido Nacionalista Vasco), and religious political parties (such as the Christian Democrat political parties in Western Europe) (Gunther and Diamond, 2003, 177–183).

The third category of political parties outlined by Gunther and Diamond are **ethnicity-based political parties** (2003, 183–185). These political parties typically do not have elaborate and extensive organizations but are characterized by their desire to "use existing state structures to channel benefits towards their particularistically defined electoral clientele" (Gunther and Diamond, 2003, 183). They seek to mobilize and benefit only the members of their own ethnic group and, in so doing, explicitly divide society into antagonistic ethnic solidarities. Examples of ethnically based political parties include South Africa 's Inkatha Freedom Party and the (Sikh) Akali Dal in India 's Punjab state.

Electoralist political parties, including catch-all political parties, are organizationally thin and characterized by the goals of electoral mobilization and success. They focus on modern campaigning techniques, such as television, opinion polling, and mass media, over the mobilization of their members. Their campaigns are run by professionals, as opposed to party members, and focus on party leaders, as opposed to ideology. The catch-all political party, in particular, is characterized by its pluralistic and tolerant orientation, thin organization, vague ideology, and focus on electoral success. These political parties seek to aggregate broad social interests and cut across social cleavages to maximize the number of votes they receive. Examples of catch-all political parties include the Liberal Party in Canada, the Democratic Party in the United States, and the British Labour Party under Tony Blair (Gunther and Diamond, 2003, 183–188).

Finally, Gunther and Diamond describe **movement political parties** as "a type of partisan organization that straddles the conceptual space between party and movement" (2003, 188). These parties are becoming increasingly prominent in Western Europe, where they most often take the form of left-libertarian or post-materialist political parties and post-industrial extreme-right political parties, but the category can also apply to newly forming political parties emerging out of social movements generally. They are characterized by their fluid organization, often based on various grass-roots groups. Often a manifestation of a negative reaction to modern society, members of these political parties may feel alienated from the mainstream political process and parties. In some cases, these may be anti-state parties (particularly those representing the extreme right) or they may merely challenge the form of democratic governance in place (Gunther and Diamond, 2003, 188–189).

The Decline of the Party?

Recently, there has been a great deal of discussion in many Western countries about the decline of the political party. Toward the end of the twentieth century, many voters in Western countries expressed dissatisfaction with their political parties. In Canada, evidence suggests that voters found political parties overly elite-dominated, insufficiently responsive, and lacking in opportunities for voters to influence their policy platforms (Cross, 2004, 171). The rise of post-materialist values, such as quality of life or the environment, is another potential reason for the decline of parties, as these issues are not generally a priority for the traditional parties. Thus, many voters look to interest groups and new social movements for better representation of their particular concerns and ideas. Finally, while there seem to be more political parties today than in the past, the differences between them appear to be decreasing. In North America, the major political parties have become catch-all parties, arguably trying to speak for everyone and failing to represent many. The decreased role of ideology in these political parties combined with the increased role for party professionals and the diminishing influence of the average member is potentially a problem. How can catch-all parties represent the diversity of citizens when they always try to occupy the middle ground? Perhaps the role of parties is changing from one of representation to one focused on governing—structuring Parliament, creating avenues for policy development, and ensuring the workings of government. While the debate continues over whether political parties are in decline or simply changing as the needs and demands of voters change, political parties do remain the dominant players at election time and continue to structure our representative institutions.

Party Systems

PARTY SYSTEMS REFER TO THE TOTAL NUMBER OF POLITICAL PARTIES PRESENT within a political system at any given time. They tend to reflect the distribution of power among the political parties and the relationship between political parties and electoral systems. In particular, studies of party systems (e.g., Lijphart, 1994) tend to examine three distinct aspects: the level of competition between parties, the number of parties present in a system, and the ideological slant of the parties of a system as a whole. Table 11.1 outlines the different party systems, their characteristics, and examples of each.

As Table 11.1 demonstrates, party systems containing fewer political parties are more likely to form majority governments, whereas party systems containing four or more political parties are more likely to have minority or coalition governments. While it is important to draw distinctions between the different party systems, it is also important to remember that they may change over time. Canada, for example, shifted from a two-party system in the decades following Confederation—when the Liberal and Conservative parties dominated the process and system and both were able to form governments at different times—to a two-and-a-half party system beginning in the 1960s, with the rise of the NDP as a regular third party. With the 1993 federal election, Canada moved into a multi-party system with a dominant party, the Liberals. For the first time, Canadians elected five parties to the House of Commons, but the only party able to win enough seats to form a government for the next decade was the Liberal Party. The move to "unite the right," resulting in the creation of the new

TABLE 11.1 *Different Party Systems and Their Characteristics*

TYPE OF PARTY SYSTEM	EXAMPLES	CHARACTERISTICS
Two-Party Systems	**The United States**—the Republican and Democratic parties	Two political parties regularly compete in elections and win seats. Majority governments are common and power alternates fairly regularly between these political parties.
Two-and-a-Half-Party Systems	**The United Kingdom**—Labour and Conservative parties dominate, with a significant third party, the Liberals. **Canada (1963–93)**—with the Liberal, Conservative, and New Democratic parties	The two major political parties win most of the seats, with one of them generally forming a majority government. A third party, however, regularly wins seats. Although the third party is unlikely to form a government, it can be quite influential, particularly in a minority government situation.
Multi-Party System with a Dominant Party	**Sweden**—the Social Democrats dominated the twentieth century, but a wide number of parties were regularly elected. **Canada (1993–2006)**—More than four parties are elected, but the Liberals form the governments and dominate the system.	Four or more political parties regularly win seats in elections. One political party, however, usually wins the most seats and forms the government, dominating the political system. In many cases, the high number of political parties winning seats results in minority or coalition governments.
Multi-Party System without a Dominant Party	**The Netherlands**—In 2006, 10 parties won seats in the lower chamber, led by the Christian Democratic Appeal (CDA) with 41 out of 150 seats.	Four or more political parties compete in election, but no one political party dominates the system. Power alternates between political parties fairly regularly. Generally results in coalition governments and consensus-based governing across party lines.

Conservative Party in 2003 and their electoral success in 2006, provided a challenge to Liberal dominance and altered Canada's party system once again.

The next section discusses electoral systems. Different electoral systems are also more likely to produce majority or minority governments, and may lead to the formation of different party systems. The important question that remains is how well the respective systems represent the population. In Canada, an increasing number of political parties have won seats in recent elections, beginning with the federal election of 1993, in which an unprecedented five political parties won seats in the House of Commons. As well, the past two elections have failed to produce a clear winner and a majority government. This situation is the result of a changing party system combined with Canada's electoral system.

Electoral Systems

ELECTORAL SYSTEMS SET THE RULES THAT DETERMINE HOW CITIZENS CAST their votes, how the votes are counted, and how they are translated into legislative seats. Different electoral systems lead to different forms of representation—for example, electing a direct representative versus voting for a party to represent you—and may appeal to different people, based on their individual and collective political values. Some electoral systems are more likely to create multi-party systems, whereas others more often lead to two-party systems dominated by catch-all parties. Some electoral systems provide the most accurate results with fewer political parties, whereas others work well with a wide variety of political parties. Choosing an electoral system, therefore, can be difficult because the same system will often work differently and produce different results in different places. Also, a system that satisfies one of our preferences may work against another. The section below outlines tools for evaluating electoral systems, as well as the major different systems and their characteristics.

Evaluating Electoral Systems

From time to time, governments may reassess and revise the rules governing elections. Recently in British Columbia, for example, in preparation for a referendum on electoral change, an assembly of citizens was asked to evaluate different electoral systems and recommend one for the province. In doing so, they were given different criteria to help them make their assessment. Similar criteria can be used to evaluate which electoral system would work best for a country, including Canada. So, when evaluating different electoral systems, we need to ask the following questions:

- Does the system produce stable and effective governments?
- Does the system help voters hold parties accountable?
- Does the system increase the power of the legislature to hold the government accountable (for example, through minority governments)?

- Does the system allow for fair and equal representation? Do all votes count equally? Are votes wasted?

- Do voters have enough choice? An identifiable representative?

- Does the system encourage participation—for example, through providing sufficient choice for voters or allowing them to elect a direct representative?

Electoral systems can be divided into different families. The remainder of this chapter explores examples from the four main families of electoral systems, discusses their relative strengths and weaknesses, and concludes with a brief discussion of electoral reform in Canada.

Plurality Systems

In a plurality system, the winner simply needs more votes than any other candidate to win the seat. The winner does not need a majority (50 percent plus one) of the votes. Canada uses a plurality system called the **single-member plurality (SMP)** system. This is one of the most common electoral systems in the world. Under this system, the territory is divided into constituencies, and each constituency elects one person (a single member) to the legislature. Individuals representing different political parties compete against each other for the seat, and the person who gets the most votes (a plurality) wins. The party that wins the most seats generally goes on to form the government. This simple system provides voters with a direct and identifiable representative and generally leads to powerful majority governments. In doing so, however, it often produces distorted results, with the winning party receiving a greater percentage of the seats than it received of the popular vote. This often rewards parties with regionally concentrated support and makes it more difficult for new parties, or parties with spread-out support, to win seats.

Proportional Representation

Proportional representation (PR) aims to ensure that the percentage of the popular vote that a party receives is translated (as closely as possible) into the proportion of seats that party is allocated in the Parliament. The seats are then allocated to the party members. In some cases, there is a pre-determined, closed list of party members; in others, the list is open and voters can vote for specific candidates, affecting their final position on the party list. Ideally, if a party wins 25 percent of the popular vote, it will get 25 percent of the available seats. In practice, however, the results may not be this accurate. One factor that affects the proportionality of an electoral system is the use of thresholds. Many countries use thresholds to ensure that parties claiming seats have a minimum level of popular support. In Sweden, for example, parties must receive a minimum of 4 percent of the popular national vote (or 12 percent within their electoral district) to claim any seats.

There are many varieties of PR systems used; however, one of the most common variations is the party list system, such as the one used in Sweden. Under this system, the country is divided into several large multi-member constituencies. Each party develops a list of candidates to run in the constituency. Citizens can vote either for a political party or an individual on the party's list, thereby affecting the ordering of the list. In this way, they influence both which party will win seats and which candidates will take possession of those seats. Taking the threshold into account, the percentage of the popular vote is then used to determine how many seats each party gets.

Ultimately, PR systems aim to be proportional—to ensure that all votes are equal and no votes are wasted. As a result of this goal, however, they often result in minority or coalition governments. PR systems may also work to improve the representation of women and/or minority groups. Parties can ensure that individuals representing politically marginalized groups are placed favourably on the lists, increasing their chances of becoming elected. In Sweden, many of the political parties committed themselves to improving the number of women represented in the Riksdag, or Parliament. Using the PR system, they ensure that a significant number of candidates running for election are women and that they are placed highly on the list, thus improving their chances of winning a seat. This has made it easier for women to get elected than in an SMP system, where each individual woman not only has to win the nomination within the riding but also has to win the seat outright. Currently, 47 percent of elected members of the Swedish Riksdag are women, compared with 21 percent in Canada's House of Commons.

Majoritarian Systems

Unlike a plurality system, in which a candidate only needs to have more votes than anyone else, a **majoritarian electoral system** requires the winner to have a majority, or 50 percent of the vote plus one. This is quite simple if there are only two political parties competing, but in many cases the existence of more than two parties requires the use of different mechanisms to achieve a majority. In some cases, individuals vote more than once. For example, in the French presidential elections, a two-round system of voting is used. Following a first round of voting, all of the candidates, except the two most successful, are dropped from the ballot. A second round of voting is then held in which voters have only two choices, one of whom will get more than 50 percent of the votes.

Other countries, such as Australia, use a system of preferential or **alternative voting**, where they rank the candidates on the ballot, indicating their first choice, second choice, and so on. This system allows citizens to indicate their preferences, rather than giving them only one choice. When the votes are counted, the candidate receiving more than 50 percent of the votes wins. If no candidate has a majority, then the candidate with the least votes is dropped from the ballot and the second choices indicated on those ballots are transferred to the remaining candidates. This process continues until one candidate has a majority. Under preferential voting, voters have more choice and vote ballot counts, but each elected representative has the support of at least half of the electorate. This system does, however, require a higher level of skill and knowledge from the voter and generally still distorts the popular vote, as in SMP systems.

Mixed Systems

Some countries have chosen to combine elements of the above systems in order to take advantage of their different strengths and offset some of their weaknesses. One example of a mixed system is in Germany, which uses a **mixed-member proportional (MMP) system** to elect its lower house. This system combines the direct representation found in SMP systems with the proportionality of PR systems. With MMP, each voter casts two votes—one for a particular party (as in proportional representation systems) and one for their local representative (as in single-member plurality systems). The available seats are divided in half. All candidates who win a plurality of votes in their constituency win a seat. The remaining seats are accorded to the political parties to ensure that the overall distribution of seats in Parliament is proportional. Under MMP, the primary strength of SMP—the direct relationship between voters and their elected representative—is combined with the proportionality of PR. These strengths may compensate for the fact that MMP uses a more complicated voting and counting system and is more likely to result in minority or coalition governments.

Strengths and Weaknesses of Electoral Systems

All electoral systems have strengths and weaknesses, some of which are mentioned above. Table 11.2 outlines the various strengths and weaknesses of these four electoral systems in more detail. Using the chart to compare the different ways of casting and counting votes, we can determine which electoral system may work best for us.

Electoral Reform in Canada

Over the past decade, Canada has witnessed increasing momentum and interest in changing both federal and provincial electoral systems. Recent referendums on electoral change have been held at the provincial level in British Columbia (2005) and Prince Edward Island (2005). A citizens' assembly in the province of Ontario also recommended a mixed-member proportional system for an October 2007 referendum on electoral reform. Although none of the referendums have been successful so far, Canadians do seem interested in electoral reform, as demonstrated by the growing amount of attention given to the issue during recent

TABLE 11.2   *Strengths and Weaknesses of Four Electoral Systems*

ELECTORAL SYSTEM	STRENGTHS	WEAKNESSES
Single-Member Plurality (SMP)	▪ is easy to understand and simple to use ▪ produces a direct relationship between the voter and the elected representative ▪ tends to produce majority governments that have the power to govern efficiently	▪ produces disproportionate results, often over-representing the winning party ▪ rewards parties with regionally concentrated support and punishes parties with diffuse support ▪ produces an overall outcome that reflects inputs inaccurately
Proportional Representation (PR)	▪ translates votes into seats directly and proportionally ▪ tends toward easier access for new political parties and more frequent election of women and minorities, which can make government more representative	▪ increases likelihood of minority governments, which may (or may not) be unstable ▪ offers no direct relationship between voters and their representative, as found under SMP
Alternative Voting	▪ gives voters more choice ▪ can lead to alliances between political parties and candidates ▪ may have more perceived legitimacy because candidates ultimately get more than 50 percent of the votes	▪ requires a higher level of knowledge and skill from voters and vote counters ▪ generally still brings disproportionate results, similar to those under SMP systems
Mixed-Member Proportional	▪ combines the representative strengths of SMP with the proportionality of PR systems	▪ is more likely to result in minority governments ▪ requires more knowledge and skill from voters and vote counters

federal election campaigns. Why do some Canadians want to change the way our votes are counted? Fair Vote Canada, an organization promoting electoral change, argues that our current single-member plurality system should be changed because it distorts the popular vote, wastes votes, and creates artificial majority governments (see **www.fairvotecanada.org/en/about_fairvoting**). Another possible reason is declining voter turnout. Arguably, a system of voting that is more proportional and in which all votes count is more likely to encourage Canadians to vote. Finally, if more than three political parties continue to compete in Canadian elections at the federal level, a different electoral system would probably work better with our new multi-party system and help offset some of the regionalism that now characterizes Canadian federal politics.

Summary

This chapter has explored how political parties, party systems, and electoral systems all shape the nature of representation and governance in democratic countries. Political parties represent the people and help to structure governing institutions. As well, different types of political parties strive to represent people in different ways. Party systems reflect the number of political parties within a system and the level of competition. The more political parties that regularly win seats in elections, the more likely it is that the country will have minority or coalition governments. Canada has experienced significant changes in its party system since Confederation and it continues to change. Finally, electoral systems determine how our votes are cast, counted, and translated into seats. They determine, among other things, whether we will have a direct representative and whether all votes are equal. As citizens, it is important to understand and evaluate how these different systems work and to ensure that our voices are represented well in our democratic political institutions.

Discussion Questions

1. Are political parties in decline in Canada? Do the current political parties in the federal Parliament adequately represent the diversity of Canadians?
2. Why do you think the number of political parties is increasing in Canada?
3. Which party best represents you? Why?
4. Using the criteria outlined for evaluating electoral systems, which system do you like best? Why?
5. Do you feel that Canada's political parties, party system, and electoral system adequately represent you? Why or why not?
6. Why do you think fewer people vote today than in the past? What can be done to change this?

References

Allum, Percy. 1995. *State and Society in Western Europe*. Cambridge: Polity Press.

British Columbia Citizens' Assembly on Electoral Reform. 2004. *Democratic Electoral Systems*. Retrieved January 8, 2007, from **www.citizensassembly.bc.ca/resources/Weekend%20Session%20Readings/Weekend3Session1.doc**.

Cross, William. 2004. *Political Parties*. Vancouver: UBC Press.

Fair Vote Canada. 2005. *About Fair Voting*. Retrieved January 8, 2007, from **www.fairvotecanada.org/en/about_fairvoting**.

Gunther, Richard and Larry Diamond. 2003. "Species of Political Parties: A New Typology." *Party Politics* 9(2): 167–199.

Lijphart, Arend. 1991. *Electoral Systems and Party Systems*. Oxford: Oxford University Press.

Further Readings

Courtney, John C. 2004. *Elections.* Vancouver: UBC Press.

Cross, William. 2004. *Political Parties.* Vancouver: UBC Press.

Smith, Gordon. 2003. "The Decline of Party?" in Jack Hayward and Anand Menon, eds., *Governing Europe* (179–191). Oxford: Oxford University Press.

Trimble, Linda and Jane Arscott. 2003. *Still Counting: Women in Politics Across Canada.* Peterborough, ON: Broadview Press.

Weblinks

Citizens' Assembly on Electoral Reform (British Columbia)
www.citizensassembly.bc.ca

Citizens' Assembly on Electoral Reform (Ontario)
www.citizensassembly.gov.on.ca

Directory of Political Parties, Interest Groups and Other Social Movements
www.psr.keele.ac.uk/parties.htm

Electionworld
http://en.wikipedia.org/wiki/User:Electionworld/Electionworld

Fair Vote Canada
www.fairvote.ca

Conservative Party of Canada
www.conservative.ca

Green Party
www.greenparty.ca

Liberal Party of Canada
www.liberal.ca

New Democratic Party of Canada
www.ndp.ca

CHAPTER 12

CITIZENS AND CITIZENSHIP

CHRISTINA
GABRIEL

The political concept of **citizenship** can mean something as simple as legal membership in a country or a full menu of rights and obligations that define an individual's relationship with fellow citizens and with the state. In this chapter, we trace the origins of citizenship as a critical political concept. We also explore the question of access to citizenship. Who historically has been included or excluded from citizenship status? Finally, we consider some of the tensions that underwrite recent uses of the term "citizenship" in contemporary politics. In particular, we focus on three primary tensions: between rights and responsibilities, universality and difference, and the national and the global.

Introduction

In 1946, Secretary of State Paul Martin, Sr. introduced Canada's first Citizenship Bill to the House of Commons. He declared that "citizenship is the right to full partnership in the fortunes and in the future of the nation" (Martin Sr., 1993, 73). Despite this declaration, more than 50 years later, many of us find it difficult to describe what it means to be a "Canadian citizen" beyond a narrow legal definition; indeed, we may find it hard to specify the content of "full partnership." Key political questions in Canada and elsewhere revolve around immigration as a source of potential citizens as well as the meaning of citizenship itself. These questions are particularly germane because the way we choose to answer them has implications for the kind of society and political community to which we aspire (Mouffe, 1992, 225).

Consequently, it is not surprising that citizenship, both in theory and application, has been a source of ongoing debate. Some social theorists have characterized citizenship as a "slippery" concept whose meaning has shifted over time and as a contested concept that consistently generates political debate and conflict (Riley, 1992; Hall and Held, 1989). At the most general level, however, differing conceptions of citizenship are characterized by some common concerns, including the inclusions and exclusions that are constitutive of membership of a particular community; reciprocal rights in and duties toward the community; and full participation in practice (Hall and Held, 1989, 175).

Citizenship as a political concept has a long history. The classical ideal of citizenship can be traced to the ancient civilizations of Greece and Rome. In the Greek city state of Athens, for example, citizenship granted the privileges and obligations of self-government to a fortunate few. A citizen, according to the Aristotelian ideal, is one who both rules and is ruled. Political participation was regarded as a civic duty. The privileges of citizenship in these ancient times, however, were bestowed upon a select group: "A citizen must be a male of known genealogy, a patriarch, a warrior, and the master of the labor of others (normally slaves)" (Pocock, 1995, 30–31). Such criteria excluded most of the Greek population—including women, slaves, foreigners, and resident aliens—from citizenship.

Although the origins of citizenship are ancient, many current conceptualizations of citizenship-as-rights are informed by the liberal political tradition dating back to the seventeenth century. The French Revolution's principles of liberty, equality, and fraternity were the grounds upon which French citizens claimed "universal recognition on the basis of common equality" (Hall and Held, 1989, 176). The American Revolution of 1776 also revived and gave renewed energy and content to the concept of citizenship. These events were deeply influenced by the English philosopher John Locke. His work "emphasized that the relationship between the people and their government was consensual and contractual" (Kaplan, 1993, 248). According to Locke's ideas, formal civil and political equality between citizens was guaranteed and protected by a limited state. Under the terms of Locke's "social contract," consent was the basis of authority. Locke was convinced that the business of government rested with the people and that they alone were responsible for their own good. They would "elect representatives, delegate powers, and agree to abide by majority decisions, but ultimately the representatives and officials hold their powers on trust and are responsible to the people" (Goodwin, 1992, 221). However, women and men without property did not figure into Locke's vision of citizenship.

The ideal of equality, nonetheless, gives the concept of citizenship its radical emancipatory potential. Previously, citizenship had been underwritten by a range of exclusions.

Take, for example, the basic political right of voting in Canada. In the years immediately following Confederation, income and property requirements, as well as the exclusion of all women, meant that only a small proportion of the population could vote. Most women won suffrage by the 1920s, but people of Chinese, East Indian, and Japanese origin were denied the vote until the late 1940s. Canada's Aboriginal peoples did not have the right to vote without extinguishing their treaty rights until 1960. Each of these groups contested their marginal status, using the language of citizenship, by making a claim for equality. In this respect, citizenship is a very powerful concept, implying that there should be no exclusion from the political community on the basis of, for example, gender or race.

Citizenship as Belonging

THIS SECTION CONSIDERS THE QUESTION OF CITIZENSHIP AS A LEGAL STATUS—WHO is born a citizen and who can access the right to be a citizen. Some argue that for citizenship to be meaningful, it should be limited; citizens should be granted rights that are unavailable to others. For example, recent American legislation has limited the right to benefits and services for legal immigrants who have not yet become legal citizens (Lister, 1997, 46). Others, in contrast, argue that citizenship should be freely available to all settled members of a community and that all individuals should be treated in the same way (Kaplan, 1993, 257). This debate has become particularly heated in the wake of large-scale migration, since World War II, to Western Europe and North America. These issues are a major challenge to conceptions of citizenship in modern liberal democracies.

Access to citizenship, in some ways, occurs along a spectrum. At one end are those born into citizenship. At the other end are groups of people resident in countries where their formal citizenship is in doubt or in question. The situation of Western European migrant workers (guest workers) is a good example. They were recruited under employment and residence permits in the post-war period. Today, they participate in the economic realm of the host country. They pay taxes and many have children who were born in the host country. But many are excluded from political participation at both the local and national levels. This situation has led to questions about the representativeness of government when large segments of the population are disenfranchised. How long does a person have to live in a country before he or she can expect political representation? The dilemma of the guest worker is not limited to Western Europe. Foreign domestics, for example, enter Canada under the provisions of the Live-in Caregiver Program. These provisions include the granting of temporary "visitor" status and the condition that domestics live with their employers for a specified period. These conditions effectively render these workers "non-citizens" (Bakan and Stasiulis, 1997). In contrast to temporary visitors, people with "permanent resident" status share many of the same rights as Canadian citizens, but they are unable to vote or run for public office. They also may be barred from certain jobs in the public service.

Tensions Underlying Citizenship

THE POLITICAL APPLICATION OF THE CONCEPT OF CITIZENSHIP IS NOT LIMITED TO legal definitions of access. It also addresses more substantive aspects of citizenship. Three are particularly noteworthy. First, the post-war conception of citizenship-as-rights is increasingly being challenged by "active" models of citizenship that stress responsibility. Second, the liberal conception of citizenship is being criticized for exclusions based on categories of difference. And last, conditions of globalization are giving rise to new forms of citizenship.

Rights versus Responsibilities

The work of British sociologist T.H. Marshall in *Citizenship and Social Class* is often taken as the starting point for thinking about the evolution of citizenship. Marshall's analysis addressed the meaning of citizenship within the context of class-based inequalities characteristic of modern economies. Do rights have any relevance, asked Marshall, if people do not have the means or capacity to make citizenship meaningful in practice? Drawing specifically on the English example, Marshall mapped three elements of citizenship that had evolved in the modern liberal democratic state. The first element, **civil rights**, emerged in the eighteenth century and referred to rights necessary for individual freedom, including "liberty of person, freedom of speech, thought and faith, the right to own property . . . the right to justice." The second element encompasses **political rights**, such as the right to vote and run for political office. These rights date to the nineteenth century. According to Marshall, the twentieth century was associated with the **social rights** of citizenship. He defined this element as "the right to a modicum of economic welfare and security . . . according to the standards prevailing in society" (1950, 10). The law and Parliament were the institutions most closely associated with the first two elements of citizenship. However, the welfare state was the institutional mechanism for social rights. Welfare state arrangements, such as public education, universal health care, public housing, and income security programs, were designed to counteract the insecurities generated by the market economy in which liberal democratic citizenship was embedded. In this respect, the welfare state added a social dimension to citizenship.

The specific configuration of national welfare states and the nature of social entitlements have varied from country to country in the post-war period. A host of factors—including the level of national resources, differing capacities of groups to advance claims, institutional practices, and ideas about the state—play a role in the degree to which countries have protected and advanced social rights. In Canada, social rights have also played an important role in fashioning post-war ideas about Canadian identity and citizenship. In a sense, social programs provided an important benchmark to assess our progress as a people. Some programs, like universal health care, were "the standard by which Canadians could judge themselves vis-à-vis

Americans. Canadians were more compassionate, more caring, and had a greater sense of social justice" (Taras, 1997, 2).

Despite differences among social welfare regimes, T.H. Marshall's key point was that citizens in need were entitled to welfare provisions, not in the form of charity, but as an entitlement of citizenship itself. In contrast to liberal ideas of citizenship, in which citizens figure as individual members of a state, Marshall's conception emphasizes collective membership in a community (Yuval-Davis, 1997, 69).

In recent times, this post-war idea about citizenship has sometimes been labelled "passive." This is because it emphasizes passive social entitlements "and the absence of any obligation to participate in public life" (Kymlicka and Norman, 1995, 286). In the United Kingdom, for example, Margaret Thatcher's Conservative government attacked the social dimensions of citizenship by praising the "active citizen." This individual discharges the duties of citizenship privately through neighbourliness, voluntary work, and charitable gifts. This particular "New Right" construction of the "active citizen" marks an important shift in the way we experience citizenship. The social rights of the disadvantaged are transferred, in part, from publicly financed entitlements into the private sphere of charity and voluntary services (Yuval-Davis, 1997, 84).

Under the post-war social rights paradigm, basic entitlements were supported by tax dollars and available to all members of society. Current New Right thinking equates social citizenship rights and "entitlement" with the idea of dependency, privileges the better-off in society, and tends to reinforce existing social inequalities. "The work obligation is presented as one that unites all citizens in a contribution to the common good." But as Lister further points out, the target of the active citizenship model is overwhelmingly the poor (Lister, 1997, 20). In the debate over rights versus responsibilities, the New Right's attempt to promote "responsible" citizenship has significantly eroded the social dimension of citizenship.

Universality versus Difference

The politics of citizenship, both in theory and practice, is also centred on the issues of "universality" and "difference." Within the concept of citizenship is an ideal premised on the basis of equality or universal status. This ideal of universality is found in such phrases as "everyone is equal before the law." Critiques by feminists, people of colour, and other disadvantaged groups, however, have raised concerns about the **universalism** attached to these concepts. These groups draw attention to the fact that formal citizenship rights do not necessarily guarantee full participation or full membership for everyone. For example, people of colour, women, people with disabilities, and gay men and lesbians have been excluded from full participation "not because of socio-economic status but because of their socio-cultural identity—their difference" (Kymlicka and Norma, 1995, 302).

The experiences of some groups and categories of people following the attacks of September 11, 2001, offer a case in point. The focus on security and terrorism resulted in the introduction of various new pieces of legislation in Canada and the

United States as well as regulatory changes in immigration and border control. Within the United States, Human Rights Watch—an independent monitoring organization that monitors rights in national and international law—reported that American officials targeted people on the basis of racial origin. It stated that more than 1000 people were detained on immigration charges, allowing officials to deny them their basic civil rights without court scrutiny (Knox, 2002, A10).

In Canada national security certificates were used to detain non-citizens and permanent residents suspected of terrorism. This measure dates back almost 30 years and predates the *Anti-Terrorism Act*. National security certificates not only allowed the state to hold individuals indefinitely on the grounds of security but also did not require authorities to reveal the evidence that supported the charges. Prior to 2001 such certificates were used against two dozen foreign nationals. After the September 11 attacks, as many as five men found themselves detained under this provision (Makin, 2007, A1, A5), which essentially held non-citizens and permanent residents to a different legal norm than citizens. Critics charged that such measures were unconstitutional and a violation of human rights (CBC News, 2004). In 2007 the Supreme Court of Canada ruled unanimously that security certificates violate the *Canadian Charter of Rights and Freedoms* and struck down key provisions of the national security certificate law. The ruling requires the federal government to devise a new law that conforms to the provisions of the Charter.

The experience of the Syrian-born Canadian citizen Maher Arar provides an additional insight into people with formal citizenship whose experiences in the post-September 11 period belie this status. Arar was returning to Canada via New York following a family holiday in Tunisia. Detained and questioned by the U.S. Immigration and Naturalization Service, he was accused of having links to terrorism and was not allowed access to a lawyer. Despite Arar's Canadian passport and his request to be returned to Canada, American officials deported him to Syria, where he was imprisoned and tortured. After ten months, Arar was returned to Canada. No charge had been laid against him in any jurisdiction (Sallot, 2004, A9). In 2004 the Liberal government established a public inquiry, under Justice Dennis O' Connor, to examine and report on the role Canadian officials played in Arar's experience. Two years later it presented its findings. Among its key conclusions was that there was "no evidence to indicate that Mr. Arar has committed any offence or that his activities constitute a threat to the security of Canada." It also concluded that it was "very likely" that the RCMP had provided information to the United States that resulted in the detention and removal of Arar to Syria (Arar Commission, 2006). The Canadian government subsequently paid $10.5 million to Arar in compensation for the deportation and torture and issued a formal written apology (MacCharles, 2007, A1, A8). Arar's case demonstrates that Canadian citizenship and a Canadian passport do not necessarily provide protection in a national security environment that links some groups of people to terrorism. In these cases, the failure to recognize citizenship status, due process, and international human rights renders some people, on the basis of group membership, "second-class" citizens.

The popular term "second-class citizens" is also used in reference to women's experiences. That is, they may claim formal citizenship rights, but this seeming parity is countered by the material aspects of their disadvantage as a group. What does citizenship mean in the context of the continuing gender division of labour or increasing feminization of poverty? Feminist accounts of citizenship have been instrumental in highlighting how this concept is deeply gendered. Noted political philosopher Carole Pateman, for example, has examined the ways in which women have been excluded or included in the category "citizen." Political theory, Pateman argues, despite its claim to universality, presupposes gender difference, and this, in turn, structures women's status as citizens. She argues that conceptions of citizenship are premised on a "patriarchal separation" between the public realm of politics and work and the private realm of gender relations and domestic life. Anything that happens in the private realm, the space traditionally associated with women, is treated as insignificant to citizenship (Pateman, 1989, 182–185). Moreover, the values citizens are expected to show, such as impartiality, rationality, independence, and political activism, are attached to men and the public realm (Lister, 1997, 70).

This public–private dichotomy, Pateman suggests, also informs the construction of the post-war welfare state. In "The Patriarchal Welfare State," Pateman takes exception to Marshall's theory of social citizenship. She argues that the very structure of the welfare state, Marshall's mechanism for the realization of social rights, far from ensuring full membership for women, casts them as "social exiles." The welfare state was constructed around the notion of a male "breadwinner/worker." It presumed that men are full-time wage earners who provide for dependent wives and children. Women, in contrast, were assumed to provide unpaid domestic care at home. They were the "dependent wives." The development of the welfare state was premised on the notion that certain aspects of care should be provided in the home by women's unpaid labour instead of through public provision (Pateman, 1989, 192). Pateman argues that these assumptions created a gendered two-tier structure in the welfare state. Men could claim "benefits available to individuals as 'public' persons" because they were paid employees. Women, however, were seen as "'dependents' of individuals in the first category" (Pateman, 1989, 188). Women's access to the rights of social citizenship was only partial.

Feminist theorist Iris Marion Young has argued that modern conceptions of citizenship can often serve to marginalize and oppress various groups of people. She begins from the point that a unitary conception of citizenship is unjust because, as she puts it, "In a society where some groups are privileged while others are oppressed, insisting that as citizens, persons should leave behind their particular affiliations and experiences to adopt a general point of view serves only to reinforce that privilege, for the perspectives and interests of the privileged will tend to dominate this unified public, marginalizing or silencing those of other groups." Young supports a democratic project that would incorporate people into the political community not only as individuals but as members of groups. Group representation becomes a method to "promote just outcomes within the democratic decision making process." Within this call is Young's conception of "differentiated citizenship," which requires the introduction of group-specific rights to confront oppression and disadvantage. She suggests that specific measures are necessary for effective recognition and representation of disadvantaged groups. Such measures would include, among other things, public support of group organizations, group representation in the generation and evaluation of relevant key policies, and veto power over specific policies that affect any one group directly (Young, 1990, 120, 124–125).

In the case of everyday politics, there have been a number of examples where policies have been directed at specific groups, rather than at individuals. Many of these have proved very controversial. Multiculturalism policy in Canada, for example, has been the source of considerable debate. The policy has been criticized as "divisive" on the grounds that it emphasizes differences between citizens and produces "hyphenated Canadians." It has also been attacked on the basis that it grants "special status" and funding to ethnocultural groups (Bissoondath, 1994). The notion of differentiated citizenship has been identified as a "radical development in citizenship theory" and one that constitutes a serious challenge to an understanding of citizenship premised on "treating people as individuals with equal rights under law" (Kymlicka and Norman, 1995, 302–303). Regardless of one's personal perspective, this growing debate about universality and difference is central to the politics of citizenship in the twenty-first century.

The National versus the Global

In the modern era, citizenship and citizenship rights and practices have been conceptualized almost exclusively in terms of membership in a nation-state. However, from the 1990s on, as Richard Falk has argued, processes of globalization have eroded the statist underpinning of conventional norms of citizenship. In particular, he emphasizes the growth of regionalism, the emergence of non-state actors such as multinational corporations and transnational non-governmental groups (1994, 177–178). In a similar vein, others have drawn attention to the phenomenon of global migration, which raises questions about the status and rights of migrants (both legal and irregular) between states and the growing trend of dual citizenship (Kofman 2003).

How do these developments affect conceptualizations of citizenship that have been built upon the foundation of a sovereign nation-state? To what extent has citizenship been detached from particular states? David Held, for example, draws attention to the "disjuncture" between citizenship, as a status with rights and duties stemming from an individual's membership in a national political community, and the growth of international law. The latter, he suggests "subjects individuals, governments and non-government organizations to new systems of regulations" (Held, 1989, 198). These emerging systems produce mixed consequences. For example, membership in the European Union has created opportunities for individual citizens of member states to challenge their own governments in such forums as the European Court of Justice. This supraterritorial means for citizens to challenge their governments has already had some effect on national legislation (Held, 1989, 199). The development of international legal regimes may contribute to the erosion of the nation-state, but the trend also provides opportunities for citizens of nation-states who seek protection from national laws.

Held has also focused on the development of new forms of transnational activities, highlighting the disjuncture between new forms of governance and the sovereign states (Held, 1995, 107–108). Nation-states have developed a host of international links in areas as diverse as trade, banking, policing and security, and environmental regulation, leading to profound changes in decision making and decision-making capacity. Canada, for instance, is a member of numerous international organizations, such as the United Nations Organization (UNO). It participates in less formal but influential coordinating meetings, such as economic summits, by virtue of its membership in the G7. And Canada is signatory to a number of trading agreements, of which the North American Free Trade Agreement (NAFTA) is the most encompassing. This sort of matrix of international links can affect the ability of nation-states to pursue policies that are truly national, including the state's very ability to guarantee rights of citizenship.

Cross-border migration associated with growing global interconnectedness also has prompted scholars to problematize the relationships between state, nation, and people that underpin conventional understandings of citizenship. Increasingly, there is a recognition that citizenship is multi-layered and enacted across a variety of scales, of which the nation-state is only one (cf. Yuval-Davis, 1999; Kofman, 2003). Yasemin Soysal (1994), for example, puts forward an influential and controversial account of post-national membership. Drawing on the case of guest workers in Europe, she suggests that universal human rights regimes play a role in the provision of economic and social rights to this group. In this case, membership is not predicated on citizenship per se but on personhood: "Individual rights, expansively redefined as human rights on a universalistic basis and legitimized at the transnational level, undercut the import of national citizenship by disrupting the territorial closure of nations" (1994, 164).

Multiple membership and dual citizenship are also increasingly important elements of citizenship politics in the contemporary era. Dual citizenship involves the "simultaneous holding of more than one citizenship or nationality" (Renshon, 2001, 6). Throughout the post-war period states in the international system have been somewhat hostile to the idea of dual citizenship. This position was framed by concerns regarding divided national loyalties, taxation issues, civil status, and military service obligations (Aleinikoff and Klusmeyer, 2002, 23). Presently, however, increasing numbers of states have adopted some form of dual citizenship. In fact, more than 90 states, including Canada, allow dual citizenship (Renshon, 2001, 5). This shift is intimately connected not only to the state's recognition of the dense matrix of transnational linkages that connect "people to family, to employment and investment . . . across borders," but also the state's acknowledgment that these ties are "mutually beneficial to sending and receiving states" (Macklin, 2006, A21).

Dual citizenship has recently come under scrutiny in Canada. Statistics Canada reports that about 553 000 Canadians are dual citizens and more than 4000 have multiple citizenship (Ward, 2006, F3). In July 2006, during the Israeli–Hezbollah conflict in Lebanon, the Canadian government evacuated as many as 15 000 Canadians from Beirut at a cost of approximately $94 million. Some of the individuals caught up in the conflict were long-time residents of Lebanon, whose ongoing physical connection to Canada was publicly questioned (Kaplan, 2006). The evacuation raised a series of concerns that did not centre solely on the costs. At issue, for many, were the loyalties of dual citizens living abroad, their obligations, and their rights, as well as the Canadian government's obligations toward them (Ward, 2006, F3). Following the Lebanon crisis, the federal government announced that it would review the provisions of dual citizenship.

Dual and multiple citizenship are linked to an increasingly interconnected global economy and so are not likely to disappear. For this reason some scholars suggest states should actively promote and manage this reality, as opposed to treating it as a "temporary aberration" (Aleinkoff and Klusmeyer, 2002, 38). For example, Don DeVoretz and Yuen Pau Woo suggest that the Canadian government should promote a stronger connection between citizenship and political participation by encouraging new immigrants to Canada and Canadian citizens living abroad to vote (2006, 3). Italy offers a case in point. It recently changed its constitution to enable some 2.7 million Italians living in other countries to vote in Italian national elections. The change not only gave expatriate citizens the right to cast a vote but also allowed them to elect their own representatives to the Italian Parliament in four extra-territorial electoral districts (Biscaro, 2006, 15–16). Of the 30 overseas candidates, 11 were Canadians or Canadian residents. Gino Bucchino, a Toronto resident, was subsequently elected to one of the overseas seats (Kaplan 2006).

Summary

This chapter explored the concept of citizenship. Conceptualizations of citizenship are generally characterized by issues of inclusion and exclusion, rights and duties, and full participation. The nature of each of these issues, however, as this chapter shows, is historically specific, shifting, and the object of political debate. Not surprisingly, citizenship as a concept has been rightly described as slippery.

While the roots of this concept are ancient, our current conceptualizations are largely informed by liberal understandings. Post-war conceptions of citizenship have been greatly influenced by T.H. Marshall's model of citizenship rights. His formulation has been the focus of considerable criticism by those who suggest that his account pays insufficient attention to the duties or obligations of citizenship. More recently, a number of diverse social groups have challenged the dominant assumptions of citizenship to argue that formal citizenship rights have not been a safeguard against socio-economic exclusion. Such groups have advocated for forms of "differentiated citizenship" to ensure full participation in the polity. In the early twenty-first century, citizenship remains a highly relevant and politically charged concept and practice. New developments signal that the membership and status associated with citizenship is becoming much more complex and multi-layered. Transnational membership and dual citizenship provide examples of two of the many ways in which conventional understanding of citizenship and citizenship rules are being challenged by processes of globalization. For these reasons, it is highly likely that citizenship will remain a contested concept.

Discussion Questions

1. To be a "Canadian citizen" is to enjoy the rights and privileges that flow from full membership of Canada as a nation-state. Discuss the ways in which some groups of people may feel excluded from the promise of full or effective citizenship in Canadian society. Are some groups in Canada "second-class citizens"?

2. In an increasingly interconnected world, should dual citizenship be actively promoted? If so, why?

3. Many citizenship debates focus on rights and duties. What types of duties should be required of Canadian citizens? Is it possible to strike a balance between rights and duties?

References

Aleinikoff, Thomas Alexander and Douglas Klusmeyer. 2002. *Citizenship Policies for an Age of Migration.* Washington: Carnegie Endowment for International Peace.

Arar Commission. 2006. "Arar Commission Releases Its Findings on the Handling of the Maher Arar Case" (press release, September 18). Retrieved from **www.ararcommission.ca**.

Bakan, Abigail and Daiva Stasiulis. 1997. "Foreign Domestic Worker Policy in Canada and the Social Boundaries of Modern Citizenship" in *Not One of the Family.* Toronto: University of Toronto Press, 29–51.

Biscaro, Antonella. 2006. "The Italian Transnational Citizen Casts a Vote and Scores a Goal." *Metropolis World Bulletin,* Volume 6, 15–16.

Bissoondath, Neil. 1994. *Selling Illusions.* Toronto: Penguin Books.

CBC News. 2004. "Security Certificates Constitutional: Court." Retrieved on March 16, 2006, from **www.cbc.ca/story/canada/national/2004/12/10/security-certificate-041210**.

Clark, Campbell. 2002. "Arab-Canadians Fear 'Persecution' at Border." *The Globe and Mail,* September 10, 2002, A8.

DeVoretz, Don J. and Yuen Pau Woo. 2006. "Dual Citizenship and Canada's New Diaspora." RIIM Commentary Series, No. 06-03.

Falk, Richard. 2004. "Citizenship and Globalism: Markets, Empire and Terrorism" in A. Brysk and G. Shafir, eds., *People Out of Place.* New York: Routledge.

Freeze, Colin. 2002. "Mistry Cancels U.S. Tour over Racial Profiling." *The Globe and Mail,* November 2, 2002, A1.

Goodwin, Barbara. 1992. *Using Political Ideas,* 3rd edition. West Sussex, England: John Wiley & Sons.

Hall, Stuart and David Held. 1989. "Citizens and Citizenship" in S. Hall and M. Jacques, eds., *New Times.* London: Verso, 173–188.

Held, David. 1989. "Decline of the Nation-State" in S. Hall and M. Jacques, eds., *New Times.* London: Verso, 191–204.

———. 1995. *Democracy and the Global Order: From the Modern State to Cosmopolitan Governance*. London: Polity Press.

———. 2000. "Regulating Globalization?" in David Held and Anthony McGrew, eds., *The Global Transformations Reader*. Cambridge: Polity Press, 420–430.

Kaplan, William. 2006. "Is It Time to Close Hotel Canada?" *Maclean's* (December 25). Retrieved April 10, 2007, from **www.macleans.ca/canada/national/article.jsp? content=20061225**.

Kaplan, William. 1993. "Who Belongs? Changing Conceptions of Citizenship and Nationality" in W. Kaplan, ed., *Belonging: The Meaning and Future of Canadian Citizenship*. Kingston: McGill-Queen's, 245–264.

Knox, Paul. 2002. "Rights Trampled in the U.S., Report Says." *The Globe and Mail*, August 15, A10.

Kofman, Eleanor. 2003. "Rights and Citizenship" in J. Agnew, K. Mitchell, and G. Toal, eds., *A Companion to Political Geography*. Oxford: Blackwell Publishing, 393–407.

Kymlicka, William and Wayne Norman. 1995. "Return of the Citizen: A Survey of Recent Work on Citizenship Theory" in R. Beiner, ed., *Theorizing Citizenship*. Albany: State University Press New York, 283–322.

Lister, Ruth. 1997. *Citizenship: Feminist Perspectives*. London: MacMillan Press.

MacCharles, Tonda. 2007. "I Wish I Could Buy My Life Back." *Toronto Star*, January 27, A1, A8.

Macklin, Audrey. 2006. "Opinion: Dealing with Dual Citizenship." *Toronto Star*, July 28, A12.

Makin, Kirk. 2007. "Security-Law Ruling Puts Parliament on Notice." *The Globe and Mail*, February 24, A1, A5.

Marshall, Robert. 2000–2001. "Paying the Price." *Maclean's*, December 25–January 1, Vol. 113, No. 52, 48–50.

Marshall, Thomas Humphrey. 1950. *Citizenship and Social Class*. Cambridge: Cambridge University Press.

Martin Sr., Paul. 1993. "Citizenship in a People's World" in W. Kaplan, ed., *Belonging: The Meaning and Future of Canadian Citizenship*. Kingston: McGill-Queen's, 64–78.

Mouffe, Chantelle. 1992. "Democratic Citizenship and the Political Community" in Chantelle Mouffe, ed., *Dimensions of Radical Democracy*. London, England: Verso, 225–239.

Pateman, Carole. 1989. "The Patriarchal Welfare State" in Carole Pateman, ed., *The Disorder of Women*. Stanford, California: Stanford University Press, 179–209.

Plant, Raymond. 1991. "Social Rights and the Reconstruction of Welfare" in G. Andrews, ed., *Citizenship*. London, England: Lawrence & Wishart, 50–64.

Pocock, John. 1995. "The Ideal of Citizenship Since Classical Times " in R. Beiner, ed., *Theorizing Citizenship*. Albany, NY: State University Press, 29–52.

Renshon, Stanley A. 2001. *Dual Citizenship and American National Identity*. Washington: Center for Immigration Studies.

Riley, Denise. 1992. "Citizenship and the Welfare State" in J. Allen, P. Braham, and

P. Lewis, eds., *Political and Economic Forms of Modernity*. Cambridge, England: Polity Press, 180–211.

Sallot, Jeff. 2004. "Judicial Inquiry Set into Arar Affair." *The Globe and Mail,* January 29, A9.

Soysal, Yasemin. 2001. "Postnational Citizenship: Reconfiguring the Familiar Terrain" in Kate Nash and A. Scott, eds., *Blackwell Companion to Political Sociology*. Oxford: Blackwell Press, 333–341.

———. 1994. *Limits of Citizenship. Migrants and Postnational Membership in Europe*. Chicago: University of Chicago.

Taras, David. 1997. "Introduction" in David Taras and B. Rasporich, eds., *A Passion for Identity: An Introduction to Canadian Studies*, 3rd edition. Toronto: Nelson Canada, 1–5.

Ward, Olivia. 2006. "Owing an Allegiance to Two Flags." *Toronto Star*, November 4, F3.

Young, Iris. 1990. "Polity and Group Difference" in *Throwing Like a Girl and Other Essays in Feminist Philosophy and Social Theory*. Bloomington: Indiana University Press, 114–137.

Yuval-Davis, Nira. (1999). "The Multilayered Citizen: Citizenship in an Age of 'Glocalization.'" *International Feminist Journal of Politics*. 1:1 June, 119–136.

———. 1997. *Gender and Nation*. London: Sage.

Further Readings

Castles, Stephen and Alastair Davidson. 2000. *Citizenship and Migration: Globalization and the Politics of Belonging*. London: Macmillan.

Lister, Ruth. 2003. *Citizenship: Feminist Perspectives*. Washington, NY: New York University Press.

Stasiulis, Daiva and Abigail Bakan. 2003. *Negotiating Citizenship. Migrant Women in Canada and the Global System*. Basingstoke, U.K.: Palgrave.

Weblinks

Citizenship and Immigration Canada
www.cic.gc.ca

Maher Arar: Commission of Inquiry
www.ararcommission.ca/eng/

Environment Canada's Primer on Environmental Citizenship
www.atl.ec.gc.ca/msc/as/primer.html

Politeia: Network for Citizenship and Democracy in Europe
www.politeia.net

CHAPTER 13

COMMUNITY

Objectives

This chapter investigates various notions of political community arising in popular discussion and political science by addressing these questions: What is community? How do communities shape politics? Is community good (and for what)? Although we may have the sense that everyone lives in some geographic community, community can mean considerably more than one's place of residence. To draw a complete picture of community, this chapter distinguishes between three bases for communities, discusses the sentiment of community, and presents the powerful but controversial political discourses of communitarianism and cosmopolitanism. Liberal and feminist views on community are reviewed, as is virtual community. Finally, the chapter suggests how community is a political strategy and a springboard for political participation.

JUDITH GARBER

Introduction

Few political concepts are employed more frequently in public discourse than that of community. What is intriguing, though, is the array of uses to which community is put. One week's *Globe and Mail* newspaper turned up articles on these related subjects: a diverse urban neighbourhood whose sense of community is threatened by a proposed Wal-Mart; the disappearance of coastal communities because of the death of fisheries; a recommendation by a community-based panel that government fund low-income housing; controversies over criminal offenders released from prisons and mental hospitals into the community; the international community's inability to decide how to handle peacekeeping in a country with a fragile government; the varying levels of acceptance of individualism within Canada's ethnic communities; and speculation about whether a peaceful protest march into a city by members of a First Nation would build cooperation with the community. For a word used so often, and so offhandedly, community turns out to be a surprisingly elusive concept.

Community always refers loosely to a group of individuals who recognize themselves, or whom others view, as holding something significant in common. This general description is, obviously, not an air-tight, universal definition. To begin with, it remains to be specified what that "something significant" is, or why it is significant. The most helpful way to approach community is to recognize it, not as one single thing, but as a collection of related ideas revolving around unity, connectedness, or sharing within groups of people. Unsurprisingly, listing the "essential elements" of "true communities" tells us little about politics, since how we define "community" depends on the context (Wood and Judikis, 2002, 12, 21). Political claims made about communal ties—about their influences upon political actions, identities, alliances, and values—are far more useful to explore.

Community in the Study of Politics

POLITICAL SCIENTISTS STUDY COMMUNITY BECAUSE IT HAS A STRONG POLITICAL core. Community is sometimes used in ways that are not particularly political, however. An interfaith spiritual community and the physics community that presents a prestigious award are examples. The concept of community, however, is inherently political because of the built-in assumption that people have a natural capacity to act publicly, together, for common purposes. Community does not require that people's political interests and participation always be oriented toward the outlets provided by governments, such as elections and law-making. However, community definitely conjures up the profoundly political notion of collective self-governance, as well as related issues concerning setting goals, distributing privileges and powers, enforcing rules, facing conflict, and reaching agreement within groups of individuals who hold something significant in common. As an element of **civil society**—that is, what is not the state and not the market—community is similar to "voluntary associations, movements, parties, [and] unions." It is a way for "individuals to . . . struggle against or agree with each other and with the centres of political and economic authority" (Kaldor, 2003, 585).

At the level of ideas, political theorists have contemplated community ever since political theory has existed. In Greece in the fourth century B.C.E., Aristotle praised community as the foundation of a healthy polis (political society). The centrality of communal structures (village, monarchy, clan, church) was not seriously challenged until seventeenth-century Enlightenment thinkers began arguing that political communities exist only to secure, in the words of John Locke, individuals' "life, liberty, and property." Even after liberalism became dominant in Britain, France, and America, influential political philosophers, including Jean-Jacques Rousseau, were "rediscovering community" (Sabine and Thorson, 1973, 529) and insisting, as Aristotle did, that people are naturally political animals. In recent decades, this debate of community versus the individual expanded to include feminists, who question the impact of community on minority groups, as well as cosmopolitans, who envision community in global terms.

At the level of practices, political scientists study community because it is a live issue. In Canadian politics, at least four visions of community vie for superiority. One promotes a national community of distinct sub-communities, including francophones, anglophones, Aboriginal peoples, and cultural minorities. Another proposes self-governing communities that exist totally (Quebec) or partly (First Nations) apart from "the Canadian community." The third seeks a dominant community guided by "traditional" anglophone-Christian culture and values. The fourth envisions Canada as a leader among a community of humanitarian, peaceful countries. Worldwide, both nationalist political leaders and fundamentalist religious leaders strive to cultivate communities that are homogeneous, assertive, and closed to outside influences. More commonly, people's conduct in the home, at work and school, over channels of communication, and on the streets is governed by rules that supposedly reflect the "community standards" and "community values" of one or more authoritative communities.

The Bases of Communities

COMMUNITY FUNDAMENTALLY CONCERNS GROUPS OF PEOPLE WHO HAVE SOMETHING in common. To make this concept specific and tangible, we can identify three major commonalities that underlie communities: place, identity, and interest. While these categories overlap, they capture distinct types of communities.

Place-Based Communities

Place-based community is "a general term for a real territorial settlement" (Gusfield, 1975, 32). Here, community refers to geographical, usually local, places with identifiable boundaries, such as city limits. "Community" is often a synonym for "municipality." Traditionally, community is associated with villages and towns, but the concept "has been generalized to the wider scope of urban communities" (Gusfield, 1975, 33). Thus, we see inner-city neighbourhoods, mobile home parks, gated housing developments, and Native reserves called communities.

What people primarily hold in common in these communities is shared space. This may cause shared interests and feelings of closeness that did not previously exist and frequently results from identifiable groups—e.g., gay men, retirees, the rich, Ukrainians—concentrating themselves in a location. This type of community does not necessarily go any deeper than geographic proximity, however, and it may not even exist in the eyes of all community "members." Laws or group rules set out conditions for belonging to place-based communities, such as property ownership (for membership in condominium associations), citizenship (for voting), an address (for attending schools), or dues payment (for using the facilities of community leagues).

Place-based community is especially useful for contrasting localities with larger, more anonymous political jurisdictions. For many people, localities are communities precisely because they are not provinces, countries, or continental trading blocs. In an important sense, this form of community emphasizes the perceived grassroots or democratic character of local places, as opposed to more distant, "higher" levels of government. Local places are seen as communities because they are believed able to facilitate people's awareness of and participation in the decisions that affect their immediate, everyday lives in common. Mexico City, Toronto, and New York, with millions of residents each, are hardly intimate places, but they are often seen as more politically accessible and thus more like communities than Mexico, Canada, or the United States, which are also geographical places. Interestingly, although there is conflicting opinion about the effect of the Internet on local communities, such as neighbourhoods (and on communal tendencies in general), evidence exists that virtual communities actually "facilitate neighborhood based interactions," including helping organize political action on place-based issues (Hampton and Wellman, 2003).

Identity-Based Communities

Groups whose members share at least one identifiable characteristic make up another significant form of community. National origin, language, religion, gender, sexual orientation, skin colour, or physical ability may underlie people's personal and, thus, collective identities, as well as their political interests and claims. This is how we come to hear so much about the francophone (or Somali or deaf or Jewish) community.

Identity-based communities can facilitate groups' self-awareness, appreciation of their culture and history, and organization for political action. Communities whose core is their identity may succeed in gaining official recognition, citizenship rights, inclusion in (or autonomy from) mainstream politics, or even the creation of a nation-state. In recent decades in various countries, indigenous peoples' communities have sought each of these things. On the one hand, in peaceful democracies, the ordinary disagreements and negotiations among identity-based communities whose practices or political claims are at odds may become pressing issues. On the other hand, in Sudan's Darfur region, systematic violence by a powerful identity-based community (along with the government) against a disfavoured identity-based community constitutes what numerous international observers believe to be war crimes.

Interestingly, certain politically potent group characteristics are rarely identified as motivating identity-based communities. Consider how infrequently we hear about the "white community" or "Christian community," as if race, religion, and culture are politically noteworthy only for certain groups. Moreover, identity-based communities may get labelled from the outside, resulting in inaccurate portraits of the group and its members' interests. The "Hispanic community," for example, homogenizes Spanish speakers with roots in various continents, and whose politics are shaped by distinctions in ethnicity, colour, class, gender, and citizenship status.

Even when viewed from within, identity-based communities may turn on constructed identities. Nationalism is a belief that there is a community of people bound by ethnicity—in effect, by blood ties and their manifestation in shared language, religion, culture, or territory. Calls for loyalty to the nation and for national sovereignty have political potency. However, Benedict Anderson (1991) calls nations "imagined communities." In this view, national identity is intangible, uncomplex, and mythical; it is more the product of a political desire for community than actual relationships among people.

Interest-Based Communities

Interest-based communities exist to benefit their members, whether the ultimate benefits are recreational, economic, or political. Belonging to a professional association or an environmental organization, for instance, may entitle you to an array of benefits, such as affinity credit cards and group discounts. Nevertheless, these can reasonably be called political communities because they are bound by a set of interests that bear directly on the members' (selfish or selfless) political goals. Members tend to carry their shared interests into public debate, and the communities try to benefit their members by forming groups or networks to influence elections, policy, and economic practices. Indeed, the popular identification of many interest groups as communities (for example, the gun-owning community and the medical community) is tied to their inserting their common interests (freedom to use firearms and maintenance of public health care) into the political sphere.

The label "community" makes political sense only when applied to groups whose common interests include political goals—politically, goldfish owners are not a community. Interests may become politicized, though, as happened with the well-publicized interest-based communities of divorced fathers or women with breast cancer. These communities began by providing emotional support and information to their members; however, they now make demands on government for, respectively, favourable child custody laws and funding for breast cancer research; on the media for sympathetic coverage; and on individuals and businesses for help with fundraising.

There are objections to calling interest-based groups communities. Increasingly, people with common interests meet and communicate entirely on-line. Whether these "virtual communities" are genuine communities is a matter of intense debate. Though profound and vital for many users, some observers judge on-line interactions, such as those that take place through blogs and social networking sites, as shallow and temporary. A related criticism of interest-based communities such as Amnesty International is that the vast majority of members merely pay annual dues and are not active in the lives of the organizations (Putnam, 2000, 155–160).

The Sentiment of Community and Social Capital

IT IS EASY TO NAME DOZENS OF EXAMPLES OF COMMUNITIES BASED ON CONCRETE commonalities among people; more abstractly, community is also a shared sentiment or feeling. Community as a sentiment "points to the quality or character of human relationships" (Gusfield, 1975, xvi). Just as one could argue that political relationships should be grounded in honesty or courage, some people insist that these relationships should rest upon community. Here, community is a sentiment that endorses shared values, common goals, participation in public life, and ongoing relationships. People bound by sentiment trust and help one another. Communal sentiment is typically attributed to groups of people who end up feeling like a community because they start out by sharing territory, whether local (Downtown Eastside Vancouver) or national (Japan). In either case, community may go beyond describing some shared characteristic to defining a whole way of life.

Political scientists and sociologists increasingly refer to these communal sentiments— and our willingness to act on them—as **social capital**. Like other forms of capital, social capital adds value wherever it is expended. Thus, society and the political system are believed to be enriched if numerous people are community-minded, and impoverished if they do not have these attachments. Among other specific benefits, social capital "allows citizens to resolve collective problems more easily" and "widen[s] our awareness of the many ways in which our fates are linked" (Putnam, 2000, 288).

On a day-to-day basis, volunteer work by community groups and philanthropy by local community foundations convey communal feelings, as does the formation of neighbourhood watches as part of community policing initiatives. Community and restorative justice programs try to instill feelings of attachment and responsibility in people who have committed crimes by sentencing them to make amends to their victims or to the whole community, instead of imposing jail sentences that isolate offenders from the community (Johnstone and Van Ness, 2007). Voting, aiding someone in distress, and even joining a bowling league are deemed significantly communal acts by some commentators (Putnam, 2000).

We also hear about the **international community**, typically in association with the United Nations and other organizations that act on the global stage to solve problems.

Here, the international community is more a group of governments than a sentiment-based community. However, the international or global community can also symbolize shared sentiments of people in different countries, as when it "expresses outrage" at governments that: take unilateral military action, permit the hunting of endangered species, or oppress political opponents. We can imagine a global public that shares moral values and common purposes—justice, health, safety, and peace—and extends empathy toward people around the world. Cosmopolitanism, as discussed below, is a term used to describe the idea of global community values.

Communitarianism

COMMUNITY HAS LONG APPEARED TO SOME PEOPLE AS A SUPERIOR ALTERNATIVE TO pervasive individualism, social and geographic fragmentation, and civic and moral impoverishment. Throughout the twentieth century, community was championed in reaction to capitalism, urbanization, and secularization. In this century, globalized economies and cultures, suburban sprawl, and the transformation of the family are spawning new political demands for revitalizing communal structures.

The call for community may take the form of a set of ideas about politics and society called **communitarianism**. Communitarians are a diverse lot; they include religious conservatives and social democrats as well as philosophers and governmental policy advisers. Some communitarians envision strong relationships within the public sphere of collective self-governance, while others focus on the private sphere (Swift, 2001, 133–136). However, the one defining feature of communitarianism is a belief in the moral claim of "we–identities as against . . . I–identities" (Taylor, quoted in Etzioni, 1996, 26).

The Civic Tradition

Communitarians speak of "the public good" and "the good society," and often develop detailed plans for realizing these goals. This is civic language, or the language of citizenship. In communitarianism, a citizen's moral and political development is rooted in rich communal frameworks, rather than in economic competition or quests for self-discovery. Individual acts and achievements gain meaning when they enhance the goals of the group. Just as athletes generally earn respect when they perform as "team players," and superior teams function well as a unit, the health of society is judged by how well it inspires political and moral commitment on the part of its citizens, or how much social capital it produces. Generally, "the public good is that which benefits society as a whole and leads to . . . public happiness" (Bellah et al., 1985, 335).

This approach to community is largely American in origin. Communitarians, who are preoccupied with identifying and faithfully following a community's "tradition," draw inspiration from the lengthy American tradition of localism existing alongside its evident liberalism. Many other countries claim vital, intact communal traditions, though. After all, how often is Canada ("peace, order, and good government") associated with community and the United States ("life, liberty, and the pursuit of happiness") with individualism? Whether or not this is an accurate picture of either country, there are plenty of Canadians worried about Canada moving away from its communitarian roots and toward an "Americanized" tradition of individual rights and freedoms (Bogart, 1994).

Civic republicans recognize that, everywhere in the world, each society has a "pattern" of values and practices supporting healthy community life. Thus, "communitarian societies do not all exhibit the same combination of order and autonomy," and some expect subgroups to commit only to selected "core values" (Etzioni, 1996, 92–93). Philosopher Charles Taylor (1993) has argued that a type of community-of-communities model is appropriate to Canadian traditions. Within individual sub-communities, whether these are based on language, culture, or another commonality, communal ties are very important. Such a diversity of strong communities is key to the public good of the larger Canadian national community.

Public and Private

Communitarians are more concerned with public, civic relationships than liberals and many other people who think about politics, but the position of the private sphere within communitarianism is important. Depending on the communitarian vision, private sphere settings may receive more attention than the public sphere.

Some communitarians, who are conservative by any North American standard, recommend taming individualism and social change by strengthening private-sector structures and intimate relations—marriage, family, religion, and neighbourhood—perhaps through home schooling or organizations like Promise Keepers, a Christian men's group (Stackhouse, 2000; Talbot, 2000). Public life is important if it upholds these private communal structures. Nevertheless, religious and "pro-family" organizations, and their members, may participate in electoral and legislative politics, by lobbying for policies such as government funding for parent-controlled charter schools and tax deductions for parent-provided child care, or by demanding that governments enforce law, order, and what they deem traditional moral values. This communitarianism is conservative in its conception of community itself because it rarely promotes equality or individual choice within the structures of intimate relationships, notably gender relations. In contrast, communitarians who are most concerned with civic life are generally receptive to openness and equality in families and other private relationships.

Yet another version of communitarianism, however, is directed toward equality in workplaces, unions, cooperatives, fraternities, communes, and other private or semi-private settings (Boyte, 1984; Wilkinson and Quarter, 1996). This is a social democratic view of community. It encourages full, equal participation and discussion in decision making, substitutes equality-producing structures for hierarchical (corporate or bureaucratic) ones, and teaches habits of equal treatment and equal responsibility.

It is also consistent with a type of feminist belief in so-called "feminine" qualities of caring and cooperation, rather than competition for power and status (Gilligan, 1982).

These more private sites link with the fully public, political sphere in that participation in factories or housing cooperatives accustoms people to active, committed citizenship. As a way of governing entire countries, this communitarian framework would still require small-scale decision-making units so that every individual would have an opportunity to make his or her voice heard. Although quite a few communitarians regard the Internet as a force of alienation from communal relations, electronic forums might support the communitarian goal of broader participation in national politics (Etzioni, 1996), as well as in neighbourhoods or interest- and identity-based "virtual communities" (Hampton and Wellman, 2003).

Cosmopolitanism

IN A WORLD WHERE COMMUNITY AND INDIVIDUAL LIBERTY ARE BOTH HIGHLY PRIZED elements of democracy, they will always be in tension. However, liberals increasingly acknowledge that community priorities may actually enhance individual autonomy, if the will of the community is expressed through democratic procedures, and if there are protections for fundamental liberties. For instance, censoring "hard-core pornography . . . harmful to the interests of members of the community" (Gutmann, 1993, 135–136) is acceptable to many liberals. Similarly, communitarians may work at "finding an equilibrium between universal individual rights and the common good . . . between self and community" (Etzioni, 1996, xviii). In practice, this might mean that the community refrains from heavily regulating or severely punishing individual lifestyle choices, unless they clash with core community values or endanger others.

Some liberals and communitarians agree that "people's shared identity of 'free and equal citizen' must . . . trump" other group identities as well as individual self-interest; in other words, both citizenship and personhood demand treating people justly. Still, the basic "importance of people identifying with *their* particular community" (Swift, 2001, 168), for communitarians, does limit the scope of the community to something smaller than the entire world. This limitation is a great concern in **cosmopolitanism**.

Cosmopolitans "think that principles of justice, and conceptions of community, must apply globally" (Swift, 2001, 169). They ask, "why must . . . democracy stop at the borders of a political community?" (Archibugi, 2001, 28). Cosmopolitanism encompasses proposals for global community, world citizenship, and global government. The two senses of "international community" presented earlier are thus highly relevant to cosmopolitanism, although major international organizations like NATO and the International Monetary Fund do not now operate in ways that represent all of the peoples and countries of the world, whether poor or rich, marginal or powerful. It is evident that cosmopolitan ideas and values challenge communitarianism. In particu-lar, cosmopolitanism appears to have a more contemporary understanding of global-ization, which makes it unrealistic and unjust for each community to "pursue its internal happiness in its own way" (Archibugi, 2001, 28).

Difference, Conformity, and Community

WHILE THEY DOMINATE THE FIELD, LIBERALISM AND COMMUNITARIANISM DO NOT encompass the entire debate about community. The demands of commonality that exist within communities may clash with the need to respect the great diversity among groups in society. Feminist and other criticisms of the impact of community on groups appar-ently "different" from the norm present a major challenge to communitarianism.

In nostalgic pictures of small-town life, people trust and identify with each other and can come to a consensus about matters of mutual concern. This scenario relies more on myth than on reality. Communities invariably contain sub-cultures, outliers, and outright dissidents, but conflicting desires and needs go against the idea of the "sameness" of a community. The presence of poor people, disabled people, people of colour, immigrants, gays and lesbians, or strangers can so threaten a community's per-ceived identity that such people may be shunned, threatened, or expelled, especially if they actually voice dissenting opinions. And women "found that if they challenged communal traditions, be they in the Greek polis, Old Quebec, or the New England village, they risked being cast out of the community as traitors, whores, or even witches" (Sypnowich, 1993, 493).

Exclusion can happen in any community. The "feminist community" appeared in the 1960s and 1970s to share a unified set of goals (liberation from the nuclear fam-ily, economic and political equality with men). Unfortunately, this notion of a single community allowed major feminist organizations to ignore or silence working-class women who were already in the labour force, women of colour who faced discrimi-nation from white women as well as from men, and lesbians who wanted access to the same legal and social benefits available to heterosexual women. These differences looked disruptive or irrelevant to a feminist community that wanted to preserve the illusion of common goals.

Communities may also have expectations for civic action that disadvantage some groups. Recall the assumption, built into the sentiment of community, that people are instinctually political, public creatures. Extensive, often face-to-face, interactions within the public sphere are one ideal of communitarianism. However, political prac-tices that are heavily oriented toward public interactions favour the most assertive, ver-bal, and credible members of the group. Sex, class, culture, and other characteristics affect the outcome of group interactions and even the desire to participate.

Summary

This chapter has shown how community is a multi-dimensional political concept. It encompasses communities based in various kinds of commonalities as well as sentiments about the goodness of human relationships, whether among citizens of a country or people around the world. Community supplies a framework for discussing, naming, and evaluating human relationships, including political ones. The term says as much about how we choose to characterize people's commonalities as it does about the commonalities themselves. It also indicates a lot about how we imagine that various kinds of people interact. Religious cults and street gangs are therefore rarely publicly referred to as communities, even if they are "a collective identity that provides a sense of security" against the outside world (Friesen, 2007). On the other hand, we persist in calling community places where neighbours detest neighbours because of who they are or what opinions they hold.

But community is also an important political strategy. Strategically, people use community to build support for their preferred solutions to political and social problems. The success of community as a political strategy depends on placing community in a flattering light. This can be done by contrasting it with things that are clearly bad, such as social chaos, or using it so vaguely as to discourage scrutiny. In the typical North American city, far more people would rally to support a new stadium for "our community's football team" than for "the billionaire media mogul's team," even if it is the same team. Politicians routinely profess sincere commitment to strengthening communities and similar no-lose ideas; if they have such credentials, they stress their experiences as community organizers and their ties to various communities (Clinton, 2003; Obama 2006).

Still, we should not conclude that community is a "glittering and nearly empty term" (Fowler, 1991, 150). A better assessment is that the term provides a relatively familiar and easy route into politics for a wide range of citizens, including people who are not politically experienced or powerful. What community politics means in people's minds may begin with a public debate among city council candidates, but it does not end there. Community also applies to residents of a Native reserve protesting against a hazardous waste facility that pollutes their air, a coalition of mothers from both sides of a divided nation searching for solutions to civil war, parents organizing to take control of their troubled neighbourhood school, immigrant women starting a self-help program to combat domestic violence, or a virtual dialogue about genetically modified crops among farmers in different countries.

For university students, participation in elections, protests, lobbying, and other forms of politics often follows naturally from ties to place-, identity-, or interest-based communities. But universities can provide additional ways for students to make a connection between community and politics through opportunities to integrate "community volunteer activities with their academic course work." On one level, "community service learning" allows students to contribute to communities locally or internationally; more broadly, it helps "to create more active and well-rounded citizens" (Charbonneau, 2004, 12) because students must think and write about the meaning of their activities. For anyone, the likelihood that community service will "alter attitudes and perceptions about community" depends on whether the motivation for such service is "choice," "incentive," "coercion," or "obligation" (Volunteer Canada, 2006, iii).

Clearly, community persuades people to act on shared interests and values in many diverse ways. Community's versatility comes from the fact that it is a flexible concept and strategy, not a rigid thing. Perhaps, then, the most interesting questions about communities revolve around whether and why they exist in the eye of the beholder, and for what purposes.

Discussion Questions

1. What are some differences between communities that people are born into and communities that people choose to enter?
2. What are the points of convergence and divergence between communitarianism and cosmopolitanism?
3. How is community used as a political strategy by politicians, the media, and citizens?

References

Anderson, Benedict. 1991. *Imagined Communities: Reflections on the Origin and Spread of Nationalism.* London: Verso.

Archibugi, Daniele. 2002. "Demos and Cosmopolis." *New Left Review,* 12 (January–February), 24–38.

Bellah, Robert N., Richard Madsen, William M. Sullivan, Ann Swidler, and Steven M. Tipton. 1985. *Habits of the Heart: Individualism and Commitment in American Life.* Berkeley: University of California Press.

Bogart, William. 1994. *Courts and Country.* Toronto: Oxford University Press.

Boyte, Harry C. 1984. *Community Is Possible: Repairing America's Roots.* New York: Harper and Row.

Charbonneau, Léo. 2004. "Educating Citizen Jane." *University Affairs,* 45 (February), 12–16.

Clinton, Hillary Rodham. 2003. *Living History.* New York: Simon and Schuster.

Etzioni, Amitai, 1996. *The New Golden Rule: Community and Morality in a Democratic Society.* New York: Basic Books.

Fowler, Robert B. 1991. *The Dance with Community: The Contemporary Debate in American Political Thought.* Lawrence: University Press of Kansas.

Friesen, Joe. 2007. "Where boundaries issues turn deadly." *The Globe and Mail,* June 16, A16–17.

Gilligan, Carol. 1982. *In a Different Voice: Psychological Theory and Women's Development.* Cambridge, MA: Harvard University Press.

Glover, Troy, Kimberly Shinew, and Diana Parry. 2005. "Association, sociability, and civic culture: The democratic effect of community gardening." *Leisure Sciences,* 27 (January–February), 75–92.

Gusfield, Joseph R. 1975. *Community: A Critical Response.* New York: Harper Colophon Books.

Gutmann, Amy. 1993. "The Disharmony of Democracy" in John W. Chapman and Ian Shapiro, eds., *Democratic Community: Nomos XXXV.* New York: New York University Press, 126–160.

Hampton, Keith and Barry Wellman. 2003. "Neighboring in Netville: How the Internet Supports Community and Social Capital in a Wired Suburb." *City and Community,* 2 (December), 277–311.

Johnstone, Gerry and Daniel W. Van Ness, eds. 2007. *A Handbook of Restorative Justice.* Portland, OR: Willan Publishing.

Kaldor, Mary. 2003. "The Idea of Global Civil Society." *International Affairs,* 79 (3), 583–593.

Kerry, Senator John. 2003. "Reviving the Ideal of Citizenship." *The Responsive Community*, 13 (Summer), 42–49.

Obama, Barack. 2006. *The Audacity of Hope: Thoughts on Reclaiming the American Dream.* New York: Crown Publishers.

Putnam, Robert. 2000. *Bowling Alone: The Collapse and Revival of American Community.* New York: Simon and Schuster.

Sabine, George H. and Thomas L. Thorson. 1973. *A History of Political Theory*, 4th edition. Hinsdale, IL: Dryden Press.

Stackhouse, John. 2000. "The New Suburbia." *The Globe and Mail*, October 28, A11+.

Swift, Adam. 2001. *Political Philosophy: A Beginner's Guide for Students and Politicians.* Cambridge: Polity.

Sypnowich, Christine. 1993. "Justice, Community, and the Antinomies of Feminist Theory." *Political Theory*, 21, 484–506.

Talbot, Margaret. 2000. "A Mighty Fortress." *The New York Times Magazine*, February 27, 34–41.

Taylor, Charles. 1993. *Reconciling the Solitudes: Essays on Canadian Federalism and Nationalism.* Montreal and Kingston: McGill-Queen's University Press.

Volunteer Canada. 2006. *Volunteering and Mandatory Community Service: Choice – Incentive – Coercion – Obligation.* **www.volunteer.ca/volunteer/pdf/MCSDP_ENG.pdf**

Wilkinson, Paul and Jack Quarter. 1996. *Building a Community-Controlled Economy: The Evangeline Co-operative Experience.* Toronto: University of Toronto Press.

Wood, George S., Jr. and Juan C. Judikis. 2002. *Conversations on Community Theory.* West Lafayette, IN: Purdue University Press.

Further Reading

Calhoun, Craig. 2007. *Community (Key Concepts).* Malden, MA: Polity Press.

Jennings, James, ed. 2007. *Race, Neighborhoods, and the Misuse of Social Capital.* New York: Palgrave McMillan.

Low, Setha. 2003. *Behind the Gates: Life, Security, and the Pursuit of Happiness in Fortress America.* New York: Routledge.

Rheingold, Howard. 2000. *The Virtual Community: Homesteading on the Electronic Frontier.* Cambridge: MIT Press.

Weblinks

The Communitarian Network
www.gwu.edu/~ccps

Global Community Initiatives
www.global-community.org

Electric Minds
www.electricminds.org

CHAPTER 14

GENDER AND POLITICS

Biology determines a person's sex, but social, cultural, political, and economic forces shape what being male or female means in everyday life. **Gender**—the social construction of masculinity and femininity—reflects power relations and is a key feature of many political struggles. Although the feminist movement has challenged some of the most rigid sex stereotypes, socially accepted gender roles still reflect the division between public life (the realm of politics and markets, dominated by men) and private life (the familial, domestic realm, dominated by women). Gendered understandings and behaviours continue to shape the life choices of women and constrain their political involvement and impact. This chapter explains why gender is political and shows how the politics of gender factor into contemporary political realities for women.

LINDA
TRIMBLE

Introduction

He was recruited; she was romanced. His was a smart move, simply business; hers was a cheap trick, utterly unprincipled. He was a high flyer, experienced, a good catch; she was a neophyte, an attractive dipstick, a harlot willing to whore herself for power. He advanced his career; she was bought. He left his party in an effort to help the government deal with tough issues; she betrayed her party (and her boyfriend) to advance her blond ambition. He is David Emerson; she is Belinda Stronach. Stronach crossed the floor of the House of Commons in 2005, joining the Paul Martin Liberals just in time to save the government from defeat on a crucial budget vote and winning a Cabinet post in the bargain. Emerson defected from the Liberals to the Conservatives days after the 2006 federal election so he could accept Prime Minister Stephen Harper's offer of a seat in Cabinet. These very similar political manoeuvres were described very differently by pundits and the press, as indicated by the words and phases cited above, which were drawn from news stories about the defections in *The Globe and Mail*, the *National Post*, and the *Toronto Star*. Both politicians were criticized for unethical behaviour, but Emerson's decision was normalized (it was "business as usual," part of the "cut and thrust of partisan politics") while Stronach's was marked as aberrant (it was consistently described as a cruel betrayal of her party and her lover). The newspaper coverage placed Emerson firmly in the public realm of business and politics, while it privatized Stronach by making reference to her looks and sexuality and, perhaps more important, by expressing both surprise and indignation that a woman would choose political power over love. The subtext is, of course, that such behaviour is unwomanly and, thus, unseemly.

Most students in university-level political science courses would contest the notion that men are "better" at politics than women or that, because of their domestic responsibilities (or inclinations), women are less capable of assuming the top political jobs. Yet this traditional understanding of gender roles has remarkable traction around the world, despite the efforts of the women's movement to disrupt the assumption that political leadership is best exercised by men. In a few Gulf Arab states, women are denied the right to vote and sit in Parliament. Even in nations where women have long been accepted as participants in political life, their assumed "natural" role as child-bearers is seen to pose a barrier to political power. The leader of the French Socialist Party, Ségolène Royal, who at the time stood a good chance of becoming France's first woman president, was asked by a rival who would look after her four children if she went for the presidency. No one queried Stephen Harper, Canada's prime minister and father of two young children, about his plans for child care while he contested the Conservative Party leadership and ran for election. Julia Gillard, a high-profile Labor politician in Australia, recently caused quite a stir when she observed that women with children find it hard to rise to the top in politics. While Barack Obama's quest in the United States for the Democratic Party's presidential nomination and, if successful, the presidency itself, is buttressed by his image as a young parent, few of the world's powerful female politicians have children, and fewer still entered politics when their children were pre-teens. Indeed, female government leaders remain a rarity, with New Zealand's prime minister, Helen Clark, one of only a handful of woman heads of state around the world.

These examples highlight the distinction between public and private roles and show that, even though women are not formally excluded from political institutions, they are not yet fully included. Political party elites, legislatures, and political leadership remain male territory, as men continue to dominate many aspects of political life. In most countries women are as politically active as men in community politics, interest group and social movement activism, electoral activities, and everyday acts of political rebellion, activities that are sometimes termed **mass politics**. In all but a few nations women remain significantly under-represented, however, in formal arenas of political power such as legislatures, city councils, the leadership ranks of bureaucracy, and the courts (Vickers, 1997, 66–69). The more difficult question is why men's control of political institutions, ideas, and decisions is still considered the natural order of things. The next section explains how male dominance of political life emerged as normal or commonplace. But why is this understanding important? Why should we care that more men than women hold positions of political power?

Political decisions shape understandings about gender with significant consequences for everyone. Those who hold political power decide whether or not birth control, abortion, and new reproductive technologies are legal and available to women. Policies can shake up the traditional division of labour in the household by providing paid parental leave for fathers. Politicians can allow men who sexually assault women to claim an "honest though mistaken belief" that the victim consented to sexual activity, or they can make laws ensuring that "no" really does mean "no." Political actors can provide economic supports, child care, and job training for mothers on social assistance, or they can force single moms into workfare programs. Employment opportunities for female immigrants can be enhanced or constricted on the basis of access to government-funded language training programs. Women (and men) with disabilities can enjoy more, or less, mobility and autonomy, depending on policy-makers' decisions about funding accessible public spaces and government services. Governments can fund universal, community-based child care programs that facilitate women's labour force participation, or they can offer women $100 per month under the guise of giving families "choices." The list is endless. Political decision-makers can challenge or uphold patriarchal structures, with very real effects on the everyday lives of men and women.

Gender, Patriarchy, and the Public–Private Divide

PATRIARCHY MEANS RULE BY MEN. IN PATRIARCHAL SOCIETIES, MEN HAVE MORE power than women and enjoy greater access to what is valued by the social group (Code, 1993, 19). Patriarchy conveys the core notion of systemic gender inequality, whether in the household or in the broader domains of economic and public life (Walby, 1996, 24).

Patriarchal thought prescribes power and authority to men, both as fathers in the household and as members of the legal profession, the business community, organized religion, and, of course, the political arena. Patriarchy has been constructed and maintained through political practices and public policy. Governments, from archaic state forms to complex modern regimes, have passed laws designed to uphold the patriarchal family and keep women in their assigned place within the household, performing domestic duties appropriate to chaste daughters or monogamous wives and mothers. For instance, Mesopotamian city states in the second and third millennium B.C.E. decreed that women, slaves, and children were legally the property of men, and they passed laws that allowed men to commit infanticide, pledge their children in marriage, and sell their wives, concubines, and children into slavery (Lerner, 1986, 88–91). In some feudal societies, political authorities upheld the so-called "rule of thumb," which decreed that a man could beat his wife, as long as he used a stick no thicker than his thumb. Control of women is a key feature of patriarchal power relations, so laws have regulated and restricted women's sexual and public behaviour. Legal strictures and cultural practices such as menstruation taboos, enforced marriage, genital mutilation, and penalties of death for errant wives ensured male domination of the female body (Miles, 1989, 103–123).

Patriarchal power relations construct sexual difference as political difference by giving legal form to the belief that women, because of their sex, are fit only to serve as wives and mothers in the domestic sphere, where they can be ruled by men. These presumptions are usually based on biological determinism and the public–private dichotomy. Biological determinism is "the belief that a woman's nature and all of her possibilities are determined by her biology" (Code, 1993, 22–23). This perspective sees women as bodies governed by hormones and reproductive destiny, not as bearers of minds with the capacity for intelligence, rationality, and free will. Biological determinism holds that biology is destiny—that, since women are "naturally" subservient and inferior to men, it is also natural for women to be ruled by men.

Social, economic, and political forces have structured these assumptions into a foundation for mutually exclusive gender roles, called the public–private dichotomy. Characteristics, roles, and standards are separated into two distinct spheres: the private sphere of family and domestic life, and the public world of business, government, culture, sports, and organized religion. Women are regarded as emotional, family-focused, irrational, dependent, other-regarding, and nurturing, and therefore "naturally" suited for private sphere roles. Men, on the other hand, are believed to be rational, independent, competitive, self-regarding, civic-minded individuals with the right stuff for engagement with public sphere activities and duties. The division between public and private remains the foundation for gender codes: different roles, characteristics, resources, norms, and expectations based on the meanings ascribed to sex differences.

Patriarchal assumptions form the foundation for laws and policies that oppress women. Oppression is "a system of interrelated barriers and forces which reduce, immobilize and mould people who belong to a certain group, and effect their subordination to another group" (Frye, 1983, 33). Post-Confederation Canadian law provides a good example of political efforts both to render women subordinate to men and to cast non-white women as subordinate to white women. Canada's earliest electoral legislation, for example, explicitly excluded women, children, and so-called "mental incompetents" from voting. The very notion of equality for women (and other marginalized groups, including the poor, Aboriginals, blacks, Indo-Canadians, and Asian-Canadians) was ridiculed as a dangerous and outlandish idea in Canada's early years. The vote was almost exclusively limited to white male property owners.

Patriarchal assumptions guided the law, denying women economic liberty in Western industrialized countries until at least the 1920s in most respects. Men were the legal heads of households, which gave them the exclusive right to control family finances (including their wives' wages), to own and sell property, to sign contracts, and to exercise guardianship rights over children (Burt, 1993, 213–214). Entry into prestigious professions, particularly medicine and law, was the exclusive privilege of men. Women who left, or were abandoned by, their husbands were not legally entitled to make any financial demands on their estranged spouses and were often left destitute as a result. Women did not have reproductive autonomy, either. In Canada, criminal laws banned the sale, advertisement, or distribution of birth control information, procedures, and devices until 1969. In short, laws and policies upheld women's economic dependence on the male head of the household and their physical confinement to the domestic sphere.

Women have never been passive victims of patriarchal ideas and structures; indeed, they have been creative in claiming their fundamental rights as citizens. Politics has provided a key arena for women's citizenship claims because citizenship is at one and the same time a status (a set of rights) and a practice (involvement in civil and political life, including informal and formal politics) (Lister, 1997, 196). In other words, women practised citizenship before they were accorded citizenship rights, thereby challenging patriarchal thinking, the public–private divide, and oppressive laws and practices. For example, women's suffrage movements were interpreted as a grave threat to the sexual order. In Australia, opponents of women's voting rights argued that, if granted political equality in law, women would neglect their duties as wives, mothers, and homemakers; moreover, they accused suffragists of promoting polyandry and free love (Sawer and Simms, 1984, 2). In contrast to these patriarchal views, feminist thought provided the foundation for women's political activism, inspiring an enduring and increasingly international social movement.

Feminism

FEMINIST POLITICAL ACTION IS ABOUT THE PURSUIT OF WOMEN'S LIBERTY, justice, equality, and solidarity. **Feminism** seeks to change the gender order so that women can enjoy autonomy and gain acceptance as socially valued members of the community. Yet feminism truly defies a compact definition. The feminist literature is diverse, complex, full of internal debates, and constantly evolving through self-criticism and introspection. There is no feminist orthodoxy. Feminism, however, must mean something; otherwise, how can we identify a feminist approach to understanding political life?

Feminism is woman-centred. This does not mean that only women can be feminists, or that feminists are concerned only with women. It means that feminism presents ways of understanding women's experiences and offers strategies for demanding changes that will improve the everyday lives of women. Feminists ask why patriarchy exists, how gender codes have been socially and politically constructed so that women are seen as subordinate to men, and what types of institutions and ideas maintain women's oppression. Feminist theories offer diverse interpretations of the nature and origins of gender-based oppression. Feminist theories also offer different ideas about how to challenge and change the discrimination and dependence women confront because of their sex, and often also because of their ethnicity, sexual orientation, class, and physical or mental ability.

Feminism is shaped by culture and thus differs from place to place. In North America, certain variants of feminism have been very active and have shaped women's social, cultural, and political movements. Radical, liberal, and socialist feminism are arguably the dominant threads, though post-modern feminism has made many important contributions to contemporary feminist thought and political practice. To briefly summarize these theoretical approaches is to grossly oversimplify complex and varied bodies of thought. Students seeking a more thorough account of feminist theories are encouraged to read further (see Tong, 1998).

Liberal Feminism

Liberal feminism is the variant of feminist thought most familiar to North Americans, who are accustomed to claims for equal rights. Liberal feminists argue that inequality for women is the result of different treatment. Patriarchal assumptions, rooted in biological determinism and manifested in the public–private dichotomy, created a set of political, legal, and economic structures that denied women a place beyond the household. As discussed above, women lacked basic citizenship rights, among them equal access to education, politics, property, and employment. Liberal feminists argue that when women are denied the right to become free, self-actualizing individuals, not surprisingly, they act like second-class citizens and form dependency relationships with men. Socialized and educated to be men's helpmates, women are unable to claim autonomy. The solution for liberal feminists is equal rights for women, accompanied by social cues and educational messages of liberty and equality. Women's subordination will end when discriminatory practices—such as denying women business loans, refusing to hire women on the grounds that they will take time off for child care, and creating barriers to women's participation in certain professions—are eradicated. Women, then, should have the same opportunities, rights, and liberties as men. Liberal feminists would point to women's continued under-representation in the top ranks of business and government as evidence that women do not enjoy equal opportunities.

Radical Feminism

Radical feminists point out that even though women have won equal rights and have entered the workforce, they continue to grapple with oppression. **Radical feminism** exposes the roots of the "sex/gender system," the set of rules, assumptions, institutions, and understandings that uphold women's subordination to men. Biological determinism, or the "biology is destiny" perspective, leads to narrowly constituted gender roles for women (as wives, caregivers, and mothers). At the same time, women's traditional roles are undervalued and even ridiculed. Consider the oft-used phrase, "I'm just a housewife." Radical feminists show how patriarchal thinking is manifested in everyday practices such as the traditional heterosexual family and expectations about gender roles. Radical feminists focus on the ways in which legal, social, and political control of women's bodies leads to sexual exploitation, promotes economic dependency on men, and denies women a political voice. Women's lack of reproductive autonomy and fear of sexual assault on the job, in the home, and in the streets maintain their subordination.

Early Canadian policies illustrate what radical feminists are talking about. Women did not have the right to control their bodies, and laws ensured their physical, emotional, and economic dependence on their fathers or husbands. For instance, until 1983, the law guaranteed a woman's consent to sexual activity with her husband. If she denied sex to her husband, legally he was entitled to force himself upon her, however violently, without recourse. In sum, radical feminists identify a key source of women's oppression as male control of women's bodies. Contemporary debates about reproductive rights and freedoms highlight the relationship between the female body and women's claim to full citizenship.

Socialist Feminism

Liberal feminists reveal legal, social, and political practices that prevent women from making free choices and competing on a level playing field with men, and radical feminists show how sexual domination oppresses women in public and private spaces. Socialist feminists emphasize economic sources of oppression, arguing that capitalism and state patriarchy intersect to reinforce women's social marginalization and economic dependency. According to **socialist feminism**, women have been consigned to unpaid household duties because capitalism benefits from a sexual division of labour wherein women serve a nurturing and reproductive function. Increasingly, women are entering the workforce to take up underpaid casual or part-time jobs, acting as a cheap, exploitable, and disposable "reserve army of labour" for the private economic sector. Governments uphold patriarchy and capitalist gender exploitation by reinforcing women's dependence on men and on low-income work. For example, workfare programs coerce single mothers into insecure, minimum-wage jobs, and "spouse in the house" rules cut women off social assistance when they form relationships with men. The Canadian Conservative government's child care initiative of

2007, which offers families $100 per month per child under the age of six, reinforces two key points of socialist feminists. By paying parents (typically mothers) for their work in the home, this policy fortifies the traditional sexual division of labour in the household. By paying them so little, the policy illustrates the continued undervaluing of domestic work.

Liberal, radical, and socialist feminists alike point to the role of the state in maintaining women's dependency. All point out that governments have done little to promote women's autonomy. Socialist feminists contribute another layer to the analysis by revealing how the state often acts in the interests of capital, which relies on the unpaid or underpaid work of women.

Post-modern Feminism

Post-modern variants of feminism are sometimes misunderstood, since they are based on theoretical premises that challenge the foundations of modern epistemology (ways of knowing). Post-modernism challenges the very existence of universal truths or common understandings about such core concepts as justice, equality, citizenship, and democracy. Post-modern thinkers believe that such "meta-narratives" are part of a symbolic order that is socially constructed through discourses (ideas, words, text, and images). As a result, reality is not set but is continually being formed, challenged, deconstructed, and reformulated. In other words, there cannot be a single unassailable version of any event or communication. **Post-modern feminism** applies this thinking to social constructs like "gender" and "woman," arguing that there can be no universal, comprehensive understanding of these concepts. For instance, women's diversity challenges the very concept of "woman," as different women have different contexts, realities, and conceptions of their own identities. This idea—that there is no single, unifying woman's reality—has become very important within the contemporary women's movement, as early feminist thought and practice tended to ignore women's multiple, overlapping realities and oppressions and to speak from the standpoint of the white, middle-class, able-bodied heterosexual woman. A quest for the unifying policy goals of the "universal woman" did not encompass the experiences, social positions, or political claims of many women who faced oppression on the basis of their sex and their ethnicity, sexual orientation, mental or physical ability, or class position. The willingness of post-modern feminists to fracture the category "woman" was reflected in a difficult, but necessary, struggle within women's groups to recognize women's diversity and confront women's oppression by other women.

Another contribution of post-modern feminism is attention to language and discourse. Post-modern feminists argue that language, not laws, represents the main instrument of patriarchy because discourse constructs a masculine symbolic order. In other words, dominant discourses underpin political decisions about laws and policies. Feminists are paying increased attention to the symbolic gender order evidenced in mass media and popular culture. In her film *Killing Us Softly III*, Jean Kilbourne (2000) deconstructs advertising, arguing that product ads construct "a mass media fantasy world populated by carefully crafted and highly restricted models of femininity." Advertising, she shows, sells values, images, and concepts of normalcy, thus writing a cultural script for "who we are and who we should be." For instance, a widely broadcast television advertisement for Wal-Mart depicted a family in crisis—kids dirty, unfed, and unhappy—because Mom was out shopping, leaving Dad in charge. In addition to shoring up the public–private divide, ads suggest women's worth is determined by how they look, and women's bodies are routinely scrutinized, criticized, objectified, and even dismembered by advertisements.

Gender and Political Representation

GENDER POLITICS IN CONTEMPORARY SOCIETIES REFLECTS BOTH THE impact of feminism and the persistence of patriarchy. In most nations women were denied the right to vote and stand for political office until the late nineteenth or early twentieth century. In Canada, white women who were British subjects were granted the federal franchise in 1918, but Aboriginal, Asian, and East Asian Canadians had to wait significantly longer to exercise this basic political right. That women were seen as biologically destined for the domestic household, not the Houses of Parliament, is illustrated by the fact that a mere 18 women entered Canada's Parliament between 1921 and 1970. In Canada, Australia, and the United States, early female legislators commonly inherited the seats of their deceased husbands, indicating that women found acceptance not as politicians in their own right but as political substitutes, the grieving "wives of" politicians. Politics was a man's game, so the women brave enough to enter the fray without being marked as male appendages were regarded as anomalous, even deviant. New Zealand MP Mary Batchelor recalled the following: "At cocktail parties I was often asked: 'Whose wife or secretary are you?'" (Waring, 1996, 6). "Are you a woman or a politician?" reporters asked Canadian MPs Flora MacDonald and Judy LaMarsh as late as the 1970s (Robinson and Saint-Jean, 1991, 136).

Despite being formally excluded from participation in political life because of their sex, women's activism over decades secured political rights, and in most nations women now participate at all levels of public life. But it was not until the contemporary women's movement gained force in the 1970s and 1980s that women's political representation increased beyond token levels. Canada's 1988 federal election brought 39 women into the House of Commons, a record 13 percent. In the United States, 1992 was hallmarked as the "year of the woman" when 24 female newcomers won office at the Congressional and Senate level. It was not until 2007, however, that a woman, Nancy Pelosi, was selected to be the Speaker of the House, the most powerful position in the U.S. Congress. The entry of 120 women MPs into the British House of Commons in 1997 represented a high-water mark for women in Westminster, with women holding 18 percent of the seats. Yet these successes do not come close to the growing numbers of women in other legislative bodies, especially in the Nordic countries, where gender parity—representation proportionate to presence in the population, with a goal of roughly 50 percent representation for women—now seems possible. When there are opportunities to build new political institutions on a constitutionally enshrined principle of equality, as in Scotland and Wales, women's electoral representation can flourish (see Mackay, 2006; Chaney, 2006).

On the other hand, progress for women is neither quick nor inevitable. In 2002, Unifem, the United Nations Development Fund for Women, reported that a scant 14 percent of the members of Parliaments worldwide in 2002 were women. By 2007 women's representation in national legislatures had risen slightly to 17 percent (see **www.ipu.org/wmn-e/world.htm**). According to Unifem, only 11 nations reached a target of at least 30 percent representation for women in their national Parliaments by the end of 2002, the target set at the 1995 Beijing World Conference on Women. By January 2007, only 19 nations had met this target. Canada, the U.S., and the U.K. were not among them and had made little progress since 2002. Canadian women's share of elected positions has increased slowly since the mid-1980s, and presently women constitute just over 20 percent of the legislators in national, provincial, and territorial legislatures. Canada is above the worldwide average for representing women in the national Parliament but has slipped considerably in the rankings over the past few years, from 36th to 47th in the world, because there has been no change in the number of women elected to the House of Commons since 1997.

Why does it matter that women continue to be markedly under-represented in the world's Parliaments? Some say it is a measure of fairness and equality. When women cannot be counted among the ranks of the politically powerful, it is assumed that their needs, interests, and goals do not matter. Moreover, to regard the under-representation of women in electoral politics as normal or acceptable is to assume that women have little of value to contribute. When a group is systematically excluded from, or under-represented in, democratic institutions of governance, those institutions lack legitimacy. "The seed of democracy lies in the principle that the legitimacy of the power to make decisions about people's lives, their society and their country" is based on representation of all those who are affected by the decisions (Ginwala, 1998, 1). Women's under-representation in political life reflects an enduring democratic deficit and a gendered leadership gap (Trimble and Arscott, 2003, 3). Notwithstanding certain exceptional cases, such as Britain's Margaret Thatcher, "women have been largely absent from images of political leaders as well as from the set of practices involved with leadership and governance" (Duerst-Lahti and Verstegen, 1995, 214). Perhaps this explains the persistence of the perception that politics and femininity are mutually exclusive. Former Canadian prime minister Kim Campbell maintains that "the qualities people ascribe to a leader overlap almost completely with the qualities they ascribe to men" (Powell, 2003). Despite her three-term electoral success, New Zealand's prime minister, Helen Clark, has endured criticisms of her appearance, speculations about her sexual orientation, and epithets such as "Dragon Lady" and "Darth Vader in drag" (McGregor, 1996).

Most important, the presence of women in democratic political institutions can affect women's everyday lives. As feminist scholars point out, when women are not equal partners in the political decision-making process, their experiences and concerns are not given equal, or even a modicum of, attention. When political institutions are shaped by unequal gender relations, the resulting policy decisions often fail to adequately address or even recognize women's needs. Studies conducted in a variety of Western industrialized nations show that women politicians see the representation of women's interests as an important part of their representative role, and they tend to bring woman-centred priorities and ideas into the legislative arena and onto the policy agenda (Swers, 2001). Evidence suggests that women who are included in the institutions and practices of political decision making do make a difference to political discourse and policy outcomes (Trimble and Arscott, 2003, 138–146). When legislative institutions are reconfigured to take equality claims seriously, and women are elected in numbers nearing parity, the substantive representation of women's interests, by female and male legislators alike, is enhanced (see Mackay, 2006; Chaney 2006).

Summary

This chapter has argued that gender matters to politics because patriarchal assumptions and the public–private divide continue to shape social, political, and economic institutions and practices. Women have entered the public world of business and government but are not yet as visible or powerful as men. A thorough investigation of the United Nations system of national accounts by former New Zealand MP Marilyn Waring (1988) revealed that women were not counted because they were regarded as "counting for nothing" when tallying a nation's economic productivity. It is only very recently that Statistics Canada decided to account for women's unpaid work in the home and community. Similarly, numerous studies have illustrated the "symbolic annihilation" of women by the mass media (Tuchman, 1978). Media treatment of women has been marked by omission, trivialization, and condemnation. Australian MP Carmen Lawrence recalls that when she became premier of the state of Western Australia, "the Sunday newspaper invited local fashion consultants to do a 'make-over' of my hair style, glasses, clothing . . . more attention was paid to my family circumstances than my professional qualifications" (Lawrence, 2002). Little had changed by 2004 when press coverage of Belinda Stronach's bid for the leadership of the Conservative Party of Canada was marked by attention to her looks and skepticism about her credentials. Women are now starting to be counted among the powerful, but their scarcity in the top jobs— as company presidents, prime ministers, and parliamentarians alike—illustrates the continued impact of gendered assumptions and sex-specific barriers.

Discussion Questions

1. Describe some contemporary gender codes evident in daily life or in popular culture. How do examples such as the ways in which people dress or act, or their depictions in music videos, sitcoms, or movies, illustrate the social construction of gender?

2. Different approaches to feminism inspire different political analyses. Apply liberal, socialist, radical, and post-modern feminist approaches to a contemporary political issue, such as pornography, marriage, or child care.

3. Why is an analysis of gender politics a key to understanding women's political representation?

4. Discuss different solutions that could be proposed to address women's under-representation in political office, depending on whether the under-representation is a result of a lack of demand (political parties prefer to recruit men) or a lack of supply (women choose not to run for office).

References

Burt, Sandra. 1993. "The Changing Patterns of Public Policy" in Sandra Burt, Lorraine Code, and Lindsay Dorney, eds., *Changing Patterns: Women in Canada.* Toronto: McClelland & Stewart, 212–242.

Chaney, Paul. 2006. "Women and Constitutional Reform: Gender Parity in the National Assembly for Wales" in Marian Sawer, Manon Tremblay, and Linda Trimble, eds., *Representing Women in Parliament: A Comparative Study.* London and New York: Routledge, 188–203.

Code, Lorraine. 1993. "Feminist Theory" in Sandra Burt, Lorraine Code, and Lindsay Dorney eds., *Changing Patterns: Women in Canada.* Toronto: McClelland & Stewart, 19–58.

Duerst-Lahti, Georgia and Dayna Verstegen. 1995. "Making Something of Absence: The 'Year of the Woman' and Women's Representation" in Georgia Duerst-Lahti and Rita Mae Kelly, eds., *Gender Power, Leadership and Governance.* Ann Arbor: University of Michigan Press, 213–238.

Frye, Marilyn. 1983. *The Politics of Reality: Essays in Feminist Theory.* Freedom, CA: The Crossing Press.

Ginwala, Frene. 1998. "Foreword" in Azza Karam, ed., *Women in Parliament: Beyond Numbers.* Stockholm: International IDEA, 1–4.

Kilbourne, Jean. 2000. *Still Killing Us Softly III.* (Video available from Media Education Foundation; see **www.mediaed.org/videos**.)

Lawrence, Carmen. 2002. Women Politicians and the Media. Retrieved March 12, 2003, from **www.carmenlawrence.com/says/papers/wompol.htm**.

Lerner, Gerda. 1986. *The Creation of Patriarchy.* New York and Oxford: Oxford University Press.

Lister, Ruth. 1997. *Citizenship: Feminist Perspectives*. New York: New York University Press.

Mackay, Fiona. 2006. "Descriptive and Substantive Representation of Women in New Parliamentary Spaces: The Case of Scotland" in Marian Sawer, Manon Tremblay, and Linda Trimble, eds., *Representing Women in Parliament: A Comparative Study*. London and New York: Routledge, 171–187.

McGregor, Judy. 1996. "Gender Politics and the News: The Search for a Beehive Bimbo-Boadicea" in Judy McGregor, ed., *News Media Politics in New Zealand*. Palmerston North, New Zealand: Dunmore Press, 181–196.

Miles, Rosalind. 1989. *The Women's History of the World*. London: Paladin.

Powell, Alvin. 2003. "Former Canadian Leader Campbell Addresses Gender Bias." Retrieved August 15, 2003, from *Harvard University Gazette*, **www.news.harvard .edu/gazette/2003/02.27/03-campbell.html**.

Robinson, Gertrude J. and Armande Saint-Jean. 1991. "Women Politicians and Their Media Coverage: A Generational Analysis" in Kathy Megyery, ed., *Women in Canadian Politics: Toward Equity in Representation*. Toronto: Dundurn Press, 127–169.

Sawer, Marian and Marian Simms. 1984. *A Woman's Place: Women and Politics in Australia*. Sydney: George Allen & Unwin.

Swers, Michele. 2001. "Research on Women in Legislatures: What Have We Learned, Where Are We Going?" *Women & Politics*, 23:1/2, 167–185.

Tong, Rosemarie Putnam. 1998. *Feminist Thought: A More Comprehensive Introduction*, 2nd edition. Boulder: Westview Press.

Trimble, Linda and Jane Arscott. 2003. *Still Counting: Women in Politics Across Canada*. Peterborough: Broadview Press.

Tuchman, Gaye. 1978. "The Symbolic Annihilation of Women by the Mass Media" in G. Tuchman, A.K. Daniels, and J. Benet, eds., *Hearth and Home: Images of Women in the Mass Media*. New York: Oxford University Press, 3–38.

Vickers, Jill McCalla. 1997. *Reinventing Political Science: A Feminist Approach*. Halifax: Fernwood.

Walby, Sylvia. 1996. "The 'Declining Significance' of the 'Changing Forms' of Patriarchy" in Valentine Moghadam, ed., *Patriarchy and Economic Development*. Oxford: Clarendon Press.

Waring, Marilyn. 1996. *Three Masquerades: Essays on Equality, Work and Human Rights*. Toronto: University of Toronto Press.

———. 1988. *Counting for Nothing: What Men Value and What Women Are Worth*. Wellington: Bridget Williams Books Ltd.

Further Readings

Brodie, Janine. 1995. *Politics on the Margins: Restructuring and the Canadian Women's Movement.* Halifax: Fernwood.

Newman, Jacquetta and Linda A. White. 2006. *Women, Politics and Public Policy: The Political Struggles of Canadian Women.* Don Mills: Oxford University Press.

Sawer, Marian, Manon Tremblay, and Linda Trimble, eds. 2006. *Representing Women in Parliament: A Comparative Study.* London and New York: Routledge.

Trimble, Linda and Arscott, Jane. 2003. *Still Counting: Women in Politics Across Canada.* Peterborough: Broadview Press.

Vickers, Jill. 1997. *Reinventing Political Science: A Feminist Approach.* Halifax: Fernwood.

Weblinks

Equal Voice (advocates for gender parity in representation; provides information and links to other equality groups)
www.equalvoice.ca

Feminist.com
www.feminist.com

The Interparliamentary Union, "Women in National Parliaments"
www.ipu.org/wmn-e/world.htm

National Organization for Women (NOW)
www.now.org

Status of Women Canada
www.swc-cfc.gc.ca

REALITY T.V.

CHAPTER 15

CULTURE AS A (CONTENTIOUS) CRITICAL CONCEPT

Objectives

The purpose of this chapter is to explore why culture is important in the study of politics and how political scientists approach the study of culture. Culture involves a shared way of life and, therefore, provides a collective frame of understanding that may influence and even potentially explain different political outcomes. This chapter provides an overview of three distinct approaches to the study of culture and politics. These are the *political culture, cultural studies*, and *cultural identities* approaches. Each of these approaches traditionally examined politics and culture within the boundaries of a given state or country. In recent years, as more attention has been paid to processes of contemporary globalization and the increasing diversity of national populations, political scientists have been forced to be more attentive to the effects of culture on politics beyond a particular country. However, the focus on culture does leave a longstanding problem for political scientists in deciding how and when to rely on "culture" as an explanation for political events and decisions. Today, the consequences of this problem are evident in certain explanations credited to "culture" that have been linked to gender inequality, global conflict, and racism.

YASMEEN ABU-LABAN

Introduction

The term "culture" is often used to refer to art, music, literature, and painting. Some distinguish between the "high culture" of classical composers, such as Mozart, or the plays of William Shakespeare, and today's "popular culture" forms, such as the rap and hip hop of Queen Latifah or the latest video clip from YouTube. Yet culture is also sometimes used more broadly to talk about language, religion, sports, advertising, and even collectivities of varied sizes, as seen in such phrases as "Western culture," "American culture," and "youth culture." Consequently, culture has been a notoriously contentious concept and has been defined in hundreds of ways. How, then, should we understand what culture means?

Political scientists generally agree that culture is something broader than just the arts and define **culture** broadly as a shared way of life. Culture is not the property of an individual but, rather, is collectively shared among human communities. Culture includes language, customs and manners, dress, rituals, behavioural conventions, and religion and other systems of belief. Precisely because culture is a collective, human creation and inherited, it has long been of interest to those who study social and political life.

The Significance of Culture to the Study of Politics

IN THE POST–WORLD WAR II PERIOD, CULTURE HAS BEEN VIEWED AS SIGNIFICANT to the study of politics for several different reasons. First, culture helps describe the differences between peoples and states, and these differences in turn may help to explain different political choices and outcomes. A classic question in the study of North America, for example, relates to accounting for why Canada has a universal health-care program, but the United States does not. It has been suggested that such different public policies between these two industrialized countries can be explained by cultural differences. Offering one such explanation, the late Seymour Martin Lipset (1990) argued that Canadians have historically been more trusting of government, have a more collective orientation, and are less individualistic than their American neighbours. Interestingly, more recent survey research, such as that contained in Michael Adams' *Fire and Ice: The United States, Canada and the Myth of Converging Values* (2003), questions the extent to which Canadians are more deferential and trusting of government than are Americans today. At the same time, Adams reports deep value differences between Canadians and Americans with respect to acceptance of difference, gender roles, and individualism.

A second reason that those studying politics are interested in culture relates to the question of power. Culture has been used to explain why some groups hold power and how and why subordinate groups do, or do not, challenge those in power. For example, in Western countries, access to education is linked with one's life chances, including the kind of job and income one is able to acquire. Pierre Bourdieu has focused on the educational system in Western industrialized countries to examine why children of middle-class parents tend to excel more than children of working-class parents (1973). Bordieu found that although schools may seem neutral, in fact, meeting classroom expectations and doing well in assessments required certain cultural understandings. Bourdieu argued that in contrast to working-class parents, middle-class parents are able to endow their children with what he called **cultural capital**. Just as money gives one the power to purchase consumer goods, cultural capital gives middle-class children the required language and cultural tools to succeed in education, to secure prestigious and well-paying jobs, and, ultimately, to continue these power disparities generation after generation.

A third reason that culture is significant to the study of politics relates to the question of democratic justice. Is it enough to say that equality is achieved when all the laws in a country treat everyone the same? Or should there be distinct rights, treatment, or recognition for some groups on the basis of cultural difference? Whether indigenous peoples and ethnic, racial, and religious minorities should have distinct recognition in the law has been the source of ongoing debate. Consider the perennial question in Canada over whether the province of Quebec, which contains a majority of people whose first language is French, should actually be recognized as a separate "nation"—a debate fuelled in 2006 within the federal Liberal Party, and across parties in the Canadian House of Commons itself.

In sum, culture is highly relevant to the study of politics because it pertains to three key areas: differences between countries, relations of power and challenges to the status quo, and questions of democracy and justice. Each of these areas, in turn, is associated with a particular approach to the study of culture. As outlined below, the question of explaining cultural differences between peoples and between countries is tied to the approach to cultural study known as **political culture**. The question of power relations is essential to a **cultural studies** approach. And, last, the focus on questions of culture, democracy, and justice is central to examining **cultural identity**.

Three Major Approaches

Political Culture

The term *political culture* was first employed by political scientist Gabriel Almond in the 1950s, when he attempted to distinguish political culture from culture generally. According to Almond, the population of any given political system is characterized by a distinct pattern of attitudes about political participation: this pattern is called political culture. Political culture was further elaborated in Gabriel Almond and Sidney Verba's well-known book *The Civic Culture*, which examined the political cultures of Mexico, the United States, the United Kingdom, and Germany to explain their comparative political stability. For each country, the authors surveyed a **representative sample** of 1000 people. Almond and Verba argued that their evidence indicated that it is generally possible to speak of "attitudes that are characteristic of a nation" and, moreover, that political culture is key to explaining stability (1963, 51). They identified three distinct types of attitudes people have about their own role in the political process:

- *parochial*—people do not expect to participate and do not make any demands;
- *subject*—people have no expectation of being politically active, but they do expect that the system will provide them with the goods and services they want; and
- *participant*—people feel they can play an active role and expect that the political system will deliver in return.

Almond and Verba's book argued that the best kind of political system has a "civic culture" that embodies a balance between democracy (as opposed to authoritarianism) and stability (as opposed to instability). The civic culture, notably, is founded on limited participation. The authors of *The Civic Culture* presumed that too much citizen activism creates instability. From their analysis, the countries that best characterize this ideal civic culture were the United Kingdom and, especially, the United States.

Several critiques of the work of Almond and Verba have emerged, however. One major criticism of the political culture approach contained in *The Civic Culture* is that it served as a justification for the status quo. The emphasis in this work was on the desirability of stability, as opposed to change. Indeed, for Almond and Verba, the limited participation of people was positive precisely because it ensured stability. *The Civic Culture* has also been criticized for being *ethnocentric* and *ahistorical*. The book actually assessed the political cultures of other countries in terms of how closely they resembled that of the United States. Moreover, the work did not address the historical differences between countries. Such historical differences, it is argued, are not captured by a "snapshot" glance at culture gleaned from administering a survey to a population at one particular point in time.

Finally, *The Civic Culture* has been criticized for its exclusive focus on national political cultures to the exclusion of relevant sub-cultures within countries, especially African-Americans in the United States. This criticism emphasizes the idea of diversity because a **sub-culture** refers to a different, or distinctive, shared way of life within the national cultural setting, characterizing a smaller grouping of people within a country.

These criticisms of *The Civic Culture* did not dissuade other social scientists from employing the concept of political culture to study the attitudes, beliefs, and rules that guide a political system and, in some cases, to look at the question of sub-cultures within countries. One notable recent example of this kind of survey work can be found in Edward Grabb and James Curtis's book, *Regions Apart: The Four Societies of Canada and the United States* (2005), which suggests that there are identifiable regional differences within each country: in Canada those in Quebec and those outside Quebec hold different views; in the United States those living in the North and the

South hold different views. The smallest gap is to be found between Canadians outside Quebec and Americans in northern states, whereas the biggest gap is between Quebecers and Americans in southern states. This is because Quebecers tend to be the most secular and supportive of a range of issues (from same-sex marriage and interracial marriage to the right to choose abortion), whereas Americans in southern states are the least supportive. This important work therefore underscores how subcultural differences matter within countries and can reveal both differences and similarities in cross-national comparisons.

Cultural Studies

In contrast to the political culture approach, which has traditionally emphasized stability, the *cultural studies* approach is premised on the desirability of transforming power relations. The cultural studies approach is interdisciplinary, meaning that analysts draw on a number of theories and methods from disciplines both in the social sciences and in the humanities. These disciplines include literary criticism, linguistics, philosophy, art history, sociology, and political science.

Nonetheless, the cultural studies approach is united by a core concern—to expose power relations and how these shape cultural practices, with a view toward challenging relations of subordination, especially in capitalist societies. The approach has been profoundly influenced by the work of Karl Marx (1818–1883) and his understanding of the importance of ideology. While the concept of ideology was used as far back as the French Revolution, in the post–World War II period the concept was largely associated with the writings and philosophy of Marx. Marx used the term to refer to those ideas that masked the uneven distribution of power between the workers (the proletariat) and the owners of the means of production (the bourgeoisie) in a capitalist system. Antonio Gramsci and Louis Althusser, two important twentieth-century thinkers inspired by Marx, elaborated on the factors that keep "bourgeois ideology" in place.

The French Marxist thinker Louis Althusser argued that, under capitalism, people are conditioned through ideology that is passed on to them by what he termed "ideological state apparatuses" (ISAs) (1971). For Althusser, the ISAs include churches, schools, parties, unions, communications, literature, arts, and the family. All, in complementary ways, encourage people to believe in the value of capitalism. For Marxists, however, the specific problem with Althusser's account was that the ideological conditioning seemed so complete that it was impossible to imagine change—in particular, how a working-class revolution could ever happen.

In much work in the Marxist tradition, culture is seen to be determined by economic relations. Antonio Gramsci (1891–1937), however, argued that culture was relevant in its own right and a key to understanding the possibility of change and revolution. Gramsci, one of the founders of the Italian Communist Party, was arrested by Mussolini's Fascists in 1926. While in prison, he wrote on the role of culture (Gramsci, 1971). Gramsci believed that social stability could not be achieved through state coercion or force. Instead, social support for capitalism, he argued, was the result of cultural consensus or **hegemony**. For Gramsci, the persistence of the capitalist system was largely achieved by the bourgeoisie's ideological domination (hegemony) of the working class. Gramsci suggested that because hegemony was never total or static but ever-changing, there was always a potential for revolutionary consciousness in the working classes.

The influence of Marx's and Marxist accounts of ideology and culture through such figures as Althusser and Gramsci is evident in cultural studies work. Most thinkers agree that cultural studies began with the publication of Richard Hoggart's 1957 book, *The Uses of Literacy* (During, 1993, 1). This book describes changes in working-class life in post-war Britain, compared with the beginning of the century. It details how just one practice—reading mass publications—had profound consequences on morals and attitudes. Hoggart was dismayed by the cultural changes brought to everyday working-class life by the ever-widening number and reach of popular newspapers and magazines. He argued that "they make their audience less likely to arrive at a wisdom derived from an inner, felt discrimination in their sense of people and their attitude toward experience" (Hoggart, 1957, 339).

In 1964, Hoggart, along with other British Marxist-inspired thinkers, established the Centre for Contemporary Cultural Studies (CCCS) at the University of Birmingham. Here, culture was defined broadly as "the entire range of a society's arts, beliefs, institutions, and communicative practices" and, therefore, explicitly included both "high culture" and "popular culture" (Nelson et al., 1992, 4). Analyses done at the CCCS tended to see culture as contested and as a modern site of class struggle. In this context, the stress was on "how groups with least power practically develop their own readings of, and uses for, cultural products—in fun, in resistance, or to articulate their own identity" (During, 1993, 7).

While cultural studies developed first in the United Kingdom, the approach has had considerable influence in countries as diverse as Canada, the United States, France, and India. In the process, it has become institutionalized within many universities and taken on issues and concerns sometimes different from the original goals of the CCCS at the University of Birmingham. Given that cultural studies was originally identified as a movement committed to bringing about change, especially socialism, its institutionalization has in itself brought about one of the major criticisms of cultural studies. It has been argued that the increasing institutionalization of cultural studies has led to the "[Walt] Disneyfication of the left," that its linkage with the working class has been muted and in some cases abandoned (Davies, 1995, 159–160).

A second major criticism of cultural studies is that it pays little attention to Third World countries that experienced colonialism and to diverse groups other than the working class that might experience disadvantage in advanced capitalist countries (such as women and ethnic and racial minorities). Since the 1990s, however, a growing body of work began to consider issues relating to gender, race, and empire (hooks, 1990; Hall, 1992; Gilroy, 2000, 2004) in relation to culture.

Cultural Identity

The third approach to the study of culture, the *cultural identity* approach, stems from the branch of political science known as political philosophy. Today, a central issue for many political philosophers concerns the nature of equality that the states deliver to their citizens. Contemporary political philosophers generally agree that discrimination against individuals on the basis of membership in a cultural group is wrong because such discrimination contravenes the principle of equality. However, there remains considerable debate over how equality is actually best achieved, particularly in Western industrialized countries where distinct cultural groups may experience discrimination, disadvantage, and inequality despite formal laws that provide for equal treatment.

Consider the case of Canada as an example. Canada is a settler-colony, founded on French and British immigration and the expropriation of land from Aboriginal peoples. Prior to European settler-colonization in the early seventeenth century, Aboriginal societies themselves were characterized by a rich range of cultural, linguistic, social, and political practices. As such, ethnic, linguistic, religious, and cultural diversity is a hallmark feature of this country's experience. According to the 2001 Census, immigrants in that year constituted 18.4 percent of the Canadian national population (Canada, 2003, 1–3). Since the 1970s, there has been a steady decline of immigrants arriving from the countries of Europe and an increase of immigrants arriving from countries in the Caribbean, Central and South America, Africa, the Middle East, and Asia. For much of Canada's history, state laws and policies explicitly limited the ability of racial minorities to access education, housing, and employment. Today, overtly discriminatory laws and policies have been eradicated. Yet there is considerable evidence that members of racial minorities and Aboriginals encounter subtle forms of discrimination and are, therefore, still disadvantaged in such areas as education, relations with the police, social services, and the justice system (Henry et al., 2000, 383–389).

The question of cultural groups and equality has also become pertinent as a result of the emergence and demands of what are termed "new social movements." During the 1960s, a variety of new social movements emerged, coalescing around the idea of identity. Feminism, linguistic rights for minorities, Aboriginal rights, disability rights, and gay rights are examples. This emphasis on identity often takes a cultural form. The increasing relevance of cultural identity in Western liberal democratic countries, as Charles Taylor notes, raises the obvious question of whether equality is best guaranteed by principles of **universalism** and blindness to difference or whether true equality requires special recognition and valuing of difference (1992, 37–44).

Difference blindness holds that through the policies and laws of the state, everyone should be treated equally and the same, no matter what differences may exist among them—whether in terms of gender, religion, ethnicity, or past history of oppression. The value attached to difference blindness is seen in many constitutions of liberal democratic countries. For example, the French *Declaration of the Rights of Man and*

Citizens, the American *Bill of Rights*, and the Canadian *Charter of Rights and Freedoms* all include universal individual rights, based on the principle that the constitution should not draw any distinction among citizens because of their cultural, social, religious, or linguistic background. The rule of law holds that the basic laws of the land should be "difference blind."

An alternative perspective holds that real equality cannot be achieved without recognizing and valuing difference and even according differential rights on the basis of group membership. Within a liberal democratic state, group-differentiated rights in the form of language rights in education, a veto power in constitutional amendments, or territorial autonomy are rights that may enable minority cultural groups to overcome potential vulnerability and disadvantage from majorities (Kymlicka, 1995). For proponents of this perspective, if everyone is treated exactly the same, without regard to their special or unique context, inequality may actually be the result. Along with Charles Taylor, two other contemporary political philosophers, Will Kymlicka and the late Iris Marion Young, are associated with passionate criticisms of difference blindness as the sole approach to equality. For example, Iris Marion Young argued that "strict adherence to a principle of equal treatment tends to perpetuate oppression or disadvantage" (1989, 251). Young asserted that, to actually overcome oppression and disadvantage, special rights need to be given to groups defined as different.

The critique of difference blindness—the advocacy of special rights and recognition—has generated its own criticism. Some argue that the official recognition of group rights on the basis of cultural identity might allow grounds to violate the rights of the individual (Fierlbeck, 1996, 21; Barry, 2000). Many continue to say that the best protection of the individual lies in difference-blind laws and rights. Critics of differentiated rights on the basis of cultural identity also raise concerns about national stability, arguing that any recognition or emphasis on diversity is destabilizing. If minority cultures are accorded separate rights and recognition, can there still be a uniting national culture, or will there be unending fragmentation and disorder? These questions have had longstanding pertinence in Canada, where the issue of national unity has been recurring and is still salient in the early twenty-first century. These questions have taken on heightened significance here and in other diverse liberal democracies in the context of the "war on terrorism," since citizens who are Muslim or Arab, or are perceived to be, have been constructed as different and as a threat (Abu-Laban, 2002).

Meeting the Challenge of Globalization

ALTHOUGH THE THREE APPROACHES HAVE DIFFERENT ORIGINS AND EMPHASES, THOSE working in all three of these traditions have been challenged as a result of the new attention paid to globalization. Contemporary processes of globalization underscore the intensification of a world-scale reorientation of economic, technological, and cultural processes and activities that transcend state boundaries. Today, capital rapidly crosses state borders, and markets have been enlarged and extended. Modern forms of transportation mean that people, too, can rapidly cross state boundaries. Contemporary communication systems, such as satellite television, cellular phones, and the Internet, allow information to pass quickly around the globe. The processes associated with contemporary globalization may affect specific countries differently. Nonetheless, as a package, these processes suggest that culture must also be considered in a context larger than the national state. Yet many analysts feel that in the absence of a world state, it is inappropriate to talk about "a global culture" as something akin to the national culture of a country. It is quite possible, however, to refer to the globalization of culture (Featherstone, 1990, 1).

Currently, many kinds of cultural flows—including ideas, images, and people— quickly transcend state boundaries (Appadurai, 1990, 295–310). The power of ideas, such as democracy or human rights, the worldwide broadcasting of images of the September 11 attacks in the United States, as well as the movement of tourists, immigrants, refugees, guest workers, and exiles each suggest how there has been a globalization of culture. Moreover, global migration has become a central form of globalization and one that serves to contribute to the internal diversity of nation-states.

Evidence of political participation at levels larger than the national state challenges the traditional study of political culture, which has emphasized people's attitudes toward national participation. For instance, among the changes that have coincided with globalization is the deepening of regional integration, as seen in the 1993 North American Free Trade Agreement between Canada, the United States, and Mexico and, especially, developments in the 25 European countries now making up the European Union. Along with a European Parliament, whose members have been elected Europe-wide since 1979, there is now a European passport, a European flag, and a European anthem. These were expressly designed to create a European (as opposed to a simply national) cultural identity. The European Union illustrates how political symbols, forms of identity, and even opportunities for electoral participation have transcended the national state, and this has spawned a new kind of scholarship around political culture that has been more attuned to the attitudes and practices of "European citizens" (Gabel and Anderson, 2002).

Globalization also raises important issues from the cultural studies perspective. It has been suggested that in many ways national governments are unable to exert control over global economic and technological processes. The Internet, for instance, has made it virtually impossible for governments to regulate or control the flow of information, particularly in the context of ever-changing technological developments. There are, thus, many new ways for less powerful groups (such as women, workers, and minorities) to try to resist the spread of capital globally. Adequately addressing how resistance is demonstrated increasingly requires looking at how groups may join together across state boundaries (see, for example, Robbins, 2005). A variety of examples suggest how such organizing is occurring. For instance, the "battle of Seattle" saw an array of students, labour groups, and other non-governmental organizations from the United States and around the world protesting the meeting of the World Trade Organization (WTO) in Seattle in December 1999. The WTO, consisting of the governments of more than 130 countries (including Canada), is committed to reducing trade barriers between countries; protestors were critical of trade liberalization for its impact on the environment, labour standards, and poverty, as well as the perceived lack of democracy in the WTO. More recently, the decision by the United States to wage war on Iraq in 2003 spawned a number of simultaneously timed massive peace demonstrations in countries around the world.

Finally, globalization spells changes for culture and cultural identity—the key concerns in much contemporary political philosophy. As one example at the level of the arts, consider world music, which has been described as music without borders. World music is characterized as coming from parts of the developing world (Cuba, Brazil, Algeria, Senegal, South Africa, India, and Pakistan), drawing from sounds the world over and making its way to Western markets. As noted by one musician, "When artists come out of their culturally bound musical traditions and start using modern instruments, they mutate the sound, they make a new stew, a new blend. This is what is called world music. There is no pure music in the world. Everything is a fusion because that's the way it is intended" (Mickey Hart as quoted in "Music," 1998, 76).

Just as world music reflects a fusion of a variety of sounds from across the globe, contemporary globalization creates a host of new opportunities for cultural inter-mixing, as capital, people, images, and ideas traverse state boundaries. What might result from such fusions? Since the late 1990s, a growing body of work (for example, Jameson and Miyoshi, 1998) is considering such questions.

Culture as a Contentious Critical Concept

THE DIFFERENT TRADITIONS HAVE, IN DIFFERENT WAYS, RESPONDED TO THE COMplexities introduced by contemporary globalization, in the process revealing how sensitivity to local, national, regional, and global levels is relevant in studying culture. However, the fact remains that "culture" in the early years of the twenty-first century is a contentious concept, and this is not merely because of debates over how best to define the term. Rather, this is because of the political uses to which culture has been put by politicians, social actors, and in some instances by analysts themselves.

Three areas stand out. First, "culture" has been viewed with suspicion by some feminists and feminist scholars. For instance, consider the work of the late Susan Moller Okin, a leading feminist political theorist. She argued that multiculturalism, by which she meant the protection by Western liberal democratic states of group rights (particularly of immigrant groups), was not compatible with feminism (Okin, 1998). She felt that advocates of multiculturalism ignore internal group dynamics, and that much gender oppression takes place in the private sphere in the name of "tradition."

Second, "culture" has been portrayed as a source, if not *the* source, of global conflict, akin to the Cold War of the mid-twentieth century. As the prominent example of our time, given the popularity of the thesis, consider Samuel Huntington's "clash of civilizations" argument, which posits inherent differences between West/Rest and Christianity and Islam, specifically. The idea of a "clash of civilizations" between countries of the West and non-West (and especially between Christians and non-Christians) has become well publicized not only in the academy but in the media and in government circles since the September 11 attacks (Abu-Laban, 2002).

Third, "culture" has been linked to racism, particularly in the racist expressions of many far-right movements today. Traditionally, racism was rooted in pseudo-scientific theories and beliefs that asserted inherent biological differences between peoples. With the defeat of Nazism and the creation of international legal instruments such as the 1948 *Universal Declaration of Human Rights* (which prohibited any discrimination based on race or colour), there was a discrediting of theories and beliefs of biological differences between people. This was also carried into the academy: since World War II, across disciplines, there has been a consensus that "there is no race but the human race." Moreover, the idea that there are biological differences between people based on "race" is controversial (which is why many social scientists put the word "race" in quotes—to signify that the term is not scientifically based but rather socially constructed and historically specific). However, racism has not disappeared. Many suggest that today's expressions of racism differ from those of the past; the "new racism" focuses less on presumed biological differences between people and more on cultural differences. This argument has been developed in part by looking at far-right parties and their discourse in contemporary Europe. Typically, far-right movements now structure their attacks in cultural terms (especially targeting immigrants whose values are constructed as inherently different) (Betz, 2002). For example, in France the far-right Front National party has articulated its anti-immigrant position by stressing cultural differences that distinguish "the French" from "immigrants," especially those that are Muslim. In this way, members of the Front National have long asserted that it is not a racist party because the focus is on cultural rather than biological differences (see Le Pen, 1985). Echoes of this fixation on culture were heard in Canada in 2007, when the town council of tiny rural Hérouxville, Quebec, introduced a controversial code of behaviour that, among other things, sought to ban the hijab (the head cover worn by some Muslim girls and women) except on Halloween.

Such different, inherently political associations of "culture" in relation to gender inequality, conflict, and racism require careful consideration on the part of analysts. For example, Okin's categorical portrayal of "culture" as harming women has been rightly challenged on a number of grounds—for instance, that her argument assumes Western culture is non-patriarchal or at least less patriarchal than that of others; that it assumes women are without agency (Honig, 1999); and not least that it inaccurately presents immigrant minorities as mired only in tradition (Bhabha, 1999). Likewise, Huntington's portrayal has also been critiqued for ignoring the diversity within cultures or "civilizations." In reality, both Christianity and Islam are marked by diverse traditions. Moreover, there is no "purely" Muslim or Christian country, since national populations are themselves characterized by religious and cultural diversity (Abu-Laban, 2001). Indeed, today, Islam is the largest religion represented in countries of Western Europe after Christianity, a feature arising from historical processes, such as colonialism, as well as contemporary migration flows (Abu-Laban, 2001). Moreover, real world conflicts evident today require serious attention to history, economics, and power relations and cannot be easily reduced in any serious analysis to just "culture." These qualifications would suggest that irrespective of the tradition analysts are working in, or even whether they try to combine aspects of political culture, cultural studies, and identity, there needs to be sensitivity to what culture may actually on its own "explain," as well as sensitivity to nuances and differences within any group.

In summary, then, there remains a big challenge across traditions to study culture in a way that does not overly simplify representations of "culture" that rest on treating any given population, or society, or religion, as homogeneous. In so far as the "new racism" (with its focus on culture rather than biology) manifests itself, there also needs to be greater consideration of how "culture" is used in the service of claims of superiority or inferiority and of unequal treatment. Not least, all analysts need to be cautious; culture may accurately provide both description and explanation in some areas, but not necessarily in all.

Summary

This chapter has addressed three ways in which the study of culture and politics has been approached in the period following World War II. The political culture approach places an emphasis on people's attitudes toward political institutions and participation. In contrast, the cultural studies approach draws from Marxism to highlight power relations and how these shape cultural practices. Cultural studies, as an approach, has traditionally been concerned with transforming relations of power. Finally, many contemporary political philosophers examine the implications of cultural identity claims made by groups in liberal democracies for equality, democracy, and justice. While these approaches are distinct, they have historically shared a common tendency to look at culture and politics within the confines of a state. In different ways, those working in each of these traditions have attempted to respond to the challenges of contemporary globalization by addressing not only the state level but levels beneath and above the state. While this is a welcome development, challenges remain, and a key one is to address culture in ways that do not simplify and treat groups as homogeneous. Additionally, political scientists studying culture need to be attuned as much to what culture does not explain as to what it does. This is especially imperative since the political uses to which "culture" can be put show no signs of abating in the twenty-first century.

Discussion Questions

1. Is there a distinct political culture to the place you live in now? If so, how would you describe it?

2. Discuss whether popular-culture forms (e.g., television programs, music, the popular press) help maintain or challenge the status quo.

3. Why do so many groups seek special recognition or rights? Can we expect such demands to grow or lessen, given contemporary patterns of globalization? Can we expect responses by governments to be supportive or not?

4. Can you think of examples of some of the ways in which "the clash of civilizations" has been used by politicians or by citizens' groups to justify a position, a policy, or a view?

References

Abu-Laban, Yasmeen. 2001. "Humanizing the Oriental: Edward Said and Western Scholarly Discourse" in Naseer Aruri and Muhammad A. Shuraydi, eds., *Revising Culture: Reinventing Peace: The Influence of Edward Said.* New York and Northampton: Interlink Publishing, 74–85.

————. 2002. "Liberalism, Multiculturalism and the Problem of Essentialism." *Citizenship Studies* 6, 4 (December): 459–482.

Adams, Michael. 2003. *Fire and Ice: The United States, Canada and the Myth of Converging Values.* Toronto: Penguin Books.

Almond, Gabriel and Sidney Verba. 1963. *The Civic Culture.* Princeton: Princeton University Press.

Althusser, Louis. 1971. *Lenin and Philosophy and Other Essays.* New York: Monthly Review Press.

Appadurai, Arjun. 1990. "Disjuncture and Difference in the Global Cultural Economy" in Mike Featherstone, ed., *Global Culture: Nationalism, Globalization and Modernity.* London: Sage, 295–310.

Barry, Brian. 2000. *Culture and Equality: An Egalitarian Critique of Multiculturalism.* Cambridge: Polity Press.

Betz, Hans Georg. 2002. "Xenophobia, Identity Politics and Exclusionary Populism in Western Europe" in Leo Panitch and Colin Leys, eds., *Fighting Identities: Race, Religion and Ethno-Nationalism (Socialist Register 2003).* London: Merlin Press, 193–210.

Bhabha, Homi K. 1999. "Liberalism's Sacred Cow" in Joshua Cohen, Matthew Howard, and Martha C. Nussbaum, eds., *Is Multiculturalism Bad for Women? Susan Moller Okin with Respondents.* Princeton: Princeton University Press, 79–84.

Bourdieu, Pierre. 1973. "Cultural Reproduction and Social Reproduction" in R. Brown, ed., *Knowledge, Education and Cultural Change.* London: Tavistock, 71–112.

Canada, Statistics Canada. 2003. "Census of Population: Immigration, Birthplace and Birthplace of Parents, Citizenship, Ethnic Origin, Visible Minorities and Aboriginal

Peoples." *The Daily*, January 23. Retrieved September 29, 2003, from **www.statcan.ca/Daily/English/030121/d030121a.htm**.

Davies, Ian. 1995. *Cultural Studies and Beyond*. London: Routledge.

During, Simon. 1993. "Introduction" in Simon During, ed., *The Cultural Studies Reader*. London and New York: Routledge, 1–25.

Easton, David. 1957. "An Approach to the Analysis of Political Systems." *World Politics*, 9, 3, 383–400.

Featherstone, Mike. 1990. "Global Culture: An Introduction" in Mike Featherstone, ed., *Global Culture: Nationalism, Globalization and Modernity*. London: Sage, 1–14.

Fierlbeck, Katherine. 1996. "The Ambivalent Potential of Cultural Identity." *The Canadian Journal of Political Science*, XXIX, 1 (March), 3–22.

Gabel, Matthew J. and Christopher J. Anderson. 2002. "The Structure of Citizen Attitudes and the European Political Space." *Comparative Political Studies*, 35, 8: 893–913.

Gilroy, Paul. 2000, 2004. *Between Camps: Nations, Cultures and the Allure of Race*. London: Routledge.

———. 2004. *After Empire: Melancholia or Convivial Culture?* Abingdon: Routledge.

Grabb, Edward and James Curtis. 2005. *Regions Apart: The Four Societies of Canada and the United States*. Don Mills: Oxford University Press.

Gramsci, Antonio. 1971. *Selections from the Prison Notebooks*. London: New Left Books.

Hall, Stuart. 1992. "Cultural Studies and Its Theoretical Legacies," in Lawrence Grossberg, Cary Nelson, and Paula Treichler, eds., *Cultural Studies*. New York: Routledge, 277–294.

Henry, Frances, Carol Tator, Winston Mattis, and Tim Rees. 2000. *The Colour of Democracy: Racism in Canadian Society*. Toronto: Harcourt Brace.

Hoggart, Richard. 1957. *The Uses of Literacy*. Middlesex, U.K.: Penguin.

Honig, Bonnie. 1999. "My Culture Made Me Do It" in Joshua Cohen, Matthew Howard, and Martha C. Nussbaum, eds., *Is Multiculturalism Bad for Women? Susan Moller Okin with Respondents*. Princeton: Princeton University Press, 35–40.

hooks, bell. 1990. *Yearning: Race, Gender and Cultural Politics*. Boston: South End Press.

Jameson, Fredric and Masao Miyoshi, eds. 1998. *The Cultures of Globalization*. Durham: Duke University Press.

Kymlicka, Will. 1995. *Multicultural Citizenship: A Liberal Theory of Minority Rights*. New York: Oxford University Press.

LePen, Jean-Marie. 1985. *Pour la France: Programme du Front National*. Paris: Éditions Albatros.

Lipset, Seymour Martin. 1990. *Continental Divide*. New York: Routledge.

"Music Without Borders: Mickey Hart Charts World Beat's Sonic Boom." 1998. *Shift Magazine* (August), 76.

Nelson, Cary, Paula A. Treichler, and Lawrence Grossberg. 1992. "Cultural Studies: An Introduction" in Lawrence Grossberg, Cary Nelson, and Paula Treichler, eds., *Cultural Studies*. New York: Routledge. 1–14.

Okin, Susan Moller. 1998. "Feminism and Multiculturalism: Some Tensions." *Ethics*, 108 (July): 661–684.

Robins, Richard H. 2005. *Global Problems and the Culture of Capitalism.* Boston: Pearson.

Said, Edward. 2001. "Islam and the West Are Inadequate Banners." *The Observer,* September 16.

Taylor, Charles. 1992. "The Politics of Recognition" in Amy Gutmann, ed., *Multiculturalism and the Politics of Recognition.* Princeton: Princeton University Press.

Young, Iris Marion. 1989. "Polity and Group Difference: A Critique of the Ideal of Universal Citizenship." *Ethics,* 99, 250–274.

Further Readings

Political Culture

Grabb, Edward and James Curtis. 2005. *Regions Apart: The Four Societies of Canada and the United States.* Don Mills: Oxford University Press.

Cultural Studies

Sardar, Ziauddin and Borin Van Loon. 2005. *Introducing Cultural Studies,* 3rd edition. London: Icon Books.

Cultural Identity

Kymlicka, Will. 1995. *Multicultural Citizenship: A Liberal Theory of Minority Rights.* New York: Oxford University Press.

Weblinks

Canadian Association of Cultural Studies
www.culturalstudies.ca

Citizenship, Democracy and Ethnocultural Diversity Newsletter (edited by Will Kymlicka)
www.queensu.ca/cded/news.html

Cultural Studies Central
www.culturalstudies.net

Interview with Samuel Huntington: "Five Years After 9/11, The Clash of Civilizations Revisited"
www.pewforum.org/events/index.php?EventID=125

THE RESULTS OF THE LATEST SAME-SEX MARRIAGE VOTE ARE IN...

artizans.com

BEEN THERE: 123 Votes
DONE THAT: 175 Votes

CHAPTER 16

THE POLITICS OF DIVERSITY

Objectives

The purpose of this chapter is to explore the concept of diversity as an important idea in contemporary theory and practice. We will examine what is meant by diversity, why it is a useful concept as well as a limited one, and why it has become significant to studying socio-political relations. To provide an overview of the debates about diversity and politics, three approaches will be considered: *classical liberalism, liberal multiculturalism,* and *radical perspectives.* These approaches provide ways to think about key political issues, including how the state should accommodate diversity, how social differences are constructed, and how to respond to power differences between groups. The chapter concludes by examining the implications of diversity in a global era.

RITA DHAMOON

Introduction

In the study of politics, **diversity** describes a multiplicity of socio-cultural peoples, social identities, or social groups. This diversity can be local (for example, diverse populations live in Toronto, Montreal, and Vancouver), national (Canada is a diverse country), or international (the world is globally diverse). The idea of diversity raises normative questions about how members of a society ought to live together, how far the state should accommodate or limit practices of diverse groups, and how to promote and preserve human rights and equity. Diversity also has empirical dimensions in that it refers to the demographics of a territory (such as an ethnic population) and specific kinds of policies or laws (for instance, the *Canadian Charter of Rights and Freedoms* addresses issues of diversity in Section 15, the equality clause, and Section 27, which emphasizes the preservation and enhancement of Canada's multicultural heritage).

The Significance of Diversity to the Study of Politics

DIVERSITY IS A SIGNIFICANT CRITICAL CONCEPT IN THE STUDY OF POLITICS for a number of reasons. First, philosophically, it raises questions about how people live together when they have diverse backgrounds, values, practices, experiences, and histories. The question of how to live together is one that shapes national politics and, at the same time, transcends the borders of the nation-state because of global issues related to the environment, human security, health, HIV/AIDS, poverty, and equity. In particular, when ways to live together are under consideration, the idea of diversity is often justified by notions of freedom, justice, respect, recognition, tolerance, equity, and rights. At the same time, diversity raises issues of power. For instance, do all diverse groups have an equitable say in the rules of society? Should they? Why are some groups seen as representations of diversity and not others? When issues of diversity are understood as matters of power difference, it becomes possible to consider why identities are constructed in particular ways and how these shape societal relations. In Canada, this promotes an understanding of relations between and among different Indigenous nations, French and English settlers, immigrant groups, temporary residents (such as domestic workers or students), and refugees. The study of diversity also encompasses the plurality of genders (male, female, transgendered), sexualities (lesbian, gay, heterosexual, bisexual, queer), racialized groups, religions, those viewed as able-bodied and disabled, languages (French, English, sign languages, Chinese, Arabic, etc.), and social classes. Diversity therefore raises a number of important issues about how the state, institutions, and we, as members of society, can evaluate and respond to various kinds of social relations.

Second, diversity is a significant concept for historical reasons. In particular, the language of diversity brings to light the differences between past and present practice, and has been one way to address various kinds of historical injustices. One example of this lies in the change in Canadian policy on ethno-cultural diversity which, in 1971, shifted from a monocultural approach (that is, a commitment to one culture) to a multicultural approach (a vision in which many cultures could be accommodated). This 1971 policy emphasized diversity through four objectives: to assist cultural groups in promoting and supporting distinctiveness; to help cultural groups overcome barriers to full participation in society; to enhance national unity through cultural exchange; and to enable all newcomers to learn at least one of the official languages (French or English) so as to become a participant in society. The real purpose of this policy remains contentious, but it symbolizes a shift from the approach taken by Canadian governments during the 1800s and most of the 1900s, when they overtly discriminated against various racialized and ethnic groups. Diversity was legally restricted by governments through such means as the 1885 *Chinese Head Tax and Exclusion Act,* which imposed a head tax exclusively for Chinese migrants; the 1908 B.C. *Municipal Elections Act,* which prevented Chinese, Japanese, and other "Asiatic" or Indian persons from voting in municipal elections in British Columbia; and the 1914 *Komagata Maru* incident, which involved a Japanese steam liner carrying 376 British subjects of Sikh, Muslim, and Hindu descent who were refused landing rights on the shores of British Columbia. While racism continues today, the 1971 multicultural policy marked a more positive approach to diversity and was followed by other formal laws and policies, including the 1988 *Multiculturalism Act,* the first national act of its kind in the world.

It is important to note that diversity is often used as a way to speak about the status of Indigenous peoples, their inherent rights, and their land claims in Canada. However, the concept of diversity does not adequately address the historical legacy of colonialism that shapes relations between Indigenous people and non-Indigenous people. This is because the concept of diversity often collapses Indigenous groups with other kinds of cultural groups without adequate recognition of prior occupation and nationhood status. As such, the language of diversity must be historically situated so as to identify the different experiences and legacies of various kinds of groups.

Third, diversity is an important concept because it relates to the ways in which citizenship is defined and determined. Historically, the legal restrictions regarding who was viewed as a desirable citizen were shaped by views that limited and regulated diversity. With regard to physical and mental disability, for instance, the 1906 Canadian *Immigration Act* ("*Immigration Act* [1906] R.S.C. c.93") allowed the deportation of immigrants after two (then three, then five) years if they were deemed a public charge or were medically diagnosed as insane or handicapped, or were simply characterized by infirmity. The act continued the previous ban on admission for the mentally disabled but also extended the meaning of mentally deficient people to restrict immigration. The purpose was to restrict the entry of those seen as irrational, dependent, and naturally unindustrious because they were viewed as having less chance of successfully "integrating" as citizens into society (Mosoff, 1999, 156). The 2001 *Immigration and Refugee Protection Act* maintained such a clause by preventing potential immigrants from migrating to Canada if they were deemed to place "excessive demands" on health and social services. This is just one example of the ways in which diversity is regulated in terms of citizenship. Diversity, however, can also provide a more positive way to approach citizenship. In particular, diversity emphasizes that citizenship can be experienced through the notion of "equality-as-difference." This notion supports the idea that equality does not arise from treating everyone in exactly the same way but emerges by recognizing that diverse experiences and identities exist, and that respect for these differences enhances social relations and a sense of belonging.

Finally, diversity is important because it sculpts various legal and political claims. The roles of the courts, governments, and other institutions are especially important in determining whether diversity should shape our institutional structures and practices. Respect for diversity has informed legal cases and outcomes, such as those regarding lesbian and gay spousal rights, the rights of Sikhs to carry religious symbols (the kirpan) in public places, and employment equity hiring policies at universities that target four under-represented groups (women, persons with disabilities, Aboriginal peoples, and visible minorities).

Critiques of Diversity

As with most critical concepts, there are a number of problems and challenges that arise from the concept of diversity and, as such, it is a contested idea. This contestation tends to stem from the link between the ideas of diversity and multiculturalism. **Multiculturalism** refers to a belief or policy that endorses the principle of cultural diversity and supports the right of different ethnic, national, and linguistic groups to retain their distinctive identities and practices. The multicultural emphasis on culture-based group distinctiveness or culturally shared ways of collective life often leads to assumptions about the homogeneity of a group and the similarities between group members who identify as or are labelled as Italian, Chinese, Muslim, African, etc. In relation to this problem of essentializing identity, the emphasis on cultural diversity conceals other aspects of identity. In particular, the almost exclusive focus on ethnicity, nationality, language, and culture obscures the ways in which identities are also shaped by modes of sexuality, gender, age, (dis)ability, class, or colour. Diversity, therefore, needs to be understood broadly so as to include multiple and interactive dimensions of identity.

Moreover, a study of diversity tends to focus on those who are seen as different from dominant groups. In Canada, this is often based on how cultural, ethnic, or racial groups are viewed as dissimilar from the two main settler groups, namely the British and the French. An understanding of diversity, therefore, emphasizes the group that is constructed as different rather than the dominant groups or the relations that construct that difference. Specifically, as post-colonial critic Homi Bhabha (1994, 34) has argued, diversity is a limited concept because it underplays the ways in which power differentials determine socio-political relations. Whereas the notion of diversity tends to emphasize **culture**, which refers to a set of learned beliefs, values, and behaviours that organize shared ways of life that are socially transmitted, or **ethnicity** in which members of a group share a sense of people-hood or identity based on descent, language, religion, tradition, and other common experiences, Bhabha contends it is necessary to examine power differences.

In particular, the concept of diversity masks the problem of racialized differences. In contrast to the concepts of culture and ethnicity, which reflect positive tendencies of identification and inclusion, the idea of **race** reflects negative tendencies of disassociation and exclusion, where people are falsely grouped according to biological notions of identity (for instance, by physical features). Whereas the idea of diversity may celebrate these as variations because they enhance a mosaic or multicultural understanding of society, as Bhabha argues, the notion of "difference" emphasizes that groups are socially constructed through power. In this regard, it is not that race does not matter, for it shapes everyday lives and experiences, but, rather, it has to be understood as a social construction that determines power differences, rather than a natural way to classify groups. This is important because the language of diversity can obscure the historical and ongoing power differences between those who are seen as white and those identified as non-white. It is, therefore, necessary to examine the ways in which various groups are assigned racial markings and attributes, a process that Robert Miles (2000) calls **racialization**. This, Miles contends, is important to do because the historical conditions of marking groups change over time. For instance, in North America, the Irish, Italians, Jews, Slavs, and Ukrainians are now considered "white," but during the eighteenth and first part of the nineteenth century, they were socially represented as non-white (Roediger, 2002; Satzewich, 2000). Thus, although the concept of diversity offers a pluralistic lens through which to understand the multiplicity of social identities, it also underestimates the problem of power differences between racialized groups. Despite these problems, the language of diversity has become a central concept in theories and practices related to identity and difference. In the next section, let us explore some of the approaches to the study of diversity.

Approaches to the Politics of Diversity

Classical Liberalism

Classical liberalism responds to diversity with skepticism. From this perspective, public and formal accommodation of group diversity by the state is neither necessary nor desirable. This is because liberal ideology already places individual rights and freedoms as paramount. Liberalism not only emphasizes the individual and his or her rights but also promotes the principles of consent, equality of opportunity, tolerance, and a clear division between the public and private spheres. On this basis, there is no need for government to publicly promote or regulate the private religious and cultural practices of groups, as this would be tantamount to unnecessary state interference in the lives of individuals. Chandran Kukathas (1988) notes that liberal principles of equality already provide individuals with basic rights, and therefore there is no need for group-differentiated rights for those who come from diverse backgrounds. The state, he argues, protects and promotes individual rights, such as the freedom of religion, precisely so that additional group rights are not necessary. Susan Moller Okin makes a similar argument in her essay, "Is Multiculturalism Bad for Women?" (1999). Okin states that while all societies are sexist and patriarchal, distinct cultural group rights for autonomy may mask the violation of individual sex equality rights for women. These women's rights, she contends, are entrenched in liberal ideas about equality.

Others, such as Brian Barry (2001), have argued that institutional commitments to diversity, especially in the form of multiculturalism, fragment and divide those living within one nation-state. By accommodating diverse institutions and practices, the notion of a unified and national citizenship is undermined. Barry states that "citizens belong to a single society and share a common fate," and therefore their specific group identities and loyalties cannot have primacy over "any broader, society-wide identity and loyalty" (2001, 300–301). Overall, all of these thinkers dispute the idea that goods and resources should be distributed according to diverse identity categories, and argue that liberalism as a value transcends cultural pluralism.

The strengths of this approach lie in identifying a serious challenge faced by governments and society—namely the significance of maintaining a sense of unity and national community. In Canada, for instance, there is ongoing debate about the nature of a Canadian national identity in the context of diversity. The classic liberal perspective also illuminates an important tension between liberal individual rights and group rights, specifically the problem of reconciling such rights when they may clash. This concern raises explicit questions about how to protect individual sex equality rights while also promoting cultural group rights.

One of the limitations of the classical liberal approach is that it over-determines this clash between individual and group rights. For example, for Indigenous women there are concerns about both the individual experiences of women and the self-determination rights of Indigenous nations (Monture-Angus, 1995). In addition, this approach falsely assumes that state institutions are neutral when responding to diverse individuals and groups. The ideal of impartiality assumes that there is one conception of justice and a single, homogeneous culture that provides the standard by which to judge other cultures. Moreover, classical liberalism underestimates the significance of cultural contexts for individuals, especially in terms of providing choices about how to live our lives.

Liberal Multiculturalism

Many of the above issues are taken up by the liberal multicultural approach. Liberal multiculturalism maintains the primacy of liberalism but takes the view that rather than leading to societal fragmentation, the allocation of recognition and differentiated group rights enables and promotes the lives of individuals and therefore the well-being of society more generally. Hence, instead of being skeptical of diversity, liberal multiculturalism calls for public institutions to tolerate and accommodate, rather than ignore or downplay, cultural particularities.

The liberal multicultural approach to diversity has been the most prominent one in Canada, both theoretically and practically. The 1971 multicultural policy and the 1988 *Multiculturalism Act* are both examples of this approach. Indeed, this Canadian version of multiculturalism has become a model response to diversity for scholars and governments across geo-political contexts, including in South Africa (Adhikari, 2004), Asia (Kymlicka and He, 2005), India (Deb, 2002), and Eastern Europe (Kuzio, 2005). Two of the most important architects of this school of thought are Will Kymlicka, who published a provocative book called *Multicultural Citizenship* (1995), and Charles Taylor, who wrote an important essay called "The Politics of Recognition" (1994). While there are notable differences between these two thinkers, they each reconceptualize and modify tenets of liberalism, rejecting monocultural and assimilationist responses to diversity. Further, they share a preoccupation with the self-determination of the Québécois and Indigenous peoples of Canada, emphasize language as a central signifier of diversity, and pay attention to the demographic fact of multicultural Canada.

One of the strengths of the liberal multicultural approach is that it begins from the premise that dialogue about diversity, specifically culture-based diversity, is necessary for society and individual self-realization. In addition, this approach does not pose diversity in opposition to unity. On the contrary, it emphasizes a mosaic model in which there can be diversity-within-unity. The mosaic allows "several bounded, nameable, individually homogeneous and unmeltable minority uni-cultures" to be "pinned onto a backdrop of a similarly characterised majority uni-culture" (Vertovec, 1996, 5). Another strength of this approach is that it distinguishes between claims made by different kinds of historically formed groups and claims. For instance, Kymlicka notes that while national minority groups, such as the Québécois and Indigenous nations, have specific historical claims (linked to land, culture, language, and occupation), polyethnic minorities (or immigrants) do not tend to make claims based on territory or nationhood status (1995, 10–33).

The problems with this approach to diversity are threefold. First, liberal multiculturalism continues to assume that the ideal of unity is ultimately universally shared. While collective national unity may be desirable for some groups, it is often minority groups, rather than mainstream society, that have to make substantial changes in their practices and institutions. Second, multiculturalism formulates diversity as a problem that arises from the presence of diverse cultures, and under-theorizes the *contexts* in which cultures are constructed, both by particular members and by external forces. These forces may be a product of racism or colonialism and have little to do with the demands of a group. As Augie Fleras points out, the over-emphasis on culture in liberal multiculturalism masks questions of racism. She states that "the mainstream no longer defines itself as racially superior but as culturally appropriate. Conversely, minorities are not dismissed as racially inferior but as culturally compatible" (2004, 431).

This takes place even though racialization continues to shape the experiences of diversity. Finally, the liberal multicultural approach emphasizes the plurality or diversity of groups rather than the power differences between these groups. For instance, the focus is on how diversity can be promoted by assigning recognition and differentiated rights to Indigenous nations in Canada, rather than on examining ways in which the allocation of recognition or rights by the state perpetuates historical colonial relations. This question of power is at the heart of the third approach to diversity.

Radical Perspectives on Diversity

Within the radical school of thought there are numerous approaches to diversity, but all share one major theme—namely a critique of liberalism. Thus, unlike the previous two approaches, the goal is not to clarify, modify, or reformulate liberalism. Instead, the primary goal is to rethink political norms in order to change the relations and contexts of power between various groups. Thus, the emphasis is on the link between history, location, and power. The very language of diversity is viewed as inadequate in addressing these themes. Himani Bannerji, for example, states that diversity is "a device for managing public or social relations and spaces," which falsely serves to suggest a happy co-existence of a multitude of identities without addressing social (and historical) relations of power (2000, 38).

To bring to view issues of history, location, and power, this third approach examines different kinds of structures and discourses of power. Taiaiake Alfred (2005), for instance, identifies the ways in which current practices and institutions continue the legacy of colonialism. He calls specific attention to the ways in which Western notions of rights and sovereignty have been used to dominate Indigenous peoples, even though such ideas are presented as emancipatory. As one illustration, the *Indian Act* continues to govern the lives of First Nations people, even though it is formally claimed that colonialism has ended in Canada. Originally, the 1876 *Indian Act* was a tool of aggressive assimilation, forced relocation, and cultural annihilation, and today, even though the act has been amended, it remains a legal way to regulate the status, membership, benefit entitlements, and living conditions of many First Nations people. Alfred suggests that the way forward is to heed the voices of Indigenous ancestors in a modern context. This, he contends, can be done in many ways, such as by "decolonizing the diet," a process through which Indigenous people can relearn traditional practices of hunting, fishing, gathering, and preparing food in a modern context. The emphasis, for Alfred, is on Indigenous ways of living with integrity, while also dismantling colonial power.

The strengths of this approach lie in shifting the focus from the "different" person or group to the many processes by which difference shapes our lives. By addressing these multiple processes, radical thinkers are going beyond the primary focus on culture in liberal multicultural thought. Some feminists, for instance, have examined the many ways in which identities become differently constructed through various processes that privilege modes of whiteness, capitalism, sexism, and patriarchy.

Another advantage of this approach is that it demands close analysis of the ways in which historical representations of identity and difference continue to shape ideas about diversity today. In this sense, it addresses historical legacies in ways that the previous two approaches dismiss or underestimate. It also emphasizes the importance of examining historical and contemporary representations of *dominant identities* as well as oppressed identities. Further, this approach takes seriously the relations between members of society, thereby displacing the primary focus of the other two approaches on how the state should respond to diversity. This not only allows a broader picture of various social dynamics but also reconfigures (racialized, gendered, sexual, disabled) subordinated groups as dynamic political agents who are already involved in practices of resistance and action, rather than simply representing them as victims who need to be accommodated by the state. Overall, this approach places an emphasis on questions of power—how it is produced, sustained, and resisted.

One of the charges against this third approach is that it often focuses on critique without always providing a clear strategy about how to reorganize social relations. Further, at times, it dismisses the value of traditional strategies, such as the legal process. The response to these criticisms is that whereas the first two approaches aim to make incremental change within the current system, radical approaches aim to make fundamental changes from both within and outside the dominant system.

Diversity in a Global Era

WITHIN THE CURRENT GLOBAL ERA, THERE HAS BEEN A GROWING EMPHASIS on changes in the international political economy and the organization of capital. Specifically, wealth is increasingly created not only or even primarily by national governments but at various global levels. In tandem with these forms of economic globalization has been a range of cultural forms of globalization. In particular, there have been growing interconnections, interchanges, and movements of people, images, and commodities across national borders.

The implications of diversity in this internationalized context are enormous. First, there is a sense that diversity is global and that we are living in a "world city." This diversity exposes people to the ideas, practices, and values of other cultures. This can be viewed as positive in that there is more cultural exchange, which has led to creative projects such as the fusion of music (for example, Bhangra and Jamaican music mixes) or the mainstreaming of cultural practices, such as wearing henna. At the same time, through the guise of diversity, these exchanges also produce negative outcomes, such as the appropriation of cultural customs, cloths, and jewelry (such as the Indian bindi). This appropriation occurs when material, symbolic, and linguistic entities become misused or reframed without adequate consideration of existing traditions and practices.

Second, this global exchange of diversity has led to the idea that identity transcends the nation-state, such that there is a shift from a national to an international consciousness. There is more talk of dual citizenship, post-national citizenship, global citizenship, or **transnational citizenship**, in which people identify with more than one nationality or nation. Even when people do not have formal citizenship from more than one country, the life of a migrant may be transnational in character through employment and family connections, a diasporic consciousness, and political practices. This notion of a transnational identity often develops because people travel and live in various parts of the world. Yet while this may be true for some people, it is important to note that this is mostly true for those who have the economic means to be mobile or, conversely, those who are forced to move for economic or humanitarian reasons. The experience of a diverse world city is therefore very much shaped by wealth.

Third, the language of diversity has been widely deployed as a tool to promote economic priorities, with both positive and negative effects. For instance, in this global era of diversity there has been a rise in the social and commercial value of various non-Western languages across the globe, especially in Western countries. Increasingly, corporations such as banks and transport companies are hiring people from different backgrounds because their language skills are good for business. At the same time, this marriage between diversity and economics has led to the exploitation of resources and labour of those living in countries deemed to be part of the Third World. For example, the Live-In Caregiver Program enables women from the West Indies and the Philippines to migrate to Canada to work, but often these racialized women are underpaid and overworked. As economic globalization has deepened, issues related to diversity become even more significant in distinguishing the world on the basis of a North–South divide.

Fourth, questions of diversity have become globally significant since the events of September 11, 2001. Following the attacks and the deaths of nearly 3000 people, there have been growing tensions about diversity. In Canada, as in other parts of the world, hate crimes have been committed against specific racialized groups, specifically Muslims and Arabs, as well as those perceived to be Muslim or Arab. As well, measures have been implemented to detain those viewed as terrorist threats, such as the Canadian Security Certificate Program, which has detained five men of Muslim origin without due process. Further, new immigration, refugee, and border controls are being instituted on an ongoing basis to monitor and regulate the mobility of targeted racialized groups through legal practices of racial profiling. In this context, rather than promoting tolerance, justice, equity, recognition, and respect, diversity provokes tension and conflict with and between members of religious, cultural, and racialized groups.

Finally, diversity has produced alliances and networks between different kinds of resistance and social movements. For example, in this global era, there have been growing movements of decolonization and anti-colonialism that have grown between those in Africa, Mexico, South America, Australia, the U.S., and Canada. In this sense, diverse geographic locations, political commitments, ways of organizing, and social organizations have come together to address issues that are globally significant.

Summary

This chapter has explored the value and limitations of the concept of diversity, both in terms of its meaning and its political efficacy. One of the recurring themes in this exploration is the role of power in producing and organizing various kinds of social and political differences. Three approaches to the study of diversity and politics were also examined—namely, classical liberalism, liberal multiculturalism, and the radical school of thought. Each approach takes a different view on the role of the state in accommodating diversity and on the significance of the relationship between identity and power. Finally, the chapter concluded by examining some of the implications of diversity in a global era. An overview of these implications indicates that diversity can produce both positive and negative responses depending on the different kinds of exchanges that take place, on economic agendas and disparities, on racialized relations and contexts, and on the political activities of civil society actors.

Discussion Questions

1. Is there one national Canadian identity? How does diversity shape this national identity, if at all?
2. Canada is a country that relies on immigration for growth. What kinds of diversity policies should the government adopt in terms of immigration?
3. Do state policies regarding the promotion of diversity, such as multiculturalism, fracture or enhance social unity?
4. Does the concept of diversity adequately capture the problem of power differences?
5. Is diversity the source of global problems, or the solution to them?

References

Adhikari, Mohamed. 2004. "'Not Black Enough': Changing Expressions of Coloured Identity in Post-Aparthied South Africa." *South African Historical Journal*, November (51), 167–178.

Alfred, Taiaiake. 2005. *Wasase: Indigenous Pathways of Action and Freedom*. Peterborough, ON: Broadview Press.

Bannerji, Himani. 2000. *The Dark Side of the Nation: Essays on Multiculturalism, Nationalism and Gender*. Toronto: Canadian Scholars' Press Inc.

Barry, Brian. 2001. *Culture and Equality: An Egalitarian Critique of Multiculturalism*. Cambridge, MA: Harvard University Press.

Bhabha, Homi. 1994. *The Location of Culture*. London and New York: Routledge.

Deb, Kushal. 2002. "Introduction" in K. Deb, ed., *Mapping Multiculturalism*. Jaipur and New Delhi: Rawat Publications.

Fleras, Augie. 2004. "Racialising Culture/Culturalising Race: Multicultural Racism in a Multicultural Canada" in C.A. Nelson, ed., *Racism, Eh? A Critical Inter-Disciplinary Anthology of Race and Racism in Canada.* Concord, Ontario: Captus Press.

Immigration Act. 1906. R.S.C. c.93.

Immigration and Refugee Protection Act. 2001. Retrieved from **http://laws.justice.gc.ca/en/I-2.5/64755.html**.

Kukathas, Chandran. 1988. "Liberalism and Multiculturalism: The Politics of Indifference." *Political Theory,* 26 (5), 686–699.

Kuzio, Taras. 2005. "Western Multicultural Theory and Practice and Its Applicability to the Post-Soviet States." *Journal of Contemporary European Studies,* 13 (2), 221–237.

Kymlicka, William. 1995. *Multicultural Citizenship.* Oxford: Clarendon Press.

Kymlicka, William and B. He, eds. 2005. *Multiculturalism in Asia.* Oxford: Oxford University Press.

Miles, Robert. 2000. "Apropos the Idea of 'Race' . . . Again" in Les Back and John Solomos, eds., *Theories of Race and Racism: A Reader* (125 –143). London and New York: Routledge.

Monture-Angus, Patricia. 1995. *Thunder in My Soul: A Mohawk Woman Speaks.* Halifax: Fernwood Publishing.

Mosoff, Judith. 1999. "Excessive Demand on the Canadian Conscience: Disability, Family and Immigration." *Manitoba Law Journal,* 26 (1), 149 –179.

Okin, Susan Moller. 1999. "Is Multiculturalism Bad for Women?" In M.C. Nussbaum, ed., *Is Multiculturalism Bad for Women?* (9–24). Princeton, NJ: Princeton University Press.

Roediger, David R. 2002. "Whiteness and Ethnicity in the History of 'White Ethnics' in the United States" in D.T. Goldberg, ed., *Race Critical Theories: Text and Context* (325 –343). Malden, MA and Oxford, U.K.: Blackwell.

Satzewich, Vic. 2000. "White Limited: Racialization and the Social Construction of 'Peripheral Europeans.'" *Historie Sociale/Social History,* 33 (6), 271–289.

Taylor, Charles. 1994. "The Politics of Recognition" in A. Gutmann, ed., *Multiculturalism: Examining the Politics of Recognition* (25–74). Princeton: Princeton University Press.

Vertovec, Steven. 1996. "Multiculturalism, Culturalism and Public Corporation." *Ethnic and Racial Studies,* 19 (1), 49–69.

Further Readings

Abu-Laban, Yasmeen and Christina Gabriel. 2002. *Selling Diversity: Immigration, Multiculturalism, Employment Equity, and Globalization.* Peterborough, ON: Broadview Press.

Bulbeck, Chilla. 1998. *Re-Orienting Western Feminisms: Women's Diversity in a Postcolonial World.* Cambridge: Cambridge University Press.

Day, Richard L.E. 2000. *Multiculturalism and the History of Canadian Diversity.* Toronto: University of Toronto Press.

Eisenberg, Avigail. 2006. *Diversity and Equality: The Changing Framework of Freedom in Canada.* Vancouver: UBC Press.

Foster, Susan and Waithera Kinuthia. 2003. "Deaf Persons of Asian American, Hispanic American and African American Backgrounds: A Study of Intra-individual Diversity and Identity." *Journal of Deaf Studies and Deaf Education,* 8(3), 271–290.

Weblinks

Canadian Heritage: "Diversity and Multiculturalism"
www.pch.gc.ca/pc-ch/sujets-subjects/divers-multi/index_e.cfm

Google Scholar: "Diversity on Campus"
http://scholar.google.com/scholar?q=diversity%20on%20campus &hl=en &lr= &cr=countryCA &oi=scholart

Ontario Human Rights Commission
www.ohrc.on.ca

Wasáse Movement
www.wasase.org

CHAPTER 17

INDIGENOUS PEOPLES

Objectives

In the late twentieth century Indigenous peoples' advocacy led the international community to discuss and articulate norms for the promotion of their rights and well-being. Although growing efforts at the international level support the view that Indigenous peoples should collectively possess certain rights, one of the most controversial issues arising from these international debates concerns who defines who is Indigenous and how different ideas of indigenousness can be included in a universal definition. This chapter explores and problematizes the concept of Indigenous peoples. It begins by distinguishing the two approaches that have been used to define this term and examining their implications and limitations. The chapter then discusses whether a universal definition can be inclusive and flexible enough to encompass the diversity of Indigenous peoples. Finally, the chapter shows that the controversy about the meaning of "Indigenous peoples" and the scope of Indigenous peoples' rights involves conflicting views about what rules apply to this category of people and about their relationship with host national states.

ISABEL ALTAMIRANO-JIMENEZ

Introduction

One of the most contentious issues arising from the emergence of the global Indigenous rights movement involves the task of defining "Who exactly is Indigenous?" In past decades, considerable thinking and debate have been devoted to defining objective standards for identifying Indigenous peoples versus the unlimited right of Indigenous peoples to self-identification. This situation has exposed both the dilemma over standard-setting in international law and the complexity of this concept. On the one hand, the formulation of strict definitional standards excludes some Indigenous groups from the protection they need. On the other, the lack of a universal definition helps some host states to continue denying the existence of Indigenous peoples within their territories.

Historically, both states and international agencies, such as the World Bank, have insisted on developing and then unilaterally imposing upon Native populations their own bureaucratically rigorous yet exclusionary definitions of who constitutes an Indigenous people. The formulation of exclusionary definitions has been one among many strategies that national states have used to systematically deny Indigenous rights. As a result of the many negative experiences Indigenous peoples and organizations have had with official definitions of Indigenous status, they have insisted that they know who they are and have instead favoured a self-identification approach. In recent years, however, self-identification has come under attack as other ethnic minorities have started to assert their Indigenous status and identity. Therefore, this approach has become a problem.

Proponents of an objective definition of Indigenous peoples point out that a subjective theory of self-identification poses the problem of granting protection to those who may not need it. They argue that to qualify as "Indigenous," people should satisfy a set of objective criteria, but so far no universal and unambiguous definition of the concept of Indigenous peoples has been accepted. Indeed, this is a political construct whose meaning is not always clear. The original meaning of "indigenous," according to the Webster's Dictionary, is "inborn" or "originating from a locality." This term, however, has come to signify the *original inhabitants in a region* before the arrival of the European colonizers. **Tribal peoples** and "Aboriginal peoples" are alternative terms to refer to those who have maintained a collective identity through association with specific territories and with those who are in a non-dominant position. As this chapter shows, meanings often vary depending on who sets the boundaries.

Objective Definitions versus Self-Identification

Although no universal definition of "indigeneity" exists, international institutions have tried to identify a number of criteria by which Indigenous peoples can be characterized globally. One of the most cited working definitions of

Indigenous communities, peoples, and nations was proposed by José R. Martinez Cobo, the first United Nations (UN) Special Rapporteur for the Sub-Commission on Prevention of Discrimination and Protection of Minorities, in his famous *Study on the Problem of Discrimination Against Indigenous Populations* (1986). This working definition offers a number of basic ideas for defining Indigenous peoples, while at the same time recognizing their right to define by themselves who is Indigenous. The definition reads as follows:

> Indigenous communities, peoples and nations are those which, having a historical continuity with pre-invasion and pre-colonial societies that developed on their territories, consider themselves distinct from other sectors of the societies now prevailing on those territories, or parts of them. (Martinez Cobo, 1986, 7/Add4)

Moreover, this definition states that Indigenous peoples are non-dominant sectors of society and are willing to preserve, develop, and transmit to future generations their ancestral territories and their ethnic identity as the basis of their continued existence as peoples. Martinez Cobo establishes that historical continuity may consist of the endurance, for an extended period reaching into the present, of one or more of the following factors:

- occupation of ancestral lands, or part of them;
- common ancestry with the original occupants of these lands;
- cultural practices;
- the use of language;
- residence in certain parts of the country, or in certain regions of the world; and
- other relevant factors (Martinez Cobo, 1986/7/Add4).

Despite the prevalence of this working definition, some observers have rejected it on a variety of grounds, including the historical continuity with pre-colonial societies and the assumption that all groups are necessarily committed to preserve, develop, and transmit their ancestral lands to future generations. For example, some dispute the use of European conquest and invasion as objective historical criteria, for not all Indigenous peoples were conquered by military means. While this element may apply to many Indigenous peoples in the Americas, others who signed treaties and made alliances with the European settlers in Canada, the United States, and Latin American countries may be excluded. Another problem with Martinez Cobo's definition arises when identifying the descendants of the "original inhabitants." In most parts of the world, descendants have undergone transformation and change in cultural identity over time, sometimes resulting in large mixed blood populations. While the Métis people (of Native and European descent) of Canada consider themselves to be and are recognized by the government as Aboriginals, the Mestizo population (of Indigenous and Spaniard descent) in most Latin American countries do not consider themselves Indigenous and are, in fact, the dominant population. Although Martinez Cobo's definition is commonly used, neither is it inclusive nor does it capture the complexity of Indigenous peoples' lives and circumstances.

Another relevant definition crafted in the late 1980s in the context of the General Conference of the International Labour Organization (ILO) can be found in Convention 169, a legal tool aimed at recognizing and protecting Indigenous rights. This instrument builds upon some of Martinez Cobo's criteria. Convention 169 applies to

> tribal peoples in independent countries whose social, cultural and economic conditions distinguish them from other sections of the national community, and whose status is regulated wholly or partially by their own customs and traditions or by special laws or regulations. . . . (Office of the United Nations High Commissioner on Human Rights, 1989)

Convention 169 also applies to

> peoples in independent countries who are regarded as indigenous on account of their descent of the populations who inhabited the country or a geographical region to which the country belonged at the time of conquest or colonization or the establishment of present state boundaries. . . . (Office of the United Nations High Commissioner on Human Rights, 1989)

While Convention 169 distinguishes between tribal and Indigenous peoples, the difference between these two categories is unclear (Mills, 2002, 51). For some countries, this issue has been contentious because the term "peoples" reflects a difference in how international law should regard Indigenous rights. Arguably, the term "peoples" in international law implies the right to **self-determination** and secession or the right to constitute a new national state. Some countries such as the United States continue to use "Indigenous groups" instead of "Indigenous peoples," a choice reflecting the belief that Indigenous populations are like any other minority group (Lindroth, 2006, 244). Another criticism Convention 169 has faced is the emphasis given to the social, cultural, and economic differences between Indigenous peoples and the mainstream society. Since Indigenous peoples are disadvantaged, states are given an active role in deciding how to improve Indigenous peoples' conditions of life. Indigenous peoples and non-governmental organizations have argued that despite emphasizing the term "peoples," the Convention fails to firmly recognize Indigenous peoples' rights to self-determination by leaving states too much residual authority over these peoples (Saugee, 1997, 365–376).

The Right to Self-Identification

Indigenous peoples have strenuously objected to both the objective approach and a universal definition of who is Indigenous. Instead, they favour subjective self-identification, arguing that the question of who is and is not Indigenous should be left to the Indigenous communities themselves rather than to the state or other official agencies. Indigenous organizations contend that a universal definition would violate their right to self-determination, including their right to define their own membership. Indigenous participants in the UN Working Group on Indigenous peoples' rights have consistently stressed the need for flexibility and respect for the desire and the right of each group to define itself according to its own specific criteria. Self-identification, the argument goes, is a flexible process that accounts for the variations of Indigenous identity across time and place. In contrast, a universal definition demands precision and certainty, which undermine the reality that group identities have evolved across time and vary from one locale to the next (Alfred, 1999, 85).

Advocates of the objective definition approach argue that subjective self-identification would, by accommodating a variety of groups and perspectives, destroy the coherence of the international Indigenous movement. From this perspective, a subjective approach relying solely on self-identification would allow for the emergence of numerous groups that might undermine the sense of Indigenous collective identity and the assertion to distinct status. Whether self-identification would indeed fragment Indigenous collective identity is subject to debate. What is clear, however, is that the issue of who is Indigenous has become increasingly politicized as Indigenous organizations have attained a distinct legal international status. From the state's perspective, the implementation of a universal declaration of the rights of Indigenous peoples in the absence of standard definitional criteria could open the door to many claims that it is unwilling to entertain.

The battle over who defines Indigenous identity exposes a serious dilemma. On the one hand, a standard, rigid universal definition could potentially lead to the exclusion of Indigenous groups seeking protection. On the other, the lack of a universal definition could lead to the abuse of the concept and potentially dilute the rights of Indigenous peoples. Certainly not all marginalized groups would like to identify as Indigenous. Some may see advantages in assimilating into mainstream groups. Others, such as the Kurds from South Kurdistan, may feel that the Indigenous struggle is too parochial, seeking instead full national independence (Colchester, 2002).

Diverse Indigenous Peoples, Universal Definitions?

ALTHOUGH THE DETAILS OF THE HISTORIES OF DIFFERENT INDIGENOUS peoples may differ, most have had a common history of oppression, subordination, and subjugation, either by former colonizers, dominant groups in their territories, or both. Because of their deteriorating socio-economic conditions, Indigenous peoples are sometimes collectively referred to as the "**Fourth World**." This designation conveys the idea that, although these groups may reside in rich nations, they live in conditions that are often worse than those commonly associated with the Third World. Despite these commonalities, the question of who is Indigenous and by which criteria this term should be defined is problematic depending on the different regional histories. In Canada, for instance, it is difficult to generalize about Native peoples as a single group. They are broadly categorized into three groups included under the umbrella term of Aboriginal peoples. The first group is the First Nations, which is not a homogeneous category but, rather, an aggregate of numerous culturally diverse nations, including the Cree, the Ojibway, and the Mohawk. The second group is the Inuit people living in the Canadian Arctic and sub-Arctic as well as in other countries, such as Denmark and Russia. First Nations and Inuit have lived for millennia in what is now Canada. The third group, the Métis, is of Aboriginal and European descent and has only recently been recognized as an Aboriginal people.

The Métis are recognized in the *Constitution Act, 1982*, as one of the Aboriginal peoples of Canada. However, if strict criteria were applied to this people, and other peoples in similar situations, such as the Garifuna of the Atlantic Coast in Nicaragua, several arguments could be made about the inadequacy of these criteria. First, under the criterion of ancestral occupancy, which is one of the most frequently used parameters, these peoples either fail to qualify or barely qualify as Indigenous. However, Canada, using ancestral occupancy as an important criterion when negotiating land claims, recognizes the Métis as one of the three Aboriginal peoples of this country. Second, Martinez Cobo's definition requires that a people be a non-dominant sector of society and also that it have historical continuity with pre-invasion societies. The Métis, and for that matter most Indigenous peoples, easily meet the first requirement but have significant problems satisfying the second one.

The non-dominant criterion also faces some additional difficulties when applied to specific peoples. Not all Indigenous peoples are non-dominant numerically in their host states. Indigenous peoples such as the Inuit constitute 80 percent of the population in Greenland, while the Quechua and other Indigenous groups constitute over 60 percent of the Bolivian population. These Indigenous groups are, nonetheless, marginalized economically or politically. One wonders, if the situation changed and those living in a subordinated position ceased being non-dominant, whether they would no longer be Indigenous?

An additional concern with objective definitions has involved the issue of distinctive cultural characteristics and the maintenance of traditional institutions. The idea of identifying Indigenous peoples by their cultural distinctiveness is a relevant one. Indeed, an important aspect of Convention 169's definition is that Indigenous peoples have maintained their own social, economic, cultural, and political institutions since colonization and the establishment of new states. Some have argued that this indicator is useless by itself for distinguishing between Indigenous peoples, **ethnic groups**, and **diasporas**.

The criterion of cultural distinctiveness, which is used in many countries, can pose even more of a problem when it is used to force Indigenous peoples to display a commitment to changeless tradition to qualify as Indigenous. In the United States, for example, Indigenous peoples such as the Mashpee have lost legal territorial claims due to the perception that they have adapted to the dominant culture and, thus, have lost at least some of their traditional values. Similarly, to assert their identity, Aboriginal peoples in Canada have to prove that they were at a certain level of social organization at the time of colonization, that they were able to understand concepts of property, and that their timeless traditions have persisted. The application of such rigid criteria to define Indigenous peoples ignores the complexity of historical change and discounts the ways in which traditions may change in response to broader environmental factors and the challenges Indigenous peoples face as a result of policies and pressures to assimilate them into the dominant culture.

The above discussion illustrates that Indigenous peoples and their specific historical circumstances are so diverse that no single definition seems capable of including them all. However, despite their shortcomings, the working definitions provided by the UN Rapporteur Martinez Cobo and Convention 169 may be seen as a starting point among international Indigenous and non-Indigenous organizations for establishing a dialogue about "who is Indigenous" and about how to overcome the dilemma exposed by the international definition-setting. Moreover, these working definitions have, in some cases, provided international support for some Indigenous peoples' desperate struggle against continued colonization and land dispossession.

In sum, despite Indigenous peoples' diversity, several general elements to identify them still remain:

- self-identification as the descendents of the original inhabitants of a territory and as different from the dominant society;
- a distinct collective history traceable through written or oral accounts;
- cultural attachment to a particular area of land and a spatialized conception of the people and their land, which can be traced through language, religion, and traditional place-naming;
- contingent vulnerability as a result of economic, social, political, and cultural marginalization, colonization, dispossession, forced relocation, revocation of Indigenous status and treaty rights, assimilation policies, and misrecognition; and
- desire of the people to continue to live as a distinct people and according to their own evolving traditional formal and informal institutions, including customary laws and kinship networks.

Political Implications of the Concept of Indigenous Peoples

THE DEMANDS OF INDIGENOUS PEOPLES FOR COLLECTIVE RIGHTS HAVE evolved alongside the broader international movement for the protection of human rights, albeit often in the face of opposition from national states. This section explains why Indigenous peoples have not been fully protected by international law and why many national states oppose this protection.

Discussions on Indigenous peoples have taken place within the frameworks arising after World War II on human rights, minority rights, and the rights of Indigenous peoples. The first type of rights refers to general human rights to which everyone is entitled. The second type applies to persons belonging to national, ethnic, religious, or linguistic minorities. These rights are formulated as the right of individuals to preserve and develop their separate group identity *within the process of integration.* The third type is a separate set of human rights that apply only to Indigenous peoples. The rights are collective and are to a large extent aimed at *consolidating and strengthening the distinctiveness and separateness of these peoples from other groups in society.* These three different types of rights did not evolve evenly, with the third remaining the most contentious.

Although the decolonization movement after World War II challenged the very idea of a people subjugating another people and the imposition of an alien culture and politic-administrative system by a dominant group, the movement did not extend to Indigenous peoples (Sander, 1995, 12–13). As part of the decolonization movement, many new independent states emerged, but Indigenous peoples in these and other independent states remained subjects. Since that time and owing in large part to sustained Indigenous advocacy by groups such as the Sami Council and the Inuit Circumpolar Conference, a substantive body of international jurisprudence aimed at recognizing Indigenous peoplehood has emerged (Colchester, 2002). At present, international law accepts, at least in principle, that Indigenous peoples have collective rights to physical and cultural survival, self-determination, self-government, land and resource ownership, and the exercise of their customary laws. Nevertheless, the ongoing demands of Indigenous peoples for the recognition of their collective rights, particularly the right to self-determination, has met stiff opposition from national states (Corbett, 1996, 40).

Although the *Draft Declaration on the Rights of Indigenous Peoples,* completed in 1992 by the UN Working Group, firmly recognizes that the core concepts of Indigenous rights are territorial rights, self-determination, autonomy, and international legal status (Kingsbury, 2001, 102), host states have been reluctant to ratify it. Erika Irene A. Daes (1995), the UN commentator, argues that by recognizing legal personality, territorial security, and international responsibility, the Draft Declaration emphasizes the collective legal status of Indigenous peoples and the need to protect their distinctive identity. This document also urges states to actively embrace this status and to provide financial and political assistance to realize Indigenous rights.

The right to Indigenous self-determination is considered to be the main tenet and symbol of the Indigenous movement (Daes, 2003, 303). Yet this right is contentious because of its secessionist connotation. Governments disagree about the definition of this right and, especially, its application. Almost without exception, however, governments have argued that if self-determination is to be used in the UN Declaration, this term should be either qualified or defined to exclude any connotation of national independence. Some countries, such as Australia, have focused on the need to protect the territorial integrity of states, calling for suitable references to be included in the Declaration. Others, including the United States and Sweden, have stressed the need to clarify the applicability of this term, which has a specific meaning under international law, to Indigenous peoples. Mexico, Chile, and Brazil have expressed concerns about using the very concept of self-determination.

Canada, in contrast, has raised questions about the relationship between Indigenous groups and state sovereignty if the international right of self-determination is included in the Declaration. The Canadian government supports the principle of self-determination for Indigenous people, but only if it is limited within the framework of existing sovereign states and only if it means giving Indigenous people more autonomy over their own affairs. From this perspective, Canada believes that the challenge is to design a concept of self-determination that obliges states and Indigenous peoples to work out arrangements for the sharing of power within the limits of the national state and existing institutions.

In responding to states' opposition to the right to self-determination included in the Draft Declaration, most Indigenous organizations have provided positive assurance that Indigenous peoples do not intend to dismember existing countries but rather to exercise their right to self-determination in a form of free association with the national states in which they live. As part of their right to self-determination, they envision the right to control their territory, natural resources, social organization, and decision-making institutions and to maintain their culture and ways of life. However, even this limited vision of self-determination presents problems for some states.

The Indigenous vision of self-determination is particularly important when considering that Indigenous peoples are still deprived of their land and life-sustaining resources in many countries, including Canada. In principle, it is now accepted that **minority rights** are not enough to protect Indigenous peoples' distinctiveness and that collective territorial rights should be included as special rights for Indigenous peoples. However, many states are reluctant to recognize Indigenous land titles, as their recognition may limit the state's ability to promote development and exploit natural resources within Indigenous territories (Altamirano, 2004).

In addition, the realization of Indigenous peoples' rights requires appropriate mechanisms and procedures that should be defined and elaborated on in national and legal frameworks. At the international level, complaint and monitoring procedures are available to promote and help implement Indigenous rights. Nevertheless, national states are not compelled to accept any recommendation. The ultimate protection of Indigenous peoples occurs at the national level, and such protection requires the state's active and positive participation. So far, the prevailing mechanisms used at the national level often consist of negotiated agreements, partnerships, and constitutional and legislative measures. In some cases, the judiciary's proactive role and the civil society's intervention have also been relevant in the support of Indigenous demands (Al Faruque and Begum, 2004, 27).

Nevertheless, by centring the discussion on the concept and meaning of Indigenous self-determination, little has been done in practice to preserve Indigenous cultural integrity. Ensuring the future viability of Indigenous peoples involves guaranteeing their autonomy and their control over lands and natural resources, religion, language, and education, all of which are fundamental to the maintenance of their cultural integrity.

Summary

This chapter has explored the complexity of establishing a universally accepted definition of Indigenous peoples. The debate over who is Indigenous and who has the power to define Indigenous identity has increasingly been politicized not only because Indigenous peoples have obtained some international legal recognition, but also because the realization of their collective rights has important political implications for national states. The difficulty of defining a universal concept of Indigenous peoples has partly to do with the fact that it is a political construction aimed at creating a subject of international law and at giving voice to culturally diverse peoples who, nonetheless, share a history of dispossession, marginalization, and domination.

Both the objective and subjective approaches to defining Indigenous peoples have limitations and face important challenges. On the one hand, definitions using strict criteria may exclude some Indigenous peoples who do not conform to the parameters but do identify themselves as Indigenous. On the other, an open self-identification policy opens the door to other minority groups seeking to take advantage of the rights and protections granted to Indigenous peoples. In overcoming the dilemma exposed by both the objective and subjective approaches, it is important to avoid oversimplifying Indigenous identities and to acknowledge that no universal definition alone will ensure cultural protection for all Indigenous peoples. Thus, any flexible definition must include Indigenous peoples' right to self-identification as a central element.

Discussion Questions

1. Is the concept of Indigenous peoples a coherent concept?
2. Is it possible to reach an inclusive universal concept of Indigenous peoples?
3. Why does the concept of Indigenous peoples have a political load?
4. Do Indigenous peoples have a just claim to "self-determination," and what might such a claim mean?
5. How do state and Indigenous positions on self-determination differ?

References

Al Faruque, Abdullah and Najnin Begum. 2004. "Conceptualizing Indigenous Peoples' Rights: An Emerging New Category of Third Generation of Rights." *Asia-Pacific Journal of Human Rights and the Law* 5(2), 1–29.

Alfred, Taiaiake. 1999. *Peace, Power and Righteousness: An Indigenous Manifesto.* New York: Oxford University Press.

Altamirano-Jimenez, Isabel. 2004. "North American First Peoples: Slipping Up into Market Citizenship?" *Citizenship Studies*, 8 (4), 349–365.

Colchester, Marcus. 2002. "Guest Editorial: Indigenous Rights and the Collective Conscious." *Anthropology Today*, 18 (1).

Corbett, Helen. 1996. "A History of the U.N. Draft Declaration on Indigenous Peoples." Unpublished Report.

Corntassel, Jeff A. 2003. "Who Is Indigenous? 'Peoplehood' and Ethnonationalist Approaches to Rearticulating Indigenous Identity." *Nations and Ethnic Politics*, 9 (1), 75–100.

Daes, Erica-Irene A. 1995. "Equality of Quality of Indigenous Peoples Under the Auspices of the United Nations-Draft Declaration on the Rights of Indigenous Peoples." *St. Thomas Law Review*, 7, 493, 496.

———. 2002. "Article 3 of the Draft UN Declaration on the Rights of Indigenous Peoples: 'Obstacles and Consensus.'" Paper presented at the Rights and Democracy Seminar of Experts on the Right to Self-Determination of Indigenous Peoples, New York.

Kingsbury, Benedict. 1998. "Indigenous Peoples in International Law: A Constructivist Approach to the Asian Controversy. *The American Journal of International Law*, 92.

———. 2001. "Reconciling Five Competing Conceptual Structures of Indigenous Peoples' Claims in International and Comparative Law" in Philip Alston, ed., *Peoples' Rights*. Oxford University Press.

Lindroth, Marjo. 2006. "Indigenous-State Relations in the UN: Establishing the Indigenous Forum." *Polar Record*, 42 (222), 238–248.

Martinez Cobo, José. 1986. *Study of the Problem of Discrimination Against Indigenous Populations*. U.N. Doc. E/CN.4/Sub.2/1986/7/Add4.

Mills, John. 2002. "Legal Constructions of Cultural Identity in Latin America: An Argument Against Defining Indigenous Peoples." *Texas Hispanic Journal of Law and Policy*, 8 (49), 46–77.

Office of the United Nations High Commissioner on Human Rights. 1989. "Indigenous and Tribal Peoples Convention Num. 169." Retrieved on October 26, 2007, from **www.ohch.org/english/law/indigenous.htm**.

Rouland, Pierre, Stephane Pierre-Caps, and Jacques Poumarede. 1999. *Derechos de minorías y de pueblos autóctonos*. Mexico City: Siglo XXI.

Sanders, Douglas. 1995. "State Practice and the United Nations Draft Declaration on the Rights of Indigenous Peoples" in Terje Brantenberg, Janne Hansen, and Henry Minde, eds., *Becoming Visible: Indigenous Politics and Self-Government*. Tromsø: The University of Tromsø, Sámi dutkamiid guovddáš—Centre for Sámi Studies.

Suagee, Dean B. 1997. "Human Rights of Indigenous People: Will the United States Rise to the Occasion?" *American Indian Law Review*, 21, 365–367.

Further Readings

Anaya, S. James. 1996. *Indigenous Peoples in International Law.* New York, Oxford University Press.

Läm, Miaban. 2000. *At the Edge of the State: Indigenous Peoples and Self-determination.* Ardsley: Transnational Publishers.

Niezen, Ronald. 2003. *The Origins of Indigenism: Human Rights and the Politics of Identity.* Berkeley: University of California Press.

Weblinks

Office of the United Nations High Commissioner for Human Rights
www.ohchr.org/english/issues/education/training/udhr.htm

International Labour Organization
www.ilo.org/public/english/region/ampro/mdtsanjose/indigenous/derecho.htm

Indian and Northern Affairs Canada (The Royal Commission Report on the Aboriginal Peoples of Canada)
www.ainc-inac.gc.ca/ch/rcap/index_e.html

CHAPTER 18

ENVIRONMENTAL POLITICS

Objectives

"The environment" is a relatively new concept, as well as political concern. In this chapter we will review the meanings of the terms "environment" and "ecology," and describe a variety of political-economic approaches to contemporary environmental problems. Although there are different ways of classifying environmental approaches, this chapter will focus on "limits to growth" approaches, highlighting seven approaches to environmental politics today. These key approaches are market liberalism, eco-Marxism, eco-feminism, eco-centrism, Aboriginal perspectives, environmental justice, and ecological democracy.

LAURIE E. ADKIN

Introduction

Although the idea of "the environment"—referring to the biophysical surroundings of humankind—is commonly used in public policy contexts everywhere in the world today, prior to the twentieth century this was not the case. Earlier societies thought in terms of "nature" and had different understandings of the relationship between nature and humans. The early Greeks viewed nature as an eternal, unchanging order, while Confucius viewed the living world as a spontaneously self-generating life force. Medieval society also saw nature in organic terms, as a living being. However, with the rise of capitalism and modern science, people increasingly viewed nature as merely providing resources for human use.

In the nineteenth century and until World War II, the terms "environment" and "environmentalism" came into popular usage to refer to the biophysical, geographical, and climatic factors thought to be responsible for shaping human development. By the early twentieth century, attention began to focus on the ways in which humans alter the natural environment. As human settlement extended to ever-greater areas of the Americas, leading to deforestation, some people began to advocate for "conservation" or "preservation" practices and ethics. Following World War II, industrialization, population growth, and rising levels of consumption per capita in the West made negative environmental effects obvious and discussion turned to the biophysical limits of such rapid economic growth.

Some significant works were published about environmental concerns in the 1950s, especially about the threat of resource scarcity. However, the publication of Rachel Carson's book *Silent Spring* (1962) drew public attention to the harm to the natural environment caused by the widespread application of insecticides and herbicides, as well as the introduction of thousands of new chemicals for consumer use. This book played an important role in mobilizing the environmental movement of the 1960s. At the same time, growing fears about the effects of radioactive fallout led to massive protests against nuclear bomb testing. From the 1960s onward "the environment" came to mean something new and became an object of citizen concern and public policy. People began to think of the environment as a collective good for which they had a shared responsibility, or for whose protection governments could be held accountable.

When we talk about "the environment" today, we generally mean both "nature"—understood as a world we share with all other life on the planet—and the biophysical conditions of human existence. The environment encompasses not only green spaces, parks, or wilderness (what we think of collectively as nature) but also urban environments, the atmosphere, the ocean, and the biosphere. We speak of local environments and recognize many environmental problems as global in scope. Global warming is an obvious example of a set of environmental challenges that no national government can meet alone.

A related term that has entered our political lexicon is "ecology." This term has crossed over from the realm of natural science to the realm of social science but at the same time bridges the two. The German biologist Ernst Haeckel (1834–1919) used the Greek words *oikos* (meaning "home") and *logos* (meaning "study") to name the science that examines the relationship between an organism and its environment (or home). Today, ecological scientists study the evolution and adaptation of organisms, the requirements for their reproduction, their interactions within specific *ecosystems*, or *habitats*, and various feedback systems at local, regional, and planetary levels. The emergence of the fields of environmental science and conservation biology has greatly contributed to our knowledge of growing environmental problems. "Ecological" today generally refers to a holistic approach to understanding the relationships among the organisms inhabiting particular spaces, and their interactions with the biophysical properties of those spaces. Qualified by such terms as "social" or "political," ecology becomes a concern with the interactions *between humans and their natural environments* (including all of the other beings who inhabit these).

Limits to Growth

THE FACT THAT PRACTICALLY EVERYONE TRYING TO INFLUENCE PUBLIC POLICY—FROM former U.S. vice-president Al Gore to Indian anti-globalization activist Vandana Shiva—claims to be an environmentalist suggests the complexity and importance of environmental issues today. A major environmental theme is the claim that there are biophysical "limits to growth" on a finite planet Earth. This claim was widely popularized in the 1970s with the publication of works such as the Club of Rome's *Limits to Growth*. Scientists and statisticians modelled trends in global population growth, food production, and resource consumption and concluded that human population and economic growth risked "over-shooting" the earth's carrying capacity. Moreover, biodiversity is diminished daily as ecosystems undergo rapid transformations and species become endangered or extinct.

Most environmentalists today believe that further economic growth in the North will sacrifice biodiversity, deepen global inequalities and conflict, and create severe hardships for future generations. Most acknowledge that populations in the comparatively affluent global North bear the lion's share of responsibility for averting environmental crises by using resources more efficiently, eliminating pollution, sharing technology, and reducing consumption. Wackernagel and Rees (1996) have developed the now-famous concept of the **ecological footprint**, defined as the total area of productive land and water continuously required to produce all the resources consumed and to assimilate all the wastes produced by a specified human population, with the prevailing technology, wherever on earth that land is located (50–51). Wackernagel and Rees calculated in 1996 that the total land area required to support the consumption of an average Canadian was *at least* 4.3 hectares, including 2.3 hectares for carbon dioxide assimilation alone. Thus, the per capita ecological footprint of Canadians was almost *three times* their "fair Earthshare" of 1.5 hectares, and more than *ten times* the ecological footprint of an average Indian citizen (0.4 hectares). (A fair Earthshare is the amount of ecologically productive land available per person on earth.)

Before turning to an examination of some key approaches to studying and remedying environmental problems, it is important to note that disagreement about the urgency of dealing with these questions still remains. A "Promethean" argument has countered "limits to growth" claims since the 1970s, asserting that humankind will always have an abundance of resources (the name "Promethean" is taken from the Greek myth). Prometheans argue that any resource scarcities will be compensated for by new technologies or new substitutes, and that human ingenuity can conquer any environmental problems that arise. This view has found favour with various politicians and can be seen in the American decision to withdraw from the Kyoto Protocol in 2001 and in the Harper government's rejection of Canada's Kyoto implementation plan. (The 1997 Kyoto Protocol established individual targets for the signatory countries to reduce their greenhouse gas emissions. Canada signed in April 1998 and ratified in December 2002.)

Approaches to Environmental Problems

EACH OF THE APPROACHES DISCUSSED BELOW OFFERS A PARTICULAR EXPLANATION for environmental problems and proposes specific policy alternatives for meeting environmental challenges.

Liberal Market Environmentalism

Market liberalism occupies a continuum of positions, from a "pure" version of free-market liberalism at one end to a more pragmatic "market-based" environmental policy approach at the other end. "Pure" market liberals believe that the "tragedy of the commons" (Hardin 1968)—that is, the overuse and depletion of natural resources—may be prevented if we privatize everything that is presently in the public realm, including air, water, and other species. Their argument is that humans value their own private property more than they value public (common) property. In the first case, we pay the price ourselves if we degrade our property (for instance, our land or water); in the second case, no one individual is accountable for the cumulative effects of common use. Moreover, market liberals suggest that the market will provide environmentally friendly products if there is sufficient public demand. For free-market environmental thinkers, citizens' groups and non-governmental organizations (NGOs) are mere "special interests" that interfere with the workings of the market by persuading governments to intervene. The actors in their universe are not citizens but consumers, producers, or entrepreneurs.

The key solutions to environmental problems of pollution or resource scarcity, the "pure" market liberals assert, are twofold: first, the creation of private property rights where none currently exist, and second, reliance on market forces (supply and demand) to measure values. Thus, if I had the right to enjoyment of clean air in the land area that I own, I could sue any party that polluted "my" air (assuming that I could prove in court that the party in question was responsible for the pollution). If park land is valued more for its wilderness value than for its timber value, then environmentalists will buy it and preserve it from industrial use. Some even argue that wildlife could also be privately owned and that ownership would be verified by branding.

Other market liberals take a less extreme view of an appropriate role for market forces in environmental policy. Some suggest "market-based" or "quasi-market" policies as a less-than-ideal but effective way to alter the behaviour of corporations and consumers. While they might prefer direct government regulation that demands, for example, immediate and substantial reductions in pollution on the part of industry, many environmentalists believe that the political climate does not exist for such policies. Instead, governments can adjust the regulatory frameworks of markets in ways that alter incentives and disincentives for behaviours that affect the environment. The main instruments are taxes and fees that make pollution, or resource consumption, more expensive and thereby create incentives for pollution abatement, greater energy efficiency, reduced consumption, or markets for products that are more environmentally friendly. Thus some environmental organizations support energy, or "carbon" taxes, to make consumption of fossil-fuels more costly and to encourage the transition to less toxic alternatives. Some organizations have called for the privatization of public utilities that provide nuclear energy, on the grounds that this would eliminate large public subsidies and make evident the true cost of nuclear power. The creation of markets in "pollution permits" (e.g., for SO_2) or greenhouse gas (e.g., CO_2) emission credits, within an overall cap on emissions per sector or region, is another "market-based" approach to reducing specific pollutants. Companies tend to support such credit or permit-trading systems because they allow them the flexibility to choose the least costly means of meeting regulatory standards (investment in pollution abatement or the purchase of credits). These types of approaches require a role for governments in setting targets or caps, in implementing new taxes or subsidies, or in eliminating existing subsidies.

Eco-Marxism

Eco-Marxists argue that the root cause of environmental destruction is capitalism. Capitalism is inherently productivist (growth-oriented) and places profit-making above any other social or environmental goals. While the free-market liberals believe that privatization of the natural environment is the solution to environmental problems, eco-Marxists point to the actual environmental damage caused by real market actors, such as corporations, in their pursuit of profit. The "greening" of capitalism through various reforms, or incentives to improve energy efficiency, according to eco-Marxists, will not be sufficient to avert serious ecological crises, because capitalism is inherently expansionist. The eco-Marxist thinker James O'Connor (1998) has argued that capitalist exploitation of nature produces "liquidity crises," as in the over-fishing of the oceans, leading corporations to seek other areas of investment (such as fish-farming) or to try to engineer nature to offset the depletion of resources and compensate for ecological degradation (such as through the genetic engineering of trees, plants, and animals). In addition, capitalism produces huge social inequalities and imposes the worst consequences of ecological degradation on the communities with the fewest resources to cope with them. Eco-Marxists argue that capitalism has proven incapable of providing the necessities of life for the peoples of the world and has been destructive of both biodiversity and cultural diversity. The kind of regulation of capitalist markets that would be required to reverse such damage, and to permit socially and ecologically sustainable societies to exist, would be so extensive that it would amount to a post-capitalist model (O'Connor, 1998).

Eco-Marxists argue that the globalization of capitalist markets has only deepened these contradictions. According to John Bellamy Foster and Brett Clark (2003), capitalism has produced a "planetary rift in the human relation to the global commons— the atmosphere and oceans" or a **global metabolic rift**." They label as **ecological imperialism** capitalists' "appropriation of the global commons . . . and the carbon absorption capacity of the biosphere, primarily to the benefit of a relatively small number of countries at the centre of the capitalist world economy." The banks and international financial institutions located in the OECD countries have imposed draconian debt-repayment programs on countries of the South, leading in many cases to the rapid liquidation of these countries' exportable natural resources. Thus the North has accumulated its own debt to the global South—an **ecological debt** resulting from "resource plundering, environmental damages, and the free occupation of environmental space to deposit wastes, such as greenhouse gases, from the industrial countries" (Acción Ecológica, 2003). The annual ecological debt of the North, owed to the South, is calculated to be at least three times the financial debt that the South currently "owes" to the North" (Foster and Clark, 2003, 196).

Eco-Feminism

While eco-feminists agree that global environmental destruction is caused by the dominant capitalist economic model and modern scientific rationalism, they associate these developments with patriarchy, or the historical domination of women by men. The key insight of eco-feminists is that both women and nature have been subjugated in modern, patriarchal societies. To explain this, Carolyn Merchant (1980) examines the relationship between the rise of capitalism and modern science in the sixteenth and seventeenth centuries, and cultural shifts in perceptions of women and nature. She discovers a transformation from an earlier, organic cosmology which conceived of a nurturing female earth, to a hierarchical, mechanistic world view that promotes the exploitation of nature. In this view, nature becomes the object of scientific inquiry and the inert matter to be exploited by men. Bacon—often referred to as the "father" of modern science, represented nature as female and the scientist as male; the task of the scientist was to penetrate nature and force her to give up her secrets. In Bacon's utopia, scientists are high-ranking, priest-like figures in a patriarchal order. Merchant's research identifies the dualisms that have become pervasive in Western culture: the concepts associated with "woman" or femininity (for example, nature, passivity, object, body, sorcery, darkness, chaos) are inferior in the dominant culture to those associated with "man" or masculinity (culture, action, subject, science, mind, light, reason).

Likewise, the life-reproducing activities of women have tended to be less valued in modern societies than activities that take place in the market sphere. For example, most of the world's subsistence agricultural production and household labour are carried out by women, who depend upon access to land, water, firewood, and other natural resources to ensure their families' survival. These are the very resources that—as Vandana Shiva argues—are often damaged, privatized, or otherwise removed from women's control by the processes of colonialism and development. In Shiva's view, "patriarchal categories which understand destruction as 'production' and regeneration of life as 'passivity' have generated a crisis of survival" (1988, 3). Development, says Shiva, is really **mal-development**, "a development bereft of the feminine, the conservation, the ecological principle" (4).

Eco-Centrism

A school of thinkers associated with the Norwegian philosopher Arne Naess coined the term "deep ecology" in the 1970s to differentiate their analysis of the cultural foundations of the ecological crisis from "shallow" proposals to merely reform some of the practices of industrial society. For deep ecologists, forests, mountains, landscapes, oceans, other species, and other aspects of nature have "intrinsic value" that is not reducible to market values. They argue that humans should seek to "cultivate a deep consciousness and awareness of organic unity, of the holistic nature of the ecological webs in which every individual is enmeshed" (Dryzek, 2005a, 184). Eco-centric perspectives share with eco-feminism the rejection of a hierarchical view of the world in which it is assumed that men should dominate nature. Instead, they advocate the principle of **biocentric equality**, rejecting **anthropocentrism** and viewing all species as equally deserving of moral consideration.

Some eco-centric concepts have been criticized, such as the distinctions between intrinsic and instrumental value, anthropocentrism and eco-centrism, culture and nature. By what, or whose, standards do we decide, for example, whether a practice (such as hunting) represents domination or co-existence? What is "nature"? While these questions are difficult to answer—or perhaps, more accurately, evoke many answers—political theorist Robyn Eckersley argues that we must continue "to explore both continuities and differences between humans and other species, between human autonomy and nonhuman agency, and what 'solidarity' and 'nondomination' might mean between humans and other humans, and between humans and nonhuman species" (2004a, 370). We know, minimally, that we are both different and interdependent—that we share a planet upon which we depend for sustenance.

Aboriginal Perspectives

First Nations' views of human–nature relationships derive from creation stories and from cosmologies in which both the animate and inanimate elements of creation may be imbued with spirit and memory. According to Deborah MacGregor (2004, 85), traditional environmental knowledge is not "a body of knowledge" but a *way of being* in relation to other beings, the environment, and the Creator. It provides ethical values and rules governing the use of nature (limits, sharing, giving back to Creation). Culture is rooted in the land, in a place, in the history lived in the place, and handed down from generation to generation. Everything in nature is imbued with Spirit; everything in nature is the gift of the Creator; all beings are connected and have reciprocal obligations to one another and to Creation. We have much to learn from such Aboriginal words as *kanikonri:io*, a Kahniakehaka or Mohawk word meaning "the good mind," which requires living in harmony with the other "nations" of the earth, and which constitutes "the path of righteousness and reason into the future" (Arquette et al., 2004, 336–337).

Environmental Justice

This approach has its origins in the United States, in struggles that have connected racism with environmental "bads." These struggles take the form of grassroots groups and coalitions that bring together the environmental and civil rights movements. Authors like Robert Bullard (1993) have documented how racialized communities suffer disproportionately from exposure to hazardous wastes, proximity to polluting industries, incinerators and landfills, and urban developments such as freeways, which eliminate green spaces and intensify noise and other forms of pollution. Black Americans and Native Americans have been particularly affected by such forms of environmental racism. White, middle-class neighbourhoods tend to have superior resources with which to resist developments that threaten their quality of life and are typically located farther from industrial areas or congested inner cities. It has also been observed that the membership and leadership of environmental non-governmental organizations (ENGOs) in North America have been predominantly white and middle-class. Such organizations have been criticized for failing to recognize the class and racial dimensions of environmental and health degradation. The opposition of poor and racialized communities to the location of incinerators and other environmental bads in their neighbourhoods, and their efforts to protect their children from pollution risks have been referred to, collectively, as the environmental justice movement. Celene Kraus (1994) has observed that the leaders of these coalitions are typically women.

Winona LaDuke (2000) has written extensively and eloquently about the devastating effects on North American First Nations of colonial development, which destroyed the ecological bases for subsistence economies, exposed First Nations to toxic contaminants—including radiation—and continues to disregard First Nations' land claims and treaty rights. There are many such cases in Canada, where First Nations have few legal means to prevent unwanted "development" on the territories to which they claim treaty rights. Non-native environmentalists are beginning to integrate support for First Nations' sovereignty into their campaigns to save wilderness areas. For example, in the 1990s Greenpeace and Friends of Clayoquot Sound worked with the Nuu-chah-nulth bands of the region in their efforts to stop the clear-cutting of old-growth, temperate rain forest.

Environmental racism also has a global dimension. Since the 1970s, polluting industries have relocated to newly industrializing countries of the South, where environmental standards and wages are smaller impediments to profit-making than in the

North. European countries ship toxic wastes to African shores. Multinational oil companies have poisoned the land, air, and water of the Ogoni people in the river delta state of Nigeria and have been accused of complicity in the repressive activities of the Nigerian government. While populations in the North seek to "green" their model of development, many of the worst forms of environmental degradation are displaced to the South.

Ecological Democracy

Some ecological theorists argue that liberal democracy must be superseded by deeper forms of democracy. This is because existing political and economic institutions are unable to deliver either social justice or ecological sustainability. Market liberalization and the prioritization of international economic competitiveness have diminished the abilities of governments to prevent environmental harms. Moreover, the short-term concerns of political parties and governments, dictated by electoral cycles, have obstructed the kind of comprehensive, long-term planning needed to deal with such problems as global climate change. Resources to influence policy-making are very unequally distributed, with large corporate and other organized interests having more weight or representation in decision-making processes than individual citizens. Some interests are systematically marginalized. And of course, as the eco-centrists point out, other species have no votes. They must rely on the voices of environmentalists to try to discern and to represent their interests.

For these reasons, ecological democratic theorists have proposed ways to level the playing field in the "deliberative" (or decision-making) processes that shape the direction of society. These include more inclusive representation of interests (making sure that every party with a stake in the issue is at the table), creating the conditions for broader participation (such as paying the expenses of citizen interveners), and permitting a greater range of knowledge and alternatives to be presented and considered (not just those of the dominant groups, or the predetermined agenda of the government). While the democratic theorists believe that much could be done to democratize decision-making processes and to produce better social and ecological outcomes, they also acknowledge that such processes may be undermined by, or subordinated to, the power and influence of market actors. This is because in a capitalist economy large corporations and financial institutions have enormous bargaining power vis-à-vis governments. In liberal public spheres, there are real inequalities of power. This observation brings us back to the eco-Marxists, who pose the problem of political and economic power very clearly, and who view the hegemonic order as deeply invested in anti-ecological pursuits.

Robyn Eckersley (2004b) has tried to conceptualize what a "green state" would look like—that is, what its political institutions and constitution might be. She proposes elements of a green constitution and a charter of citizens' environmental rights and responsibilities, while also recognizing the necessity of economic and societal changes. Ecological values need to be internalized, or normalized, she argues, just as economic ones have been in liberal democracies. It is up to the "green public sphere" to bring about this cultural shift, "in the same way that the bourgeois public sphere facilitated the shift toward the widespread diffusion of liberal market values" (245). To this end, ecological economists, political analysts, and activists in many movements around the world have proposed numerous reforms for economic restructuring as well as political democratization. Comprehensive programs have been developed by green parties, and some of their elements have been adopted by other political parties.

In Eckersley's view, "transnational green public spheres," social movements, and green parties together will bring about transitional reforms, just as social movements in the nineteenth and twentieth centuries did in order to construct social democratic states. The time is ripe, she suggests, because it has become increasingly clear that liberal democratic states are incapable of resolving ecological problems.

Summary

This review has presented some of the approaches that make claims about the existence of environmental problems, their causes, and their solutions. There is some agreement among these approaches; for example, all but the Prometheans and the pure market liberals accept that humans will confront some limits to resource consumption. Their differences, of course, are significant. If we believe the Prometheans, we need do nothing but continue much the way we have been doing; if we believe the eco-Marxists, radical societal changes are necessary.

Depending on their ideological orientations, the resources available to them, and the nature of their civil societies, governments have been more or less receptive to the conflicting claims of these environmental approaches. Governments in Northern Europe have been the most amenable to implementing green plans or sustainable development targets. The European Union has adopted supranational environmental regulations under sustained pressures from European green parties and publics concerned with health and environmental risks. The "Anglo-American" or market-liberal democracies have proven much more resistant to any comprehensive approach to "ecological modernization." Conservative governments in the United States, Canada, and Australia have consistently refused to meet international targets for greenhouse gas reductions.

The fact that these same countries are among the largest per capita consumers of the world's resources has led some to ask whether a "global apartheid" system is emerging, in which "one part of humanity is assigned a large ration [of limited resources] while another part gets only a small ration" (Altvater, 1998, 33). Moreover, some populations are more responsible than others for the excessive use (over decades of industrialization) of the planet's "sinks" for wastes such as greenhouse gases yet are refusing to reduce significantly their exploitation of this global commons (the earth's atmosphere). The eco-Marxist and environmental justice approaches remind us to be alert to class and racial inequalities at all levels—from the local to the global.

The eco-feminist and eco-centric discourses have had, perhaps, the most difficulty in penetrating mainstream debates about "sustainable development." Feminist research on the ways in which women are more adversely affected by the commercialization of agriculture, ecological degradation, or the effects of climate change has begun to "be heard" in some policy domains.

Deep ecologists, Aboriginal cultures, and non-Western philosophical traditions that ask us to think about our relationships with other species in terms of interdependence, reciprocity, and biocentric equality have, to date, made little headway in public policy debates. Even the position that nature or other species have "intrinsic value," apart from any instrumental value they may have to humans, is difficult for environmentalists to voice in land-use consultations and other contexts. Far more successful has been the "developmentalist" discourse of governments and corporations, utilizing the language of "integrated resource management" or "sustainable development," in which "no growth" is "not an option."

The approaches that we have reviewed bring different insights to bear on one of the most pressing questions of our time: the environmental sustainability of human economic development. Is there a point at which we will irreversibly damage the earth's ability to sustain the human population? We need to ask questions about the equity dimensions of environmental pollution and limits to growth. What are the implications of the claim that, if everyone on earth lived like the average Canadian or American, we would need at least *three* earths to provide the necessary resources and to absorb the wastes we would produce?

Current debates about the implications of global warming are part of such larger questions. The efforts of scientists, ENGOs, and "green publics" around the world have pushed governments to enter into such international treaties as the 1992 United Nations Framework Convention on Climate Change (UNFCCC) and the 1987 Montreal Protocol (which phased out the production of ozone-depleting substances). A quick look at the list of civil society organizations on the list of "parties and observers" of the UNFCCC provides an indication of the range of actors trying to influence policy at national and international levels—from the World Business Council on Sustainable Development to Greenpeace International and a host of other international ENGOs, to scientific and other organizations from the Canadian Arctic to the Amazon Basin. Transnational networks of environmentalists and Aboriginal peoples (such as Climate Action Network International; the Global Forest Coalition; Action for Solidarity, Equality, Environment and Development, Europe; the Third World Network, the Coordinator of the Indigenous Organizations of the Amazon Basin; the Indigenous Environmental Network; the Inuit Circumpolar Council; and the South African Climate Action Network, to name just a few) continue to pressure for action on climate change. Employing the critical interpretations of global capitalism and its environmental costs that have been outlined in this chapter, these actors believe that social justice, both globally and generationally, as well as planetary health and biodiversity are at stake in the outcomes of these struggles.

These questions demonstrate the ways in which "environmental" conflicts have always been about much more than the preservation of nature or the prevention of pollution. Environmental conflicts are embedded in world views, economic systems, political institutions, and human needs, and their resolutions are transformative for all of these.

Discussion Questions

1. Who should we believe: the "limits to growth" environmentalists or the Prometheans?
2. Who should be responsible for ensuring that the environment and human health are not harmed by the numerous chemicals being produced and marketed?

References

Acción Ecológica. 2003. "Ecological Debt: South Tells North 'Time to Pay Up.'" Retrieved October 26, 2007, from **www.cosmovisiones.com/DeudaEcologica/a_timetopay .html**.

Altvater, Elmer. 1998. "The New Global Order and the Environment: Defining the Issues" in Roger Keil, David V.J. Bell, Peter Penz, and Leesa Fawcett, eds., *Political Ecology: Global and Local.* London and New York: Routledge, 19–45.

Arquette, Mary, Maxine Cole, and the Akwesasne Task Force on the Environment. 2004. "Restoring Our Relationships for the Future" in Mario Blaser et al., eds., *In the Way of Development: Indigenous Peoples, Life Projects, and Globalization.* London: Zed Books; Ottawa: International Development Research Centre.

Bellamy Foster, John and Brett Clark. 2003. "Ecological Imperialism: The Curse of Capitalism" in Leo Panitch and Colin Leys, eds., *The New Imperial Challenge: Socialist Register 2004.* London: The Merlin Press, 186–201.

Bullard, Robert D., ed. 1993. *Confronting Environmental Racism: Voices from the Grassroots.* Boston: South End Press.

Carson, Rachel. 1962. *Silent Spring.* New York: Houghton Mifflin Co.

Dryzek, John S. 2005a. *The Politics of the Earth*, 2nd edition. Oxford: Oxford University Press.

———. 2005b. "Political and Ecological Communication" (excerpt from article of the same name, originally published in *Environmental Politics*, vol. 4, no. 4 [1995], 13–30) in John S. Dryzek and David Schlosberg, eds., *Debating the Earth: The Environmental Politics Reader*, 2nd edition. Oxford, U.K.: Oxford University Press, 633–646.

Eckersley, Robyn. 2004a. "Ecocentric Discourses: Problems and Future Prospects for Nature Advocacy." *Tamkang Review*, vol. 34 no. 3–4 (Spring–Summer): 155–186.

———. 2004b. *The Green State: Rethinking Democracy and Sovereignty.* The MIT Press.

Hardin, Garrett. 1968. "The Tragedy of the Commons." *Science*, 162: 1243–1248.

Krauss, Celene. 1994. "Women of Color on the Front Line" in Robert D. Bullard, ed., *Unequal Protection: Environmental Justice and Communities of Color.* San Francisco: Sierra Club Books, 256–271.

LaDuke, Winona. 2000. *All Our Relations: Native Struggles for Land and Life.* Boston: South End Press.

McGregor, Deborah. 2004. "Traditional Ecological Knowledge and Sustainable Development: Towards Coexistence" in Mario Blaser et al., eds., *In the Way of*

Development: Indigenous Peoples, Life Projects, and Globalization. London: Zed Books; Ottawa: International Development Research Centre.

Merchant, Carolyn. 1980. *The Death of Nature: Women, Ecology, and the Scientific Revolution.* San Francisco: Harper & Row.

O'Connor, James. 1998. *Natural Causes (Essays in Ecological Marxism).* New York: Guilford Press.

Shiva, Vandana. 1989. *Staying Alive: Women, Ecology, and Development.* London: Zed Books.

Wackernagel, Mathis and William Rees. 1996. *Our Ecological Footprint (Reducing Human Impact on the Earth).* Gabriola Island, BC: New Society Publishers.

Further Readings

Dobson, Andrew and Robyn Eckersley, eds. 2006. *Political Theory and the Ecological Challenge.* Cambridge University Press.

Dryzek, John S., David Downes, Christian Hunold, and David Schlosberg, with Hans-Kristian Hernes. 2003. *Green States and Social Movements: Environmentalism in the United States, United Kingdom, Germany and Norway.* New York: Oxford University Press.

European Green Party. 2006. *A Green Future for Europe.* Programme adopted at the October 2006, Second Congress of the European Green Party. Retrieved October 26, 2007, from **www.europeangreens.org/cms/default/dok/153/153995.a_green _future_for_europe@en.htm**.

Weblinks

Environment Canada
www.ec.gc.ca/envhome.html

Global Greens
www.globalgreens.info/index.php

Green Party (Canada)
www.greenparty.ca/

Climate Action Network—International
www.climatenetwork.org

Pembina Institute (Canada)
www.pembina.org/index.php

United Nations Framework Convention on Climate Change
http://unfccc.int/2860.php

(For Canada's status, see
http://maindb.unfccc.int/public/country.pl?country=CA.)

Global Perspectives

The politics of the early twenty-first century are marked by a movement of power and capacity from the state to international and global levels. For centuries, the state was the most significant unit in the study of politics. This global era, however, has witnessed the reorganization of political power in the form of global cities and transnational regions. Moreover, this period is increasingly characterized by turbulence, transformation, and instability. The current global order (or disorder) has been variously described as the end of history or the clash of civilizations or the new imperialism. What is certain is that globalization has drawn the fates of the North and the South closer together, exposing in stark relief the growing and indefensible disparities in well-being and life chances between the minority and the vast majority of the world's population. The current era has also witnessed new forms of conflict, raising new questions about the role and nature of political violence. This section examines violence, ranging from the singular act of a terrorist to war as an arena for political action. Although violence has always been part of the toolkit of international politics, its heightened significance speaks loudly to the failure of international institutions to resolve political conflicts on local and global scales.

CHAPTER 19

POLITICAL VIOLENCE

Objectives The objectives of this chapter are to explain four concepts: (1) the relations between power and violence; (2) two types of more or less institutionalized and legal forms of political violence—war and terrorism—paying special attention to genocide and state terrorism; (3) the political function of the term "terrorism"; and (4) relations between political violence and the processes of globalization in the contemporary period.

SEAN F. McMAHON

Violence has a longstanding relationship with politics, and wars have long been associated with it. Less obvious is the fact that many of our most cherished political institutions, such as legislative assemblies and, indeed, the modern state, resulted from the exercise of violence. The attacks of September 11, 2001, and their aftermath in Afghanistan and Iraq only served to highlight further the connections between violence and politics on a global scale. This chapter examines violence as an important correlate of politics. More specifically, it examines two types of **political violence**: **war** and **terrorism**. The chapter concludes with some observations about the changing face of political violence in the era of globalization.

Introduction

Major American cities are racked by gang violence. On September 11, 2001, four airplanes were crashed into the World Trade Center in New York, the Pentagon, and a field in Pennsylvania. On March 20, 2003, the United States invaded Iraq. All of these are acts of political violence. This chapter is an introduction to the concepts of violence and politics. More specifically, it examines two types of more and less institutionalized and legal forms of political violence, war and terrorism, and the ways they are deployed to achieve political ends in the contemporary period (Marshall, 1999, 27). It does so by asking four questions: (1) What is political violence? (2) What is war? (3) What is terrorism? (4) What is the relationship between violence and globalization? Through the course of this examination I caution against the all-too-frequent and loose use of the term "terrorism." While the phrase "political violence" encourages inquiry into the histories and political motivations of those who use violence for political ends, "terrorism" is a term that often serves political purposes by obscuring questions of history and motivation.

What Is Political Violence?

POLITICS IS ABOUT POWER. AT ITS MOST BASIC, VIOLENCE IS THE USE OF PHYSICAL force to cause injury. Political violence is the use of physical force to affect power relations. People often treat power and violence as synonyms. They think that power is the ability to inflict violence and that a measure of power is the ability to cause massive injury. This is inaccurate. Violence is often combined with power in the practice of politics, but the two concepts are not the same. It is this combination that is of interest to such authors as Hannah Arendt and Charles Tilly. According to Arendt, violence has an instrumental relationship with power (Arendt, 1970, 46). In other words, violence is a tool. Physical force is used by power to repel foreign invaders. Moreover, violence is used as a tool to injure those in positions of power or to injure those who would challenge those in positions of power. Revolutionaries such as Che Guevera and Nelson Mandela used violence to challenge the prevailing corrupt and discriminatory governments that characterized pre-revolutionary Cuba and apartheid South Africa. These governments also used violence against these revolutionary figures and masses of citizens, many of whom were only indirectly involved in insurrection, if at all. Ultimately, however, what counts is the power supporting the violence, not violence alone. Arendt argues that violence unsupported by power will never accomplish political goals or serve as an effective means to a political end. Furthermore, violence cannot create power but only destroy it (Arendt, 1970, 49, 56). In other words, violence cannot stand in place of political power, but it can undermine political power.

Power is premised on the support of significant sectors of society. A lone man with a gun is not powerful. A man with a gun backed by social groups such as wealthy classes, the military, or mass popular support has the power to use violence successfully.

Similarly, even the most violent authoritarian leaders govern because they are supported by a certain social group or groups (Arendt, 1970, 50). Authoritarians can use violence because they exercise power. Despite media representations to the contrary, this is true even of a dictator, such as Saddam Hussein. This violent regime rested on the implicit and explicit support of the United States, the Ba'ath Party, and Sunni Muslims in Iraq.

That said, no government can exist that is premised exclusively on violence (Arendt, 1970, 50). Governments, however, can and do use more or less violence against their own populations. It is generally understood, though, that governments are most likely to resort to violence against populations when they are losing their grip on power. The spectacle of tanks in the streets facing down protestors or the practice of making opposition leaders go "missing" are signs that governments have lost their legitimacy and popular support. The more power that is lost, the more violence will be used. The substitution of violence for power will not reverse the government's loss of power because, as noted above, violence cannot build power (Arendt, 1970, 54). In fact, the use of violence may undermine popular support for the government and, thus, its legitimacy and power. This also means that a popularly supported group challenging the government has the power to successfully use violence against the government. For example, in Nicaragua in 1979, the Sandinista movement had popular support and, as a result, was able to use violence successfully to topple the Somoza regime.

Arendt also considered the important question of when it is legitimate to use violence. For Arendt, violence is never legitimate but can be justifiable. Conversely, power requires no justification and is legitimate because people have come together to act in concert. The distinction is that violence relates to some future end, while power is based on the past act of coming together. The justification for violence comes from the promise of future changes brought about through violent means (Arendt, 1970, 52). For Arendt, violence is justifiable in easing human suffering. A military intervention to end **genocide** would be an example of justifiable violence.

The idea that violence can destroy power casts violence in a negative light. It must be recognized, however, that violence can also be understood as a productive and positive exercise. For example, Tilly argues that it was the control and subsequent use of violence by fledgling European states that led to the consolidation of power and, more importantly, the making of the modern state (Tilly, 1990, 70). This is an essential feature of Weber's oft-cited definition of the modern national state: "a human community that successfully claims monopoly on the legitimate use of physical force within a given territory" (quoted in Gerth and Mills, 1958, 78). With the end of feudalism, regional power holders and/or notables no longer controlled the means of violence in society or the capacity to wage private wars. The state disarmed the populations and made illegal private armies. Effectively, the state consolidated the means of violence and power at the expense of domestic rivals (Tilly, 1990, 76). This does not mean that the state eliminated violence. Instead, the state institutionalized and regulated its use in the form of domestic police forces and standing armies. The contemporary "peace-building" exercises in both Afghanistan and Iraq aim to achieve precisely this outcome.

Standing armies became the essential feature of the state, and their construction and maintenance, in turn, generated bureaucratic mechanisms for popular conscription and courts (Tilly, 1990, 70, 75). The ruler's use of political violence in the form of war expanded the structure of the state itself. For example, the need to supply and pay the army and rebuild after wars necessitated that the state collect and store revenue. This led to the development of state treasuries and state-wide systems of taxation. Public assemblies developed in much the same manner.

Toward the end of the eighteenth century, states stopped using mercenaries in their armies. Instead, the state conscripted its own citizenry into the army. As states taxed citizens and demanded that they fight for the state, the citizenry began to make demands of the state. One demand in particular was for popular working-class franchise—if the citizens were good enough and old enough to die for the state, they were good enough and old enough to vote. As electorates grew and elected assemblies became ever more central to the conduct of political life, lawmakers were pressured to appeal and be accountable to ordinary citizens (Tilly, 1990, 83). Many of the bureaucratic features of the modern state, such as state treasuries, systems of taxation, and public assemblies, were the by-products of the exercise of violence.

What Is War?

IT IS OFTEN OBSERVED THAT WAR IS AN INTEGRAL AND TIMELESS PART OF THE HUMAN condition. The Greek city states fought the Peloponnesian War from 431 to 404 B.C.E. The Muslim and Ottoman empires fought wars from the seventh century up until the twentieth century. Europe experienced the Napoleonic Wars of the late eighteenth and early nineteenth centuries as well as World Wars I and II in the twentieth century. In the early twenty-first century, Project Ploughshares reported that there were 37 armed conflicts ongoing in 29 countries as varied as Colombia, Sudan, Russia, and the Philippines. How should we understand this destructive force that is older than recorded history itself?

Carl von Clausewitz offers the standard threefold conceptualization of war. First, war is a social and political activity of states. Second, says Clausewitz, "war is an act of force to compel our enemy to do our will." Third, "war is an act of policy" (Clausewitz, 1989, 75, 87). For Clausewitz, then, war is a military tool used by states that meets ends left unsatisfied by other political mechanisms, such as diplomacy. War, however, is not an autonomous activity; it is always linked to larger political imperatives, such as sovereignty, imperialism, territorial expansion, and hegemony. It is in this sense that Clausewitz most famously declared that "war is a political instrument, a continuation of political intercourse carried on with other means" (Clausewitz, 1989, 87).

Despite offering the standard conceptualization of war, Clausewitz was not the first to study this particular political activity. Greek historian Thucydides analyzed the Peloponnesian War between the Greek city states of Sparta and Athens as a war in which Sparta defended its dominant position among the city states against the ascending power of Athens. Medieval religious scholars were the next to treat the issue of war. They did so in the form of "just war" theory. St. Augustine argued that one Christian could kill barbarians in the defence of another Christian. St. Aquinas developed and refined Augustine's thought further into the principles of justness of war (*jus ad bellum*) and the just conduct of war (*jus in bello*). According to Aquinas, for a war to be just (*jus ad bellum*), it had to meet six standards: (1) war must be declared by legitimate authority; (2) the cause of the war must be just; (3) the party declaring war must have the right intention; (4) war must be the last resort; (5) the war must be proportional; and (6) the war must have a good chance of succeeding. Once a just war is initiated, it must be conducted according to rules (*jus in bello*), including discrimination between combatants and non-combatants, and due proportion, which requires that parties not use excessive means to achieve military goals.

The contemporary United Nations institutionalizes the tenets of "just war" theory. For example, echoing the tenet that war must be the last resort, Article 2.3 of the *United Nations Charter* declares that all states shall settle their disputes by peaceful means. Furthermore, Article 41 states that members of the Security Council can use measures not involving force to realize its decisions, and Article 42 outlines forceful measures that can be taken if the Article 41 measures are inadequate. Moreover, the idea that the fighting of wars should be governed by some rules is expressed in such international institutions as the *Rome Statute* (which created the International Criminal Court) and the *United Nations Convention on the Prevention and Punishment of Genocide*. The *Rome Statute*, for example, identifies rape and sexual slavery as war crimes and, thus, forbidden for use as weapons against an enemy.

The *United Nations Convention* confirms that genocide is a crime under international law under all circumstances during times of peace or war. The convention defines "genocide" to mean any of the acts committed with the intent to destroy, in whole or in part, a national, ethnic, racial, or religious group. Among the list of aggressive acts considered as genocidal are killing members of the group, causing serious bodily or mental harm to members of the group, deliberately inflicting on the group conditions of life calculated to bring about its physical destruction in whole or in part, imposing measures intended to prevent births within the group, and forcibly transferring children of the group to another group (**www.unhchr.ch/html/menu3/b/p_genoci.htm**). Another rule of war is that the destruction of an entire group cannot be the intended outcome of the use of violence. Both the *Rome Statute* and the *Convention on Genocide* demonstrate conclusively that all is *not* fair in love and war.

War is politics by other means. Rather than the instrument being the ballot box (in the case of domestic politics) or diplomacy (in the case of international politics), the instrument is organized violence, generally executed by a military, although private contractors—or mercenaries by any other name—increasingly populate contemporary conflict zones, such as Iraq. Attempts to regulate war, however, have not always been successful. The *United Nations Convention* did not prevent genocide in Rwanda or in the former Yugoslavia in the late twentieth century. Like any other political activity, be it the selection of party leaders, national elections, or international trade, people have instituted rules to govern the conduct of war.

Recently, steps have been taken to enforce these rules of war. The International Criminal Court came into effect in 2002. This permanent court takes the place of ad hoc international criminal tribunals. It enforces the rules of war by holding individuals responsible and accountable for the commission of war crimes, such as genocide. In addition to the enforcement of the rules of war through the punishment of perpetrators, the court also aims to deter future war criminals. After initially participating in the treaty creating the court, the United States has subsequently withdrawn from the treaty and declared that it will not be bound by the court.

What Is Terrorism?

AT THE 1972 MUNICH OLYMPICS, 11 ISRAELI ATHLETES WERE TAKEN HOSTAGE AND killed by a Palestinian splinter group called Black September. In 1985, Air India Flight 182 was bombed while en route from Montreal to New Delhi, killing all on board. Three years later, Pan Am Flight 103 was blown up over Lockerbie, Scotland. In 1995, a religious group named Aum Shinrikyo unleashed Sarin gas in the Tokyo subway system, killing 12 people. Most would agree that all of these examples are acts of terrorism and that the perpetrators of these acts are quite clearly terrorists. Of course, such easy and straightforward conclusions prompt important questions: What is terrorism? What is a terrorist?

The term "terrorism" was first applied during the French Revolution. British statesman Edmund Burke used the term to describe France's Jacobin government, which, from 1793 to 1794, was dominated by Robespierre, the Reign of Terror, and the frequent use of the guillotine. Since then, definitions of the term have proliferated, largely because of the highly contentious and politicized nature of this type of political violence. Defining terrorism has often faltered on the adage, "One man's terrorist is another man's freedom fighter." Even the American government cannot agree on a definition of the term. For example, the U.S. State Department, the Federal Bureau of Investigation (FBI), the Central Intelligence Agency (CIA), and the Defense Department all define terrorism differently. In the wake of the September 11 attacks, the American government set about defining domestic terrorism in legislation. In Section 802 of the *USA PATRIOT Act* (2001), Congress defined domestic terrorism as acts dangerous to human life that are a violation of the criminal laws of the United States or any state; that appear to be intended to intimidate or coerce a civilian population, to influence the policy of a government by intimidation or coercion, or to affect the conduct of a government by mass destruction, assassination, or kidnapping; and that occur primarily within the territorial jurisdiction of the United States (*USA PATRIOT Act*, 2001).

The contentious nature of defining terrorism also kept the Canadian government from offering a definition until the passage of the *Anti-terrorism Act* in 2001. There are four facets of this definition. First, terrorism is an act or omission committed for a political, religious, or ideological purpose. Second, the act must be intended to intimidate specific social groups or the public generally or to compel an individual or institution to do or to refrain from doing any act. Third, the act must intentionally endanger a life, cause death or serious injury, endanger the health or safety of the public, cause substantial property damage, or disrupt the delivery of essential services. Finally, a terrorist group is an entity that has as one of its purposes or activities facilitating or carrying out any terrorist activity (*Anti-terrorism Act*, 2001).

Similar to governments, contemporary academe also has failed to develop a consensus about an acceptable definition of terrorism. Definitions vary from the use or threatened use of force designed to bring about a political change to the illegitimate use of force to achieve a political objective by targeting innocent people (White, 2002, 10). These are the most simple and imprecise definitions. Martha Crenshaw, offering a more developed definition, sees terrorism as the systematic use of unorthodox political violence by small conspiratorial groups with the purpose of manipulating political attitudes, rather than physically defeating an enemy (Crenshaw, 1983, 2). She argues further that the intent of terrorist violence is psychological and symbolic. The violence is premeditated and purposeful, and employed in a struggle for political power (Crenshaw, 1983, 2).

Common Themes

All of these definitions pose problems of interpretation, including identification of non-combatants and victims, the illegitimate use of force, and the differences between an act of terrorism and an act of war. Despite these ambiguities, there are several characteristics or themes common to most definitions of terrorism. Following are four of the most frequently cited characteristics: (1) an act of terrorism is violent and uses force; (2) the act is intended to serve a political end or purpose; (3) the victims of the act are often random or arbitrary; and (4) the act is intended to instill fear in a larger audience. Alex P. Schmid, however, has produced a composite definition that is the most inclusive of the broad range of activities often labelled as terrorism. First, Schmid states explicitly that both non-state and state actors practise terrorism. Terrorism is not practised exclusively by clandestine organizations. Second, the victims of terrorism are not the primary target of the violence. Third, terrorism is a communication process. The latter two points are closely related to the fourth characteristic: terrorism communicates a message far beyond the fate of the victims. In fact, the victims are not the intended recipients of the message; the message is conveyed to an audience that is the primary target of demands, intimidation, or coercion (Schmid and Jongman, 1988, 28).

Noam Chomksy and Edward W. Said add another important element to the definition of terrorism. It is premised on the idea that defining terrorism is dependent on the definer or, perhaps more accurately, on whoever has the power to define terrorism. Chomsky suggests that a terrorist act is one committed against "us"; it is terrorism when "we" are the victims. It is not the scale of the violent act or the body count that determines whether the act is labelled a terrorist act (Chomsky, 2002, 1). When "we" are bombed by "them," it is an act of terrorism, and "they" are the terrorists. When "we" bomb "them," it is a pacification campaign, or low-intensity warfare, and "they" are collateral damage (Booth and Dunne, 2002). "We" are never terrorists and, most certainly, never perpetrate acts of terrorism. In keeping with this idea, Said speaks to why the labels "terrorism" and "terrorist" are applied to the actions of others. He says that identifying someone as a terrorist isolates him or her from time, from causality, and from prior action and thereby portrays him or her as inherently and gratuitously interested in destruction for its own sake (Said and Hitchens, 1988, 154). A terrorist, according to this perspective, is someone who lives outside history, who is without legitimate grievances, who has not suffered dispossession or deprivation, and who is only interested in killing for killing's sake.

The cry of "terrorism" should be used with considerable caution precisely because of the political function the term is made to serve. Labelling someone a terrorist all too easily prevents us from searching for the root causes of the person's violent actions. Instead, we come to simplistically reduce the root causes of terrorism to terrorists alone. We are encouraged to assume that the reason there is terrorism is that there are terrorists—and not poverty or state repression or foreign occupation. Unfortunately, this reductionist gaze leads to equally simplistic policy responses. It suggests that the only way to be rid of terrorism is to eradicate the terrorists themselves, rather than the root causes. Without dealing with the larger issues, single-minded assaults on terrorists only succeed in creating more determined terrorists focused on changing unsustainable material and political circumstances.

State Terrorism

Examples of state terrorism abound, such as the well-publicized examples in the last century of Chilean president Augusto Pinochet's death squads and the United States' Contras in Nicaragua. On September 11, 1973, the United States backed a coup that replaced Chile's democratically elected president, Salvador Allende, with Pinochet. Under Pinochet, state security services and death squads targeted all forms of political opposition—members of political parties (primarily leftists), union and religious leaders, agrarian reformers, and anyone else considered to be an opponent of the regime. These death squads were responsible for the disappearance, killing, and torture of thousands of people.

Similarly, in 1981, the United States initiated an aggression against the socialist Sandinista government of Nicaragua. The instrument of this aggression was a mercenary army, called the Contras, trained, funded, and supplied by the United States. Over the next five years, the Contras, working from their bases in Honduras, killed and tortured more than 11 000 Nicaraguan peasants and villagers. In both cases, the state used paramilitary groups to intimidate and kill both random and symbolic targets in order to convey messages of obedience (Chile) or opposition (Nicaragua) to larger segments of society. In fact, the former director of the American Central Intelligence Agency, testifying before Congress, said as much when he called the American Contra war "state-sponsored terrorism" (Chomsky, 1988, 27).

It is commonly asserted that "terrorism is the weapon of the weak," meaning that such acts as bus bombings and airplane hijackings are the only violent means available to non-state actors lacking resources and an organized state military. If we look at the historical record, however, we see that terrorism has often been used by militarily powerful states, rather than weak non-state actors. From the sixteenth to the nineteenth century, for example, colonial powers such as Britain, Portugal, and Spain used state terrorism to eradicate indigenous populations in Africa, Asia, and South America. In the past century, the United States has practised state terrorism in, among other places, Nicaragua, El Salvador, Vietnam, and Cambodia. Finally, Israel continues to use state terrorism in an attempt to subvert the Palestinians' quest for nationhood. Historically, militarily powerful state actors have made recourse to terrorism.

If we return to the relationship between violence and power suggested by Arendt, we see an interesting similarity between non-state and state terrorism. Recall that the successful use of violence requires political power that is embedded in other popular support. Al-Qaeda intimidated and bombed while Saddam Hussein tortured and killed. However, neither of these actors had significant popular support in Afghanistan or Iraq. In fact, these actors tried to compensate for their narrow power bases through the use of violence. While able to make use of violence, these non-state and state actors were politically weak. In this case, terrorism is, in fact, the weapon of the *politically* weak.

Globalization and Violence

SOME AUTHORS ARGUE THAT WAR HAS FUNDAMENTALLY CHANGED IN THE ERA OF globalization. Mary Kaldor, for example, asserts that the violence in such places as Yugoslavia, Rwanda, and Sierra Leone constitutes "new wars." These new wars blur traditional distinctions among war, organized crime, and large-scale violations of human rights (Kaldor, 1999, 2). "New wars" are bound up with the interconnectedness of globalization and its related processes, which both integrate and fragment, homogenize and diversify, and globalize and localize (Kaldor, 1999, 3). What results is a reversal of the development of the modern state as conceptualized by Tilly. States in an era of globalization no longer exclusively consolidate power and do not monopolize the means of violence. Furthermore, these "new wars," in contrast to old wars, are about identity politics and not geopolitical or ideological goals (Kaldor, 1999, 6). The aim of "new wars" is to eliminate people of different identities, the Tutsis in Rwanda, for example. As a result, civilians, not soldiers, are the targets of violence in the "new wars." A century ago, the ratio of military to civilian casualties in wars was eight to one; now, the ratio is approximately one to eight (Kaldor, 1999, 8). Increasingly, civilians suffer the violence that was historically reserved for soldiers.

Other authors, such as David Keen, have noted that in the era of globalization, the ends to which violence is directed have changed. Violence is often now used, not with the intent of seizing control of the state, but of legitimizing actions that during times of peace would be criminal. Furthermore, violence is deployed as a means of restructuring economic relations (Keen, 1998, 11–12). In the case of Angola, for instance, the civil war has enabled the otherwise marginalized rebels to enrich themselves through control of the diamond mines in their territories. In the absence of war, these resources would be exploited or, indeed, redistributed by the Angolan ruling class. In this instance, the goal of winning a war in the traditional sense has been replaced by different objectives.

This idea that the end of violence may not be the seizure of state power is reflected in the September 11 attacks. Al-Qaeda did not have as its end control of the American state. Neither was the attack followed by an invading force. The four hijacked planes did not fundamentally threaten the American state. Instead, Al-Qaeda used violence to strike a blow at the symbols of American economic and military might so readily associated with globalization. Among other things, the attacks were aimed at convincing the government of the United States to withdraw its forces from Saudi Arabia.

Al-Qaeda's actions were facilitated by many of the processes of globalization. In fact, much of contemporary violence is expedited or even promoted by globalization. The increasing ease, speed, and opacity of financial transactions facilitated Al-Qaeda fundraising and allowed for the strategic disposition of those funds, just as the globalized economy encourages the lucrative trade of Sierra Leone's diamonds, Cambodian timber and gems, and Colombian drugs and oil. The increased movement of peoples among states enabled the Al-Qaeda hijackers to move among Saudi Arabia, Afghanistan, Germany, and the United States with relative anonymity. Furthermore, the increasing transfer of goods globally means that Soviet-made small arms end up in the hands of child soldiers in Somalia, Uganda, and Burundi. Another important connection between violence and the processes of globalization involves modern communication technologies that bring wars into living rooms as the wars unfold in real time. However, these technologies come into play most spectacularly in the case of terrorism. The Internet and satellite television produce truly global audiences for such events as those of September 11, 2001.

Summary

This chapter has examined a few of the complex and unfolding relationships between violence and power and between war and terrorism. Violence is an important correlate of politics, and the strength of this relationship is not waning in the twenty-first century. Neither has it been diminished by the processes of globalization. The ongoing American aggression against Iraq highlights some of the ideas presented in this chapter. First, this war demonstrates that the use of violence, even by the world's dominant state, does not produce power or legitimacy. In fact, the use of violence begets more violence with unintended effects. Second, the accusation of terrorism is dependent on who has the power to define the term. The United States does not define ground operations and aerial bombardments that randomly terrorize, maim, and kill civilians as state terrorism. Rather than being defined as victims of terrorism, the civilians are defined as collateral damage. Third, the United Nations does have rules to govern the conduct of war. However, these rules are not always obeyed, and transgression of these rules can go unpunished. Fourth, war can be an effective means of securing valuable resources, such as oil.

This chapter's consideration of political violence, terrorism, and war prompts further questions, including these: Under what conditions is violence justified? How does a legitimate regime emerge? What are the politics around using the term "terrorism"? To whom do the rules of war apply? How are the rules of war enforced? Finally, how will the processes of globalization continue to alter political violence? The politics of the early twenty-first century beg an open debate and action on these questions because they are increasingly critical to human security in a globalizing era.

Discussion Questions

1. What is the relationship Arendt establishes between violence and power? Critically assess this relationship.

2. In the fight against unjust regimes, such groups as Nelson Mandela's African National Congress employed acts of political violence that were characterized as terrorism. Is terrorism always morally reprehensible? Or does the justness of the end legitimize the use of terrorist means?

3. How can violence be understood as a positive and productive exercise? Provide modern examples of by-products of war-making.

4. Will human societies always engage in war? What are the alternatives?

References

Anti-terrorism Act. 2001. Canada. December 18.

Arendt, Hannah. 1970. *On Violence.* New York: Harcourt, Brace World.

Booth, Ken and Tim Dunne, eds. 2002. *Worlds in Collision: Terror and the Future of Global Order.* New York: Palgrave.

Chomsky, Noam. 1988. *Culture of Terrorism.* Montreal: Black Rose Books.

———. 2002. *Pirates and Emperors, Old and New: International Terrorism in the Real World.* Cambridge: South End Press.

Clausewitz, Carlvon. 1989. *On War.* M. Howard and P. Paret, eds. Princeton: Princeton University Press.

Crenshaw, Martha. 1983. *Terrorism, Legitimacy, and Power: The Consequences of Political Violence.* Middleton, CT: Wesleyan University Press.

Gerth, Hans H. and C. Wright Mills, eds. 1958. *From Max Weber: Essays in Sociology.* New York: Oxford University Press.

Kaldor, Mary. 1999. *New and Old Wars: Organized Violence in a Global Era.* Stanford: Stanford University Press.

Keen, David. 1998. *The Economic Functions of Violence in Civil Wars.* Oxford: Oxford University Press.

Marshall, Monty G. 1999. *Third World War: System, Process, and Conflict Dynamics.* New York: Rowman & Littlefield Publishers, Inc.

Said, Edward William and Christopher Hitchens. 1988. *Blaming the Victims: Spurious Scholarship and the Palestinian Question.* London: Verso Books.

Schmid, Alex P. and A.J. Jongman. 1988. *Political Terrorism: A New Guide to Actor, Authors, Concepts, Data Bases, Theories and Literature.* New York: North-Holland Publishing Company.

Tilly, Charles. 1990. *Coercion, Capital and European States, AD 900–1990.* Cambridge: Blackburn.

UNHCR. Retrieved January 25, 2004, from **www.unhchr.ch/html/menu3/b/p_genoci.htm.**

USA PATRIOT Act. 2001. United States of America. October 24.

White, Jonathan R. 2002. *Terrorism: An Introduction,* 3rd edition. Canada: Wadsworth.

Further Readings

Chomsky, Noam. 2002. *Pirates and Emperors, Old and New: International Terrorism in the Real World.* Cambridge: South End Press.

Fisk, Robert. 2005. *The Great War for Civilisation: The Conquest of the Middle East.* London: HarperCollins Publishers.

Lyons, Robert and Scott Straus. 2006. *Intimate Enemies: Images and Voices of the Rwandan Genocide.* Cambridge: Zone Books.

Said, Edward. 2000. *The End of the Peace Process: Oslo and After.* New York: Pantheon Books.

Worcester, Kenton, Sally Avery Bermanzohn, and Mark Ungar. 2002. *Violence and Politics: Globalization's Paradox.* New York: Routledge.

Weblinks

COW—Correlates of War Project
www.umich.edu/~cowproj

Electronic Intifada
http://electronicintifada.net/new.shtml

Iraq Body Count
www.iraqbodycount.org

University of Maryland's Center for International Development and Conflict
Management (CIDCM)
www.cidcm.umd.edu

SIPRI: Stockholm International Peace Research Institute
www.sipri.org

UN PARKING

CANADA

artizans.com

CHAPTER **20**

THE WEST AND THE REST

Objectives

The dichotomy of the West versus the Rest, a construct of the colonial period, has been revived and reinforced by post–Cold War international politics, and especially by the tragic events of September 11, 2001. This chapter critiques two ways in which the idea of the West and the Rest is used in contemporary politics. The first approach, usually associated with the writings of American conservative Francis Fukuyama, asserts that Western liberal democracy has triumphed over its challengers, especially communism, and that there are few alternatives for the Rest  (non-Western countries) other than to join with the West in embracing Western neo-liberal values and liberal democratic forms of government. For Fukuyama, "the end of history" means that Western liberal democracy will prevail across the globe in the twenty-first century as the superior way to govern global diversity. The second approach, advanced by another American conservative, Samuel Huntington, advances a quite different interpretation of the West and the Rest. He argues that different civilizations, especially Islam and Confucianism, fundamentally conflict with Western values and that civilizational differences necessarily will result in conflict between the West and the Rest. Both of these approaches have resonated in American and global politics, especially since September 11. In this chapter, we examine

MOJTABA MAHDAVI

the long lineage of the West–Rest dichotomy, including its most recent appearances in two essays that later became books: Francis Fukuyama's *The End of History?* and Samuel Huntington's *The Clash of Civilizations?* Neither approach, we will see, adequately captures the complexities of our global community. Finally, we will discuss what can be done to get past the West-versus-the-Rest dichotomy.

Introduction

In the past two decades, the world has been shocked first by the fall of the Berlin Wall in 1989 and then by the collapse of the World Trade Center on September 11, 2001. Although there are many explanations for these separate events, both have contributed to the revival of old assertions about the superiority of the West and the inferiority of the Rest. In previous eras, politicians and scholars used this way of representing the world as a justification for Western colonialism, arguing that it was the "civilizing mission" of the West, and the "white man's burden," to bring Western values and institutions to inferior and less advanced peoples. In our contemporary post-colonial world, however, this colonializing gesture has been dressed up in new language. The West is represented as the only society that defends democracy and human rights, while the Rest purportedly lack or resist such noble modern values. Central to these and related assertions is the suggestion that any resistance to Western values, institutions, and power is the mark of rage, irrationality, and backwardness, and, thus, the West is justified in advancing its model of progress globally.

Before the collapse of Soviet communism, politicians used the "us versus them" distinction to justify the Cold War between twentieth-century capitalism and communism. In the early twenty-first century, this construct now identifies new enemies of the West, notably the Orientalist East and Islamic and Confucian civilizations. After the tragic events of September 11, politicians have substituted "the War on Terrorism" for the Cold War on communism. The West–Rest dichotomy, thus, is not new. In fact, it dates back to the colonial period in the early sixteenth century and has survived in various forms ever since.

What Is "the Rest"?

IF THE WEST TYPICALLY REFERS TO COUNTRIES THAT HAVE EVOLVED WITHIN a liberal and capitalist governing framework, what is "the Rest"? The Rest refers to countries located in four regions of the global South (that is, countries that generally lie to the south of what we call the West): Africa, Asia, Latin America, and the Middle East, most having a long history of Western colonialism. The motivations of the West—in various eras, the Spanish, the Portuguese, the British, the French, the Dutch, and most recently the Americans—to colonize the Rest are perhaps best captured in metaphor by "the three G's" of gold, god, and glory (Mazrui, 1986). *Gold* represents colonialist demands for accumulation of capital, cheap raw materials and labour, including slave labour, and expanding markets for Western goods. *God* stands for religious or cultural justifications of colonialism as well as the destructive role of Western missionaries, who assaulted indigenous traditions, often guided by explicitly racist assumptions about the "white man's burden" to civilize the "little brown" barbaric nations. *Glory* points to the colonial arrogance and competition among imperial powers in their global struggle for power and prestige. The great empires of the West were in no small way built through the political and cultural domination and economic exploitation of the Rest.

In the late 1950s and early 1960s, the era of Western colonialism drew to a close as one colony after another was granted self-rule to emerge as a newly independent country. Although the colonial powers formally withdrew from their colonial possessions, they maintained a vested interest in protecting their long-term control over political and economic resources in the former colonies. The old form of colonialism was revived in a new ideological form. This time the pretext was development and modernization. The former colonies would be retained within the West's orbit by ensuring that they adopted Western values, goals, and institutions rather than by direct rule.

After World War II, the United States became extremely worried by the attraction to socialism witnessed in the growing number of newly independent countries, including India and many newly independent countries in Africa. The dilemma facing the West was how to transform these countries into nominally sovereign nation-states and, at the same time, continue to exert political dominance. Thus, the only legitimate model put forward was a non-communist model of development, a Western liberal-capitalist model.

Western countries and international development agencies embraced **developmentalism and modernization theories** and policies that advanced Western values as a universal paradigm to be followed by the rest of the world. The Western path to development and democracy, it was argued, would save the Third World (developing and under-developed countries) from the dangers posed by the Second World (the Communist bloc, headed by the Soviet Union). Just as important, developmentalism would emancipate these countries from their traditional values, which were seen to stand as impediments to the spread of both liberalism and capitalism. Developmentalism was concisely conceived as a Western alternative to the socialist path of development. In practice, it turned out to be an ideological arm of American expansionism during the Cold War.

We cannot fully explore the intellectual foundations and political implications of developmentalism and modernization theories and policies here. Suffice it to say that they advanced three foundational assumptions about "us versus them." First, the modern West was, by definition, developed and a model to be emulated, while the Rest was under-developed. Second, the causes of under-development were seen to be rooted in the traditional culture and institutions of the Rest. Third, the Rest had to abandon its traditions and adopt Western practices; otherwise, the West and the Rest would remain under-developed.

Although developmentalism dominated thinking about the appropriate relationship between the West and the Rest in the post-war years, it did not go unchallenged. Serious doubts were raised about the universal application of these theories and policies. It could be readily observed that in many countries, modernization did not lead to democracy but, instead, to various forms of authoritarianism, middle-class revolutions, and/or fundamentalist politics. Moreover, others argued that modernization had simply set in place a new form of unequal relations between the West and the Rest that had been previously established in the colonial period.

The persistence of under-development and the continuing lack of liberal democracy in the global South—along with the inability of developmental and modernization theorists to present compelling explanations for these failures—contributed to the rise in the 1960s and 1970s of a new set of radical theories, such as dependency and world-system theories. Andre Gunder Frank (1969, 2–15), one of the founding fathers of **dependency theory**, argued that the nature of the West–Rest relationship could be best explained by dividing the world into two categories: the North "metropolis" and the South "satellite." He further argued that the colonial legacy and unequal international structures created conditions in which the satellite remained highly dependent on the metropolis and that, contrary to modernization theory, development in the North actually caused under-development in the South. Development and dependency, Frank argued, are mutually reinforcing.

An extremely conservative reaction against mainstream developmentalism came from Harvard political science professor Samuel Huntington in 1968. He also rejected a universal positive correlation between development and democracy in developing countries and boldly challenged the idea that non-Western civilizations would follow the Western path of liberal democracy. Stability, he argued, had priority over democracy and development in Southern countries, and politicians in the West should focus on public order rather than social and political change, even if that meant supporting authoritarian regimes. For Huntington, it was "not the absence of modernity but the effort to achieve it which produces political disorder" (1968, 41). During the Cold War, Huntington's theory of political order prescribed to decision-makers that pro-Western governments and stability in the Rest must be privileged over promoting political change and democracy, which could ultimately challenge Western domination and create conflict.

"End of History" or "Clash of Civilizations"?

UNFORTUNATELY, THE "DEVELOPMENT DEBATE" HAS NOT BEEN RESOLVED. During the past two decades, there has been renewed theorizing, especially in the United States, about the appropriate relationship between the West and the Rest. Reflecting on the collapse of Soviet-style communism, for example, Francis Fukuyama proclaimed in his 1989 essay, "The End of History?" (and later in his book *The End of History and the Last Man* [1992]) that Western liberal capitalism had defeated its two major opponents—fascism and communism. The collapse of the Soviet Union, Fukuyama argued, signalled nothing less than "the end of history as such: that is, the end point of mankind's ideological evolution and the universalization of Western liberal democracy as the final form of human government" (1989, 271). The West had won.

Resting at the centre of Fukuyama's thesis was the idea that Western liberal democracy had proved itself to be the best and, indeed, the only viable option for the governance of the many and diverse countries of the contemporary world. *The End of History* thus revived the old developmentalist claim that Western liberal capitalism is a universal paradigm, one that could be and should be embraced by countries in the North and the South. Although Fukuyama suspected that there might be lingering resistance to the liberal-capitalist model, he predicted that the Rest would eventually see the error of their ways and embrace the intellectual and material value of liberal capitalism. Like the West, the Rest would come to understand that the modern world had arrived at the end of history because "the basic principles of the liberal democratic state could not be improved upon" (1989, 272).

The End of History found many critics, not the least of which was Samuel Huntington, who warned against Fukuyama's overly optimistic view of history and the universality of the Western paradigm. His objection to the principle of "Endism" rested on Huntington's argument that the "weakness and irrationality" of the Rest stood as an enduring obstacle to the global spread of Western values and institutions. "The hope for the benign end of history," Huntington argues, "is human. To expect it to happen is unrealistic. To plan on it happening is disastrous" (1989).

Huntington developed his critique in his 1993 essay, "The Clash of Civilizations?" and later in his book *The Clash of Civilizations and the Remaking of World Order* (1996). His central thesis was that conflict, not cooperation, best characterizes post–Cold War politics. Moreover, he claimed that the fundamental source of conflict in this new world order will be cultural rather than economic or ideological. "The great divisions among humankind and the dominate source of conflict will be cultural . . . The **clash of civilizations** will dominate global politics. The fault lines between civilizations will be the battle lines of the future" (1993, 22).

Huntington reasoned that the world consists of seven or eight major civilizations: "Western, Confucian, Japanese, Islamic, Hindu, Slavic-Orthodox, Latin American, and possibly African civilizations" (1993, 25). For Huntington, the domination of the West over the Rest was an ongoing source of conflict between the two: "The next world war, if there is one," he suggested, is likely to be "the conflict between 'the West and the Rest' and a response of non-Western civilizations to Western power and values" (1993, 41). In the post–Cold War era, "the Velvet Curtain of culture," he explained, "has replaced the Iron Curtain of ideology." For Huntington, "this is no less than a clash of civilizations—the perhaps irrational but surely historical reaction of an ancient rival against our Judeo-Christian heritage, our secular present, and the world-wide expansion of both" (1993, 31–32).

For Huntington, fundamental and innate differences between civilizations necessarily lead to conflicts. "The efforts of the West to promote its values of democracy and liberalism as universal values, to maintain its military predominance and to advance its economic interests endanger countering responses from other civilizations" (1993, 39). The hegemony of the West, he contended, promotes "the growth of civilization-consciousness" on the part of the Rest and "de-Westernization and indigenization" such as the rise of Asian-ization in Asia and (re-) Islam-ization in the Muslim world (1993, 26). The greatest conflict, he suggested, will occur between the West and either Confucian or Islamic civilizations—or both.

Given these non-negotiable facts of contemporary politics, according to Huntington, the West has only two options. First, the West should consolidate its power and defend itself against the Rest; and second, the U.S. should consolidate its relations with Europe and Latin America, maintain friendly ties with Japan and Russia, and protect its interests against non-friendly civilizations, in particular Islamic and Confucian civilizations. In doing so, moreover, the West should exploit differences among these civilizations and maintain its economic and military superiority (1993, 48–49). In other words, Huntington's advice to contemporary Western policy-makers was to follow the old policy of *divide and rule* over non-Western civilizations.

Although it is difficult to assess the direct impact of Huntington's work on Western policy-makers, especially in the United States, it is probably no coincidence that the Bush administration has frequently pulled out the "clash of civilizations" card to justify its War on Terror and its unilateral foreign policies. American conservative politicians have often suggested that "our enemies hate 'us' because they hate our *values* and our *civilization*."

Neither "End" nor "Clash"

THE END OF HISTORY AND THE CLASH OF CIVILIZATIONS ARE TWO SIDES OF the same coin: both theses turn the West and the Rest into two monolithic categories. *The End of History* implies that the West offers a universal paradigm of development and democracy: the West is the best, and the Rest, lacking its own models of development, should and will follow the West. *The Clash of Civilizations* also suggests that the West is the best and thus must prevail over cultures with different histories, values, and institutions.

The two theses are seriously flawed, however, for three reasons. First, the "End of History" thesis assumes that there is only one path to modernity: the one already trod by the West and down which the Rest must follow. In this view, the cultures and traditions of non-Western societies are residual factors, "leftovers" from a pre-modern, backward time. The Rest or the global South itself is a residual category because its character, cultures, traditions, and institutions are examined in terms of Western standards, not in terms of its own values. The reference point is the West: the Rest is defined not in terms of what it is but in terms of what it lacks. This **Western-centred**

viewpoint ignores that societies can modernize themselves by reinterpreting their own traditions and cultures.

Second, the "Clash of Civilizations" thesis relies on a vague, abstract, and wholesale notion of "civilization identity." It discounts that there is always a contest over the definition of "civilization" and who represents a civilization. Civilizations are not unitary entities; there are official and unofficial, current and countercurrent voices within each civilization. Each civilization is a dynamic plural entity, not a "shut-down, sealed-off" unit (Said, 2001). In other words, there is no single West, just as there is no single Rest.

Finally, Samuel Huntington argues that Western civilization (or culture) is unique and fundamentally different from other civilizations, especially Islam. For Huntington, it is not "Islamic fundamentalism" but the "fundamental" essence of Islam that makes it incompatible with modernity and democracy. Huntington's simplistic argument is that the "Islamic mind" and democracy are mutually exclusive and inalterably grounded in culture. Yet one of Huntington's many critics, Fred Halliday, reminds us that "there is nothing specifically 'Islamic' about" obstacles that hinder democracy in Muslim societies, though some of these obstacles "tend to be legitimized in terms of Islamic doctrine." Any argument about incompatibility or compatibility between Islam and democracy adopts "the false premise that there is one true, traditionally established 'Islamic' answer to the question, and this timeless 'Islam' rules social and political practices. However, there is no such answer and no such Islam'" (1996, 116). For Halliday, Islam is so broad that "it is possible to catch almost any fish one wants. It is, like all the great religions, a reservoir of values, symbols and ideas. . . . the answer as to why this or that interpretation was put upon Islam resides . . . in the contemporary needs of those articulating Islamic politics" (1994, 96).

It is, therefore, legitimate to challenge the assumption that the West and Islam, even the West and Islamism, have been in a constant fundamental clash. The West supported the totalitarian Ba'thist regime of Saddam during, and arguably before, the Iran–Iraq War (1980–1988). It has consistently supported the Egyptian autocratic regime under Sadat and Mubarak since President Sadat made a peace with Israel. It has had longstanding relationships with the Arab oil monarchies, in particular Saudi Arabia. Since the nineteenth century, the West has supported—to use Fatema Mernissi's phrase—the "palace fundamentalism" (2003) of the Saudi regime, the ideology, considered fanatical by non-adherents, known as Wahhabism, which is taught in the radical Islamist schools (*madrasas*) in Pakistan that gave birth to the Taliban.

The symbiotic relationship between Western liberal democracies and "palace fundamentalism," for example, challenges the simplified binary of the liberal democratic West versus the traditional autocratic Rest. The relationship between the West and the Rest is far more complex than clash or cooperation. There are several examples of clash *within* civilizations, not between civilizations. The Iran–Iraq War and the Iraq–Kuwait War (1990) are two cases in point, where two countries within a "civilization" have been in conflict. More important, in the 1990 and 2003 American-led wars against Iraq, some Arab countries remained on the American side, while France and Canada of the "Western civilization" opposed the American war against Iraq in 2003. These examples underline that states, not civilizations, are the primary actors of international politics. States will act in their best interests and forsake their traditional civilizations in favour of political, economic, and military interests (Ajami, 1993).

Many scholars have offered alternatives to Huntington's confrontational civilizational thesis. Some argue that contemporary global instabilities are more appropriately understood as a "Clash of Globalizations" (Hoffmann, 2002). Benjamin Barber (2002) offers a similar line of argument by suggesting that we are in an era of the collision between **Jihad** and **McWorld**. The collision, he asserts, is occurring between "the forces of disintegral tribalism and reactionary fundamentalism" (Jihad) and "the forces of integrative modernization and aggressive economic and cultural globalization" (2002, 245). More specifically, "The Jihadist's quarrel, Barber argues," is not with modernity but with the aggressive neo-liberal ideology . . . they are not even particularly anti-American." They "suspect that what Americans understand as prudent unilateralism is really a form of arrogant imperialism." This is not, therefore, a clash of civilizations "but a dialectical expression of tensions built into a single civilization" created by McWorld; this is a "war within civilization" (2002, 248–249).

In a similar vein, Michael Hardt and Antonio Negri argue that "**Empire** is the new world order" (2000, 3). Empire "is the political subject that effectively regulates [the] global exchanges, the sovereign power that governs the world" (2000, xi). Empire is reducible neither to the United States nor to another form of imperialism (2000, xiv). Unlike imperialism, Empire is not imposed on people; rather, it is a complex web of institutions and socio-political and economic relations through which people participate in the making of Empire. We participate in the construction of Empire by our active participation in the political rule (good citizen) and economic regime (good consumer). We live in the post-modern age, and Empire is the dominant rule of this age. It has no foundation, no centre. "Empire is the non-place of world production where labor is exploited" (2000, 210). The "new proletariat" is "multitude" with no centre, no place; like Empire, it is, at once, everywhere and nowhere at the same time. Multitude is "counter-Empire" (2000, 207); it is no longer a traditional working class but a joint global axis of resistance against complex networks of Empire (2000, 55). In our post-modern age, the paradigm of the West versus the Rest has transformed into the relations of "Empire versus Multitude."

Contemporary global tensions are perhaps more accurately described not as a clash of civilizations, but, instead, as a **clash of fundamentalisms** (Ali, 2002), a clash between two versions of political extremism, a clash between two tiny aggravated minorities who exploit religious or cultural rhetoric for political purposes. This clash can also be characterized as a clash between market fundamentalism and religious fundamentalism. In either case, this is a "clash of ignorance" (Said, 2001), in which democracy and social justice are "caught between a clash of movements each of which for its own reasons seemed indifferent to freedom's fate" (Barber, 2002, 245).

Summary

This chapter has examined the rise and revival of the political construct of "the West versus the Rest," especially the theses offered by Francis Fukuyama and Samuel Huntington. This chapter argued, however, that neither the "end of history" thesis nor the "clash of civilizations" thesis adequately captures the complexities of culture or the sources of conflict in contemporary global politics. The current conflicts in the world are not between civilizations but, rather, occur between political actors who often are pursuing specific political goals that are not tied to culture or civilization per se.

What is to be done to achieve a better, more peaceful world? Benjamin Barber suggests that we must begin by "readjudication of north–south responsibilities" (2002, 247). We need to democratize global economic and political institutions. A true victory in the current global conflicts lies in democratization of globalization. "The war against jihad will not," Barber argues, "succeed unless McWorld is also addressed" (2002, 247).

Jonathan Sacks suggests that we must begin by appreciating the "dignity of difference" (2002). The dignity of difference stands for self-respect and respecting others. It implies self-critique and criticizing others and promotes dialogue among ourselves and others. It requires a careful critique of global and local models. This means that each culture or nation should engage in a critical dialogue with its own traditions and formulate the universal values of democracy and social justice in a local language that can be implemented through local or homegrown institutions. The dignity of difference never suggests that we should not learn from other cultures, or that they have nothing new and valuable to offer to our own culture. The dignity of difference calls for a "third way" and not solely "my way." Put differently, the best way to eliminate the West-versus-the-Rest dichotomy is a "third way," one in which the West is not the best and the Rest can take the best of the West. As the great Martinican poet Aimé Césaire (1983, 77, quoted in Said, 2003, 86) reminds us, "no race possesses the monopoly of beauty, of intelligence, of force, and there is place for all at the rendez-vous of victory."

Discussion Questions

1. Is Western modernity/democracy a universal paradigm, or should non-Western countries seek a particular path of modernity/democracy?

2. Which thesis of the post–Cold War period presented in this chapter best explains the complex picture of our world?

3. How convincing is the argument that the major conflicts in the world are better explained by the following theses: "Jihad versus McWorld," "a clash of globalizations," "a clash of fundamentalisms," and "Empire"?

4. In what ways can we eliminate the old and dangerous dichotomy of the West versus the Rest? Discuss intellectual and political solutions.

References

Ajami, Fouad. 1993. "The Summoning." *Foreign Affairs.* September/October.

Ali, Tariq. 2002. *The Clash of Fundamentalisms: Crusades, Jihad and Modernity.* London: Verso.

Barber, Benjamin R. 2002. "Era of Jihad vs. McWorld" in Kim Booth and Tim Dunne, eds., *Worlds in Collision: Terror and the Future of Global Order.* New York: Palgrave McMillan, 245–262.

Césaire, Aimé. 1983. *The Collected Poetry.* Translated, with an introduction and notes, by Clayton Eshleman and Annette Smith. Berkeley: University of California Press.

Frank, Andre Gunder. 1969. *Capitalism and Underdevelopment in Latin America.* New York: Monthly Review Press.

Fukuyama, Francis. 1989. "The End of History?" *The National Interest,* 16, 3–18.

———. 1992. *The End of History and the Last Man.* New York: Avon Books.

Halliday, Fred. 1994. "The Politics of Islamic Fundamentalism: Iran, Tunisia and the Challenge to the Secular State" in A.S. Ahmed and H. Donnan, eds., *Islam, Globalization and Postmodernity.* London: Routledge.

———. 1996. *Islam and the Myth of Confrontation.* London: Tauris.

Hardt, Michael and Antonio Negri. 2000. *Empire.* Cambridge: Harvard University Press.

Hoffmann, Stanley. 2002. "A Clash of Globalizations." *Foreign Affairs.* July–August, 81: 14, 104.

Huntington, Samuel, P. 1968. *Political Order in Changing Societies.* New Haven: Yale.

———. 1989. "No Exit: The Errors of Endism." *The National Interest.* University Press.

———. 1993. "The Clash of Civilizations?" *Foreign Affairs,* 72:3, 22–50.

———. 1996. *The Clash of Civilizations and the Remaking of World Order.* New York: Simon and Schuster.

Mazrui, Ali. 1986. *The Africans.* Video no. 4.

Mernissi, Fatema. 2003. "Palace Fundamentalism and Liberal Democracy" in Emran Qureshi and Michael A. Sells, eds., *New Crusades: Constructing the Muslim Enemy.* New York: Columbia University Press, 51–67.

Sacks, Jonathan. 2002. *The Dignity of Difference: How to Avoid the Clash of Civilizations.* London and New York: Continuum.

Said, Edward. 2003. "The Clash of Definitions" in Emran Qureshi and Michael A. Sells, eds., *New Crusades: Constructing the Muslim Enemy.* New York: Columbia University Press, 68–88.

———. 2001. "The Clash of Ignorance," *Nation,* October 22.

Further Readings

Ahmed, Akbar, S. 2007. *Journey into Islam: A Crisis of Globalization.* Washington, D.C.: Brookings Institution Books.

Hardt, Michael and Antonio Negri. 2004. *Multitude: War and Democracy in the Age of Empire.* New York: Penguin Books.

Hobsbawm, Eric and Terence Ranger. 1983. *The Invention of Tradition.* Cambridge: Cambridge University Press.

Norris, Pippa and Ronald Inglehart. 2004. *Sacred and Secular: Religion and Politics Worldwide.* New York: Cambridge University Press.

Rejali, Darius. 2007. *Torture and Democracy.* Princeton: Princeton University Press.

Said, Edward. 1978. *Orientalism.* New York: Pantheon Books.

Wallerstein, Immanuel. 1993. "The Present State of the Debate on World Inequality" in M.A. Seligson and J.T. Passe-Smith, eds., *Development and Underdevelopment.* Boulder: Lynne Rienner Publishers, 217–230.

Weblinks

Benjamin Barber, Jihad vs. McWorld
www.theatlantic.com/doc/199203/barber

Edward Said, "The Clash of Ignorance"
www.thenation.com/doc/20011022/said

UNESCO—Dialogue Among Civilizations
www.unesco.org/dialogue/en/shu-essay.htm

Fawaz A. Gerges and Joanne J. Myers, "America and Political Islam: Clash of Cultures or Clash of Interests?"
www.cceia.org/resources/transcripts/116.html

Gilles Kepel and Joanne J. Myers, "Jihad: The Trail of Political Islam"
www.cceia.org/resources/transcripts/135.html

John Esposito and Joanne J. Myers, "Unholy War: Terror in the Name of Islam"
www.cceia.org/resources/transcripts/137.html

CHAPTER 21

GLOBAL (DIS)ORDERS

Objectives

Contemporary global politics has been shaken in recent years by rampant terrorism, multilateral and unilateral military reprisals, and mounting civil strife. These turbulent times reveal cracks, if not a breakdown, in the prevailing global order and have led to ever-louder demands for the creation of new norms and institutions of global governance. As this chapter describes, this is not the first time in world history when prevailing systems of global governance have eroded in the face of pronounced structural change and clashing belief systems. In past centuries, world leaders and citizens have been challenged to find new international mechanisms to tame the conflicts and disorders of their times.

W. ANDY
KNIGHT

To understand how such disorder has been dealt with in the past, this chapter provides a survey of both the breakdowns in past world orders and the subsequent attempts to govern the turbulence that was generated by periods of fundamental change. A cursory review of the structural changes from pre-Westphalian to Westphalian world order is undertaken followed by a brief discussion of the introduction of global governance systems aimed at re-establishing world-order equilibrium amid the global disorder of contemporary times.

Introduction

The terrorist attacks in the United States on September 11, 2001, reminded us of the extent to which dominant theories in international relations are inadequate for explaining the world around us. Realism, a popular approach to the study of international politics, stresses the sovereignty and centrality of national states that act in their own interests in global politics. The realist approach may have been useful in providing an explanation for the precarious stability of the Cold War era but finds it hard to comprehend the relevance and force of transnational non-state actors in the contemporary world. International relations experts are known to disagree about the nature of our contemporary world order. Some argue that since the end of the Cold War and the intensification of globalization forces, we are witnessing a decided shift in the underlying structures of world order. Some describe the new world disorder with the term "turbulence."

The end of the Cold War saw the erosion of the structural and ideological underpinnings of the bipolar superpower conflict that dominated the previous half-century. Apart from relaxing global tensions, this new structural condition ostensibly reduced the major security threat that the world faced during the Cold War—notably, the threat of nuclear war between two heavily armed military camps (mutual assured destruction, or MAD). But the face-off between the superpowers had provided a milieu in which many conflicts that were seething underneath the Cold War blanket were figuratively frozen. Lifting that blanket, in some cases, resulted not only in a thaw but also in a percolation of incipient conflicts, many of which became violent civil wars. This period of global structural change also fuelled an American triumphalism, which celebrated the apparent defeat of communism and the emergence of "a **unipolar moment**" (Krauthammer 1990–1991, 23).

The formidable position of the United States was aided by the fact that the formerly powerful Soviet Union disintegrated "into an unstable constellation of fifteen independent states" (Klare, 1998, 59). The initial thawing of the Cold War also seemed to unfreeze a number of seething conflicts around the globe, resulting in civil wars and internecine violence in such places as Afghanistan, Rwanda, Somalia, and the former Yugoslavia. In the aftermath of the collapse of the Soviet Union, it was estimated that there were approximately 93 conflicts around the world, in which 5.5 million people were killed—75 percent of those being civilians (Keating and Knight, 2003, 1–4). Almost all of these were intra-state conflicts, thus partially explaining the disproportionate number of civilian casualties.

A culture of violence emerged in the latter part of the twentieth century as hypernationalism and long-suppressed ethnic conflicts reared their ugly heads. Some examples of this culture are the debacle in Somalia, the Rwandan genocide, the mounting toll of civilian deaths in the Democratic Republic of the Congo, Sierra Leone, Liberia, and Mozambique, and the continued violence in other places, such as the Middle East, Asia, and Chechnya. Other human tragedies and gross human rights violations occurred in so-called "failed states," where the total absence of governance structures meant that civilians were particularly vulnerable to futile violence. Millions of innocent people became refugees and displaced persons, fleeing the violence, and thousands of children were recruited as child soldiers by both government and rebel forces. The destruction of national infrastructures and of governmental and societal institutions worth billions was a result of internecine violence and natural and man-made disasters during this immediate post–Cold War period. To this new dimension of insecurity were added the longstanding and continuing problems of unchecked population growth, crushing debt burdens, barriers to trade, drug trafficking, the trafficking in women and children, and a growing disparity between rich and poor. Poverty, disease, famine, natural and man-made disasters, oppression, and despair compounded the problems and led to a new preoccupation with what was labelled "broadened and deepened" transnational security threats. One analyst, who had anticipated this scenario, predicted, "We will soon miss the Cold War" (Mearsheimer, 1990). This picture of the immediate post–Cold War period has been described as one of turbulence and global disorder, if not an emerging anarchy (Kaplan, 2000).

Toward a New World Order?

OTHER OBSERVERS, WHILE RECOGNIZING THE TUMULTUOUS AND SIGNIFICANT events that accompanied the conclusion of the Cold War, insist that what seems like global disorder in the early phase of the post–Cold War era actually represents a temporary adjustment—a transitional period. Such a transition is to be expected when the world order undergoes change of the magnitude experienced since 1989. But when one observes the trends in world politics over a relatively long period of time, one may discern certain patterns of order within what seems to be disorder (Rosenau, 1990). Stephen Gill calls this condition "patterned disorder" (Gill, 1994, 170). In fact, some politicians were convinced during the early 1990s that a "new world order" had emerged, with the United States situated at the centre.

The results of the 1990–91 Gulf War, which pitted Iraq against an insuperable U.S.-led coalition, lent credence to the notion that the United States was now the sole global superpower. The U.S. was in a position to bring order to global disorder as the world's policeman or, more menacingly, to shape the global post–Cold War world order in its own likeness. Even American president George H.W. Bush got caught up in the headiness of the moment and prematurely declared, in 1991, the emergence of a "new world order." In his view, American power could be wielded, in concert with "coalitions of the willing," to bring order and stability across the globe. Clearly, only the United States was in a position to do this, or so it was assumed by the Bush-senior administration. As it turned out, Bush lost the next election, and it did not take long before there was further evidence of the "new world disorder."

Critics suggested that the announcement of a new world order was premature, if not a chimera (Slaughter, 2001). Realists, in particular, have long argued that the essential features of the international system have not changed since the time of

Thucydides. They are convinced that the international system always has been, and continues to be, anarchic. This is so, according to those who hold this position, because there are no supranational institutions that can impose order on national states, the dominant systemic actors in the world order. States have always been bent on survival and self-preservation. As a result, the international system is filled with security competitions and confrontations and what is generally referred to as "security dilemmas." Kenneth Waltz is one supporter of this notion that the world has not been transformed since the end of the Cold War. His work stresses the continuities that are observable in world politics (Waltz, 2000, 39). Similarly, John Mearsheimer suggests that international anarchy did not change with the thawing of Cold War conditions. In his opinion, states are still the principle actors in world politics, and, as long as that is the case, the future is likely to look very much like the past, with military competition between sovereign states as the distinguishing feature of world politics (1992, 214).

But there are others who disagree with the above position, arguing that the underlying structure of the international system has shifted in recent years. They point to evidence of such change in technology-driven developments, such as the information revolution, the proliferation of telecommunications systems worldwide, and the evident shrinkage of the globe as a result of globalization and growing complex interdependence. As a result, they argue, states are losing their monopoly over instruments of power and regulation. Concurrently, non-state actors (some benign, others malign) are taking advantage of this vacuum of power and absence of regulatory ability to increase their power vis-à-vis the state. Jessica Matthews, for instance, argues that "the end of the Cold War has brought no mere adjustment among states but a novel redistribution of power among states, markets, and civil society." National governments are not simply losing autonomy in a globalized economy but, instead, are sharing powers, including political, social, and security roles at the core of sovereignty with non-state actors (1997, 55).

However, a more nuanced position holds that both continuity and change are exhibited during times of transition. James Rosenau, for instance, advances the notion that the contemporary era can be described as "a historical breakpoint." In his words, "Global life may have entered a period of turbulence the likes of which it has not known for three hundred years and the outcomes of which are still far from clear." He suggests further that today's changes are "so thoroughgoing as to render obsolete the rules and procedures by which politics are conducted, thereby leaving observers without any paradigms or theories that adequately explain the course of events." While some may dismiss these changes as mere anomalies, Rosenau is convinced that these "anomalies" are more pervasive than the recurrent patterns and that the discontinuities are more prominent than the continuities (Rosenau, 1990, 5–6).

Overwhelming evidence, particularly since 1989, points to systemic changes in world order. But there is also evidence that during times of systemic instability, political actors have risen to the challenge by proposing and adopting governance mechanisms to contain turbulence and bring equilibrium to the seeming disorder. The next section provides a survey of the evolution of global governance in response to transformative shifts in world orders since 1648. This survey shows that the innovative capacity of political action is ever-present during moments of crisis, even though the prescriptive governance solutions have not always been adequate to meet the challenges of the times.

Global Governance and World Order

KIMON VALASKAKIS MAKES THE CASE THAT THROUGHOUT HISTORY THERE have been essentially three recognized systems of global governance. The first is the exercise of authority by a hegemonic power as exemplified by Pax Romana, Pax Britannica, or Pax Americana. The second is tied to the notion of balance of power. In this case, countervailing forces bring a measure of order to a system. In the Westphalian world order, for instance, the balance of power system found root in national state sovereignty. In a sovereign-states system, there is no overarching power to impose settlement from above. Therefore, sovereign states maintain some order in the system by negotiation, by forming alliances, and by going to war. The third is a system of governance that operates through a pre-arranged set of criteria. Valaskakis uses federalism as one example of this form of governance. Federalism is a system of governance in which the jurisdictions of central government and those of subjugated units are clearly outlined in advance (2001, 46–47). A survey of world order over time reveals at various turbulent junctures the introduction of different types of global governance systems in an attempt to bring order to the disorder.

From Pre-Westphalian to Westphalian Order

Beginning with the early Modern Period, in pre-Westphalian Europe, one is struck by the extent to which the world order exhibited a type of turbulence and structural change similar to the one our current world order is experiencing. This pre-Westphalian era was a period of declining empires, retreating feudal lords, and an emerging class of traders and capitalist entrepreneurs (Valaskakis, 2001, 48). The Holy Roman Catholic Church represented God's rule on earth and had established itself as the hegemonic power that acted as an instrument of European governance. However, by the early 1600s, there were already signs of tremendous turbulence in this early world order. One indication of this was the first pan-European war, which severely weakened the influence of the Church and led to its eventual replacement with about 300 sovereign princes.

The old order, disintegrating because of the disorder of the religious wars, was slowly replaced by a new pan-European order based on the equal sovereignty of newly created states. This European-states system eventually expanded to encompass the entire globe, reaching its zenith around 1945 with the creation of the United Nations (UN) system— the only universal governance system of which 192 states today are members. So, one can safely label the period 1648 to 1945 as the Westphalian world order.

Sacrosanct claims of sovereignty characterized the Westphalian world order. This order consisted of a proliferating number of sovereign states, each supposedly in unchallenged control of its territory, resources, and population. With no overarching governance body to mediate between these sovereign entities, self-restraint gave way to numerous inter-state clashes in the 150 years following the signing of the Westphalian Treaty. It has been estimated that between 1650 and 1800, there were about 67 significant wars, many of which involved the "great powers" of the time. To address this problem, and to maintain a semblance of order, a system of international governance and law was created.

First came the codification of rules of diplomacy at the Vienna Congress in 1814–15, after the defeat of Napoleon by a coalition composed of Austria, Britain, Prussia, and Russia. These rules established a consensus about regular peaceful relationships between most European states. Out of this Congress also emerged a concert system of governance to deal with future threat to the system. In Article VI of the Treaty of Chaumont, the four great European powers agreed to "renew at fixed intervals . . . meetings for the examination of the measures which at each of these epochs shall be considered most salutary for the repose and propriety of the Nations and for the maintenance of the peace of Europe" (Hinsley, 1967, 195). The idea of preventing war through regular meetings of the states in the system was, indeed, novel. However, these Congress meetings also institutionalized the status quo, making it difficult for necessary systemic change to take hold. This tension between stability and change pitted Britain (sympathetic to the forces for change) against the Holy Alliance of reactionary rulers of Austria, Prussia, and Russia (bent on maintaining the status quo).

The importance of the control of territory to the European sovereign entities led to a rivalry over the so-called "new world"—a number of "ungoverned" territories in Africa, Asia, the Americas, and the Caribbean. The colonial expansionary period allowed some European states to amass great wealth as they acquired new territories and pillaged the wealth and resources of indigenous peoples through conquest. Britain became "great" during this colonial period, with France not too far behind. Great Britain rose to global pre-eminence by 1815. Aided by the industrial revolution, this country held a disproportionate share of the world's manufacturing production. With a combination of growing wealth and an expanding colonial empire backed by a formidable Royal Navy, Britain became a global hegemon within the Westphalian world order.

That hegemon also became the "holder of the balance" in the balance-of-power system of the colonial period. As Hans Morgenthau put it, "The balancer is not permanently identified with the policies" of the other states in the system. In fact, "its only objective within the system is the maintenance of the balance, regardless of the concrete policies the balance will serve." It does so by throwing its weight on one side or another to ensure a relative equilibrium of the system (2001, 147–148). Britain's role as balancer, or arbiter of the system, during the colonial phase of the Westphalian world order is generally described as "Pax Britannica"—a term reserved for the period of peace that resulted from Britain's tenure as the dominant global power.

Eventually, the Congress system of governance became a loose regime, labelled the Concert of Europe, which addressed problems reactively as they arose. It did not deal with those problems at regular meetings in a pre-emptive fashion—as was initially intended. The Paris Peace Conference was convened to bring an end to the Crimean War in 1856. The Congress of Vienna in 1864 addressed the Schleswig-Holstein War, the conference at Prague brought an end to the Seven Weeks War in 1866, and the one at Frankfurt in 1871 similarly helped to end the Franco-Prussian War. The Concert of Europe also used its status to try to force a long-term settlement of the Balkan question in 1878 at the Berlin Congress. At a later Berlin Congress (1884–85), the Concert divvied up much of the African continent among European imperial powers.

The Concert system proved effective at maintaining balance in the expanding international system by recognizing emerging powers and broadening the governance system beyond Europe. It thus internationalized the Westphalian order. The Concert granted recognition to the United States, an emerging power, in 1783 with the Treaty of Paris, and to several Latin American states in 1823. The Ottoman Empire and Rumania were granted admission to the Concert system in 1856 by the Treaty of Paris, and Japan was added in 1853. The expansion of the international governance system became even more evident in 1907 when the Hague Conference drew 44 states, including 18 from Latin America.

Turbulence in the Westphalian World Order

The Concert of Europe provided a governance framework for an expanding international system for almost a century. While small conflicts erupted from time to time, the Crimean War was the only major international war during that period. The Concert was, therefore, successful as long as it could maintain order within the international system. But once it was unable to facilitate the peaceful settlement of disputes between the European states, it quickly lost legitimacy and relevance. The Concert's demise was due, in large part, to the turbulence that accompanies shifts in the underlying structure of a world order. The Westphalian world order, as noted above, was initially a pan-European order. As that European order became internationalized with the entrance of new states into the system, the resulting tensions called out for the creation of a new governance system—one that would be more relevant to the changing times.

Added to this governance problem was the need for functional agencies during the early phase of globalization, to manage the coordination of a number of transnational issues in the socio-economic sphere. The Convention of Octroi in 1804 created a centralized supranational administration to control navigation on the Rhine. An international commission for the Elbe was created in 1821. The Treaty of Paris in 1856 established a Commission for the European Danube in an attempt to supervise the free navigation of that river after national administration proved unable to deal with the modern world of shipping and international trade along that water system.

This trend in functional governance continued with the creation of the International Telegraphic Bureau (later named the International Telegraphic Union) in 1868, the General Postal Union (later renamed the Universal Postal Union) in 1874, the International Bureau of Weights and Measures in 1875, the International Union for the Publication of Customs Tariffs in 1890, and the Metric Union and international Health Offices in 1881 and 1901. A concurrent trend was the emergence of public international unions, private international associations, and hybrid bodies, such as the International Labour Organization (ILO), formed in 1919. Already, by the 1900s, there were clear signs that the Westphalian order, which had embedded the notion that states were the only actors of significance in world politics, was beginning to be challenged by the multiplication of actors on the world stage.

Functional cooperation proved insufficient for keeping the Westphalian world order from undergoing turbulence and change. Between 1914 and 1945, that world order seemed more like a world disorder shaken by two major world wars, the 1929 stock market collapse, the 1930s economic Depression, the rise of fascism, economic protectionism, and the League of Nations' demise.

Actually, the establishment of the League was an attempt at bringing order to the post-Concert disorder. During the course of World War I, several individuals and civil society groups worked with some governments to propose a plan to save the world from another major war. American president Woodrow Wilson was one of the world leaders who felt strongly that a new governance system was needed to bring a semblance of order back to the international system. At the Versailles Peace Conference, Wilson chaired a special commission on the League of Nations. The blueprint for this new international governance body drew heavily on perpetual peace plans of earlier eras, the experience of the Congress and concert systems, and the experimentation with functional transnational regulatory instruments (Knight, 2000, 65–81).

The Covenant of the League of Nations became the governing constitution of this world body and reflected hope that a lawful, just, and peaceable world order would eventually be the outcome of international cooperation among the members of the states system. It adopted in the 1920s the *Geneva General Act for the Settlement of Disputes*, a Permanent Court of Arbitration, and a Permanent Court of Justice to provide the states with mechanisms for resolving conflicts. In forming a Financial Commission, the League made an attempt to regulate the expanding world economy and to "reconcile reparations with financial stability, reduce trade barriers, and reconstruct the international monetary system" (Tehranian, 2002, 12).

The League was plagued by several problems. First, it was not a truly global body because the colonized world was not a part of this arrangement. Second, despite Wilson's efforts, the United States never became a member of the League. Third, the League was not flexible enough to accommodate the demands of the revisionist powers—the Soviet Union, Mussolini's Italy, Nazi Germany, and Imperial Japan. These powers disliked the global status quo and rejected extant institutions, including the League, treaties, diplomacy, international law, and the international economic order. Japan attacked China and occupied Manchuria in 1931. The League failed to respond to that act of aggression. Italy launched an attack on Ethiopia in 1935, and again the League proved impotent to act. In 1933, Hitler withdrew Germany from the League and began a series of aggressive measures that basically went unchecked by the League.

In many respects, one can view World War II as a by-product of the dialectical current produced from the clash between continuity and change, as well as status-quo forces and upstarts. Germany had emerged out of World War I as a totally dissatisfied power. Not only was it defeated on the battlefield, its territorial ambitions were thwarted by the status-quo powers. In addition, the Versailles Treaty, which formally brought an end to the war, forced Germans to pay for the economic costs of the war through reparations. Widespread dissatisfaction in Germany over this "victor's justice" became fertile ground for a rearmed Adolf Hitler to sow his seeds of hatred and stir up the bed of domestic unrest and global disorder.

Since the League was unable to constrain Germany and Japan, the world was thrust into a cataclysmic war only 20 years after the conclusion of what was commonly referred to as the "war to end all wars." As distinguished historian E.H. Carr succinctly put it then, "The characteristic feature of the twenty years between 1919 and 1939 was the abrupt descent from the visionary hopes of the first decade to the grim despair of the second, from a utopia which took little account of reality to a reality from which every element of utopia was rigorously excluded" (1939, 224). This explains to a large extent the great pains taken in the closing days of World War II to construct a global governance system that would balance the utopian hopes of humanity for prolonged and sustained peace with the realism of state leaders who felt that deterrent and enforcement measures were required to keep delinquent actors in line.

In August 1941, just months before the United States entered World War II, U.S. president Franklin D. Roosevelt joined British prime minister Winston Churchill in putting together the Atlantic Charter. This Charter formed the basis for the Declaration of the United Nations, which was signed on January 1, 1942, by 26 governments. The premise of the Declaration was the need to establish a permanent governance system that would ensure general global security after the war was over. At the Yalta Conference in February 1945, Roosevelt, Churchill, and Stalin laid out the basis for the UN Charter, the constitutional document that would guide the operations of the United Nations—a new global governance institution—and lay out the parameters of the post–World War II world order.

Diplomatic negotiations at a conference in San Francisco on April 25, 1945, resulted in agreement on the UN Charter. This document enshrined veto power for five permanent members of the organization's apex body, the Security Council (the United Kingdom, China, France, the Soviet Union, and the United States). It also intimated that Japan, Germany, and Italy were "enemy states." Fifty states signed the Charter, representing all geographical areas of the globe. For the first time, the global governance institution demonstrated signs of becoming truly universal. Today, the UN membership stands at 192 states.

The Cold War climate stymied the UN's ability to perform as expected, according to the UN Charter. The animosity between the United States and the Soviet Union was played out in the UN Security Council and other organs of the world body. Excessive use of vetoes by both superpowers limited the UN's ability to maintain the peace. The post–Cold War era initially offered great promise of a more assertive UN. However, the expansion of the security concept, the prevalence of new security threats, including transnational terrorism and transnational crime, the agitation by non-governmental organizations to have a greater say in global governance, and the problems associated with unregulated globalization all reveal the need for major transformations in the way the UN governs. Failure to do so could result in the organization's being sidelined, as we witnessed recently in the cases of Kosovo and Iraq, or in the development of new systems of global governance.

Reform of the UN is critical to any discussion of ways to address the current global disorder. It is still the only universal governing framework for the globe, but it cannot function properly as an enforcer of the global rule of law unless its member states, particularly the most powerful ones, empower it to do so. The choices for dealing with the new world disorder are becoming clear. Either we choose to strengthen the UN and the multilateral system of governance or we allow a governance system of Pax Americana to fill the void. Unfortunately, the choice may not be entirely in our hands as citizens of the globe. It will take a combination of acquiescence on the part of the world's hegemonic power (the United States) and the development and acceptance of a post-hegemonic conceptualization of global governance to find an acceptable means of bringing equilibrium back to the international system.

Summary

This chapter indicates clearly that the world has undergone critical turning points and turbulent periods in the past. We are, today, living in one of those periods of turbulence and transition. Existing dominant theories of international relations often fail to explain contemporary world politics. This causes us to consider the need for new approaches to understanding world politics and to develop new ways of thinking about the problem of transition, conflict, and change in world order. Our current era exhibits signs of a structural disjuncture. While, on the one hand, there are tendencies toward global integration and global governance, there are, on the other, also propensities toward fragmentation and global disorder. While "old political, economic, and social structures are under stress or breaking down," we have only begun to imagine the foundations for a new global order (Gill, 1994, 170).

Discussion Questions

1. What evidence is there that we live in a new world disorder?
2. What are the differences of opinion within the scholarly and practitioner communities about the current state of world order?
3. How has human agency been instrumental in developing global governance mechanisms to address the turbulence of world disorders?

References

Carr, Edward Hallett. 1939. *The Twenty Years' Crisis, 1919–1939: An Introduction to the Study of International Relations.* New York: Harper Torchbooks.

Gill, Stephen. 1994. "Structural Change and Global Political Economy: Globalizing Elites and the Emerging World Order" in Yoshikazu Sakamoto, ed., *Global Transformation: Challenges to the State System.* Tokyo: United Nations University Press.

Hinsley, F.H. 1967. *Power and the Pursuit of Peace.* Cambridge: Cambridge University Press.

Kaplan, Robert D. 2000. *The Coming Anarchy: Shattering the Dreams of the Post Cold War World.* New York: Random House.

Keating, Tom and W. Andy Knight, eds. 2004. *Building Sustainable Peace.* Edmonton: University of Alberta Press.

Klare, Michael. 1998. "The Era of Multiplying Schisms: World Security in the Twenty-First Century" in Michael T. Klare and Yogesh Chandrani, eds., *World Security: Challenges for the New Century*, 3rd edition. New York: St. Martin's Press.

Knight, W. Andy. 2000. *A Changing United Nations: Multilateral Evolution and the Quest for Global Governance.* Houndmills: Palgrave.

Krauthammer, Charles. 1990–91. "The Unipolar Moment." *Foreign Affairs,* 70.

Matthews, Jessica. 1997. "Power Shift." *Foreign Affairs,* January–February, 76.

Mearsheimer, John. 1990. "Why We Will Soon Miss the Cold War." *The Atlantic Monthly*, Volume 266, No. 2 (August).

————. 1992. "Disorder Restored" in Graham Allison and Gregory F. Treverton, eds., *Rethinking America's Security: Beyond Cold War to New World Order.* New York: Norton.

Morgenthau, Hans. 2001. "Different Methods of the Balance of Power" in Karen Mingst and Jack Synder, eds., *Essential Readings in World Politics.* New York: W.W. Norton Company.

Rosneau, James N. 1990. *Turbulence in World Politics: A Theory of Change and Continuity.* Princeton, NJ: Princeton University Press.

Slaughter, Anne-Marie. 2001. "The Real New World Order" in Karen Mingst and Jack Snyder, eds., *Essential Readings in World Politics.* New York: W.W. Norton Company.

Tehranian, Majid. 2002. "Globalization and Governance: An Overview" in Esref Aksu and Joseph A. Camilleri, eds., *Democratizing Global Governance.* Houndmills: Palgrave/Macmillan.

Valaskakis, Kimon. 2001. "Long-term Trends in Global Governance: From 'Westphalia' to 'Seattle'" in *Organization of Economic Cooperation and Development, Governance in the Twenty-First Century.* Paris: OECD.

Waltz, Kenneth. 2000. "Structural Realism After the Cold War." *International Security,* 25 (Summer).

Woolf, L. 1916. *International Government,* 2nd edition. London: Allen Unwin.

Further Readings

Aksu, Esref and Joseph A. Camilleri, eds. 2002. *Democratizing Global Governance.* Houndmills: Palgrave Macmillan.

Archer, Clive. 1983. *International Organizations.* London: George Allen Unwin.

Cox, Robert W. 2002. *The Political Economy of a Plural World.* London: Routledge.

Rosneau, James N. 1990. *Turbulence in World Politics: A Theory of Change and Continuity.* Princeton, NJ: Princeton University Press.

Weblinks

On the Concert of Europe
www.pvhs.chico.k12.ca.us/~bsilva/projects/concert/concessy.html

On the League of Nations and the United Nations (BBC)
www.bbc.co.uk/history/worldwars/wwone/league_nations_05.shtml

CHAPTER 22

INTERNATIONAL RELATIONS

Objectives

Finding explanations for why national states act the way they do on the international stage has been a central preoccupation for students of international relations (IR). This chapter uses the case of the origins of the 2003 War in Iraq to demonstrate the central premises of three dominant analytical models—realist, liberal, and radical—in the study of international relations. The chapter shows that these models of world affairs are grounded in quite different understandings of human nature, national states, and the contours of power in the international system. The origins of the War in Iraq demonstrate that explanations of international conflict and peace are complex, involving multiple levels of analysis, systemic inequalities among national states, divergent motivations of international actors, and the idiosyncratic characteristics of key leaders.

JURIS
LEJNIEKS

Introduction

American foreign policy in the immediate aftermath of the attacks of September 11, 2001, can be described as a policy success by some measures. The United States put together a global coalition to overthrow the Taliban regime in Afghanistan, which had been harbouring Osama bin Laden and his Al-Qaeda organization. The coalition included critical state actors such as Russia, China, Pakistan, India, and Japan, along with the usual NATO government support. The Taliban regime was overthrown, and there was broad agreement that Afghanistan should be rebuilt economically and politically. When the George W. Bush administration went to war against Iraq and the Saddam Hussein regime in March of 2003, however, Washington's attempts to build another broad coalition ran into serious resistance. Many of the same states that had supported the war against the Taliban, such as France, Germany, and Russia, were now opposed. Although Tony Blair committed significant numbers of British troops to the new war, the failure to build a broader coalition was a major diplomatic defeat that continues to bedevil American foreign policy in its efforts to rebuild post-war Iraq. Moreover, as the War in Iraq drags on with few successes and growing failures, the invasion is widely regarded both inside and outside the United States as a foreign policy blunder of historic proportions, with far-reaching consequences and few obvious solutions.

Why was there opposition to the War in Iraq? It is often recounted that the regime of Saddam Hussein had displayed a flagrant disregard for the rights of its own citizens. It had a history of using weapons of mass destruction (WMD) against the Kurds in northern Iraq and Iranian troops during the war with Iran. Also, Iraq disregarded the wishes of the international community by ignoring a number of UN Security Council resolutions in the aftermath of the Gulf War. The regime of Saddam Hussein was an obvious target for international condemnation and action, including a decade of economic sanctions, but that condemnation did not extend to the use of force as proposed by the United States in 2003.

A number of possible reasons have been put forward for the lack of broader international support for America's policy of regime change in Iraq. Among the reasons offered are the Bush administration's inability or reluctance to wait a few more weeks to achieve a second Security Council resolution; the over-emphasis on a military, as opposed to a diplomatic, solution; and the Bush administration's strident rhetoric and uncompromising attitude toward its allies and the United Nations. The invasion of another state is never an easy proposition, especially when that state clearly has not instigated aggression, as Iraq had done in the early 1990s against Kuwait. Legitimizing the use of force is even more difficult. Underlying the legal issue of **legitimacy** is the question of the Bush administration's motives for pursuing the War in Iraq and whether or not Bush was willing to accept any alternative to the military solution and the deposing of Saddam Hussein. It appeared to the world that the United States was committed to overthrowing Saddam and that no level of Iraqi compliance with American and UN demands would suffice.

Analyzing International Relations

THE SPECULATIONS ABOUT THE BUSH ADMINISTRATION'S MOTIVATIONS are numerous and depend on public statements both by Bush and his supporters and by his critics and the more speculative arguments about the underlying and

unstated Bush policy. Here are some possible "reasons" for the American commitment to war:

- the probability that Iraq had WMDs that were an imminent security threat to the
  United States;
- the United States' obligation to uphold and enforce UN resolutions that the UN
  Security Council had been unable or unwilling to enforce as an organization;
- the attack on Iraq was part of the broader American-led "War on Terrorism" and
  Iraq's alleged or potential links to Al-Qaeda;
- the promotion of regional stability in the Middle East by the democratization of
  Iraq; and
- the toppling of Saddam Hussein, which would put an end to a murderous regime.

Unstated reasons, because they have not been publicly voiced by the Bush administration, include these:

- the desire by Bush to finish the job that was started by Bush senior during the
  Gulf War;
- supporting Israel by eliminating a potential future threat to its security;
- providing a long-term, secure, and cheap energy (oil) source for the American
  economy;
- the influence of the religious right in U.S. politics; and
- Bush's personal belief system, which some suggest is heavily influenced by his
  religious convictions.

The problem for students of international relations is to choose which one of the
above explanations is the "correct" explanation for the invasion of Iraq. Though it
may be impossible to determine the "correct" explanation because we may be missing
critical facts and opinions on which to base our analysis, a number of tools have been
developed for the purpose of addressing such questions with accuracy. Students of
international relations, similar to political decision-makers, evaluate and act on
incomplete data. Despite the often-noted lack of data, the task of explanation is
assisted by our ability to structure our information in several different ways. The rest
of this chapter explores two ways: the use of levels of analysis and the use of analytical
models, particularly the realist, liberal, and radical models that have dominated the
study of international relations.

Researchers in the IR field often frame their explanations in relation to three levels of analysis. First, at the individual level, the focus is on the perceptions, personalities, and world views of key individual decision-makers (George W. Bush and Saddam
Hussein) or other important participants (U.S. vice-president Dick Cheney, for example). Second, at the state or national level, the focus is on state characteristics, such as
type of government, political culture, economic structures (the military-industrial
complex, for example), or identifiable national interests, such as security needs or the
corporate sector. Third, at the systemic level, the focus is on the structure of the

international system and the nature of the distribution of power among the actors that make up the system, especially whether it is anarchical (and thereby lacking in security) or cooperative, and whether it is unipolar, bipolar, or multipolar. This latter distinction focuses on whether the weight of power in the international system rests with one state (unipolar), two dominant states (bipolar), or a variety of, if not all, national states (multipolar).

Levels of analysis are important because they help us categorize our empirical data and focus our attention on a range of possible explanations. For example, at the level of the individual, we can ask questions such as these: What is the influence of individual (decision-maker) beliefs on state behaviour? Was Bush acting out of some basic personal beliefs, perhaps his religious convictions, when he ordered the invasion of Iraq? At the national or state level questions might revolve around whether domestic political conditions prompted a policy shift; more specifically, was U.S. foreign policy driven by a more fundamental shift to the right in its political makeup? At the systemic level, the focus would turn to the role and the status of the United States in the international system of states and such questions as whether the United States, as a waning or insecure power, acted unilaterally and militarily to reassert its pre-eminent position in the international system.

A second major tool that we employ to explain war and peace is analytical models. An analytical model is a set of propositions that explain events by connecting relevant concepts. We generate propositions by positing a relationship between independent and dependent variables. The statement that the War in Iraq was caused by the Bush administration's insecurity based on the perception of immediate threat from Iraq's WMDs is an example of such a proposition. The proposition, however, ultimately depends on the nature of the analytical model employed. In the study of foreign policy and international relations, we normally employ one of a number of available analytical models. Although many models of international relations have been developed over the years, often in response to shifting international conditions, three perspectives have dominated the field: realism and two of its variants, neo-realism and hegemony; liberalism and liberal institutionalism; and the radical model, which finds its genesis in Marxist theory.

Realist Models

REALISM RESTS UPON A NUMBER OF INTERRELATED ASSUMPTIONS. PRINCIPAL among these assumptions are that (1) humans are egotistical and power seeking, (2) politics is a struggle for power in the pursuit of national interest, (3) the state is the pre-eminent actor in the international system, and (4) progressive change more often occurs in domestic politics than in international political life.

At its core, realism is pessimistic about human nature—human beings are self-interested, egotistical, and power seeking, and this basic fact about our species necessarily results in aggression and conflict. The second assumption addresses the key concept of power. There are a large number of definitions of power because of its controversial nature, but here I define power as "the capacity to act in global politics." Realists contend that the central preoccupation of international political activity is the immediate pursuit of power, since acquiring, maintaining, and demonstrating power allow us to meet political and economic objectives. Hence, international relations are characterized by rivalry and conflict, where all states pursue and defend their national interests and all states pursue the same broad national interests to a greater or lesser extent. A state's pre-eminent national interest is the pursuit of its own self-preservation, since the international system is anarchical and security is in short supply.

Other broad national interests are the economic well-being of the population and the pursuit of specific national values, such as economic freedom and democracy in the American case. National interests are achieved through the application of power, which, at times, depends on military capability, since the ultimate resolution of conflicts is war. Very powerful states, such as the United States, may not have to wage war to be influential as they can influence the behaviour of others simply because they possess significant power and have shown the will to use it. But power is relative because some states possess more power than others and not all power can be used in all international contexts. Just because the United States possesses nuclear weapons does not mean that it can use them, or threaten to use them, for example, in a fishing dispute with Canada.

Realists maintain that states are the most significant actors in the international system because they are more powerful than other international actors, including such inclusive **intergovernmental organizations (IGOs)** as the United Nations. States have the capacity to tax their subjects and use these resources to pursue foreign policy objectives. Further, they can mobilize their populations to create militaries that serve to protect or expand the state and its sovereignty. States are sovereign in the sense that they are not obliged to do what other states tell them to do. According to the doctrine of state sovereignty, there is no higher authority even in today's international system than the national state. And since there is no world government, realists argue that the international system is inherently anarchical and characterized by turmoil, discord, and conflict.

Realists also assume that since human nature is immutable, international politics is immutable. International politics is, thus, perpetually characterized by self-reliance and the struggle for power. The international system is inherently conflictual; peace is only a temporary condition and is always in jeopardy. Realism presents itself as an analytical model that holds for all times because the basic nature of state relations never changes. There is no progressive evolution toward a global community.

A major variant of realism is neo-realism, also known as structural realism. The major difference from realism lies in the neo-realist emphasis on the international system itself instead of the state and its leaders. For neo-realists, the structure of the international system is still characterized by a lack of overarching authority, but equally important is the distribution of capabilities within the system. It is the nature of the system and the distribution of capabilities, or relative distribution of power, that defines the nature of international events. All states are basically alike in their functions—they all perform the same basic tasks despite different constitutions, ideologies, or cultures. They differ significantly only in regard to their power. Hence, change in the international system occurs when great powers rise and fall, along with a shift in the balance of power. Neo-realists contend that the only way to minimize conflict among actors is the maintenance of a balance of power.

The hegemonic model is a popular variant of neo-realism that focuses on the preponderance of power held by one state in relation to all others in the international system. According to this model, the hegemon provides the values and the rules, in other words, the leadership—that maintain effectively functioning political and economic systems defined by peace, stability, and prosperity. It is a system that serves the interests of the hegemon and some of the other states in the system, depending on their political and economic relationship to the hegemon. The hegemon must maintain its unique position because instability arises when a hegemon weakens and a challenger moves to erode the influence of the hegemon. Instability is dangerous because it disturbs both the international and regional balances of power, thus creating conditions for war. Proponents of the hegemonic perspective also contend that a critical obligation of the hegemon's leadership is the maintenance of a prosperous international economic system. Since the global economy today is defined by capitalism, this means the maintenance and expansion of the benefits of free trade. Hegemony is not only for the benefit of the hegemon; a benevolent hegemon provides economic benefits to all other actors.

To sum up, the realist model assumes power-seeking and antagonistic individuals who organize themselves into political actors that we call states. The resulting international system is one of anarchy that finds stability either through a balance of power or the domination of one state, the hegemon, over all others. Either the state or the international system determines whether or not the system will be peaceful or prone to conflict.

Liberal Models

LIBERALISM AND LIBERAL INSTITUTIONALISM CHALLENGE THE REALIST PERspective because they focus on the individual and cooperation. In contrast to realist models, liberal models are optimistic about human nature because they assume that human behaviour is ultimately based on reason. Individuals thus may use reason to recognize and develop shared interests with others and engage in cooperative activities for their mutual benefit. Indeed, rather than anarchy and conflict, liberals contend that through reason, law, and institution-building, international society can work together to build a more peaceful and sustainable world.

Liberals, like realists, recognize that human beings are self-interested but, because humans are also rational, humankind is perfectible or at least capable of improvement.

Human reason can triumph over human fear and the drive for power. This human nature has a powerful influence over international behaviour. In the long term, international cooperation will dominate the propensity for self-interested conflict. The international system, from a liberal perspective, is characterized by relative peace, the promotion of global interdependence, and the spread of human rights. Increasingly, common problems, such as global warming or the AIDS epidemic, are understood as international problems that can only be solved through the collaboration of national states in the North and the South. States work together first out of self-interest, and increasingly, by the very success of that cooperation, working together becomes habitual and overrides narrow state self-interest.

Since liberalism is ultimately committed to both political and economic freedoms for the individual, liberals also promote democracy, since it provides the greatest freedoms and rights for individuals. But democracy provides a great deal more than individual liberty. Democracy also promotes economic development by increasing political stability and decreasing government influence and possible corruption in the economy. For students of international relations, however, the most important aspect of liberalism is that democracies foster international peace. Ordinary people, as opposed to princes, generally oppose war because they pay for war with higher taxes and often with their very lives. Furthermore, democratic peace theory posits that democracies do not fight wars against other democracies, since they are more likely to act cooperatively to settle mutual disagreements. Implicit in this model is the idea that increasing the number of democracies in the world increases the possibility for a more peaceful world.

The liberal institutionalist model is grounded in the idea that cooperation takes place increasingly within the context of transnational actors. The result is an international system characterized, not just by interdependence, but by interdependence through specialized institutions. Institutions are essential, since the increased speed and spread of transportation and telecommunications have changed world politics dramatically by changing the global agenda from a narrow military security perspective to the need to emphasize shared problems that must have shared solutions. Common problems are no longer just the most immediate threats, such as security and epidemics, but are now increasingly longer-term problems, such as population growth, depletion of fish stocks, and environmental issues (such as global warming). The consequences of these threats are a "global commons" problem because they affect all states, whether they contribute to the problem or not. Evidence of the importance of institutions is their growth. Currently, there are several hundred IGOs, such as the United Nations and the Organization of American States (OAS), but nongovernmental organizations (NGOs), such as the Red Cross and Greenpeace, are even more numerous and expanding. Their numbers now exceed 26 000 worldwide.

Despite the growth of transnational actors, solutions to global problems are exacerbated by economic inequality because economic globalization has increased the gap between the rich states of the North and the poor states of the South. The growing gap is not only morally unacceptable; it also accentuates other global problems.

The global poverty gap contributes to growing immigration and refugee problems, and environmental issues, such as access to food and energy supplies. Increasingly, as well, poverty contributes to local violence among peoples who have nothing to lose, with the danger of violence spilling over into neighbouring states or a whole region. Liberal internationalism argues that addressing these issues is fundamental to global peace, security, and prosperity.

Liberal institutionalists argue that, because of their pessimistic view of human nature, realists ignore the growth and strength of international civil society. While there is no world government, the functioning of transnational institutions and the acceptance of norms of international law is leading to common habits of cooperative behaviour of both state and non-state actors, including individuals. Compliance with norms and rules is the result of a complex interaction between self-interest and morality. States and other international actors adhere to rules since it is in their long-term interest to do so, not only because of tangible benefits but also because other actors' adherence to rules makes the international system more orderly, predictable, and peaceful. In contrast to realist models, liberal models consider international organizations (including intergovernmental and non-governmental groups) to be as important as states. In the international system, these models project the replacement of international anarchy with interdependence and a growing international civil society.

Radical Models

RADICALISM HAS MANY VARIANTS, BUT RADICAL APPROACHES HAVE SOME CORE themes. First, politics, both national and international, reflect the forces of economic production. Second, capitalism, the driving force of the contemporary international political economy, promotes human exploitation and inequality. And third, prevailing economic and political relations must be replaced by more egalitarian economic and political systems. "Radicalism," here, does not have the usual connotation of extremism. Rather, radicalism proposes solutions to underlying or root causes. It is normative because of its commitment to change. The change comes in the form of the elimination of global capitalism to establish a new international economic system based on a different distribution of power that ends exploitation of the weak by the strong.

The radical approach emphasizes the consequences of what is termed the "new imperialism." Imperialism in the contemporary context does not imply the existence of an empire because there is no direct and formal political control over other peoples as was the case historically. Formal control has been replaced by less formal control, but control no less for the benefit of the imperial power. Imperialism today is self-sustaining. The imperial power establishes the economic and political rules of the game, and weaker states have to make choices on the basis of those rules. The mechanism of control is the global capitalist economy, which is dominated by the United States, other developed Northern states, and the international institutions that they have formed, such as the World Bank and the International Monetary Fund (IMF). These international financial institutions have inordinate influence over the daily lives of the poor of Africa, the Middle East, and Latin America, as well as their governments.

While the specific methods of control vary, the imperialist objective is to keep the poor states of the South in their place on the lowest rung in the global division of labour. Although called free trade, the global exchange of goods and services is unequal. The South sells natural resources, agricultural products, and labour-intensive manufactured goods, often using outdated production methods. In turn, the North exports high-profit, high-technology manufactured goods (such as computers and medical equipment) and essential services (such as banking). Neither do the states of the North practise free trade when it harms their own economic interests. The governments of the North interfere in the marketplace when it is to their advantage, by subsidizing research and development or protecting important economic sectors from external competition because they are important to security of supply or because they have a competitive edge in the export market.

The radical perspective underlines that direct political control of the South is not necessary because economic imperialism is essentially self-sustaining. To earn hard currency to repay debt or acquire essential imports, including military equipment, the South must sell its goods. It cannot withdraw from the international economic system without serious economic or political consequences. But because the exchange with the North is unequal, the South keeps falling further and further behind economically. When hard export earnings are insufficient for current needs, the states in the South must either borrow or depend on international aid. Default is a difficult option because that would cut off the debtor nation from further international borrowing.

There are times when economic conditions are so serious that a state must borrow from the IMF to maintain liquidity. As a condition of the loan, the IMF extracts concessions called structural adjustment programs or, more recently, poverty reduction strategies. These programs are designed to attract private investment and raise export earnings by changing domestic economic policies and can range from the adjustment of exchange rates, more often than not currency devaluation, to cutting expenditures by cutting social programs to balance the budget, to cutting domestic subsidies for struggling industries. The result is a political control exerted through the influence of international institutions, in this case the IMF. Further control comes with ties among the elites of the North and the South states. Elites in the South are personally enriched by their status in their economic system and resulting political status. Sometimes, they are further enriched by bribery or, for example, more subtly through having themselves or their children educated in the most prestigious schools and universities in the North. Imperialism uses culture (or soft power) to inculcate the idea that capitalism is not only a way to get rich but also the best and most efficient way to structure economies. When capitalism is internalized, the imperialist system is not challenged.

At the 2004 World Social Forum, Indian political economist Arundhati Roy condemned the new imperialism, arguing that the complex contemporary system of multilateral trade laws and financial agreements effectively institutionalizes global inequality.

"Why else," Roy asked, "would it be that the US taxes a garment made by a Bangladeshi manufacturer twenty times more than a garment made in Britain?" "Why else would it be that countries that grow cocoa beans, like the Ivory Coast or Ghana, are taxed out of the market if they try to turn it into chocolate? . . . Why else would it be that after having been plundered by colonizing regimes for more than half a century, former colonies are steeped in debt to those same regimes and repay them some $382 *billion* a year?" Roy concludes that "no individual nation can stand up to the project of corporate globalization on its own" (2004, 13).

There are moments in world affairs when imperialist power is exerted more overtly. This can be accomplished through foreign aid programs, including the training and equipping of militaries and police forces. In some cases, direct intervention is deemed necessary. Anti-imperialists often point to such examples as the American intervention in Iran (1953), Guatemala (1954), the Dominican Republic (1965), Granada (1982), and Panama (1989). These interventions range from the prevention of revolution, especially socialist or communist, to suppressing revolutions, to overthrowing governments that threaten vital economic interests. The current tensions between the U.S. and anti-imperialist Venezuelan president Hugo Chavez can be read in this light.

Radicals identify capitalism as the driving force behind imperialism. Capitalism needs empire for the supply of raw materials, such as oil, which are often available only in the South. Multinational corporations need the opportunity to invest in the South in order to cut costs and increase profits. Minimal governmental intervention in the poor states, lack of environmental regulations, low taxes, and low wages all contribute to the corporate bottom line. Finally, capitalism needs expanding markets because their productive capacity is greater than their domestic market can absorb. Without international expansion, the imperialist economy can go into recession.

Radicalism differs from realism and liberalism in a number of important ways. First, radical approaches locate the source of international behaviour in domestic and international capitalist systems. Human behaviour is structured through these larger systems of production and exchange. While the state is an important international actor, it is an agent of economic interests defined by dominant socio-economic classes, transnational elites, and multinational corporations. According to a radical perspective, the international system is not characterized by anarchy (realism) or interdependence (liberalism) but, instead, by a rigid stratification of power and wealth among the states of the North and the South. Most important, the radical perspective is normative in the sense that it opposes the global capitalist system, imperial domination, and the resulting exploitation and impoverishment of the vast majority of the world's population.

Back to the War

WE NOW RETURN TO THE REASONS WHY THE UNITED STATES WENT TO WAR against Iraq, with the subsequent execution of Saddam Hussein, international condemnation about the loss of innocent Iraqi lives, and growing concerns within the

U.S. about the toll in American lives and the cost to American taxpayers. A realist would focus on such explanations as the alleged presence in Iraq of weapons of mass destruction, alleged Iraqi support for Al-Qaeda, American support for Israel, the American pursuit of stability in the Middle East, and America's need to ensure a secure supply of energy for long-term economic security. The essentially unilateral act by the United States reinforces the realist explanation for the war.

We may want to argue that the lack of proof regarding WMDs or Al-Qaeda ties negates both these reasons for the war as well as a realist interpretation of the occupation. But a study of decision making shows us that the key issue in such cases is not reality so much as the perception of reality. In this instance, it does not make any difference whether the WMDs were there, as long as the Bush administration believed them to be there (although there is considerable debate as to whether they really believed this or simply chose to believe it in support of other motivations). But even without the WMD argument, Middle East security is essential to the United States because of the presence of energy that fuels the American economy. Further, from an American perspective, Israel is the only democratic and reliable ally in the Middle East—and this is not to mention the influence of the powerful pro-Israel lobby in the United States. Increasing the number of democracies in the Middle East, even by one, increases the chances of stability in that region, especially in view of the growing power of Iran. Since the potential for positive change in the Middle East without military intervention was seen as minimal, or even potentially threatening to American interests, the United States decided to act. Ultimately, of course, the United States has the power to act unilaterally and pursue its national interests, however defined.

Liberal analysts can pursue one of two strategies in evaluating American policy. They can point to the upholding of Security Council resolutions and the objective of Middle East stability as significant liberal goals. In addition, there is a long-term benefit to a liberal international system through the elimination of the non-democratic and repressive regime of Saddam Hussein. A second strategy from a liberal perspective is to condemn the American-led War in Iraq as a pursuit of realist objectives at a time when state security concerns should be secondary to more important global threats. The fact that the United States acted almost unilaterally and did not give UN inspectors sufficient time to finish their work supports this interpretation. By implication, the American claim of support for UN resolutions and the moral argument regarding the toppling of a murderous regime are so much rhetoric for a basically self-interested pursuit of national interest. American unilateralism also suggests that the United States was acting as a hegemon, especially considering its unbending attitudes toward the views of its potential allies.

The radical perspective is clear. The War in Iraq was an attempt by the United States to secure a long-term oil supply by establishing a friendly regime in the Middle East. In addition, American companies (such as Halliburton) benefited directly and immediately through the economic rebuilding process in Iraq. Regional economic stability was enhanced by the elimination of an undependable regime, possibly resulting in a new regime that is not a threat to Saudi Arabia and the energy-driven economic system of the region. The dilemma for the radical analyst is that there is no direct (clearly stated by the administration) evidence for their position. The radical argument rests on the capitalist nature of the international economic system and the influence of economic elites, such as Vice-President Cheney, on American foreign policy. The differences between the United States and its allies are nothing more than evidence of different capitalist economic interests that translate into differences over Iraq policy.

Whatever the explanation, the War in Iraq also demonstrates that the outcomes of foreign policy adventures are often uncontrollable and unintended. If the United States invaded Iraq to make the world more secure, the policy has been an abysmal failure. Iraq has proven to be a training ground for international terrorists. Similarly, if the goal was to provide democratic stability in the Middle East, again quite the opposite has been accomplished. American alliances in the region have been strained, and countries hostile to both the United States and Israel have been strengthened. Finally, the American economy has not been strengthened. It remains vulnerable to external fluctuations in oil supply, while the cost of the war has contributed to the mushrooming American debt. For some sectors of the American economy, such as the military-industrial and security-technology sectors, the War in Iraq (and the War on Terrorism more generally) has proven to be a windfall. At the same time, the American economy as a whole has been rendered vulnerable to foreign investors and governments that hold American debt. More than this, many of the overly confident architects of the war have resigned their posts in government, while President Bush's approval ratings are among the lowest ever recorded. The lessons of the Iraq War, in other words, underline the complexities of international relations in the contemporary era and the limitations of hegemonic politics.

Summary

It is generally argued that the administration of George W. Bush returned to realism after the Clinton administration's attempts to turn American foreign policy in a more liberal direction. The Bush administration was committed to strengthening the American military, as is evidenced by its emphasis on a ballistic missile defence system. It also has refused to join the International Criminal Court because of the possibility that its military personnel could be charged while serving American interests abroad. Other evidence of realism is the disdain that the administration has shown for international institutions and norms. It refused to join the Kyoto Protocol, withdrew from the Anti-Ballistic Missile Treaty, and continues to be critical of the land mines treaty because of its argued need to maintain land mines in South Korea, to prevent a land attack by the very large North Korean army.

After September 11, 2001, the War on Terrorism increased America's belief that military power is the major deterrent against terrorist attacks. In fact, there is a significant hegemonic strain in American policy, especially since that date. The Project for a New

American Century—an organization that included Vice-President Cheney, former Secretary of Defense Donald Rumsfeld, and former Deputy Secretary of Defense Paul Wolfowitz—emphasizes a global challenge and role for the United States as the leader in maintaining peace and security in Europe, Asia, and the Middle East. This thinking takes as its point of departure the assertion that the terrorist threat is not just to the United States but also to the rest of the world, and that the United States has a moral duty to fight freedom's fight wherever it may be. It is, thus, up to the United States, because of its unique abilities and its commitment to democracy and freedom, to maintain stability and peace in the international system. Subsequent events have made folly of this grand design in political engineering and exercise in hegemonic hubris.

While it is possible to explain American policy in radical terms, it is a more difficult task because the evidence is more circumstantial. The other difficulty for the radical perspective is that while it is opposed to American foreign policy, it does not prescribe what the United States should do, except in some very general ways. The argument that the United States must stop intervening in the internal affairs of other states becomes an argument for American isolationism. The United States had isolationist tendencies prior to World War II and was, consequently, criticized for its late entry into that war. The anti-imperialist argument translates into debt forgiveness and protectionism for the South's economic interests even as the world's economies are increasingly tied together. For students of international relations, the question is which perspective to choose, and on what grounds? Our review of models of international relations suggests that multiple levels of analysis, as well as moral and empirical factors, are embedded in the way we choose to interpret contemporary world politics.

Discussion Questions

1. Has terrorism become the new Cold War for the United States?

2. Do you think that international organizations are better able to deal with global problems than states? Why?

3. Which model (realist, liberal, or radical) do you choose to use to critically evaluate state behaviour? Why?

4. To what extent do you think the results of the 2008 U.S. presidential election were determined by the War in Iraq?

References

Roy, Arundhati. 2004. "The New American Century." *The Nation*. February 9, 11–14.

Further Readings

Doyle, Michael. 2006. *Making War and Building Peace.* Princeton, NJ: Princeton University Press.

Hardt, Michael and Antonio Negri. 2001. *Empire.* Cambridge, MA: Harvard University Press.

Mearsheimer, John J. 2003. *The Tragedy of Great Power Politics.* New York: W.W. Norton and Company.

Weblinks

BBC News: "Iraq Commentaries—After the War: Was War Justified?"
http://news.bbc.co.uk/1/hi/world/middle_east/3033959.stm

English School: "Reconvening the English School of International Relations Theory"
www.leeds.ac.uk/polis/englishschool

International Relations (IR) Theory
www.irtheory.com

The Project for the New American Century
www.newamericancentury.org

CHAPTER 23

INTERNATIONAL ORGANIZATIONS

Objectives

International organizations are a central part of global politics. To gain a fuller understanding of them in all of their variety and complexity, this chapter provides an introduction to international organizations and an overview of their place in world politics. Every country in the world belongs to international organizations. These organizations, in turn, are shaped by the major organizing principles of world politics, among them state sovereignty, anarchy, and global governance. This chapter discusses these principles as well as the origins and evolution of international organizations. It describes the critical distinction between intergovernmental organizations (IGOs) and non-governmental organizations (NGOs). Finally, the chapter identifies some of the central preoccupations influencing the future role of these organizations in world politics.

TOM KEATING

Introduction

As we enter the twenty-first century, thousands of international organizations are active on the world stage. Every country in the world is a member of at least one international organization, and most countries participate in many. Canada, for example, is a member of numerous international organizations, ranging from the United Nations to the Arctic Council. In addition, many individuals belong to organizations whose membership and activities cross national borders. International organizations have a long history but proliferated most dramatically in the second half of the twentieth century. They have become a permanent and, often, influential feature in the daily lives of billions of people around the planet. It is possible to learn a great deal about international organizations by studying particular IGOs, such as the United Nations (UN) or the European Union (EU), and NGOs, such as the International Committee of the Red Cross or Amnesty International. The immense variety of organizations, however, suggests a different approach, one that examines features common to many different organizations.

As an integral part of world politics, international organizations have been influenced by many of its organizing principles and practices. It is particularly beneficial to understand the meaning and significance of state sovereignty, anarchy, global governance, and multilateralism.

Historical and Political Sources

INTERNATIONAL ORGANIZATIONS HAVE BEEN TRACED BACK TO 1397. SINCE THE time of Dante, in the early fourteenth century, international organizations, including proposals for world government, have been advocated as alternatives or complements to a system of independent sovereign states. International organizations have been invented and reinvented repeatedly in attempts to find effective means for facilitating and regulating international political, economic, and social interactions. Proposals for institutions that closely resemble the United Nations and the European Union date back to the seventeenth century (Hinsley, 1963). Many of these proposals were concerned primarily with eliminating or reducing international conflict among European states. While the authors of these proposals—Sir Thomas More, William Penn, and Immanuel Kant, among others—might be impressed with the extensive network of international organizations that exists today, they would likely be disappointed that these organizations have been unable to prevent warfare within and between states. By the latter half of the nineteenth century, international organizations were more likely to be devoted to matters of international commerce than to conflict. Today, the more numerous and influential international organizations are those involved in matters of international trade and finance.

As with most political institutions, international organizations do not operate in a vacuum. They are part of a vast array of political, economic, social, and cultural activity that takes place on the global stage. Particularly noteworthy are two prominent features of the global political arena in which international organizations operate: state sovereignty and anarchy (Schmidt, 1998). The first distinguishes the participants in world politics, separating national governments or states as they are most commonly labelled and private individuals, groups, and corporations that also participate in world politics. **State sovereignty** refers to the legal (*de jure* sovereignty) and empirical (*de facto* sovereignty) condition whereby states recognize no higher authority either domestically or externally and are thus free to act as they wish. Sovereignty emerged as an influential governing principle after the Thirty Years War, which ended with the Peace of Westphalia in 1648. The war and the resulting peace settlement legitimated the autonomous and sovereign power of states over and against that of the Church and the Emperor, as well as potential domestic challengers. Sovereignty is an absolute term suggesting both autonomy and capability, but few states possess absolute sovereignty. Most states are constrained in their actions by the power of other states, by the restrictions imposed on them through international agreements and organizations, and by various domestic checks and balances. The widespread acceptance of the principle of state sovereignty, however, has meant that states must give their consent to be bound by international law and other commitments that might arise from being members of international organizations.

The principle of state sovereignty reflected and reinforced a second feature of world politics, the absence of a single central authority or government to regulate world politics and enforce international law. **Anarchy** refers to the absence of government or a formal authority. Sovereign states operate in a system in which there is no permanent authority that makes and enforces laws to regulate their behaviour or that of other actors in world politics. As a result, states (increasingly with private individuals, groups, and corporations) make their own rules and determine how and by whom they are to be administered and enforced. The process by which rules are made and enforced in world politics is both complex and fascinating because of the absence of clearly defined authoritative procedures and institutions. This process is often referred to as **global governance**, defined as "governing, without sovereign authority, relationships that transcend national frontiers" (Finkelstein, 1995, 369). Attempts to establish more authoritative institutions of government at the global or regional level necessarily implies restrictions on the freedom of sovereign states to do as they please, something that many states have resisted. Thus the establishment of international organizations and the process of global governance generally involve a delicate and complicated balance between the preservation of state sovereignty and the development of authority structures at the international level. Yet it is also apparent that governance is no longer under the exclusive control of states.

The term **multilateralism** describes both the process and the end result of these efforts to establish rules and organizations to resolve common problems and support cooperation among states and other actors in world politics. At its simplest, multilateralism refers to a diplomatic process involving more than two states. Multilateralism also describes a particular form of international politics, one that can be distinguished from bilateralism or imperialism. It refers to a form of cooperation among states marked by three distinct characteristics. First, the costs and benefits of cooperation are shared by all participating states. Second, cooperation is based on certain principles of state conduct that influence the relations among states. Finally, states are committed to this cooperative behaviour for the long term and do not necessarily expect immediate results (Ruggie, 1993). Multilateralism thus entails a specific form of global governance, one that has a significant role for international organizations. Critical scholars have also called attention to the increased influence of non-governmental (or civil society) organizations in the process of global governance. These authors have referred to the involvement of these actors alongside states as exemplifying a "new multilateralism," a process of cooperation and governance that is initiated and sustained by groups emerging out of civil society (Schechter, 1999).

Classifying International Organizations

AN INTERNATIONAL ORGANIZATION MAY BE DEFINED AS A FORMAL INSTITUTION that facilitates regular interaction between members of two or more countries. Such a definition would yield thousands of entities. There are, however, several criteria by which one can sort out the numerous international organizations that populate this planet. One important initial distinction is to identify two separate categories of international organizations. The first, **intergovernmental organizations** or IGOs, consist of national governments or states. Currently, there are between 300 and 400 IGOs actively involved in world politics. The United Nations is the pre-eminent example of an IGO. The EU, the World Trade Organization (WTO), and the North Atlantic Treaty Organization (NATO) are other well-known examples. A second category of international organization is **non-governmental organizations** or NGOs, sometimes referred to as civil society organizations. These organizations have as their members private citizens or national affiliates of groups composed of private citizens. In the mid-1990s there were over 10 000 NGOs. Most NGOs are of little interest for students of world politics, while others occasionally emerge as important political actors for selected issues. Many others, such as the Red Cross, Greenpeace, and Amnesty International, have an active and ongoing involvement in world politics. Later in this chapter we will return to take a closer look at these NGOs and their involvement in contemporary global politics. For now, however, we will examine the origins and evolution of intergovernmental organizations and the major perspectives on their role in world politics.

Intergovernmental Organizations

IGOs have become a permanent feature of world politics in the twentieth century. As mentioned, one of the primary motivating factors in establishing these organizations has been a desire to limit or prevent warfare between states. For many people concerned about the recurrence of warfare, some form of world government offers the best solution to continued bloodshed or the best method for achieving peace and prosperity. Consequently, scholars and practitioners have devised elaborate plans for international organizations as the core of a world government (Hinsley, 1963). Not surprisingly, the most elaborate efforts to establish IGOs have taken place during or immediately following major wars (Holsti, 1998). For example, the two major institutional experiments of the twentieth century, the League of Nations in 1919 and the United Nations in 1945, were set up after the world wars. During World War II, the commitment of national governments to establishing an international organization was so strong that discussions on the UN began as early as 1942, long before the outcome of the war was known. The preamble of the UN Charter identifies preserving the peace as its primary objective. While peace may have been the primary motive for many in creating international organizations, the vast majority of organizations have been created to serve economic and social needs. In his review of international organizations, Craig Murphy identified their principal tasks as fostering industry and managing social conflicts. He also identified two secondary tasks for these organizations: strengthening states and the state system, and strengthening society (1994, 32–37). Murphy links the creation of international organizations to changes in the international political economy, commencing with the second industrial revolution in the late eighteenth century. These changes helped to create international markets in industrial goods by linking communications and transportation infrastructure, protecting intellectual property, and reducing legal and economic barriers to trade (1994, 2).

The vast and at times contradictory range of activities that have engaged international organizations is illustrated in the UN and its network of Specialized Agencies. The UN is a multi-purpose organization involved in a number of areas, such as economic development (UN Development Program), health (World Health Organization), communications (International Telecommunications Union), human rights (Office of the UN High Commissioner for Refugees), and other social concerns such as refugees (UN High Commissioner for Refugees), women (UN Development Fund for Women), and children (UN Children's Fund). The UN has been the principal forum in which newly independent states seek confirmation of their independence and sovereignty. At the same time, it has been pursued by human rights advocates as the organization through which the rights of individuals against the state are to be advanced and ultimately protected, and it has been used by civil society organizations to gain recognition and participation in the process of global governance.

International Economic Organizations

Among the more significant specialized IGOs have been those established to serve more limited and specialized mandates in the area of international trade and finance. The WTO, for example, which was established in 1995, focuses primarily on matters related to international trade. It developed out of the Bretton Woods negotiations of 1944 and the General Agreement on Tariffs and Trade (GATT), first signed in 1947. The GATT's original objective was to reduce and eventually eliminate tariff barriers to international trade. This mandate has evolved into a wider yet still fairly limited range of trade-related issues. The restricted mandate of the WTO, however, has been challenged by observers who maintain that it is not possible to separate trade from associated issues such as the environment and labour practices. In fact, one of the themes of the so-called "Battle in Seattle" in 1999 was that the WTO should take responsibility for the associated costs of trade. The attempts to have the organization deal with the effects of trade have been strongly resisted by many member governments of the organization and by its secretariat. The Bretton Woods negotiations also established the International Monetary Fund (IMF) and the International Bank for Reconstruction and Development (IBRD), most commonly known as the World Bank. The former was designed to regulate international capital transactions and national monetary policy; the latter was intended to provide capital for economic reconstruction in Europe. Both have evolved into major players in the global economy of North–South relations, playing an increasingly intrusive role in the domestic political economy of poorer states. Membership in these organizations has increased steadily over the past three decades, to the point where more than two-thirds of the world's states are members. There has also been a significant growth in the number of regional and ad hoc institutions in this area, including most prominently the EU, the North American Free Trade Agreement (NAFTA), and the Group of Eight (G8), which includes most of the globe's leading economies. Many of these institutions have devised rules that restrict the freedom and autonomy of member governments. The intrusive activity of these organizations has led some to argue that they represent a new form of constitutionalism for their member governments. This new constitutionalism refers, in part, to the ability of these organizations to subvert or override domestic constitutions in imposing restrictions on the economic and political practices of member governments. As discussed below, this in turn has led to demands for greater democratization and accountability on the part of these institutions.

Regional Organizations

The UN and other IGOs can be distinguished on the basis of their memberships. Organizations that, like the UN, are open to all states, are described as universal. Other organizations restrict membership to particular states on the basis of regional, historical, or strategic considerations. For example, the Organization of African Unity (OAU), now the African Union, established in 1963, is restricted to African states. The Organization of American States (OAS) includes states in the western hemisphere and for years was considered to be an instrument of U.S. foreign policy. Since the end of the Cold War, however, the OAS has reflected a greater involvement by other states in the region, including Canada, which joined the organization in 1989. NATO unites states in Europe and North America that share common security interests, whereas the Association of Southeast Asian Nations (ASEAN) was created to meet the regional security interests of its members. Regional organizations have, in certain instances, emerged as important alternatives to the more universal institutions, particularly in matters of trade and finance. The EU, NAFTA, and the Asia-Pacific

Economic Cooperation (APEC) forum stand as the most important regional organizations in the international political economy. These, and other regional organizations, raise additional concerns and debates about the relationships between and among IGOs as they compete for recognition and influence (Fawcett and Hurrell, 1995).

General Features of Intergovernmental Organizations

IGOs vary extensively in their structures, procedures, capabilities, and budgets, but there are some common elements worth mentioning. Most organizations have a permanent secretariat that oversees the day-to-day operations of the organization. Members of the secretariat are drawn from member countries and become the employees of the organization. Frequently they view their roles as those of international civil servants, representing the interests of the organization as a whole rather than of their home states (see, for example, Yi-chong and Weller, 2004). Most of these organizations are led by a secretary general, a president, or a director who is selected by the member governments of the organization. The budgets of IGOs are based on the contributions of member governments. IGOs do not have any independent sources of revenue and thus remain dependent on member government contributions.

The representation of states in IGOs is generally based on the principle of political equality. At the same time, the decision-making structures and procedures of these organizations commonly reflect inequalities in status and power of member states, allowing the more powerful greater opportunity to influence the decisions of the organization. In some organizations this inequality in status is formally acknowledged. For example, the UN Charter recognizes the political equality of all of its members, but only the UN Security Council can make decisions that are binding on all member states. The United States, Great Britain, France, China, and Russia, as permanent members of the Security Council, have each been given a veto that allows any one of them to prevent the Council and hence the UN from undertaking an action with which it disagrees. In the IMF and the World Bank, inequality of status is recognized by granting member states voting shares based on their monetary contributions, much as with private corporations and their stockholders. Other organizations, such as NATO, that lack such formal mechanisms often take decisions only if and when the most powerful member governments support the decision.

While the support of major powers is most often required if an international organization is to undertake effective action, this does not necessarily mean that major powers always dominate the process of global governance. On occasion, the agreement and support of more powerful states can be obtained through the efforts of smaller states or members of the organization's secretariat. For some observers, IGOs provide the best opportunity for less powerful states to influence the course of global politics. The influence of these states, especially when they act together through coalitions, is apparent in such areas as the post-Seattle international trade negotiations and the extensive negotiations at the UN on the law of the sea in the 1970s. The decision-making process in most IGOs is based on some combination of negotiation, consensus-building, and formal votes. The sources of influence within this decentralized and diffused policy-making environment are extremely varied. Obviously a state's relative power in the world at large has an effect on its ability to wield influence. Beyond this, states can employ a variety of techniques, such as diplomatic skills or technical expertise, to shape the outcome of the decision-making process within IGOs. Unlike national legislatures, IGOs contain no organized political parties, but coalitions of states that share views often cooperate to achieve specific objectives. These coalitions have become an active part of the process of global governance in IGOs. As early as the 1960s, in the UN, 77 poorer countries formed a coalition known as the Group of 77 to pressure other UN members to devote more attention and resources to global economic inequalities. Coalitions were an important and influential feature of negotiations in the GATT during the 1970s and 1980s and continue to be used by member governments in the WTO. An added feature of this process is the increasingly active participation of NGOs and corporate interests.

One of the ongoing dilemmas involved in international organizations is the balance between the sovereignty of member states and the power of the organizations to take and enforce binding decisions that infringe on this sovereignty. Part of the difficulty arises from the fact that most IGOs are explicitly designed to protect and reinforce the sovereignty of their member governments. Most IGOs contain some reference that recognizes the independence, sovereignty, territorial integrity, and formal equality of member governments. This, in turn, makes it difficult for these organizations to take action against a member government unless that member government consents to such action. These conditions are, however, changing. "The old notion that what goes on within the state is a matter of sovereign privacy . . . has been swept away. In its stead, we have installed the doctrine that world order entails political stability, democratic governments, respect for human rights, general economic well-being, ethnic harmony, and peaceful resolution of conflicts within states, no less than cooperative and peaceful relationships among them" (Claude, 2000). NATO's air assault on Serbia in the spring of 1999, taken in response to the Serbian government's violent reaction to separatist movements in Kosovo, is a vivid illustration of a more assertive and intrusive role for organizations. These developments have raised new issues and responsibilities for international organizations without any concomitant attempt to expand the capacity or authority of these institutions to address them.

Non-governmental Organizations

NGOs have been defined in various ways. One of the more encompassing definitions has been incorporated into two UN resolutions referring to "any international organization which is not established by intergovernmental agreement . . . including organizations which accept members designated by government authorities, provided that such membership does not interfere with the free expression of views of the organizations" (UN General Assembly Resolutions 288 [X] and 1296 [XLIV]). The term "NGOs" is also generally restricted to non-profit organizations and thus excludes multinational corporations and other, more nefarious commercial organizations such as drug cartels that operate in more than two countries. Many groups have taken to calling themselves civil society organizations (CSOs) to distinguish themselves more explicitly from governments. It should be noted that many NGOs have absolutely nothing to do with world politics as it is most commonly understood. As an individual you might take some interest in the World Ninepin Bowling Association or the World Rock 'n' Roll Confederation, but these groups are likely to contribute little to ending the conflict in the Middle East or alleviating poverty in Haiti. On the other hand, the World Jewish Congress or Oxfam might be able to make a significant contribution to these goals.

In contrast to IGOs, among which there is a considerable amount of similarity in organizational structure and decision-making procedures, there is an amazing variety of these qualities among the thousands of NGOs. Most NGOs have developed out of concerns for specific issues. Amnesty International, for example, emerged as a result of the work of a British lawyer, Peter Benenson, who in the early 1960s began to advocate for the humane treatment of prisoners in foreign countries. It has since developed into one of the world's most active and effective defenders of individual rights and, in 1977, was awarded the Nobel Peace Prize. The Red Cross, which originated in the mid-nineteenth century as a result of the concern of another individual, Jean Henri Dunant, for the welfare of injured combatants, was given the first Nobel Peace Prize in recognition of its work in providing humane treatment for victims of conflict. Médecins Sans Frontières illustrates the disregard that NGOs often display for principles such as state sovereignty and non-intervention, as it has responded to humanitarian emergencies regardless of the state or the situation. It, too, has been recognized for its work with the Nobel Peace Prize in 1999. In 1997, another NGO, the International Campaign to Ban Landmines (ICBL), was awarded the Nobel Peace Prize in recognition of its work to pressure governments to sign the Ottawa Treaty, a convention establishing a comprehensive ban on anti-personnel land mines. This group developed as a result of a number of individual efforts in different countries to challenge governments to eliminate these weapons. The ICBL developed a close working relationship with members of the Canadian government, and this cooperation was instrumental in launching the Ottawa Process and the successful conclusion of the treaty in December 1996. The Ottawa Process illustrates the dynamics of NGO involvement in global governance. The ICBL worked with a coalition of NGOs from around the world. The ICBL was led by an American, Jody Williams, but found it easier and more effective to work with officials in Ottawa than those in Washington, which eventually refused to support the Ottawa Treaty.

Not all NGOs win peace prizes. Most of them are rather modest operations established by groups of concerned individuals in different countries to pressure governments to adopt policies that support their particular causes. Their political activity is generally focused in three directions. First, they seek to influence national governments to adopt foreign policies that support their cause. Second, they lobby intergovernmental institutions to promote their policy concerns. Finally, they publicize their concerns with the intent of generating popular support and funds.

NGOs are becoming increasingly important political actors in world politics. Groups such as Amnesty International, the Red Cross, CARE, Oxfam, Save the Children, Greenpeace, the World Wildlife Fund, to mention just a few—have taken an increased interest in the activities of international organizations and national governments and have sought to articulate their concerns and demands to an international audience. Additionally, some NGOs are in the centre of international politics in such areas as conflict prevention and resolution, economic development, and human rights. In recognition of this increased involvement, certain NGOs have pressed for more direct participation in the policy-making process of global governance. The Canadian government has been among the most supportive in advocating for improved access for NGOs at the UN and other IGOs. More extensive, direct, and effective involvement on the part of NGOs would see political activity that has traditionally been nationally based replaced by policy-making at the international level, involving representatives of national governments acting through IGOs, and representatives of NGOs representing the interests of the "public." To date, NGOs have acquired consultation status with some IGOs, most notably in the UN. NGOs have also become particularly active around various UN conferences that have been held in recent decades on such issues as population, women, human rights, and social development. The UN Security Council also consults with representatives of selected NGOs in areas such as human rights and peacekeeping. All of this activity reflects an increasingly significant role for NGOs in the process of global governance. As Claire Cutler has written,

> The actors, structures, and processes identified and theorized as determinative by the dominant approaches to the study of international law and organization have ceased to be of singular importance. Westphalian-inspired notions of state-centricity, positivist international law, and "public" definitions of authority are incapable of capturing the significance of non-state actors, like transnational corporations and individuals, informal normative structures, and private economic power in the global political economy. (Cutler, 2001, 27, 133)

Competing Perspectives on International Organizations

THERE ARE MANY DIFFERENT THEORETICAL DEBATES SURROUNDING THE PRACTICES of international organizations, multilateralism, and global governance. We will briefly review four of the most prominent arguments about the sources and potential role of international organizations in world politics. First, a realist view holds that IGOs play, at best, marginal roles in world politics, and are little more than a reflection of the interests of the governments that created them (Mearsheimer, 1994–95). Viewed from this perspective, IGOs have no independent influence and last only so long as they are useful to states. States, primarily concerned with maximizing their own power, remain the most significant actors in world politics. States therefore use IGOs to protect or enhance their own power position in the system. Some realists argue further that a dominant power (hegemon) uses IGOs to organize support and compliance from other states. In their view a hegemon is essential for the creation and maintenance of IGOs (Gilpin, 1981; Keohane, 1984). Realists maintain that IGOs act only in response to the pressures of their member governments and therefore are very much at the mercy of the most powerful states in the international system. NGOs, in contrast, are relatively insignificant players in world politics and can only be effective to the extent that they gain the support of powerful national governments.

An alternative view, liberal institutionalist, holds that international organizations are both important and influential on the world stage. This view holds that states cooperate out of a sense of common purposes that emphasize absolute gains and converging self-interests. Additionally, some liberals hold that states are not only concerned with maximizing their own gains relative to other states in the system but are more generally concerned with the effects of cooperation on the system as a whole. While accepting the importance and influence of states, liberals also argue that organizations, once created, acquire a degree of independence from their member governments and are effective in shaping the behaviour of these governments. International organizations are, in this view, considerably more than a mere reflection of states' interests and power. Some liberals go further in arguing that there has been a transfer of authority from states to international organizations such that these organizations have taken on responsibility for areas previously under the jurisdiction of national states.

A final collection of views takes a more critical perspective on international organizations. Proponents of these critical approaches argue that international organizations hold the potential to bring about a radical transformation in the practice of world politics (Cox, 1992). IGOs provide an opportunity for less powerful states to pursue their own interests and perhaps design policies in opposition to those being pursued by more powerful states. This view also emphasizes the potential for NGOs to alter the course of world politics in the critical areas of political and economic reform. More than the other two approaches, these critical approaches emphasize the historical and political context in which international organizations now operate and identify them as a possible source of governance that is more democratic, just, and humane than the existing international system (Falk, 1995).

Current Issues and Debates

THERE ARE A NUMBER OF IMPORTANT ISSUES SURROUNDING INTERNATIONAL organizations in the twenty-first century. One is institutional reform. While much of the interest in reform was sparked by the fiftieth anniversary of the UN in 1995, it has also been inspired by the end of the Cold War in 1989 and the increased activism of IGOs and NGOs in the global political economy. Institutional reforms touch on many issues, from the more practical concerns with budgets and administration to the more complicated and politically charged issues of NGO representation and democratization. Numerous studies, commissions, and reports have been undertaken in the 1990s that examine organizational reform in IGOs, such as the UN, the WTO, and the EU. The attention to reform reflects a perceived growth in the influence and relevance of these institutions. As a result, matters of accountability, transparency, and legitimacy of decision-making structures and processes, alongside concerns about representation and democracy, take on greater significance.

The debate over representation and democracy in NGOs pertains to the need for and mechanism by which national communities and, ultimately, individual citizens are to be represented in these organizations. As international organizations assume greater responsibility for public policy, questions are raised about the extent to which and means by which the public is to be represented in these organizations. Attention is increasingly being given to the need to democratize these organizations, to open up their decision-making procedures to allow for representations by NGOs or other representatives of private citizens, in addition to the national governments currently represented (Held, 1995). In the European Union a Parliament was established in 1977. Members of the European Parliament are elected directly by constituents in all of the member states of the EU. Proposals for popular assemblies and for elected Parliaments along the lines of the European Parliament have been suggested for other organizations but have yet to be adopted. Alternatives that have been tried or proposed include such mechanisms as regular consultations between representatives of IGOs and NGOs, and periodic meetings of NGOs and other groups such as has occurred around various UN conferences. Each of these proposals seeks to provide a more direct link between individuals and IGOs.

A final significant and related area of concern is the scope of responsibilities to be accorded these institutions in the arena of global governance. Many people have looked to international organizations as a preferable alternative to a world of sovereign states. For them, international organizations should expand their responsibilities to govern an ever-widening set of policy arenas. To some extent this has been occurring. A number of areas of international and domestic politics are now regulated by international organizations. This is especially evident in Europe, where the EU has assumed responsibility for vast areas of domestic politics. For the most part, however, responsibility for those areas that most affect our daily lives—such as education, health, and social welfare—remains with the nation-state. Moreover, if and when international organizations have intervened in domestic affairs, it has generally been at the behest of their member states. Nevertheless, increasingly international organizations whose mandate was not initially concerned with domestic matters have moved into these areas. For example, international trade and financial institutions increasingly intervene in domestic social affairs by imposing monetary and fiscal constraints on national governments. The result has been to blur the division of responsibilities and power between national governments and international organizations. Former Canadian prime minister Joe Clark once remarked that "the rules of the GATT are as important to Canadians as the rules of the Canadian constitution." The net effect has been to increase the salience of international organizations and international agreements in national policy debates. This is particularly true of poorer countries but is to varying degrees significant for all countries that are extensively involved in the global political economy. The increased involvement of international organizations in areas previously within the domestic jurisdiction of national governments suggests that there has occurred a diminution of state sovereignty.

This development raises challenging questions about the acceptable degree of institutional interference in the domestic affairs of states. For example, many advocates would like to see international organizations interfere to protect the human rights of oppressed peoples in countries such as Burma (Myanmar), Rwanda, or China. At the same time, others worry about the possibility that international organizations might interfere to protect the interests of foreign investors or to interfere with domestic environmental and labour standards. Additionally, there are profound differences among member states over the nature and scope of intervention by international organizations. Many governments in the developed capitalist countries support international organizations that act in support of free market principles, while governments of weaker countries are concerned that more powerful states will use international organizations to control their policy options. The balance between effective international institutional intervention and respect for state sovereignty will be one of the major considerations shaping the future role of international organizations.

Summary

International organizations have become a permanent and prominent feature of world politics. There has been a tremendous growth in the number and variety of international organizations, especially in the last half of the twentieth century. "International organizations" refers to non-profit organizations, of which there are two general categories: governmental organizations of two or more states and non-governmental organizations of individuals or groups from two or more countries. There are more than 300 intergovernmental organizations and more than 10 000 non-governmental organizations active in the world today. Intergovernmental organizations can be further classified according to membership (universal or regional) and objectives (multi-purpose or single-purpose).

Intergovernmental organizations have originated out of a concern for the elimination of war and a shared concern for managing transborder problems. Many advocates of a more peaceful international system have argued for the need for international organizations to provide for global peace, order, and justice. Others argue that international organizations merely reinforce the position of powerful states and interests in the international system. Three competing perspectives—realist, liberal institutionalist, and new multilateralist—posit different views on the salience and influence of international organizations and their relationship with national governments. While interpretations on the role and influence of international organizations varies, it is evident that as a result of the salience of cross-border issues such as environmental pollution, the AIDS epidemic, refugees, and economic globalization, international organizations will become an ever-increasing part of world politics in the years ahead.

Discussion Questions

1. Should more responsibility be given to international organizations to manage political and economic and social affairs at the international level?
2. Would a world government be a good thing? What would it look like?
3. Have international organizations such as the World Trade Organization acquired too much power?
4. How could IGOs be made more democratic, allowing for more direct representation and participation of NGOs and/or private citizens?
5. How effective has the United Nations been in facilitating peaceful cooperation among states?

References

Cameron, Maxwell A., Robert Lawson, and Brian Tomlin, eds. 1998. *To Walk Without Fear*. Don Mills, ON: Oxford University Press.

Cox, Robert. 1992. "Multilateralism and World Order." *Review of International Studies*. 18:61–80.

Falk, Richard. 1996. *Humane Governance*. University Park: Pennsylvania State University Press.

Fawcett, Louise and Andrew Hurrell, eds. 1995. *Regionalism in World Politics: Regional Organization and International Order*. Oxford: Oxford University Press.

Finkelstein, Lawrence. 1995. "What Is Global Governance?" *Global Governance*, 1: 366–372.

Gilpin, Robert. 1981. *War and Change in World Politics*. Cambridge: Cambridge University Press.

Haas, Peter. 2002. "UN Conferences and Constructivist Governance of the Environment." *Global Governance*, 8, 74.

Held, David. 1995. *Democracy and the Global Order*. Stanford: Stanford University Press.

Hinsley, F.H. 1963. *Power and the Pursuit of Peace*. Cambridge: Cambridge University Press.

Keating, Tom. 2001. *Canada and World Order*. Don Mills, ON: Oxford University Press.

Keohane, Robert. 1984. *After Hegemony.* Princeton: Princeton University Press.

Mearsheimer, John. 1994–95. "The False Promise of International Institutions." *International Security,* 20:82–104.

Murphy, Craig. 1994. *International Organization and Industrial Change.* Cambridge: Polity Press.

Ruggie, John. 1993. *Multilateralism Matters.* New York: Columbia University Press.

Schechter, Michael. 1999. *Future Multilateralism.* New York: Palgrave.

Schmidt, Brian C. 1998. "Lessons from the Past: Reassessing the Interwar Disciplinary History of International Relations." *International Studies Quarterly,* 42:433–460.

Scholte, Jan Aarte. 1999. "Global Civil Society: Changing the World?" May, p. 2. **www.warwick.ac.uk/fac/soc/CSGR/wpapers/wp3199.PDF**.

Winham, Gilbert. 1990. "GATT and the International Trade Regime." *International Journal,* 45:796–822.

Yi-chong, Xu and Patrick Weller. 2004. *The Governance of World Trade, International Civil Servants and the GATT/WTO.* Cheltenham: Edward Elgar.

Further Readings

Bennett, A. LeRoy. 1995. *International Organizations: Principles and Issues,* 6th edition. Englewood Cliffs, NJ: Prentice Hall.

Commission on Global Governance. 1995. *Our Global Neighborhood.* Oxford: Oxford University Press. Also see the Commission's website at **www.cgg.ch**.

Keck, Margaret and Kathryn Sikkink. 1997. *Activists Beyond Borders: Advocacy Networks in International Politics.* Ithaca, NY: Cornell University Press.

Weiss, Thomas, David P. Forsythe, and Roger Coate. 1997. *The United Nations and Changing World Politics,* 2nd edition. Boulder: Westview.

Weblinks

International Committee of the Red Cross
www.icrc.org

OneWorld.net: NGO Listings
www.oneworld.net

United Nations
www.un.org

World Trade Organization
www.wto.org

CHAPTER 24

GLOBAL POLITICAL ECONOMY

Objectives

Although there have been previous moments when international economic flows have had important political implications, such as the free trade era of the nineteenth century, processes of economic globalization today are challenging conventional political formulas in an unprecedented manner. The intense globalization of financial flows, trade, and production are all helping to reshape political authority and state policy. The objective of this chapter is to introduce the concept of global political economy and to explore some of the complex debates emerging out of the contemporary wave of economic globalization. In particular, this chapter seeks to highlight the *political* dimensions of the global economy and to discuss the historical emergence of "political economy" as a field of study that focuses on the intersection of political and economic power.

ROB
AITKEN

Introduction

This chapter introduces global political economy (GPE) as a concept and an approach to understanding some of the critical changes in today's economy, society, and politics. Political economy has historically examined the relationship between politics and economics or, put differently, the relationship between political and economic power. In response to the dramatic intensification of cross-border economic flows in the 1970s and 1980s, GPE emerged both as a field of study concerned with the politics of the global economy and as a concept designed to place these developments in critical context. This chapter is divided into four separate parts. The first section outlines the concept of political economy, tracing both its early origins as well as some of the ways in which it has been used to describe the complicated realm of economic globalization. Although GPE emerged as a response to the intense economic changes of the past 35 years, this section highlights the ways in which critical thinkers in the GPE tradition draw on a set of concepts that emphasizes the relationship between the economy and the study of politics. This set includes such critical concepts as dependency, imperialism, world systems, and mercantilism. The second section of this chapter places globalization in historical context by highlighting the kind of political economy that emerged after World War II. Understanding today's world of globalization requires a sense of how it differs from the way in which the global economy was organized and managed in the post-war period. The third section of the chapter turns to the new world of "economic globalization" by exploring some of the features of the new global economy and the political forces that shape it. The chapter concludes by posing some of the big questions central to GPE and to debates around the concept of globalization. What are the consequences of globalization? What implications does globalization have for our understanding of politics and political authority? At the international level, more importantly, how should we characterize globalization? Is globalization a "natural" process, the result of the political power of a particular group or the logical outcome of empire? GPE is a concept and a field of study that offers a particular perspective on these complicated and evolving questions.

Political Economy

THE STUDY OF POLITICAL ECONOMY HAS A COMPLICATED AND COMPLEX history. At one level, the term was used throughout the nineteenth century to denote a wide range of thinkers interested in the study of the economy. It was used, for example, to describe both the classical tradition in economics and, later, the kind of analysis put forward by Karl Marx and socialist critics of capitalism. Over the course of the twentieth century, however, the term **political economy** took on a distinctive meaning as a field of study concerned with the ways in which economics and politics intersect. Put a bit differently, political economy, at its most general level, refers to the study of the intersection of political and economic forces: the confrontation between states and markets, power and wealth, or the worlds of politics and economics.

Although traditional approaches to political economy all paid significant attention to the international economy, they could not have anticipated the scope of the global economic processes that dominate our world today. By the 1970s, the dramatic intensification of international economic changes posed a series of challenges to the conventional field of political economy. The spectacular increase of global financial flows, trade, and other international political and economic activities created the need to refocus political economy from the national to the international to better take account of the changing nature of the global economy. It is in this context that GPE was founded, both as a new field of inquiry and as an object of study. The global political economy refers both to the space of the global economy beyond national frontiers as well as the study of that new space and its implication for political, economic, and social life. In general terms, GPE refers to the study of both the intersection of politics and economics at the global level as well as the underpinnings and political effects of economic globalization.

GPE has also focused attention on a very specific process: the *political* construction and management of the global economy. What does it mean to say that the global economy is politically constructed and managed? Unlike mainstream economics, which tends to conceive of the economy as a set of activities separate from political life, writers in GPE understand the global economy as a political project—that is, as a site that is managed *by* and *in the interest of* particular groups or sets of social forces. In this sense the economy is conceived as a political construction and as an object that is actively managed in a way that benefits some while injuring others. Political economists in the critical GPE tradition attempt to uncover the ways in which national and global economies have been constructed and managed to benefit certain groups and disadvantage others.

One writer who has been influential in this critical understanding of GPE is Karl Polanyi (1886–1964). Polanyi, a historian, anthropologist, and political-economist, argued against the "free market" view of the economy, which suggested that the market was natural and "self-regulating" in ways that required no government intervention. Polanyi insisted that the economy is always the reflection of political differences and contests. In this sense, markets are, in Polanyi's terms, "artificial," in that they are less the product of natural processes and more the result of political actors seeking politically beneficial arrangements. As Polanyi noted, the "free" market "was not the result of any inherent tendency of markets towards excrescence, but rather the effect of highly artificial stimulants administered to the body social" (Polanyi, 1944, 57). Polanyi's detailed historical study of the rise and demise of *laissez-faire* in the nineteenth and early twentieth centuries demonstrated that free trade embodied the reigning ideas of economic and political elites and imposed and sustained these ideas through governmental regulation and public policy. There was, in other words, nothing natural about so-called natural economic forces and self-regulating markets.

More recently, Robert W. Cox has picked up on Polanyi's argument by noting that power in the global economy is not simply a question defined in economic terms (which firms can exercise decisive leadership in markets) but also a political question about how certain social classes are able to shape markets in the first place and derive power from those markets to cement their position in society. For Cox, it is production, control over the ways in which material economic resources are produced and distributed, that is the basis of all other forms of political or social power. "The social power of dominant classes," notes Cox, "may be thought of as originally grounded in the control of production, the material basis of all societies" (Cox, 1987, 18). This understanding of power, common to the critical GPE tradition, is often referred to as **historical materialism**.

Although interest in GPE emerged out of the intensification of international economic transactions and flows beginning in earnest throughout the 1970s, it also often draws on a much longer and older list of concepts. There has been, for example, a long-circulating debate about the concept of **mercantilism**, the predominant understanding of the national and international economy in the sixteenth and seventeenth centuries. Mercantilists assumed a fixed volume of world trade and depicted the international economy as a competitive site in which states vied with each other to achieve a positive balance of trade. As such, mercantilists advocated a global economy dominated by protectionist state policies, as well as policies that often promoted exports and discouraged imports. More important, mercantilist policies often led imperial countries into competitive struggles with each other for "overseas" markets and territorial possessions.

In addition, dominant themes within GPE, such as power differences in the global context and global political and economic inequalities, have long been a fixture of many critical voices in political science and in other social sciences. The question of **imperialism,** for example, has often been central to the way in which writers working in GPE have framed their analysis of the politics of the global economy. The organization of the world's economy today, and its persistent inequalities and power differences, cannot be separated from the long histories of imperialism that continue to shape the ways in which many countries are inserted into the world economy. Beginning, most strikingly, with Lenin in the early moments of the twentieth century, the matters of empire, capitalism, and the global economy have been intimately connected (Lenin, 1973). Similarly, there have also been longstanding discussions relating to **dependency**. Throughout the 1960s and 1970s, in particular, critical writers, many from the "developing" world, began to decry the persistent political and economic inequalities that seemed to be a fundamental characteristic of the international system. In a slightly different fashion, Immanuel Wallerstein developed a theory of world systems to describe the emergence, over many centuries, of a world capitalist system in which the countries at the centre of the system, what Wallerstein described as the "core," obtained supremacy over the world economy and its resources and, indeed, continue to benefit disproportionately more than the countries that lie at the "periphery" of the world system. Concepts such as mercantilism, imperialism, and dependency are examples of the ways in which GPE scholars have explained the historical development of capitalism and how it has changed over time.

Bretton Woods and Embedded Liberalism

ALTHOUGH WRITERS IN THE GPE TRADITION HAVE TENDED TO USE A VARI-ety of concepts to highlight different aspects of global political, cultural, and economic relations, they all raise questions relating to the historical and political organization of global economic practices. The reorganization of the global political economy after World War II, in particular, attracted a great deal of critical interest among many GPE scholars. At the famous international conference held in 1944 at Bretton Woods, New Hampshire, the allied powers, led by the United States and the United Kingdom, sought to reconstruct the world economy to avoid repeating the political and economic instabilities of the interwar period. British and American policy-makers, in particular, sought to avoid what they conceived as the disastrous pursuit of two opposite but equally destabilizing programs: economic nationalism (or isolationism) and *laissez-faire* free trade. As the chief British negotiator at Bretton Woods, John Maynard Keynes, noted, excessive competition and "the progress of economic imperialism" were "a scarcely avoidable part of a scheme of things" in an international order of *laissez-faire* and free trade (Keynes, 1933, 757). To avoid the costs of a system of free trade, and the costs generated by the equally unstable system of economic isolationism pursued by many countries during the economic crises of the 1930s, Keynes and American negotiators proposed a post-war international economic order that was *open* to international economic flows but at the same time was also *managed* in a way that allowed some degree of domestic protection. This delicate balance, negotiated at Bretton Woods, sought to create a more stable international system in which national governments could pursue certain autonomous policies of domestic economic stability, including demand management, active fiscal policies, and, in some cases, more generous social protection or social security schemes. National governments also would be obligated to participate in a world economy that would be managed through new multilateral institutions: the General Agreement on Tariffs and Trade (GATT), the International Monetary Fund, and the World Bank. In the words of one important analyst, John Ruggie, Bretton Woods established a new regime of **embedded liberalism**. It was a "compromise," in which the leading powers sought to "maneuver between two extremes" and to construct a kind of liberal world economy that would be embedded in national societies and respond to their needs for domestic stability and social protection (Ruggie, 1982).

Embedded liberalism is a clear example of a moment when a particular political coalition was able, in some form, to reorganize the global economy in line with its particular interests. The emergence of a "compromise" at the Bretton Woods conference, and throughout the whole process of post-war planning, was not the result of some neutral development or natural market forces. Rather, embedded liberalism was a *political* project that reflected the interests and desires of a particular constellation of social forces, or what Italian socialist Antonio Gramsci referred to as a *historic bloc*. In particular, the political vision of embedded liberalism was advocated by a group of otherwise disparate social and class interests, most clearly active in the United States, including elements of productive capital (large productive or manufacturing interests), state officials and bureaucrats associated with Keynesian policies or the Depression-era policies of President Roosevelt's New Deal, and elements of organized labour that had reconciled themselves to the vision of a liberal capitalism moderated by some elements of social and worker protection.

Globalization and a Borderless World?

BY THE 1970S, THE CAREFULLY CONSTRUCTED COMPROMISE NEGOTIATED AT Bretton Woods began to collapse. A number of developments in the 1970s, complicated and multi-faceted, resulted in the move away from the Bretton Woods arrangements. At one level, the American role in the new economy began to come under some pressure. Bretton Woods was an explicitly United States–centred system, and the emergence of significant American economic weaknesses over this period provoked questions, from many, about the stability of the American economy at the centre of the global system. Increasing competition from European and Japanese firms, persistent inflation, increasing unemployment, rising energy prices, and a gradual worldwide economic slowdown all characterized the early 1970s and marked a break from the "long boom" that had followed the end of World War II. The early and mid-1970s also witnessed the emergence of fiscal deficits among many Western countries for the first time, in any sustained way, since the end of the war. Perhaps most important, however, it was the changing role of the American dollar as the centre of the global monetary system that most destabilized the post-war order established at Bretton Woods. After World War II, the U.S. dollar, the "greenback," was established as the universal currency in the international system, and for the most part other national currencies were "pegged" to it in somewhat fixed ways. By the 1970s, serious problems began to threaten this arrangement. Not the least of these, the U.S. government removed the "gold window" and effectively ended the system of fixed exchange rates that had been key to the kind of global economic stability envisioned at the Bretton Woods conference.

The collapse of Bretton Woods set in motion a long period of complicated changes in the organization of the international economy. For example, a system of "floating" exchange rates emerged in which world exchange rates were set by private currency markets rather than being pegged to the American dollar. There also emerged a number of other new and transformative trends—among them, the intensification of globalized and "offshore" production processes, the gradual implementation of "free trade" agreements that restricted the ways in which national governments could favour domestic producers, the dramatic rise of international trade, the deepening of flexible labour markets, and the general "opening" of national economies to international economic transactions and flows of all kinds.

Perhaps the most spectacular development in this move toward **globalization** has been what Eric Helleiner has referred to as the "re-emergence of global finance" (see Helleiner, 1994). Although the international movements of financial capital—through credit, bank loans, speculative capital, money, and investment—were relatively contained through the Bretton Woods period, the new regime of floating exchange rates, among many other factors, eventually led to the dramatic emergence of very large and unstable global financial markets and large flows of financial capital into and out of these markets. By 2004 it was estimated, for example, that there was at least $1.9 trillion (USD) in daily turnover in foreign exchange markets, a volume that far exceeds the abilities of most governments to regulate (Bank for International Settlements, 2005, 2).

Just as the move toward an economic order organized around the vision of embedded liberalism reflects the interests and political influence of a particular set of social forces, so, too, does the move toward a borderless world of economic globalization. One of the central concerns of writers working within GPE has been to investigate the ways in which this most recent round of economic globalization has been neither a natural nor a technologically ordained process. Rather, economic globalization has been a decidedly political project. The move toward a global economy in these terms has both relied upon and been justified by a particular set of ideas relating to **neo-liberalism**. This economic and political project differs from the embedded liberalism of the post-war moment in many important ways. Although they both subscribe, broadly speaking, to liberal conceptions of how the economy should be organized, neo-liberalism rejects the notion that the economy itself should be regulated by the state. For neo-liberals, state interventions designed to stabilize the economy through fiscal and monetary policies or to protect society with social security, welfare, and health insurance distort the natural tendencies of the market and foster "dependency" among citizens. In contrast, neo-liberals have increasingly sought a global free-trade model in which the "market," and not the state, is used to organize the economy and many other areas of social, political, and economic life. As Cox puts it, neo-liberals have sought "the achievement of a market utopia on the world scale" (Cox, 1996, 191).

Beginning with the economic crises of the 1970s, various academics, politicians, business activists, and other organizations promoted neo-liberal ideas and encouraged governments to embrace the neo-liberal conception of a market utopia. This network of neo-liberals, including two important Nobel laureates—Milton Friedman and Friedrich von Hayek—helped make sense of the shifts of the 1970s in the language of neo-liberalism and were instrumental in the complex process through which neo-liberal ideas became dominant. Unlike the political coalition that coalesced around the vision of embedded liberalism, neo-liberalism is often associated with financial capital (banks, investment houses, auditors), globally oriented business sectors, and transnational elites.

The emergence of a form of economic globalization, structured around the ideas and ideals of neo-liberalism, has been a political process, not only because it has been championed by a very particular set of social forces, but also because it has had a significant set of political effects. The imposition of liberalized markets for trade and finance and a greater reliance on the market as a mechanism of governing economic and social life has not been an uneventful or neutral process. Although barriers to the flow of trade and investment have, in some ways, declined over the past decades, there has also been an increase in social and economic inequalities, both in the developing world and in "advanced industrial societies." The Global Policy Forum, for example, notes that when "we look more closely at the numbers, we find that . . . extreme poverty is not declining and is even increasing" (Bissio, 2005, 14). This is just one of a series of startling social and economic indicators suggesting that globalization has often been accompanied by increased levels of debt, poverty, and exclusion.

The move toward liberalized markets has not, however, gone uncontested. Over the past 15 years, in particular, a range of social movements, NGOs, and civil society groups have launched successful political campaigns designed to challenge, resist, or question the logic of neo-liberal globalization. Extremely diverse, the movements opposed to neo-liberal globalization have often been frustrated with "conventional" politics and, instead, have taken their struggles to the street in a wide range of protests, direct-action campaigns and, frequently, various forms of civil disobedience. The ability of a coalition of activists—committed to human rights, organized labour, social justice, environmental integrity, indigenous rights, "fair trade," and democracy—to disrupt the Third Ministerial of the World Trade Organization in Seattle in 1999 is often seen as a key moment in the emergence of a sustained opposition to neo-liberalism.

Although they have often been grouped by a number of overarching terms, including the "anti-globalization," "global justice," or "global democracy" movement, the disparate groups opposed to neo-liberal forms of globalization have recently attempted a more ambitious organization of their political action. The World Social Forum (WSF), formed in 2001, represents itself as an "open meeting place" for the diverse movements that oppose neo-liberalism and as a mirror image of the World Economic Forum (WEF), whose annual meeting at Davos, Switzerland, hosts the globe's economic and political elites. Purposely not pitching itself as a political party or a conventional representative body, the WSF has emerged as a leading space in which activists and organizers can learn from each other, share experiences, and support each other's struggles. A "non-confessional, non-governmental and non-party" space, the WSF is rapidly becoming a key setting for the construction of alternatives to neo-liberal forms of globalization and is committed to the idea that "another world is possible." One of the recent meetings of the WSF, which meets annually in the developing world, convened in Karachi, Pakistan (March 24–29, 2006), and attracted well over 35 000 people to strategize and stand in solidarity with each other against neo-liberal globalization (Conway, 2004).

The New World Order:
Neo-Liberalism or American Empire?

SCHOLARS WORKING WITHIN GPE HAVE ASKED IMPORTANT QUESTIONS ABOUT
the historical emergence and implications of neo-liberal forms of globalization.
Undoubtedly, the predominance of neo-liberalism is key to understanding contemporary global politics. In many ways, neo-liberalism seems a very dominant set of ideas
in establishing the parameters of today's political questions and debates. At a more
concrete level, neo-liberal ideas and practices are increasingly promoted by a web of
globalized elites who populate large corporations, international business schools, consulting firms, international institutions like the World Bank or the World Trade
Organization, and international "think tanks," such as the Trilateral Commission or the
more secretive Bilderberg Group (see Robinson, 2004).

Despite this predominance, however, there is a tension in today's GPE between the
kinds of policies generated in relation to neo-liberal concerns and those that are conceived in connection to the increasingly important thrust of what many critics are calling
the ethos of American empire. The goal of a neo-liberal market utopia has often been
sidelined by American policies that are increasingly imperial in tone. Punctuated most
importantly by the 2003 invasion, and subsequent occupation, of Iraq, "American
empire" has become a shorthand to describe a kind of policy toward global economic
and political issues that focuses less on the creation of a global free market system and
more on the assertion of American supremacy in political and strategic terms. In the
aftermath of the events of September 11, 2001, the policies of the Bush administration
have tended to break with the neo-liberal thrust and stress, in contrast, the importance
of American national interests and issues of American strategic concern. This includes
not only the American military initiative in Iraq, itself characterized by important economic issues relating to the control of oil resources and the future of the carbon economy, but also an increasing skepticism, among members of the Bush administration, of
any element of globalization that is not managed directly by the United States. In addition, the Bush administration has increasingly turned to a conception of unilateral action
in the global arena, a departure from the neo-liberal emphasis on a rules-based multilateral trading system. Finally, the Bush administration has turned to protectionist policies that ignore or only selectively accept the concerns or judgments of key neo-liberal
institutions, such as the World Trade Organization. Canada's longstanding trade dispute
with the United States over softwood lumber is a prime example of this.

This perceived trend has provoked some to ask whether current American policies
constitute a kind of return to imperialism. Many writers suggest that the term "empire"
best characterizes the logic that is now ascendant in the global political-economic context.
Although "empire" is a complicated term, it refers to the exercise of political, economic,
or cultural control of the territory, resources, or population of state or society by another.
This logic of empire is not animated by global business and neo-liberal elites seeking to

carve out a market ideal. Rather, it is driven by strategic and military calculations and, in particular, by an American administration convinced of its own capacities to establish basic rules for global political and economic norms, and to project its own national interests above all else. As Walden Bello notes, "there has been a sharp struggle between the more globalist fraction of ruling elite, stressing the common interest of the global capitalist class in a growing world economy, and the more nationalist, hegemonist faction that wanted to ensure the supremacy of US corporate interests" (Bello and Malig, 2004, 88).

These competing conceptions of global life confront students of GPE with an interesting puzzle. Which logic—neo-liberalism or empire—will dominate the GPE of the short and medium term? Are these two impulses different, or can they be reconciled with each other? What is the relationship between neo-liberal political impulses and the vision of international life embodied in the policies of the Bush administration and the "War on Terror"? It is the relationship between these two impulses, and the ways in which they both are affected by other sites of political struggle, such as the World Social Forum, which will form the key to many debates about the global system in the early twenty-first century.

Summary

Political economy is a field of study centrally concerned with the intersection of political and economic power. Although the roots of political economy stretch back into the early nineteenth century, it has recently been necessary to expand this field of inquiry to take into account issues of economic globalization more fully. This chapter has introduced the concept of global political economy as a field of study and as a concept designed to address the ways in which global economic practices are politically managed and constructed.

One way to address this process of political management is to pay particular attention to the social interests that have been central to the ways in which the global economy has been organized and reorganized over time. The reorganization of the world economy after World War II, for example, was accomplished by a group of social interests, productive capital, state managers, some elements of organized labour, that were keen to promote a kind of "embedded liberalism." This contrasts with a more recent attempt, since the 1970s, to reorganize the economy along neo-liberal lines. This neo-liberal project, supported by particular social forces, has been centrally concerned with the construction of a global "market utopia."

Finally, this chapter has emphasized that GPE pays attention not only to the ways in which the economy is politically constructed but also to the ways in which it is politically contested. The attempt to forge a market utopia over the past few decades, for example, has often been met by opposition from groups that have been displaced or hurt by neo-liberal reforms. The move to neo-liberalism has not only been complicated by the forms of resistance it has provoked but also by an increasingly imperial set of policies promoted by the American government over the past few years. It is in these contexts that GPE is an increasingly important field, which tries to make sense of the complex political issues related to economic globalization and the possible futures of the global society.

Discussion Questions

1. What makes political economy different from other areas of political inquiry?

2. In your view, does it make sense to separate the study of economics and the study of politics?

3. In today's world, what is the role of *economic* factors and forces in the ways in which *political* power is exercised?

4. How has economic globalization been a political project? In whose interest are neo-liberal forms of economic restructuring?

5. Why are movements such as the "global justice movement" concerned about the direction of economic globalization? What, in your view, are the prospects for creating an alternative to neo-liberal forms of globalization?

References

Bank for International Settlements. 2005. *Triennial Central Bank Survey.* Basel: Bank for International Settlements.

Bello, Walden and Maylou Malig. 2004. "The Crisis of the Globalist Project and the New Economics of George Bush" in Alan Freeman and Boris Kagarlitsky, eds., *The Politics of Empire: Globalisation in Crisis.* London: Pluto Press.

Bissio, Robert. 2005. *Social Watch 2005: Roars and Whispers.* Montevideo: Social Watch Secretariat/Third World Institute.

Conway, Janet. 2004. "Citizenship in the Time of Empire: The World Social Forum as a New Political Space." *Citizenship Studies,* 8, 4: 367–381.

Cox, Robert. W. 1987. *Production, Power and World Order: Social Forces in the Making of History.* New York: Columbia University Press.

———. 1996. *Approaches to World Order.* Cambridge: Cambridge University Press.

Hardt, Michael and Antonio Negri. 2000. *Empire.* Cambridge: Harvard University Press.

Helleiner, Eric. 1994. *States and the Re-Emergence of Global Finance: From Bretton Woods to the 1990s.* Ithaca, NY: Cornell University Press.

Keynes, John Maynard. 1933. "National Self-Sufficiency." *The Yale Review,* XXII: 4.

Lenin, V.I. 1973. *Imperialism, the Highest Stage of Capitalism: A Popular Outline.* Peking: Foreign Languages Press.

Polanyi, Karl. 1944. *The Great Transformation: The Political and Economic Origins of Our Times.* Boston: Beacon Press.

Robinson, William I. 2004. *A Theory of Global Capitalism.* Baltimore, MD: Johns Hopkins University Press.

Ruggie, John. 1982. "International Regimes, Transactions and Change." *International Organization,* 36.

Further Readings

Appelbaum, Richard P. and William I. Robinson, eds. 2005. *Critical Globalization Studies.* New York: Routledge.

Rupert, Mark and M. Scott Solomon. 2006. *Globalization and International Political Economy: The Politics of Alternative Futures.* New York: Rowman and Littlefield.

Scholte, Jan Aart. 2005. *Globalization: A Critical Introduction.* London: Palgrave.

Weblinks

Global Policy Forum
www.globalpolicy.org

The World Bank
www.worldbank.org

The World Social Forum
www.forumsocialmundial.org.br/index.php?cd_language=2

CBC *Ideas* podcast on Karl Polanyi, "Markets and Society" (discussion of the theoretical and conceptual basis of critical political economy and GPE)
www.cbc .ca/ideas/calendar/2005/07_july.html

Political Economy Research Centre, University of Sheffield (good starting point for studying the academic discipline of GPE)
www.shef.ac.uk/perc

CHAPTER 25

GLOBAL CITIES

Cities are the fulcrum of civilization. They have been the loci of national economies and often are understood as personifying the national character. This chapter explores the reconfiguration of cities and city-regions in an era of intensifying globalization. It examines the emergence of the global city, new international hierarchies among cities, growing disparities of wealth and influence, both within and among cities, and the activities of new social movements that are simultaneously rooted in local and transnational networks. In a global age, city-regions anchor the international economy even as they provide vital services for their own populations. This chapter explores the tension between the policy objectives of local communities and their leaders on the one hand, and on the other, wider-area economic actors and the central governments. Cities also are widely celebrated as the birthplace of democratic participation. Can it be that, in this new global age, democratic practices thought to have been eroded in recent years may again be revived within the confines of global cities? A second objective in this chapter is thus to explore the following proposition. In the high-stakes, often zero-sum games of world urban concentration driven by private-sector economics, the rebirth of the local community as a fully democratic counter-weight will require two things. First, its authorities must possess sufficient

JAMES
LIGHTBODY

Objectives

resources to mount public policies effectively, and second, there must be a decentralization of political power that goes sufficiently beyond familiar pandering rhetoric that city governments will be taken seriously.

Introduction

In general terms, this chapter explores global interconnectedness. Specifically, it looks at how this phenomenon has placed new policy demands on city-regions even as it has limited their capacity to respond to these demands. In today's world there are over 300 city-regions with a population of more than one million—six in Canada alone, and at least 20 with more than ten million residents. The twentieth century status quo within city-region policy-making has been drawn into question over the past two decades with the arrival of new citizens from across the globe and with the increasing assessment of local public policies in the light of comparative international experience.

Over that same period a recognizable city-regional political culture has become apparent even as each city-region remains vulnerable, on its own, to global market fluctuations, with their attendant capital shifts and labour force choices. The divergence among cities is one of degree, however, often expressed through institutions and political practices. What is known for sure is that globalization and urbanization are inextricably linked as phenomena and both are tied to cut-throat corporate competition and the growing demands of consumerism. A collateral policy fact of the new urban life is that income inequality has dramatically deepened.

Global Cities

THE TERM "WORLD CITIES" WAS COINED BY BRITISH URBAN PLANNER SIR Peter Hall in 1966. These are now defined as post-industrial production sites primarily encompassing international firms providing corporate services and finance. **Global cities** are a sort of sub-national regional social formation formally described as "dense nodes of human labor and communal life" (Scott, 2002). Their clout is based on the locational choices of transnational corporations. Globalization has been accompanied by population concentration within relatively few very large centres, so that a general system of world city-regions has emerged.

An ambitious attempt to catalogue global city-regions based on their pattern of relationships has been undertaken by the Globalization and World Cities Study Group and Network at Loughborough University. The Loughborough group used three measures: content analysis of the world's leading financial media; assessment of the structure of branch offices of large "producer services" operations, especially law, accounting, and advertising; and personnel migration patterns (Hall, in Scott, 2002, 65). For example, the group compiled data on the "international migration of highly skilled and specialized professional and managerial workers" that graphically showed how concentrated in New York the international financial system had become. The migration of professional workers is an interesting measure, since it reflects voluntary choice of location in which attaining citizenship in the host country is not the principal motivation (in contrast with persons seeking refugee status, for example). The Loughborough group established a score for each city, an "Inventory of World Cities," and ranked 122 sites as either alpha (10 cities), beta (10), or gamma (35). The remaining 67 are considered to hold "some evidence" of world city status. The top four alpha cities are London, Paris, New York, and Tokyo (Scott, 2002, 71). In Canada, Toronto stands as a beta city, Montreal is a low-ranking gamma, and Vancouver embraces "some evidence" of world city formation akin to Brisbane, Cairo, and Montevideo (but ahead of Hanoi and Tijuana).

Global cities are centres for post-industrial corporate services and international finance, distinguished by their place in an established pattern of inter-city transactions and relationships. They are demarked by their high concentration of advanced corporate services for the highest levels of transnational commerce, or for "industries producing the organizational commodities necessary for the implementation and management of global economic systems" (Sassen, 1998, 203).

Local Response to Global Pressures

The **new localism** is a term used to explain a variety of collective initiatives in economic development and political action at the level of the community. An analogous term used in 1970s cities was "neighbourhood government." The new localism has emerged since changes in information technologies that purportedly encourage local action have not axiomatically yielded direct democratic participation—either in Zimbabwe, for instance, or Canadian city-regions—any more than market capitalism necessarily promotes democratic choice in Malaysia, Florida, or Alberta. Still, as citizens reject the authority of longstanding national leadership arrangements, they have also begun a variety of new collective initiatives at the community level. These aim to establish minimum conditions so that people can take control of their own lives. In an ideal setting they would create communities based on the common good, equality, and a sustainable relationship with the environment.

Community activists may find their political behaviour newly legitimized by connections to knowledge compatriots abroad. **"Glocal"** is a hybrid term used variously to describe "innovative strategies" focused on global issues by empowering local communities. One cornerstone NGO, the Global Forum, is based on a network of city-to-city partnerships between mayors for development purposes (social, cultural, economic, and architectural), often in conflict with "the dominant or hegemonic urban regime." Localism may mitigate insensitive nation-state practices and open up participatory avenues—at least in city-regions (where the world is watching). In reality, "glocal" operations are often far more prosaic, centred on enabling local residents to construct (or rebuild) waterworks, schools, community hospitals, and other local infrastructure. The obvious belief is that real decision-making responsibility is increasingly necessary at lower levels in a global age. For Canada's cities this would mean a more genuine devolution of central authority, permissive of a localism that could deliver, for example, child and elder care and recreational and cultural facilities, not as universal policies but in a fashion immediately fitting for the locale.

A second common catchword here is **governance**, which means, strictly, a co-option of state, market, and civil society into the managing of large urban areas. The politics and policies governing place are important for global cities. Recent European experience reveals a heightened identity assigned to city-regions by their citizens because they are not only places of economic growth and opportunity, but also cosmopolitan meeting and market places providing a valued interpersonal alternative to transnational power networks. Even the most advanced information industries require a physical location for the concrete processes that are situated in specific places. New service industries in particular further appear to require an agglomeration of specialized, or boutique, service providers, especially since they tend to buy such specialties through sub-contracting.

The networked communities of the new world economy evolve on a daily basis, their shape shifting as technology permits, to the point that some demographers now speak of a single, borderless "world city" or "exopolis," as elites rooted in knowledge networks are easily able to transcend political boundaries electronically. The new knowledge elites have found that traditional metropolitan boundaries for physical space have lost significance for the work (and play) they perform within other layers, or orders, of magnitude. Political boundaries, however, still retain limited value for those municipal office holders trapped by space, time, and function. Even here, one global tendency for coping with the new reality that cities are a less viable unit of local social organization is institutional consolidation. Ironically, in a time of new localism initiatives, adjacent municipal organizations have sought out region-wide coalitions as a means of dealing with the possibilities and countering the threats of globalization.

If new localism resourcefulness can be sustained in global cities, then genuine debates will come to be rooted in the neighbourhoods of the world. The municipal has, incredibly, become a major constituency in global politics, and there may come a time when a network of mayors and councils will be heard as they circumvent the national level and move directly onto the international stage. Effective self-government means more than political space and partial autonomy; it requires some recognition of relative equality, genuine opportunities for self-realization, and a politics that encompass a range of issues that matter, directly, to residents.

Impact of Globalization on Canadian Cities

Four of the world's mega-cities (populations of more than 10 million) are located in First World countries. The World Bank has projected that, over the next 50 years, 42 new mega-cities will emerge, with only one to be found in countries of the global North. The largest agglomerations already on the horizon are Tokyo (nearly 30 million people); Mumbai, India; Lagos, Nigeria; Dhaka, Bangladesh; and Sao Paulo,

Brazil. China plans to manage population growth by shifting peasant migration into 40 large cities of 30 million or more inhabitants. All of these cities—except Tokyo, which has expanded less rapidly—will be characterized by urban sprawl, unemployment, violence and social disorder, and large underclass barrios.

Alongside the new wealth in global cities has come great inequality. One source of the anti-globalization movement's often violent challenge to the new world order lies in an inequality map of global deprivation. Measuring the income gap between the wealthiest fifth of the population in the world's richest country and that in the poorest reveals that the ratio has moved from 3 to 1 in 1820 (the Industrial Revolution) to 74 to 1 at the start of the twenty-first century (Lightbody, 2006, 524). Increasingly in the global economic era, a permanent underclass has grown as earnings have either remained static or declined. What does appear non-debatable is that the extremes of poverty and inequality of wealth have been most closely juxtaposed in the world's global cities.

Even in Canadian city-regions, low-income numbers increased in the 1990s (although only by half of one percent), in contrast with the 1980s, when the low-income rate declined. In the 27 Canadian census metropolitan areas (CMAs), the gap between richer and poorer neighbourhoods widened in the 1990s, although the proportion of poorer quarters (six percent of all) had remained static for 20 years. Incomes increased more in already wealthy neighbourhoods, a reflection of the fact "that income grew more quickly among high than low-income families" (Lightbody, 2006, 525).

Canadian city-regions have not assumed the noxious characteristics of those countries that have most fully pursued international neo-liberal policies. Within the largest city-regions of these countries, the middle classes are fading while working classes are being "re-proletarianized." In these communities the newly rich plant themselves behind the high walls of plantation-style suburban developments, where private funds pay for civic services. However, the greatest relative poverty levels today are to be found not within poorer countries but in the most post-industrial. The poorest fifth in the United States today earns less than a quarter of the average income, and the trend in the United Kingdom arches similarly. The United States has the most unequal distribution of any advanced country in the world while, globally, social democrats decry the "globalization of poverty."

For Canada's city-regions, the 1990s were a time of consolidation for both family income (growth of one percent) and low-income rates; this had followed a 1980s decade of growth in the former (five percent) and decline in the latter. In the 1990s, incomes grew most for already high-income families, while the lower income groups actually lost ground. A third of recent immigrants had low incomes in 2001, twice the overall average and a significant increase from 23 percent in 1980. This repeats a global pattern in which newcomers without officially recognized skills and knowledge are assigned to a lower status workforce by persons who perceive themselves and their own groups as having a social and economic advantage. In global cities where workplace avenues out of relative poverty are closed, social mobility, even across generations, becomes stagnant. This is the new global urban division of labour where elites, the bourgeoisie, the marginalized, and the impoverished—across territorial boundaries—have been reordered into globalization's winners and losers.

Social Diversity in Global Cities

At one time city-regions in Canada and the United States stood pre-eminent, burgeoning with newcomers from a wide slice of the world's peoples. However, the individuals walking the streets of Toronto or Vancouver these days do not differ much from those walking the streets of Sydney, Frankfurt, London, New York, or any other globally ranked city.

The 2001 census reveals that roughly 45 percent of the total population of immigrants living in Canada come from Europe. Because of open immigration policies and low levels of natural increase, our foreign-born population had grown to 18.4 percent, the highest proportion since 1941 (17.5 percent). In comparative terms today, the U.S. proportion was 7.9 percent; France, 6.3; the U.K., 3.4 percent; and Australia, 22 percent. Of Canada's 27 CMAs, 10 have a foreign-born population of 20 percent or more. The five Quebec CMAs, not including Ottawa-Hull, were all below this number.

Global cities attracting capital growth become international centres of attraction for migration. Effectively, this means they become new communities with few collectively shared and inherited customs, where individuals must forge social bonds as they work and live. In migrant-dependent societies like Canada's, many newcomers find themselves relegated to lower status for a time, and the data reveal that the unemployment rate among recent arrivals is much higher than for those born in Canada, which is itself higher than that of longer-term resident immigrants. Earnings follow a similar path. At least initially this lower economic standing is accentuated by social differences rooted in skin colour, religion, and custom. Yasmeen Abu-Laban adds the caution that, "In global cities, issues surrounding immigration, multiculturalism, and racism have a special resonance and currency that may not be present in other urban locales in Canada" (1997, 83).

Political Ideology and Global Cities

The sustained economic growth across the globe since the end of the 1970s is widely believed to be the end product of an ideology commonly known as **neo-liberalism**. When applied, this philosophy puts its priorities on deregulation, the privatizing of state enterprises, free reign given to market forces, the conversion of tangible assets into more itinerant financial instruments, and a belief in "lean" government. A worldwide force for government on the cheap has been achieved by rolling back institutions (often through deploying public–private partnerships), under-funding state capacities, defusing accountability through privatizing state operations, and even depoliticizing NGOs by professionalizing their activities and personnel. In Canada, the harsh provincial cutbacks to financial support of Canadian city activities in the 1990s were but one local application of global orthodoxy. The political ideology of "public choice" also finds its source in these crude belief patterns.

More specifically, in global cities companies in new fields, such as specialized electronic components, have created internal pressures on local governments to upgrade or provide services and public infrastructure to meet clean industries' market requirements. Cities have had to create new categories in land planning, such as Special Industrial Zones, and have had to find lands to accommodate this. Even conventional Research and Development Parks may no longer fit new requirements. The semi-conductor industrial field, for example, is not able to locate in or near areas occupied by medium and heavy industry, or any commercial or transportation activity that creates vibrations, airborne contaminants, and heavy or disruptive traffic patterns. In Canada, city politicians also should be informed of research in the U.S. and Western Europe that affirms that retaining existing firms is more effective in stimulating local economic growth than activities that try to capture new global investments.

New pan-national social movements (environmental, women's, anti-racism issue networks) mean that business is not the only global actor anymore. Such movements provide local actors with information, intelligence, and heightened legitimacy. Individuals engaging in these "politics of identity," largely through new social movements, uncover political space in their own persons, in environmental causes, and in human rights. All of this can spur specific local initiatives focused on the city-regional institutions of their own particular communities. On the other hand, some networks newly organized in these policy realms will tend to find that their common interests lay not so much with fellow citizens, even those with education and access in their home communities, as with knowledge compatriots abroad. Leadership elites of this type have business or professional travel and contacts that cause them to assess local practices and political institutions against those that perform better in other locales. Political space shrinks, in a sense, as borders become porous and global concerns are expressed in local action.

Political Implications of Cities Being Globalized

On the basis of detailed inter-country comparisons, the Organisation for Economic Co-operation and Development (OECD) has confirmed an observable reality that not all regions are equally endowed with development potential. This has led that organization to three conclusions: (1) it is unwise continually to buttress a declining industrial base; (2) specific territories have their own particular advantages, whose potential can be maximized; and (3) city-regions—for reasons of accessibility, efficient form, mobility, and population skills—are normally appropriate centres for larger territorial development. Yet placing the necessary cost-effective service provisions and infrastructure support into effect generally remains a local, not central, government mandate. Since resources are seldom sufficient for all, central (federal) governments will have to choose to designate which city-regions are growth priorities, and there will be those that lose out. To designate any city-region as a "failure" is a very difficult political task for any level of democratic governing.

Place and Power

IN THIS NEW ERA IN WHICH SOCIAL AND ECONOMIC—AND POLITICAL—BEHAVIOUR increasingly ignores the boundaries of traditional states, place still remains important to citizens; it is anchored by global city-regions. In this context some writers have gone so far as to forecast the general decline of the traditional nation-state. It is their argument that in regions such as Europe, the quest for a new and relevant local identity has revealed that national governments are less than appropriate authorities when urban systems are directly dependent on an integrated world economy. Global cities reinforce such perceptions as they become demonstrably capable of working autonomously in the transnational marketplace.

Populous global city regions such as London, New York, and Tokyo that centre the financial and services networks of the global economy have discreetly challenged the future of national sovereignty and its potential for disruption in the making of "purely local" choices. It is perhaps ironic that the neo-liberal tendency of central governments to decentralize important state functions to cities, often with little financial support, has indirectly enhanced the latter's capacity—as increasingly autonomous social, economic, and political communities—to participate in the competition of global markets. And, during roughly the same time frame, international migration dramatically increased the heterogeneity of the world's larger cities. Just as Canada's economic developments after World War II once acted as an urbanizing magnet for the rural under-employed, globalization has drawn the multi-faceted international contact points of the world into the world's cities.

Almost anywhere, city councils tend naturally to reflect their electors' views that their economic destiny abroad is in conflict with the sparse interest of rather distant central officials who, at their most benign, are understood to be somewhat uninterested in providing information about local economies to foreigners. In a sense, cities, even global cities, have a bit of a free ride, in that they are not expected by citizens to provide the full gamut of state operations because they are sub-national governments. Hence, cities can more easily cherry-pick their preferred agenda items, and these preferred goals are dedicated resources and relatively more of them. For cities distant from the national core, this includes not only trade and infomercial activities abroad but also an almost mandatory opportunity to move into direct inter-municipal connections with trading partners.

Local Activism

Ours is a world of greater overall prosperity than ever. It is also one in which social justice remains the exception and widening economic inequality the norm. We also know that the former is in the world's public eye in global city-regions, the very place in which the latter condition is most extreme. Shifting standards for comparison and action explain away domestic inequalities by pointing to worse disparities elsewhere, presumably minimizing public support for better state poverty reduction strategies. On the other hand, any improvement to policies for labour conditions or increasing sub-standard incomes (e.g., minimum wages) is held in check by implicit threats from capital to exit for the competitive, low-wage, small-tax nations seen nightly on the news.

Especially for bigger cities, the evaluation of urban institutions' performance by cosmopolitan elites has increasingly been tied to standards established in the external communities with which they are familiar. Indigenous standards are likely to be precedent-driven, traditional, and incremental—not wrong but not innovative. Important questions generated by extra-locally sourced debates can produce fundamental skepticism within local policy communities about the relative effectiveness of these longstanding global city activities.

In developed countries, local democratic activists in global cities have mobilized to challenge the "world-class" aspirations of some community leaders when the consequences for neighbourhoods become immediate. The benefits of unrestrained economic growth are seldom equally accessible to all, and the consequences become policy targets. Tenants, in particular, usually have to pay higher rent, and job expansion for the better-qualified provides the economically marginal with few improved employment opportunities. The diversion of resources to provide growth-supportive new infrastructure frequently leaves citizens with deterioration in the quality of what they already have. For the poor, who, either in decayed city-core centres or slum barrios in the suburbs, tend to live or work near both pollution and congestion, further environmental degradation can be devastating. Internationally prestigious sporting events and expositions may have similar consequences. Often the centre-city poor are either forced to relocate to suburbs, which can be considerably distant from work and social networks or, if not relocated, will find their neighbourhood shops and services targeting a different and well-heeled clientele.

Well-known examples of this type of reaction were among the activities following the release of the Brundtland Report (1987), which is most widely known for popularizing the broad political concept of sustainable development. It set the groundwork for the 1992 "Earth Summit" in Rio de Janeiro. This conference, attended by heads of state and an estimated 50 000 official observers and citizens, led to a set of proceedings that provided a world stage for the global media, and under their glare the various participants agreed to a global action plan (Agenda 21) committing to sustainable development and four related international treaties.

The events also legitimized social movement pressure on governments to act. By now, over 150 countries have some sort of advisory panel to conciliate competing actors and interests in the review of national policies. In Canada, for example, by the 1990s forest industries in British Columbia had been forced into a collaborative planning process for crown lands (94 percent of the provincial territory), not by sporadic local environmental blockades and protests, but by the growing threat of international product boycotts mounted by a world environmentalist network based in global city-regions. This ultimately produced significant changes in provincial land use. At the local level, over 2000 cities and towns internationally have by now created local action committees both to operationalize Agenda 21 plans and to assess the current practices of home communities against the world standard.

Political Impacts

GLOBAL CITIES HAVE LEARNED THAT INTER-CONNECTIVITY HAS POLITICIZED a whole new range of issue arenas, new policy networks surrounding them and, in consequence, closer and immediate international surveillance. Accessible worldwide communications permit NGOs an effective means to organize across boundaries. The scheduled meetings of international organizations (such as the World Bank, the World Trade Organization, or the G8) provide a public forum for international protest, almost always in an urban setting. Such conflict between the established order and social movements that seek change weakens the authority for either to have the decisive say in all public business; in turn, this can open new opportunities for autonomous policy innovations by cities.

New Issue Arenas

In the case of Canada, 94 percent of 2.2 million new arrivals between 1991 and 2001 settled in city-regions (about three-quarters chose Toronto, Vancouver, or Montreal, and three in five foreign-born residents of Canada live in the three largest CMAs). Toronto attracted the highest number of newcomers, who, by 2001, constituted 41.4 percent of its population. By 2001, 85 percent of all immigrants lived in an urban area, but only 56 percent of native-born Canadians did so. This points to a significant demographic separation as native-born Canadians evacuate to spatially separated suburbs, leaving the central city for new arrivals.

Global cities face policy consequences as new arrivals internationalize the policy agenda. Newcomers immediately suffer an "income penalty" partly because of inadequate language skills, non-recognition of credentials earned in origin countries, and the genteel practice of discrimination. For an adjustment period they will require a measure of employment support and access to city social services, a community commitment to language education, and realizable means to align professional qualifications with community standards. Some policy consequences, such as demands for racial equity in employment and culturally aware policing, are obvious and direct; others may not be, as when a greater number of new urban immigrants necessitates improvements in public transit. The internationalizing of Canadian city-regions has increased demand for more effective public transit, even in suburbs.

City-regions in the integrative front lines can experience stress on policing brought on by the introduction of old-world struggles to new environs, as with the Sikhs and Tamils in Canada, or Algerian and Moroccan Arabs in France. Some city-regions have had only limited (mostly unprofitable) experience in grappling with wider clashes that stem from divergent cultural expectations. This has been especially the case where values rooted in collective orientations collide sharply with the strict individualism of Western liberalism. Policy frustrations on both sides intensify as immigration introduces collective-tradition communities that are larger, more affluent, and better organized.

Citizenship itself may also be valued differently in a global age. Global cities, by definition, are cosmopolitan not only in attitudes and activities but also in ethnicities, languages, and religions. In their struggle for basic democratic rights at city governing levels, newcomers have seldom hesitated to turn to non-governmental actors with commitments to globalization of human rights, and occasionally they have exploited victories at the local level to win stronger rights for citizens at the national level. Will immigrants to Canada be empowered to participate in local decision-making processes before gaining national citizenship rights? Cities will learn first.

Global versus Local Citizenship

Globalization has the ability to shrink world space and to concentrate that space within urban centres. Constant connection through electronic communication means that specific individuals can simultaneously interact no matter where they are on this planet, while being oblivious to the burning house of next-door neighbours. What this overall setting has meant for metropolitan areas is that their global cosmopolitans are isolated both from their underclass neighbours and from those outside the policy communities of specific interest to them. They tend to be out of traditional policy-making loops while tightly connected to the new.

One insidious consequence of the new global model of concentrated media ownership and subsequent centralized convergence of news-gathering activity has been a marked decline in the resources directed to local community. Even in global cities, coverage of city news, community leaders, and public policy debates is seldom adequate. In the developed liberal democracies, local institutional memory of the context for past policy choices is crippled as priorities shift from the serious to the comedic and the community's news is reduced to entertainment.

The slow emergence of a "global civil society" since 1948—bound by covenants and international agreements, monitored by the UN and NGOs, networked human rights activists and progressive political gladiators at all levels of authority in all states—has compelled even the most local of policy-makers to keep an outward eye. The new language of Agenda 21, for example, has passed through the policy gateway for all levels of governing; one consequence has been pressure to force more holistic policy-planning practices upon even those in local city politics. For example, while politicians in central governments face generalized political pressures to unite families, to respond to refugee claims, and to devise longer-term human resources strategies for immigration and settlement, city-regional policy-makers confront immediate issues quite literally on their doorsteps. Abu-Laban succinctly lists the policy concerns of urgent import to immigrants: "finding affordable housing, accessing health and counseling services, receiving English-language training, dealing with family intergenerational conflict, and finding employment" (1997, 83).

In the age of the global city, the successful promotion of the specific locational advantage of city-regions (especially in instances where national states are perceived as distant, not knowledgeable, or politically unresponsive) appears in part contingent upon the emergence of city-regional regimes led by the business community. Still, those that are confined to the business community alone will fail. Experience reveals that flourishing informal alliances have embraced labour, ethnic, and cultural communities; effective leadership in post-secondary education and research; and so forth, to achieve sufficient critical mass and common voice to be heard in a rough, competitive world. Yet even the best-intentioned community leadership in desperate locales can be diverted from the realization of strategic plans by quick-fix booster shots (such as world expositions), inadequate potable water or poor transit, and an educational system with too little public support.

Summary

The World Bank estimates that by the year 2025 there will be 2.5 billion more city dwellers than there are today, and most of this growth will occur in the developing world. Canada's National Round Table on the Environment and Economy put it this way: "cities of the world will need to cope with the rough equivalent of two more 'Chinas' worth of population within one generation" (Lightbody, 2006, 532). Concurrently, there is a pressing inadequacy in technological competence, logistical know-how, and sheer administrative capability within developing world cities confronted with unrestrained urban growth.

The policy uncertainties that result will raise important questions. Are mayors actually city leaders, and what is the reach of their political authority? Which citizens are they consistently most likely to represent? Will central governments continue to erode the formal authority of the municipal? Is the municipal level more likely to be innovative? But, then again, will such innovation be at the expense of real equity in public policy applications? By definition, global city-regions exist within a global space, and their capacity to meet human needs effectively while in hard-nosed competition with other cities for economic advantage will come to be the critical measure of the success of twenty-first century civilization.

Discussion Questions

1. Do you see evidence of "new localism"–style activities in your home city?

2. Should global cities seek independence from their surrounding nations?

3. Is it fair to evaluate what your city hall is doing by comparing it with cities elsewhere in the world?

4. Is it wise policy for Canadian cities to continue to pursue "world-class" games and expositions?

References

Abu-Laban, Yasmeen. 1997. "Ethnic Politics in a Global Metropolis: The Case of Vancouver" in Timothy L. Thomas, ed., *The Politics of the City: A Canadian Perspective.* Scarborough: ITP Nelson, 77–95.

Lightbody, James. 2006. *City Politics, Canada.* Peterborough: Broadview Press.

Sassen, Saskia. 1998. *Globalization and Its Discontents.* New York: The New Press.

Scott, Allen J., ed. 2002. *Global City-Regions: Trends, Theory, Policy.* Oxford: Oxford University Press.

Further Readings

Held, David and Anthony McGrew. 2002. *Globalization/Anti-Globalization.* Cambridge: Polity Press, Blackwell.

Lightbody, James. 2006. *City Politics, Canada.* Peterborough: Broadview.

Pieterse, Jan Nederveen. 2004. *Globalization or Empire?* London: Routledge.

Sassen, Saskia. 1998. *Globalization and Its Discontents.* New York: The New Press.

Sassen, Saskia, ed. 2002. *Global Networks, Linked Cities.* London and New York: Routledge.

Weblinks

The Brundtland Commission (and sustainable development)
www.unesco.org/education/tlsf/theme_a/mod02/uncom02t01bod.htm

Global Cities Institute
www.rmit.edu.au/rd/global-cities

Globally Speaking: Global Cities
www.abc.net.au/global/cities/default.htm

The Glocal Forum
www.glocalforum.org

CHAPTER 26

REGIONALIZATION AND GLOBALIZATION

Objectives

This chapter introduces the critical concept of **regionalization** and explores its growing importance in contemporary global politics, focusing especially on the development of the North American region. The chapter begins with a discussion of the relationship between regionalization and globalization. Contrary to popular perceptions that the multiple and complex processes of globalization are progressively shaping the planet into a single and homogeneous political space, we find that the world is simultaneously being carved up into large and distinct regions, many of which are governed through international treaties and trading agreements. An explanation of the reasons why the trend toward regionalization has become pervasive in the contemporary world will follow, showing that it has also led to competition for economic and political areas of influence. Regionalization, as the chapter describes, has impacts on both international relations and domestic politics, and has tended to advantage dominant economic actors and economies. As a result, regionalization is increasingly resisted by less developed countries that are seeking alternatives that promote human development rather than corporate profitability.

JULIÁN
CASTRO-REA

Introduction

This chapter focuses on regionalization, another contemporary trend in international politics that has received far less attention than globalization in political science texts and in the popular media. By regionalization, we mean the creation and development of associations among countries, generally in contiguous geographic spaces, mainly for, but not limited to, economic purposes. These associations are generally formalized through legally binding international treaties or intergovernmental agreements, such as free trade agreements. Prominent examples of the latter are the North American Free Trade Agreement (NAFTA) and the Association of Southeast Asian Nations (ASEAN). The European Union (EU) is the most developed example of regionalization both because of the degree of economic integration that has been achieved during the past half-century and because of the creation of supranational institutions, including a democratically elected European Parliament and a common European currency—the euro.

Because regions generally are formed by countries that share common borders or continental landscapes, it is tempting to think that regions evolve naturally as a result of cultural and economic interchanges between countries, which over time nurture shared values, objectives, and interests. However, geo-political regions are neither natural nor inevitable; they are invented, created, and differently constructed. They are the products of political decisions made by governments in response to very real political and economic interests and their assessments of advantage in an ever-more competitive international setting. Region-making is carried out by states, which actively seek closer association with other states to realize goals that would be difficult to achieve by any one single national state.

It is by no means obvious how regions are shaped into geo-political units. Take, for instance, the Asia-Pacific Economic Cooperation (APEC). This "region" joins together 21 disparate countries in Asia, Oceania, and the Americas, whose only common feature is having a shore on the Pacific Ocean. Most of these countries also belong to other regional associations, such as NAFTA or ASEAN, with which they have much closer cooperation agreements. As we can see from this example, regions are cut in an arbitrary manner, dictated by political decisions made in each member country, and often overlap, if the interests of concerned states point in more than one direction.

Parallel Trends

GLOBALIZATION AND REGIONALIZATION ARE TWO TRENDS THAT APPEAR TO PULL THE world in opposite directions. Globalization is often understood as a homogenizing process that erases national boundaries and makes all states and their populations interdependent on a global scale. Regionalization, in contrast, effectively carves the planet into a series of supranational geo-political entities that are exclusive of one another. Paradoxically, however, globalization and regionalization are not contradictory processes. Instead, through both its origins and its operations, regionalization helps to further advance contemporary globalization processes.

The ongoing formation of the North American region provides a good example of how regionalization and globalization work hand in hand. The formal regionalization of North America began with the 1989 Canada–United States Free Trade Agreement (CUSFTA), which was expanded to include Mexico with the 1994 North American Free Trade Agreement and has been more recently elaborated in the Security and Prosperity Partnership of North America (SPP). This partnership agreement was signed by the leaders of Canada, United States, and Mexico in Waco, Texas, in 2005. The SPP commits the three countries to further harmonize regulatory, energy, and security policies for the North American continent. The leaders of NAFTA countries, termed "the three amigos," meet each year to review their progress toward continental policy harmonization.

From the outset, CUSFTA explicitly invoked article 24 of the General Agreement on Tariffs and Trade (GATT).[1] Article 24 allows GATT member countries to grant preferential trade terms to a limited number of GATT partners, provided that in so doing they do not increase their exchanges with this limited collection of states at the expense of the rest of the world. This is called "**trade diversion**" in international trade law. Instead, regionalized countries must together enhance their overall global trade ("**trade creation**" in international law) if they want to live up to GATT's expectations. This way, CUSFTA members committed to making global trade in its entirety benefit from the increased efficiency that regional cooperation was expected to promote. This commitment was extended to Mexico when this country joined NAFTA.

CUSFTA opened the path to the proliferation of **open regionalism** in various parts of the world. It is called "open" so it can be distinguished from earlier experiences of international economic cooperation, where member countries increased exchanges among themselves rather than with the rest of the world. Open regions, in contrast, seek to increase the international competitiveness of member states both within and outside the region. Indeed, some regional member states end up intensifying their exchanges with the rest of the world relative to the period before they created a region. Canada's experience is a good case in point. Between 2001 and 2006, this country increased trade with its partners in North America from almost $585 billion to over $597 billion (CAD). However, during the same period its global exchanges went from $747.2 billion to $836.7 billion (CAD). That is, Canadian trade expanded both within and outside North America, but expansion was more substantial outside

---

[1] The GATT was conceived by the Bretton Woods Conference as part of a larger plan for economic recovery after World War II. The GATT's main purpose was to reduce barriers to international trade through reduction of tariff barriers, quantitative trade restrictions, and subsidies of trade. The GATT was approved in 1947 during the United Nations Conference on Trade and Employment in Havana, Cuba. On January 1, 1948, the agreement was signed by 23 countries, including Canada and the United States. Originally, the GATT was supposed to become a full international organization called the International Trade Organization, but it remained simply an agreement. Since 1994, the functions of the GATT have been replaced by the World Trade Organization.

the North American region, both in relative and absolute terms (Canada, Department of Foreign Affairs and International Trade, 2007b).

Contemporary regionalization encourages international economic exchanges and thus contributes to globalization. As important, by engaging in open regionalism, countries commit to operating in the global economy under a set of rules agreed upon within and under the supervision of the World Trade Organization (WTO). These rules apply to all regional entities. Thus, regionalism is not about clubs of countries withdrawing from the world economy to limit their trade to exchanges among themselves. Rather, it means that clusters of countries agree to compete under the same regulations, thus contributing to the development of a single international political economic regime.

North America as Regional Trend-Setter

REGIONALIZATION IN NORTH AMERICA IS IMPORTANT NOT ONLY AS ONE MORE example among others. In fact, this region created a model that would set a new standard for regionalization after the end of the Cold War. For a variety of reasons we will discuss later in this section, this standard would end up being followed or even actively promoted in other regions.

Regionalization in North America was mostly a decision made in the United States, which became a reality once the neighbouring countries became receptive to the idea. As early as 1979, some politicians in the United States—including runner-up Republican presidential candidate Ronald Reagan—publicly endorsed the project of an economic alliance with Canada and Mexico. At the time, the project was rejected by Mexican and Canadian leadership, but it would not take long before it was seriously considered, rising to the top of Canada's political agenda in 1985 and Mexico's in 1990 (Barry, 1995).

The decision to pursue regionalization was strategic because the U.S. aimed both to revamp its global power, in decline at the end of the Cold War, and give a boost to its declining industry in face of competition from the European and Asian regions. In a sense, then, North American regionalization can be seen as a response to emerging regional powers. NAFTA was indeed a way of creating a larger platform for the recovery of American economic competitiveness, by pooling resources—human, natural, industrial, and technological capacities—of all three North American countries and by creating economies of scale (Deblock and Rioux, 1993; Cicantell, 2001). By **economies of scale** we mean increased efficiencies of production as the number of goods being produced increases. Economies of scale lower the average cost per unit since fixed costs are shared over an increased number of produced goods (Investopedia.com, n.d.). This is achieved through the reorganization of corporate activities across international borders, aimed at taking advantage of better supplies of materials, cheaper workforces, and larger markets—all of which are critical to corporate competitiveness in the contemporary global economy. As important, the United States wished to break the stalemate of global trade negotiations within GATT, entangled for seven years in the "Uruguay Round" of negotiations.[2] NAFTA was designed to demonstrate to the rest of the world that such controversial issues as investment, intellectual property rights, agriculture, and dispute settlement mechanisms could be successfully incorporated into trade agreements.

NAFTA would influence international trade because of the central place the United States occupies in the world system. The European Union and its preceding organizations were seen as exceptions, responding to uniquely European goals of fostering cooperation and mutual trust to avert another war. European integration evolved gradually, starting with the creation of the European Coal and Steel Community (ECSC) in 1951, followed by the expansion of cooperation to all economic sectors with the European Economic Community in 1958, and culminating in the European Union, established in 1993. Moreover, the European experience was not a case of clear open regionalism. Because of its strong transnational institutions, the EU was often criticized for not living up to GATT's requirement of creating more outward- than inward-oriented trade. In other words, the European Union often appeared to be engaged in trade diversion rather than trade creation.

In many ways, North America is a region like no other, primarily because of the commanding presence of the world's only superpower within it. The United States' dominance over the world is not only material, in terms of trade and military might, but also extends to shaping political institutions, domestic markets, legal frameworks, and even cultures around the globe. North American regionalization was then in a position to break the trail open, showing the rest of the world the way ahead by committing to a globally oriented region. Later on, the superpower made use of its large market to entice potential new partners to engage in bilateral or plurilateral (that is, involving more than two countries) trade liberalization. Indeed, soon after NAFTA was signed, the United States concluded an array of trade liberalization agreements with a host of different regions and countries. The United States also actively promoted the extension of the NAFTA model to the rest of the hemisphere through the Free Trade Area of the Americas (FTAA). When this initiative failed in the face of the resistance of some governments in the area, the American government proceeded to carve out separate agreements with supportive governments in the hemisphere. As a result, the United States is presently part of five regional and 17 bilateral trade agreements.[3] In this way, the United States has positioned itself as a trade hub in a liberalized environment, with many

---

[2] The Uruguay Round was a round of GATT negotiations so named because it was launched in Punta del Este, Uruguay, in 1986. It had come to a halt because the GATT's members could not agree on how to deal with contentious issues, such as agriculture, intellectual property rights, foreign investment, and financial services. It was only concluded at the Marrakech conference in December 1993, once NAFTA was about to be implemented.

[3] For a full list of trade agreements in which the United States participates, see **www.ustr.gov/Trade_Agreements/Section_Index.html**.

spokes. These spokes are economically dynamic countries that vie for increased presence in the U.S. market and for more U.S. investment, without necessarily having easier access to each other's markets or capitals.

Competition among Models of Regionalization

ALTHOUGH THEY ARE BOTH MARKET-ORIENTED AND CONTRIBUTE TO GLOBALIZATION, major differences persist between the European and North American models of regionalization. Perhaps the greatest difference is the degree of state economic intervention that is associated with each of these models. The European Union is much more prone to high levels of taxation, industrial and regional development policies, and standardized labour legislation than is North America. Sometimes called "Social Europe," the European Union has also maintained a more comprehensive social welfare policy regime than its North American counterpart.

The EU has also created a vast network of institutions mandated to deal with common regional issues. These institutions are only indirectly accountable to the governments of member states. Their jurisdiction is regional (Europe-wide) rather than national and, in principle, they are accountable to European citizens. While these institutions are often criticized for being too bureaucratic and remote, they do provide avenues for democratic accountability that are simply absent in the North American case. North America has left regional issues as matters of negotiation among the governments of its member states. Citizens are represented through their governments, almost exclusively by the executive branches, and they have only limited access to the handful of North American institutions that have been tentatively set in place. For instance, North American citizens can file claims to the continental Commission for Environmental Cooperation, but they can't request disclosure of proceedings or of panels set up to settle commercial or investment disputes.

In other words, North Americans, unlike their European counterparts, have no direct accountability mechanisms other than the ones offered by regular domestic politics. The governance of the North American region largely operates through its overarching binding intergovernmental agreements, such as NAFTA and the recently crafted Security and Prosperity Partnership (SPP). These are constitution-like documents that North American governments commit themselves to respect even when they conflict with domestic legal orders, electoral platforms, or public opinion (Clarkson, 2002). Moreover, in practice, these agreements do not even operate the same way for every member country, as the United States regularly does not abide by the rules set down in them. The best case in point is Washington's reluctance to comply with successive rulings, issued by NAFTA's trade dispute panels, ordering the U.S. to stop imposing extra duties on Canadian imports of softwood lumber and give back to producers duties unduly levied.

As already noted, the United States has attempted to spread its model of regional governance through bilateral agreements, especially since the failure of the FTAA. Within the Americas, Chile, Panama, Peru, and Colombia all have accepted the American model. This model also prevails in Southeast Asia, where the superpower makes its influence felt through its participation in APEC. American influence is also felt strongly in the Middle East, through agreements with states such as Jordan, Israel, and, more recently, Afghanistan and Iraq.

But American efforts to set up hub–spoke relationships with other countries have not proceeded without resistance or competition. First, the EU has competed for influence in many areas of the globe, building on previous links with former colonies and making use of Economic Partnership Agreements (EPAs), uniquely European cooperation agreements that blend trade with aid. Other countries have developed regional relationships that resemble the EU model. Our hemisphere's southernmost countries, grouped in the Southern Common Market (Mercosur), for example, have opted for regional dynamics more akin to the European model, thus reinforcing their historical transatlantic ties. The Caribbean, a region historically attached to Europe but economically intertwined with the United States, is torn between the two models.

Some countries, including Venezuela, Ecuador, and Bolivia, have rejected outright the NAFTA model. Finally, the emerging economies of China and India also are competing with both the European Union and United States to establish trading relationships, especially with resource-rich African countries. China and India, for the most part, have not placed the same kinds of stringent conditions on African trading partners as those often demanded by the U.S. or international financial institutions, such as the World Bank and the International Monetary Fund. In February 2007, Chinese President Hu Jintao toured eight African states—Cameroon, Liberia, Sudan, Namibia, South Africa, Seychelles, Zambia, and Mozambique—to nail down development projects and business deals discussed during a China–Africa summit held in Beijing in November 2006 (Anonymous, 2007).

Domestic Impacts of Regionalization

TO THE EXTENT IT REQUIRES CLOSER COOPERATION AND HARMONIZATION OF ECONOMIC policies of more than one country, regionalization is not only about redefining international relations and global flows of trade and commerce. It also affects the states internally, by pushing them to adapt to the new disciplines and requirements of regionalization. Adaptation obviously affects mostly domestic economies, but it also has impacts on politics, societies, and cultures of the countries involved. These impacts are particularly clear in Mexico and Canada because for more than a decade these countries engaged precisely with the country that exerts the strongest influence in the contemporary global economy. As a result, it is increasingly necessary for Canada and Mexico to factor the U.S. component into domestic decision-making.

NAFTA rules also have direct impact on domestic governance in these two countries. A good example is the far-reaching measures designed to protect foreign investment from government actions, as defined in the agreement's chapter 11. These measures allow foreign investors to sue host states whenever they consider their ventures and profit prospects have been adversely affected by legislation or policies. If affected, these investors are deemed to have been "expropriated," according to chapter 11 wording. Under this chapter, it is irrelevant whether legislation or policies aim to protect the public good. NAFTA signatories are legally obliged to compensate foreign investors if their business plans were frustrated. U.S.-based corporations have resorted to this chapter more often than their Canadian and Mexican counterparts.[4] In fact, lawsuits, real or expected, exert a constant check on the activities and decisions of Canadian and Mexican governments. In a number of instances, Ottawa and Mexico City have effectively been forced to pay compensation. The best-known is the Metalclad case, where the Mexican government was forced to pay $16.685 million (USD) to an American corporation because the enactment of environmental and public health protection measures conflicted with the corporation's plan to build a toxic waste landfill.[5]

A clear indication of how far-reaching these impacts can be is found in Canadian and Mexican reactions to the attacks of September 11, 2001. In the aftermath of the attacks, the United States increased control of its borders and enhanced its domestic security policies. Under pressure from Washington to do the same, and claims from business affected by border restrictions, the Canadian and Mexican governments reformed policies and institutions in issues ranging from putting security at the top of public priorities to restricting mobility of people across borders, and from enhancing government control over citizen dissent, protest, and organization to defence spending.

Two separate bilateral agreements were adopted to beef up border security: the United States–Canada Smart Border Declaration of December 12, 2001, and the United States–Mexico Border Partnership Agreement of March 22, 2002. These agreements clearly express how the United States put pressure on its neighbours to accommodate its new concerns, but they also represent the implicit acknowledgement by the U.S. of the impossibility of effective unilateral action to protect its territory. Canada and Mexico also introduced changes into their domestic security apparatuses. Canada implemented an Anti-terrorism Plan, allocating $5 billion (CAD) to enhance surveillance and border checks. In 2002, Ottawa created the Border Infrastructure Fund with a budget of $600 million over five years. More important, this country introduced three major legislative changes: the *Anti-terrorism Act* (Bill C-36), introduced in October 2001, the *Public Safety Act of 2002*, and a revised *Immigration and Refugee Protection Act* (Bill C-11), effective June 2002. The combined

---

[4] As of February 2007, out of a total of 42 legal suits filed under NAFTA's chapter 11, 28 were claims of U.S. corporations against the governments of Mexico or Canada (elaboration from Canada, Department of Foreign Affairs and International Trade, 2007a).

[5] All details and legal documents pertaining to this case can be found in Mexico, Secretaría de Economía (2007).

effect of this new legislation has increased the government's capacity to gather information, scrutinize the flow of immigrants, and supervise financial transactions.

Additionally, mirroring the U.S. example, in April 2004 a comprehensive national
security policy was announced, for the first time ever in Canada (Canada, Privy
Council Office, 2004). The new policy creates a permanent National Security Advisory
Council and grants coordination powers to a newly created Department of Public
Safety and Emergency Preparedness. The policy addresses six strategic areas: intelligence, emergency planning and management, public health, transport security, border security, and international security. All new measures will be funded with
$690 million, in addition to the $7.7 billion already spent on security-related issues
since September 11.

Beyond these impacts across a wide array of public policies, from a political standpoint September 11 had critical effects on democracy—including human rights, civil
liberties, and electoral politics—and sovereignty in the two countries neighbouring
the United States (Castro-Rea, 2007). Canada and Mexico could not resist pressures
to conform to this new security environment because their governments felt that the
prosperity of each country was at stake. As we can see, regionalization enhances interdependence, which in turn makes weaker partners more vulnerable to the demands
of the stronger partner.

Summary

Regionalization is a process of growing importance in contemporary global politics. It
runs parallel and contributes to globalization, carving the world up into large and
distinct regions, many of which are governed through international agreements. Regions
do not emerge naturally: they are created according to the interests and strategic calculations of member states. They contribute to globalization, but they also compete
against each other for global influence. Regionalization affects both international relations and domestic politics but has, overall, tended to entrench existing disparities of
wealth and power, giving advantage to dominant political and economic countries. The
Canadian and Mexican experiences under NAFTA are indicative of this tendency. As a
result, American-style regionalization has been increasingly resisted by less developed
countries that are seeking alternatives.

For these reasons, it is not an exaggeration to say that regionalization is an integral
part of globalization. If current prospects are positive for regionalization, this does not
mean the trend cannot be stopped in the medium or long term. Countries marginalized
from the process of regionalization may call the process into question in multilateral fora,
such as the WTO. Moreover, the number of countries wary of U.S.-style regionalization is
on the rise, and these countries are either opting for the European model or stepping back
altogether from regionalization and its requirements for policy harmonization. In the
Americas, recently elected governments in Argentina, Brazil, Bolivia, Ecuador, and
Venezuela are distancing themselves from the model of regionalization inspired by

NAFTA. These opponents basically argue that the restrictions that these types of agreements impose are designed with economically powerful countries in mind, ignoring the development needs of weaker economies and ultimately leaving less competitive regions, economic sectors, and workers to fend for themselves when they are bypassed by the market. The resistance of these critics may be followed by other disgruntled countries around the world, especially once they realize trade liberalization is not a panacea for development and increased standards of living for everyone.

Alternative scenarios are actively being discussed among academics (Bello, 2002) and among global civil society organizations (North-South Institute, 2007). They include regionalization models that address human needs first and foremost, instead of focusing exclusively on increasing business opportunities and economic competitiveness. The latter objective, critics argue, is ultimately synonymous with catering to the needs of multinational corporations and countries of the wealthy North. These alternative scenarios have yet to have a significant impact in the governance of the global economy, but as the many failures of corporate-oriented regionalization become increasingly apparent, their influence will surely grow.

Discussion Questions

1. How are globalization and regionalization related to each other? Do they compete with one another or do they help each other?
2. Is it positive or negative for a country to get involved in a region?
3. What were the objectives pursued by the United States within NAFTA?
4. Who will likely prevail in the competition for world influence: NAFTA or the EU? Why?
5. What would a government require if it were to implement alternatives to regionalization?

References

Anonymous. 2007. "China Woos Cameroon." *Business Monitor International*, February 26.

Barry, Donald. 1995. "The Road to NAFTA" in D. Barry, Mark O. Dickerson, and James D. Gaisford, eds., *Toward a North American Community? Canada, the United States, and Mexico* (3–14). Boulder: Westview.

Bello, Walden. 2002. De-globalization: Ideas for a New World Economy. London: Zed Books.

Canada, Department of Foreign Affairs and International Trade. 2007a. Retrieved February 2007 from **www.international.gc.ca/tna-nac/nafta-en.asp**.

Canada, Department of Foreign Affairs and International Trade. 2007b. Retrieved July 2007 from **www.international.gc.ca/eet/pdf/PFACT_Ann_Merch_Trd_Ctry_2006_May_2007-en.pdf**.

Canada, Privy Council Office. 2004. *Securing an Open Society: Canada's National Security Policy*. Ottawa: PCO.

Castro-Rea, Julián. 2007 (forthcoming). "Assessing North American Politics After September 11: An Overview of Impacts on Continental Security, Democracy, and Sovereignty" in Jeffrey Ayres and Laura Macdonald, eds., *Contentious Politics in North America: National Protest and Transnational Collaboration Under Continental Integration*. Toronto: University of Toronto Press.

Ciccantell, Paul. 2001. "NAFTA and the Reconstruction of U.S. Hegemony: The Raw Materials Foundations of Economic Competitiveness." *Canadian Journal of Sociology*, 26-1, 57–87.

Clarkson, Stephen. 2002. *Uncle Sam and Us: Globalization, Neoconservatism and the Canadian State*. Toronto and Washington: University of Toronto Press-Woodrow Wilson Center Press.

Deblock, Christian and Michèle Rioux. 1993. "NAFTA: The Trump Card of the United States?" *Studies in Political Economy*, 41, 7–44.

Investopedia.com. (n.d.) "Economies of Scale." Retrieved February 2007 from **www.investopedia.com/terms/e/economiesofscale.asp**.

Lewis, Patsy. 2005. "An Assessment of the Development Potential of the FTAA and EPA for Small Developing States." Paper presented to the conference Re-Mapping the Americas: Globalization, Regionalization and the FTAA, University of the West Indies, St. Augustine, Trinidad and Tobago (October).

Mexico, Secretaría de Economía. 2007. Retrieved February 2007 from **www.economia-snci.gob.mx/sphp_pages/importa/sol_contro/consultoria/Casos_Mexico/Metalclad/Metalclad.htm**.

North-South Institute. 2007. Retrieved February 2007 from **www.nsi-ins.ca/english/default.asp**.

Secretariat of the African, Caribbean and Pacific Group of States. (n.d.) Retrieved February 2007 from **www.acpsec.org**.

United States, Office of the United States Trade Representative. (n.d.) Retrieved February 2007 from **www.ustr.gov/Trade_Agreements/Section_Index.html**.

Further Readings

Foot, Rosemary S., Neil Macfarlane, and Michael Mastaduno, eds. 2003. *US Hegemony and International Organizations*. Oxford: Oxford University Press.

Katzenstein, Peter J. 2005. *A World of Regions: Asia and Europe in the American Imperium*. Ithaca: Cornell University Press.

Schulz, Michael, Fredferick Söderbaum, and Joakim Ojendal. 2001. *Regionalization in a Globalizing World: A Comparative Perspective on Forms, Actors and Processes*. London: Zed.

Urmetzer, Peter. 2003. *From Free Trade to Forced Trade: Canada in the Global Economy*. Toronto: Penguin Canada.

Wilkinson, Rorden. 2006. *The WTO: Crisis and the Governance of Global Trade*. London: Routledge.

Weblinks

Asia Pacific Economic Cooperation
www.apec.org

European Commission
http://ec.europa.eu/index_en.htm

Foreign Affairs and International Trade Canada
www.international.gc.ca/commerce/menu-en.asp

NAFTA Secretariat
www.nafta-sec-alena.org/

World Trade Organization
www.wto.org

CHAPTER 27

RETHINKING POVERTY IN A GLOBAL ERA

Objectives

The stubborn persistence of poverty in a global era reinforces Henry George's observation made over a century ago: "The association of poverty with progress is the great enigma of our times" (George, 1880, 6). George's observation remains prophetic today. Never before has the world created so much wealth or been more capable of a fairer and more equitable distribution. Yet the current era of globalization is characterized by a "paradox of plenty" (Brodie, 2004): increased wealth creation is accompanied by rising levels of poverty and destitution, which are spatialized, gendered, and racialized (Lowell, 2006; Newell, 2005). This paradox is not unique to contemporary globalization. In the nineteenth century, capital expansion under Pax Britannica saw an increase in world trade and an improvement in wages and working conditions in the global North. These same global processes left stagnant, and at a subsistence level, the wages and working and living conditions in the global South (Bata and Bergesen, 2002, 2–6). By the late-twentieth century, the dominant trend was income concentration and a widening gap between rich and poor countries. While scholars differ on how to conceptualize this polarity—for example, "uneven globalization," global "winners" and

MALINDA
S. SMITH

"losers" (Kennedy, 1993), or "global apartheid" (Booker and Minter, 2001; Bond, 2006), there is consensus that poverty is uneven within and across geopolitical spaces.

This chapter explores various meanings and dimensions of poverty in an era of intensified globalization. It has several objectives. First, it provides a genealogy of poverty, mapping its contested conceptions, from low income and consumption to notions of human development and social exclusion. Second, the chapter explores the social dimensions of poverty, which have often been overlooked in more conventional analyses. Third, it examines efforts to rethink poverty as if these social dimensions mattered. Finally, the chapter concludes with a brief survey of proposals to ameliorate poverty and achieve what might be called a new "global social contract."

Introduction

As with so many critical concepts in the social sciences and humanities, what poverty is and what it means are contested. Definitions of "poverty" are shaped by notions of civilization, cultural norms, and values (Bush, 2007). Differences arise over how poverty is defined and measured as well as about the policies designed to reduce and, ultimately, eradicate it. Understandings of poverty are shaped by the unit of analysis and by space, time, and severity. The unit of analysis may be an individual, a social group (grouped by gender, age, or race, for example), a country, a region, or the globe. The spatial dimensions of poverty include the incidence and severity of poverty within countries, such as between rural and urban areas, and across global regions, such as between North and South. Poverty is shaped by time, with conditions of poverty being either temporary or chronic. Another dimension of poverty relates to its intensity or severity, such as between relative deprivation and absolute destitution. What any definition of poverty minimally entails is recognition "that significant numbers of people are living in intolerable circumstances where starvation is a constant threat, sickness is a familiar companion, and oppression is a fact of life" (Kanbur and Squire, 1999, 1).

Although inequality and poverty often are discussed in tandem, they are conceptually distinct. In an era of neo-liberalism, inequality has become a constitutive feature of the global economy (Bush, 2007, 1–22). Inequality is inclusive of both poverty and social welfare. Global poverty denotes the existence of people worldwide whose basic needs (such as food, clean water, and shelter) are not met and whose standard of living is below the norm, as determined by the societies or regions in which they live. Global poverty is a problem because people are living below subsistence, in conditions of immeasurable suffering, and this negatively affects their life chances. Ultimately, global poverty is a profound waste of human potential.

Global inequality, by contrast, refers to the skewed distribution worldwide of income, consumption, and other indicators of socio-economic well-being. Income and consumption are unequally distributed between the poor countries in the South and the rich countries in the North, and this concentration of wealth is deepening. Inequality thus calls into question the fairness of the global economy and the legitimacy of institutions of global governance, particularly the World Bank and the

International Monetary Fund (IMF). The two concepts—inequality and poverty—are interconnected insofar as a major factor in the increase in global poverty is unequal distribution of wealth and power, including access to and control of resources, such as land and water, as well as labour power and mobility (Bush, 2007, xiii, 81–114). Both concepts pose ethical challenges for academics, policy-makers, non-governmental organizations, and social justice activists committed to a more just world order.

Income inequality between rich and poor countries continues to increase in the twenty-first century. Where the income gap between the world's rich and poor countries was 3:1 in 1820, by 1950 it was 35:1, by 1997 it was 74:1, and by 2002 it was 82:1. A mere 20 percent of the world's population in the rich countries owns 86 percent of the world's gross domestic product (GDP). The combined wealth of the world's three richest *individuals* is greater than the combined GDP of the world's 48 poorest *countries*. While global per capita output has risen by 90 percent over the past 30 years, this is not the case for Africa, where the real per capita income has declined. It is now lower than it was in 1970. Africa is home to most of the countries in which at least 50 percent of the population live below the poverty line (World Bank, 2007). Of the 53 countries the Bank identifies as low-income or poor, 34 are in Sub-Saharan Africa. As well, 28 of the 30 least livable countries, as determined by quality of life, are on the African continent (UNDP, 2006).

While the data for the Middle East and Latin America are less grim, they do show that per capita income in these regions is stagnant or growing at a pace that is significantly lower than in the global North. In Asia, often advanced as the good news story for regional economic development, the picture is uneven. The majority of the world's poor live in India and rural China. In South Asia, home to 515 million poor people—more than the populations of Canada, the United States, and Mexico combined—the outlook is bleak. Poverty is concentrated in rural areas and primarily affects women, indigenous peoples, and ethnic minorities, who face cultural discrimination and lack access to land, water, and social services (Thapa, 2004). One regional development report noted that "during the globalisation phase about half-a-billion people in South Asia have experienced a decline in their incomes" (*Times of India Online*, February 14, 2002). The report concluded that globalization has conferred benefits on "a small minority of educated urban population," but overall income inequality has increased.

A Genealogy of Poverty

THROUGHOUT HISTORY, STUDENTS OF POLITICS, PHILOSOPHERS, AND ECONOMISTS, among others, have tried to make sense of poverty. In *Leviathan* (1651), philosopher Thomas Hobbes suggests that an individual's consent to a social contract would enable her to escape a life that was "poor, nasty, brutish, and short." A supreme authority would guarantee civil order, industry, and the conditions for wealth creation. In *The Wealth of Nations* (1776), political economist Adam Smith argued that national wealth was created through a market-based economy, free trade, and an "invisible hand" that would ensure balance within the economic order. By contrast, in *Capital* (1867), Karl Marx saw neither an authoritarian regime nor an invisible hand as necessary or sufficient for understanding the contradictory tendencies in the accumulation of capital that led to the creation of wealth for a few and, simultaneously, the impoverishment of the majority.

The examples of the late Mother Theresa, the "Saint of the Gutter," and various Roman Catholic friars and Buddhist monks draw attention to non-materialist conceptions of poverty. A spiritual understanding of poverty may require a vow of poverty, which is a voluntary, personal renunciation of private and communal material property as a means to achieving well-being. Ethical conceptions of poverty may entail judgments about "moral bankruptcy" and assumptions that an individual's laziness or personal choices lead to debilitating vices, such as gambling or addictions, and, ultimately, to poverty. Conversely, absolute destitution and starvation can lead to crime, and ethicists have debated whether it is best to understand thievery in such cases as a personal choice or the outcome of structural inequities. On the one hand, some conceptions of poverty draw our attention to voluntary action and personal choice as causes of poverty, whereas other conceptions point to structural and societal factors that impose limits on escaping poverty. As well, historically there have been conflicting political and social responses to the poor, ranging from empathy and compassion to pity, moral disdain, and even fear.

Understanding the "who" of poverty has shifted over time and space. During the Middle Ages, for example, there was a social class of **paupers** whose well-being partly depended on a sense of moral obligation in their fellow citizens; paupers met or supplemented their basic needs through the charity of churches or private philanthropy. There were moral overtones to the early nineteenth century **Poor Laws**. First introduced in the United Kingdom, these laws served as a way of getting the poor off the streets and into poorhouses, where they would be taught the "value of work" and thus avoid laziness or vagrancy. The poor themselves were blamed for their plight, rather than economic or social structures.

Since the mid-1940s, the IMF and the World Bank adopted a narrow conception of poverty, based primarily on economic indicators. Poverty was conceptualized in terms of gross national product (GNP), household income, consumption, and monetary access to the market. The World Bank defines poverty as "the inability to attain a minimum standard of living." This minimum standard of living benchmark was further subdivided into two other criteria: (1) the ability to purchase minimum daily nutritional requirements as determined by the society in which one lives, and (2) the ability to meet basic needs that are shaped by an assessment of "the cost of participating in the everyday life of society" (World Bank, 1990, 26). In both cases, the World Bank prioritized income and consumption over broader notions of social well-being.

In the 1990s, the World Bank and the IMF reluctantly acknowledged that their post–World War II development strategies had failed to reduce poverty or limit the uneven impact of globalization. Eduardo Aninat, the IMF's managing director, stated, "Overall, the number of very poor—those living on less than $1 per day—has stayed roughly the same over the past decade; only limited progress has been made in reducing the share of the world population living in poverty" (Aninat, 2000). Yet the statistics cannot capture the whole story of the extreme conditions of destitution, ill-health, hunger, chronic under-employment, and human insecurity in which half of humanity lives.

Mapping Social Dimensions of Poverty

TODAY, POVERTY IS A COMPLEX, MULTI-CAUSAL PHENOMENON, WHICH IS SPATIALIZED, gendered, and racialized worldwide. Notions of poverty take into account social well-being and involve comparisons between (and within) different countries and regions. Poverty is often distinguished between relative and absolute measurements. **Relative poverty** takes into account the unequal distribution of income within a given society. Roach and Roach (1972, 23) suggest relative poverty relates to those at "the bottom segment of the income distribution." This notion suggests that a person may be able to acquire adequate food, clothing, clean water, and shelter but that this exhausts his or her resources, leaving nothing for other things, such as telephone, transportation, or even reading materials. Trying to capture the cross-cultural variations in the daily lived experiences of the poor is difficult. Can we compare—and if so, how—deprivation in an affluent society such as Canada with, for example, the experience in an impoverished society such as Haiti or Nicaragua? In Canada and the United States, some people are poor relative to others in these societies. However, the poor in the North American region may be considered wealthy in relation to the poor in South Asia. **Absolute poverty**, on the other hand, measures physical deprivation. In 1978, World Bank president Robert McNamara coined the concept to characterize a condition "so limited by malnutrition, illiteracy, disease, squalid surroundings, high infant mortality, and low life expectancy as to be beneath any reasonable definition of human decency" (quoted in Singer, 1979, 158). Absolute poverty has at its "absolutist core" the belief that if there is hunger or starvation, avoidable disease, lack of access to education, or a life of shame, then it does not "matter what the relative picture looks like" (Sen, 1983).

Despite claims of the "death of distance" accompanying neo-liberal globalization, physical and social geography do matter in global mappings of the incidence and severity of poverty. Over the decade between 1993 and 2002, the number of "$1 a day poor" declined in rural areas by 150 million but increased in urban areas by 50 million (Ravallion, Chen, and Sangraula, 2007). The **urbanization of poverty**, expected to increase as one in two people are born into urban spaces, varies across the world's regions. The highest percentage of rural poor is concentrated in Asia (633 million), followed by Sub-Saharan Africa (204 million), and Latin America and the Caribbean (76 million). While East Asia has the smallest number of rural poor, in Eastern and Central Europe, there is a ruralization of poverty (Ravallion, Chen, and Sangraula, 2007). An additional 1.5 billion people live below the poverty line of $2 per day, and their numbers are expected to increase by 25 million per year. In total, some 3 billion people—half of the world's population—live on less than $2 per day. This economic insecurity gives rise to significant migration, with some 3 million people annually migrating from poor to rich countries, and even greater numbers between poor countries such as from Bangladesh to India, or Egypt to the Persian Gulf states (World Bank, 2004; Population Reference Bureau, 2006, 2005).

Poverty is also shaped by a complex intersection of gender and age. Some 70 percent of those living in extreme poverty are girls and women (UN, 1995a, 4), giving rise to the idea of the **feminization of poverty**. According to Nilüfer Cagatay (1998, 3), the feminization of poverty is a short-hand concept that captures at least three things: first, there is a higher *incidence* of poverty among women; second, there is greater *severity* in the experience of poverty by women; and, third, the incidence of women's poverty is *increasing* at a faster rate when compared with the incidence among men. Women are disadvantaged in both urban and rural areas in their access to nutrition, education, health services, and employment and wages. This disadvantage arises from at least three overlapping factors: first, the rise in the number of female-headed households; second, cultural factors that shape intra-household and labour market inequalities among women and men; and, third, neo-liberal macroeconomics such as structural adjustment programs (SAPs), which have disproportionately harmed the well-being of girls and women (Moghaden, 2005).

Both the very old and the very young, especially girls and women, are adversely affected by poverty. One in two children worldwide—one billion—lives in poverty, with the majority living in the global South (UNICEF, 2005). UNICEF names this global phenomenon "childhood under threat," with young lives shaped by silent and forgotten killers: poverty, conflict, and preventable diseases such as HIV/AIDS, malaria, and pneumonia. Children live in hazardous conditions in overcrowded shantytowns and urban slums, where they lack basic necessities such as shelter, adequate nutrition, and access to schooling (UNICEF, 2000, 1). Stolen childhood results when young lives are marked by the intersection of poverty, violence, exploitation, and abuse. This includes the trafficking and sexual exploitation of children (often, but not exclusively, young girls); indentured and forced child labour; or the kidnapping of children to serve as soldiers or to become "bush" or "rebel wives" and, in turn, give birth to further stigmatized "rebel babies" (Baldi and Mackenzie, 2007). Gender and age intersect both in the incidence of poverty and in efforts to combat poverty. In its 2007 report, UNICEF notes that "gender equality produces a double dividend: it benefits both women and children. Healthy, educated, and empowered women have healthy, educated, and confident daughters and sons. The amount of influence women have over the decisions in the household has been shown to positively impact the nutrition, health care and education of their children" (UNICEF, 2007, 2–3). Gender equality not only positively correlates with the well-being of children; "without it, it will be impossible to create a world of equity, tolerance and shared responsibility—a world that is fit for children."

An under-theorized area in the international literature is the **racialization of poverty** and global inequality (Kothari, 2006; Razack, 2004). Manning Marable suggests the problem may be understood as one "of global apartheid: the racialized division and stratification of resources, wealth, and power that separates" the world's rich, located primarily in the global North, "from the billions of mostly black, brown, indigenous, undocumented immigrant and poor people across the planet" (Marable, 2004). The world witnessed the ugly intersection of race, poverty, and marginality when Hurricane Katrina devastated the city of New Orleans and part of the Gulf Coast of the United States on August 29, 2005, exposing Third World conditions within the so-called First World. The slow response of the Bush administration to the plight of those whose lives were devastated by Katrina exposed what some critics refer to as the "two Americas," one made up of those who are rich and mostly white, and the other of those who are poor and mostly racialized minorities such as blacks and Latinos. It led U.S. Secretary of State Condoleezza Rice to admit that, even in the richest country in the world, "There are still places that race and poverty are a huge problem in the United States, and we've got to deal with that" (CNN, 2005; Fletcher, 2005).

Stephen Lewis, former UN special envoy for HIV/AIDS, argues that the epidemic's devastating impact on Africa has not been taken seriously by Western countries because of silent racism. According to Lewis, "In my soul, I honestly believe that an unthinking strain of subterranean racism is the only way to explain the moral default of the developed world, in refusing to provide the resources which could save the mothers of Africa" (Lewis, 2002, 4; Kubacki, 2006). Lewis argued that it is this same racism and the way it intersects with poverty that also led to the failure to act to prevent the 1994 genocide in Rwanda. Lewis's view echoes that of Lt.-General Roméo Dallaire, who led the UN peacekeeping mission to Rwanda when the international community withdrew its forces as the genocide was under way. In his memoirs, Dallaire (2003) attributes the genocide to xenophobia, but the failure to protect likewise was shaped by racism and global indifference to Rwanda's impoverished people, who might have fared better if they had oil or other resources, rather than being merely "humans."

Rethinking Poverty as if the Social Mattered

THIS SECTION EXPLORES ANOTHER ASPECT OF POVERTY, ONE THAT TRIES TO account for anti-poverty thinking that takes seriously the conditions of "humans" and their social well-being worldwide. It provides a brief survey of the broadening of anti-poverty thinking to account for "the social," including the emergence of human development, social capital, and social exclusion.

The meaning of poverty began to broaden in the 1990s with the introduction by the United Nations Development Programme (UNDP) of the idea of **human development**. It drew attention to "the social" in development and provided an understanding of development and poverty beyond economic indicators and basic needs. This change in thinking was strongly influenced by Nobel Prize winner Amartya Sen and his influential book *Development as Freedom* (1999). In it, he argued, "Development requires the removal of major sources of unfreedom: poverty as well as tyranny, poor economics as well as systemic social deprivation, neglect of public facilities as well as intolerance or overactivity of repressive states" (1999, 3). Similarly, the UNDP's conception of human development prioritized non-monetary and social-well-being indicators, such as access to health care and knowledge, political and cultural freedoms, and participation in the everyday life of the community. Given the shared aim of expanding capabilities, both the World Bank and the UNDP came to conceive of development as freedom. However, where the Bank focuses almost exclusively on economic freedom and financial and material well-being, the UNDP tries to capture a broader conception of freedom, one that is inclusive of social, political, and cultural freedom, as well as notions of social citizenship rights.

By the mid-1990s, conceptions of poverty also encompassed an understanding of risk and vulnerability as determinants of transient or chronic poverty. One form of vulnerability arises from variable employment, income, and living standards. Vulnerability also arises from the lack of social and political rights that create conditions of fear and insecurity. Risks can arise from complex factors, including environmental and health hazards, such as crop failure and famine; personal insecurity, such as sexual exploitation or land eviction; and macroeconomic shocks. Those with more resources are better able to deal with exposure to risk and have greater access to risk-coping mechanisms, including social safety nets.

Thinking on poverty has further broadened to encompass the concept of **social capital** (Bourdieu, 1986; Coleman, 1988; Fine, 2001a). In a nutshell, social capital suggests that "relationships matter" and that "who" we know, including our social networks, constitutes a kind of capital.

While the debate about the relevance of social capital for development began in academic circles in France and the United States in the 1970s and 1980s, a variety of actors soon picked up the concept and used it in different ways. The World Bank and other official bodies, such as the Organisation for Economic Co-operation and Development (OECD), initially embraced the concept of social capital as a way of integrating social theory with economic theory, claiming that human well-being depended on economic development (Field, 2003, 9; Woolcock and Narayan, 2000). Promoted by the World Bank, social capital soon became associated with faith in civil society organizations as essentials to the success of a host of good governance and anti-poverty initiatives.

In the political economy of development literature, proponents suggest social capital is the "missing link" in development discourse, policy, and practice. According to the opening lines of the World Bank's PovertyNet website, "*Social capital* refers to the norms and networks that enable collective action . . . social cohesion—social capital—

is critical for poverty alleviation and sustainable human and economic development" (PovertyNet, 2004). Under its explanation of what social capital is, the site suggests, "Social capital is not just the sum of the institutions which underpin a society—it is the glue that holds them together" (PovertyNet, 2002). Critics argue that the World Bank's conception of social capital in development underplays the unequal distribution of wealth as well as social relations of domination and exploitation in the accumulation of financial and social capital (Fine, 2001b).

The mid- to late-1990s also witnessed the emergence in Europe of the idea of **social exclusion** in theorizing on poverty. The concept of social exclusion widened the conceptual gap in how poverty is understood in the North and the South. The earlier conception of poverty within the European Commission (EC) referred to limited material—social and cultural resources that excluded a person's participation in a "minimum acceptable way of life"—as determined by the states in which they live (Schultz, 2002, 120). Like human development, social exclusion is much broader than income-poverty. The concept first emerged in French policy discourse as a way of addressing "new poverty"—that is, the problems that arise from inadequate social insurance and social safety nets for the chronically un- and under-employed.

There are competing conceptions of social exclusion. Despite a diversity of definitions, social exclusion as a concept offers a broader understanding of the "multiple forms of social disadvantage—income, social, political, and cultural—and thus encompasses theories of citizenship and racial-ethnic inequality as well as poverty and long-term unemployment." Today, the narrower definition of income and subsistence is used primarily in explanations of poverty in the global South. The more multi-causal conception of poverty is used in the EU and global North. An important cautionary note is whether, over time, the spatially specific definitions of poverty will distort our understanding of "who" the poor are—in the global North and the global South—as well as lead to a kind of geopolitical–conceptual gap in understanding "why" some people are poor.

Toward a New "Global Social Contract"?

THIS SECTION PROVIDES A BRIEF COMMENTARY ON THE CONTRADICTIONS between neo-liberal globalization and a desire to reduce poverty and achieve social well-being. Successive waves of economic globalization, failed anti-poverty strategies, and the many unfulfilled international promises to eradicate poverty have contributed to the problem's deepening worldwide. The modern anti-poverty agenda gained international prominence with at least two developments in the mid-1960s. United States President Lyndon B. Johnson declared a "war on poverty" in his State of the Union address of January 8, 1964. Second, Robert McNamara made global poverty eradication the priority of his World Bank presidency.

Over the next 30 years a number of global commitments were made to reduce poverty, including the international development targets (IDTs) set at Copenhagen in 1995, the introduction of Poverty Reduction Strategy Papers in 1999, and the Millennium Development Goals (MDGs) in 2000. Sadly, Oxfam International (2000) characterized this history as one of "missed targets" and "broken promises."

The shift to a social and a pro-poor agenda required rethinking the anti-poverty strategy that had dominated policy thinking since World War II. This strategy was heavily influenced by neo-classical economics and the Washington Consensus (Fine et al., 2001). The World Bank and the IMF promoted economic growth as the strategy by which development would occur. This strategy at best prioritized "getting the market fundamentals right" and at worst showed an indifference to poverty and social well-being (Taylor, 2006). Whatever the country, this one-size-fits-all strategy promoted a series of neo-liberal policy prescriptions that called for deregulation, currency devaluation, trade and financial liberalization, privatization of parastatals, and reduction of public enterprises (Smith, 2006). Little to no distinction was drawn between public enterprises that performed a primarily social function and those that did not. One devastating result was drastic cuts to public expenditure in the areas of health, education, and social services, which were further exacerbated by the introduction of user fees that restricted access to the poor, especially in rural areas.

The consensus at the 1995 World Summit for Social Development (WSSD) in Copenhagen was that the social aspects of poverty mattered. The gathering called for greater social investment to reduce poverty, illiteracy, and health deprivation. Some 117 governments reached consensus on a global agenda for poverty reduction. They committed to reducing global poverty by half by the year 2015. The WSSD's Declaration and Program of Action characterized poverty reduction as "an ethical, social, political and economic imperative of human kind." The WSSD also endorsed the 20/20 Initiative, which called for South governments to spend 20 percent of their domestic budgets and Northern governments 20 percent of their foreign aid budgets on funding anti-poverty and social programs in education and health. A year later, the "donor's club," constituted primarily by the Development Assistance Committee (DAC) of the OECD, affirmed the Copenhagen consensus on poverty reduction. The DAC also committed to related targets in areas of social well-being, including literacy, education, and health services.

Despite a plethora of declarations, commitments, and targets, little progress has been made in eradicating global poverty. The intransigence led to global social protests from Seattle in 1999 to the "Make Poverty History" campaign unveiled at the 2006 G8 Meeting at Gleneagles, Scotland. Confronted with the profound policy failures, local and global protests, and the call for their dismantlement, the World Bank and the IMF unveiled a new "pragmatic neo-liberalism," which was to include elements of a social agenda. Beginning in 1999 the policy shift included the IMF's adopting poverty reduction as one of its core objectives, and the release by the president of the World Bank of a *Comprehensive Development Framework*, which has been called a "new development paradigm" that underwrites a new "architecture of aid" (Wolfensohn and Fischer, 2000).

In 1999, the World Bank and the IMF adopted Poverty Reduction Strategy Papers (PRSPs) as a major element of their new development thinking. The IMF describes PRSPs as "the macroeconomic, structural and social policies and programs that a country will pursue over several years to promote broad-based growth and reduce poverty" (IMF, 2005). PRSP principles include local ownership, partnership among stakeholders, enhanced participation, and results orientation. To address previous criticisms of an externally imposed, top-down, and uniform approach, the IMF requires that these principles, along with Putnam-inspired notions of social capital, be incorporated into new anti-poverty strategies fashioned in each country. Debtor countries in the global South must adopt PRSPs to receive debt relief and concessional loans.

In September 2000, the UN Millennium Summit opened in New York with a call by world governments to eradicate poverty, and some 149 countries committed to do so as well as to achieve the related Millennium Development Goals (MDGs). All the major international organizations released substantial reports on poverty.[1] The World Bank and the IMF also decided that PRSPs would now require a program of action to achieve the MDGs, particularly the goal of reducing poverty by half. There has been uneven progress in achieving global anti-poverty and social well-being targets, with variations across regions, within countries, and between social groups (see Table 27.1). Two examples are illustrative: first, despite the optimism of the 2007 MDG review, there is real pessimism about whether much of Africa will achieve the MDG targets by 2015 (UN DESA, 2007). A second example is the Copenhagen target, incorporated into the MDGs, to achieve gender equity for girls in primary and secondary education by 2005; this target was not achieved.

Despite this alphabet soup of policy changes, the new anti-poverty and social policy agendas appear as "add-ons" that fit uncomfortably with the IMF and the World Bank's macroeconomic agenda. It remains to be seen whether the PRSPs and MDGs can square with the neo-liberal macroeconomic policies and desired social outcomes. Moreover, the commitment to financing development, through increased official development aid called for in Copenhagen and various G8 Summits, often is expressed and rarely is achieved. At a 2002 Financing for Development Conference in Monterrey, Mexico, 22 countries of the OECD's DAC committee made a commitment to increase official development aid (ODA). In 2006, only five of the OECD's 22 countries—Denmark, Luxembourg, Netherlands, Norway, and Sweden—achieved the UN foreign aid target of 0.7 percent of gross national income (OECD, 2007). In 2006 ODA declined by 5.1 percent from the previous year, to $103.09 billion (USD). As well, with the exception of debt relief, ODA to Africa was static. One of the most significant changes in ODA occurred in Canada (a drop of 9.2 percent), which resulted from a decline in debt relief and humanitarian aid to Africa.

---

[1] The World Bank subtitled its report *Attacking Poverty* (2000/2001), and in 2003 and 2004, its reports all prioritized poverty reduction. In March 2000, UNICEF released *Poverty Reduction Begins with Children*. A month later, the UNDP followed with *Overcoming Poverty* (2000) and again in 2003 with *Millennium Development Goals: A Compact Among Nations to End Human Poverty*.

Table 27.1 Millennium Development Goals (MDGs): 2007 Progress

Goals and Targets	Africa		Asia				Latin America & Caribbean*
	Northern	Sub-Saharan	Eastern	South	Southern	Western	
Goal 1 Eradicate extreme poverty and hunger							
Reduce extreme poverty by half	TE	TNM	TM	TM	TE	NP	TNM
Reduce hunger by half	TE	TNM	TE	TE	TNM	NP	TE
Goal 2 Achieve universal primary education							
Universal primary schooling	TE	TNM	NP	TNM	TE	TNM	TM
Goal 3 Promote gender equality and empower women							
Equal girls' enrolment in primary school	TE	TNM	TM	TM	TE	TE	TM
Women's share of paid employment	TNM	TNM	TE	TNM	TNM	TNM	TE
Women's equal representation in national parliaments	TNM	TNM	NP	TNM	TNM	TNM	TNM
Goal 4 Reduce child mortality							
Reduce mortality of under five-year-olds by two-thirds	TE	NP	TE	TE	TNM	TNM	TE
Measles immunization	TM	TE	NP	TNM	TNM	TM	TM
Goal 5 Improve maternal health							
Reduce maternal mortality by three-quarters*	TNM	NP	TE	TNM	NP	TNM	TNM
Goal 6 Combat HIV/AIDS, malaria, and other diseases*							
Halt and reverse spread of HIV/AIDS	TNM	NP	NP	TNM	TNM	TNM	TNM
Halt and reverse spread of malaria*	TE	NP	TNM	TNM	TNM	TE	TNM
Halt and reverse spread of tuberculosis	TE	NP	TNM	TNM	TNM	TE	TE
Goal 7 Ensure environmental sustainability							
Reverse loss of forests**	TE	NP	TM	NP	NP	TNM	NP
Halve proportion without improved drinking water	TE	NP	TE	TE	TM	TM	TM
Halve proportion without sanitation	TE	NP	TE	TE	NP	TE	TE
Improve the lives of slum-dwellers	TE	TNM	TNM	TE	TE	TNM	TE

continued

Table 27.1   Continued

Goals and Targets	Africa Northern	Africa Sub-Saharan	Asia Eastern	Asia South	Asia Southern	Asia Western	Latin America & Caribbean*
Goal 8 Develop a global partnership for development							
Youth unemployment**	TNM	TNM	TM	NP	TNM	NP	NP
Internet users	TE	NP	TE	TE	TNM	TE	TM

Country experiences in each region may differ significantly from the regional average. For the regional groupings and country data, see **mdgs.un.org.***

Legend

Target already met or very close to being met.   TM

Target is expected to be met by 2015 if prevailing trends persist, or the problem that this target is designed to address is not a serious concern in the region.*   TE

Target is not expected to be met by 2015.   TNM

No progress, or a deterioration of reversal.*   NP

Notes

*The available data for maternal mortality and malaria do not allow a trend analysis. Progress in the chart has been accessed by the responsible agencies on the basis of proxy indicators.

**The assessment is based on a new methodology and therfore not comparable with previous assessments.

SOURCE: Table modified from UN Department of Economic and Social Affairs (DESA), Statistics Division, "Millennium Development Goals: 2007 Progress Chart" (2007), http://unstats.un.org/unsd/mdg/MDG_Report_2007_Progress_Chart_en.pdf.

"Madness" is how former World Bank president James Wolfensohn characterized global spending priorities in the new millennium (Fickling, 2004). "We have got it tremendously wrong," Wolfensohn stated about the global community's response to poverty and under-development compared with, for example, military and defence spending. For instance, over a trillion dollars a year is spent on defence, 20 times more than is spent "on trying to give hope to people" (Fickling, 2004). This disparity suggests that rich countries do not take seriously their global commitments to poverty reduction.

Two years before he became Britain's prime minister, Gordon Brown published an editorial in which he stressed the global challenges posed by poverty and HIV/AIDS, and why it was important for rich countries to act. "Four people a minute die of AIDS. Eleven million children are orphaned in Africa alone. Another 20 million are expected to lose one or both parents in the next six years." He therefore expressed an urgent call to the North "to act on the scourge of poverty and disease" (Brown, 2004). Less was spent on development aid and poverty reduction in 2004 than was being spent 40 years previously. Further, despite "free trade talk," in 2005 rich countries spent some $283 billion on domestic agricultural subsidies, which represented 29 percent of total farm income (Modeley, 2006); this is less than the same countries spend on foreign aid to poor countries. The major challenge to ameliorating poverty, then, is not resources but a lack of political will. As the history of anti-poverty initiatives suggests, there is much reason for pessimism. Whether there is the political will to achieve what Brazilian president Luiz Inácio Lula da Silva called "a New World Social Contract," to eradicate hunger and poverty and improve social well-being at home and worldwide, remains to be seen (da Silva, 2004).

Summary

This chapter has explored the paradoxes, persistence, incidence, and severity of poverty in an era of unprecedented wealth creation. Twenty-first-century poverty is a complex, multi-causal phenomenon that is spatialized, gendered, and racialized on a global scale. The chapter mapped the multiple factors that continue to shape poverty, including space, place, and time. The paradox of poverty amid plenty laid waste to familiar claims that economic growth would underwrite poverty alleviation and that social well-being would accompany economic growth. Efforts to rethink poverty and its reduction have been shaped by a growing recognition that the social matters. This recognition has generated important thinking on human development, social capital, and social exclusion, as well as a plethora of international anti-poverty commitments, including the MDGs and PRSPs. Despite these commitments, the history of global initiatives to end poverty has been littered with broken promises and dashed hopes. If there is a "lack," it is not of ideas or resources; rather, it is in the area of global leadership and political will to create a new global social contract to make poverty history.

Discussion Questions

1. What do you think is the most compelling explanation for the incidence of poverty?

2. Why is it important to rethink poverty in terms of the social?

3. Do you think the divergent approaches to explaining poverty—subsistence income in the South and social exclusion in the North—will lead to a geopolitical–conceptual gap that affects (a) how we understand poverty; (b) who we consider poor; and (c) why some people are poor?

4. To what extent are the feminization and racialization of poverty problems in your community or country?

5. Do you think it is likely that poverty will be eradicated in your lifetime?

References

Aninat, Eduardo. 2000. "Making Globalisation Work for the Poor." Remarks by Mr. Eduardo Aninat, Deputy Managing Director of the IMF at the German Foundation for International Development, Berlin, March 14, 2000.

Baldi, Giulia and Megan Mackenzie. 2007. "Silent Identities in Sierra Leone" in R. Charli Carpenter, ed., *Born of War: Protecting Children of Sexual Violence Survivors in Conflict Zones*. Bloomington, CT: Kumarian Press, Inc.

Bankston, C.L. and M. Zhou. 2002. "Social Capital Process: The Meanings and Problems of a Theoretical Metaphor." *Sociological Inquiry*, 72, 2, 285–317.

Bata, Michelle and Albert J. Bergesen. "Global Inequality: An Introduction." *Journal of World-Systems Research*, 7, 1 (Winter 2002), 2–6.

Bessis, Sophie. 1995. "From Social Exclusion to Social Cohesion: A Policy Agenda." Management of Social Transformations (MOST), Policy Paper No. 2 (2–4 March). Retrieved on February 18, 2004, from **www.unesco.org/most/besseng.htm**.

Bond, Patrick. 2006. "North Versus South: Expect More Global Apartheid—and South Africa's Collaboration—in 2006." *MR Zine* (Monthly Review).

———. 2004. *Against Global Apartheid: South Africa Meets the World Bank, International Monetary Fund and International Finance*. London: Zed Books.

Booker, Salih and William Minter. 2001. "Global Apartheid." *The Nation* (July 9).

Bordieu, Pierre. 1980. "Le capital social: notes provisoires." *Actes de la récherche en sciences sociales*, 2–3.

———. 1986. "The Forms of Capital" in J.G. Richardson, ed., *Handbook of Theory and Research for the Sociology of Education*. New York: Greenwood Press, 241–258.

Brodie, Janine. 2004. "Globalism and the Paradoxes of Social Citizenship." *Citizenship Studies*, 8, 4 (November).

Brown, Gordon. 2004. Speech by the Chancellor of the Exchequer Gordon Brown at the conference "Making Globalisation Work for All—The Challenge of Delivering the Monterrey Consensus," United Kingdom Treasury, London, February 16.

Bush, Ray. 2007. *Poverty and Neoliberalism: Persistence and Reproduction in the Global South.* London and Ann Arbor, MI: Pluto Press.

Byrne, David. 1999. *Social Exclusion.* Buckingham: Open University Press.

Çağatay, Nilüfer. 1998. "Gender and Poverty." UNDP Social Development and Poverty Elimination Division, Working Paper Series No. 5 (May).

CNN. 2005. "Rice: Disaster Shows 'Ugly Way' Race, Poverty Collide." CNN.com, Tuesday, September 13. Retrieved from **www.cnn.com/2005/POLITICS/ 09/13/katrina.rice/index.html**.

Coleman, J. 1988. "Social Capital in the Creation of Human Capital." *American Journal of Sociology*, 94, 95–120.

Dallaire, Roméo. 2003. *Shake Hands with the Devil.* Toronto: Random House Canada.

da Silva, Luiz Inácio Lula. 2004. Speech delivered at the conference "Making Globalisation Work for All—The Challenge of Delivering the Monterrey Consensus." United Kingdom Treasury, London, February 16.

Fickling, David. 2004. "World Bank Condemns Defense Spending." *Guardian Weekly*, Saturday, February 14. Retrieved February 14, 2004, from **www.guardian.co.uk/ print/0,3858,4858685-103681,00.html**.

Field, John. 2003. *Social Capital.* London and New York: Routledge.

Fine, B. 2001a. *Social Capital Versus Social Theory: Political Economy and Social Science at the Turn of the Millennium.* London and New York, Routledge.

———. 2001b. "The Social Capital of the World Bank" in B. Fine, C. Lapavitsas, and J. Pincus, eds., *Development Policy in the Twenty-First Century: Beyond the Washington Consensus.* New York: Routledge, 136–54.

Fletcher, Michael A. 2005. "Katrina Pushes Issues of Race and Poverty at Bush." *Washington Post*, Monday, September 12: A02.

Fukuyama, Francis. 1996. *Trust: The Social Virtues and the Creation of Prosperity.* Free Press.

George, Henry. 1880. *Progress and Poverty*, 4th edition. New York: Blackwell.

Gordon, D. and P. Spicker, eds. 1999. *The International Glossary on Poverty.* London: Zed Books.

Gordon, D. and P. Townsend, eds. 2002. *Breadline Europe: The Measurement of Poverty.* Bristol: The Policy Press.

International Monetary Fund. 2005. "Fact Sheet-Poverty Reduction Strategy Papers (PRSP)." Washington, D.C.: IMF, September, **www.imf.org/external/np/exr/ facts/prsp.htm**.

Kanbur, Ravi and Lyn Squire. 1999. "The Evolution of Thinking About Poverty: Exploring the Interactions." World Bank, Washington, D.C., September.

Kennedy, Paul. 1993. "Preparing for the 21st Century: Winners and Losers." *The New York Review of Books*, 40, 4 (February 11).

Kothari, Uma. 2006. "An Agenda for Thinking About 'Race' in Development." *Progress in Development Studies*, Vol. 6, No. 1, 9–23.

Kubacki, Maria. 2007. "UN Envoy Says Racism Behind West's Inaction Against HIV/AIDS." *Ottawa Citizen*, September 7.

Levitas, Ruth. 1998. *The Inclusive Society? Social Exclusion and New Labour.* London: Macmillan.

Lewis, Stephen. 2002. Speech of the UN Special Envoy on HIV/AIDS, African Religious Leaders Assembly on Children and HIV/AIDS, Nairobi, Kenya, June 10.

Lowell, Peggy. 2006. "Race, Gender, and Work in São Paulo, Brazil, 1960–2000." *Latin American Research Review*, 41, 3 (2006): 63–87.

Marable, Manning. 2004. "Globalization and Racialization." *ZNet*, August 13, 2005, 1–5.

Newell, Peter. "Race, Class and the Global Politics of Environmental Inequality." *Global Environmental Politics*, 5, 3 (August 2005): 70–94.

Organisation for Economic Co-operation and Development. 2007. "Development Aid for OECD Countries Fell 5.1% in 2006," online at **www.oecd.org/home, April 3, 2007**.

Oxfam International. 1995. *Poverty Report.* Oxford: Oxfam UK.

———. 2000. "Missing the Target: The Price of Empty Promises." Report to the Special Session of the General Assembly to Review and Access Implementation of the Declaration and Programme of Action, Adopted by the World Summit for Social Development, Geneva, June 26–30.

Population Reference Bureau. 2006. "World Population Data Sheet: International Migration Is Reshaping United States, Global Economy." Washington, D.C.: World Population Bureau. **www.prb.org**.

———. 2005. "2005 World Population Data Sheet." Washington, D.C.: World Population Bureau. **www.prb.org**.

PovertyNet. 2002. "What Is Social Capital?" The World Bank Group, PovertyNet, last updated October 10, 2002, at **www1.worldbank.org/prem/poverty/scapital/whatsc.htm**.

PovertyNet. 2003. "Social Capital for Development." The World Bank Group, PovertyNet, Social Capital Home, last updated October 7, 2004, at **www1.worldbank.org/prem/poverty/scapital/index.htm**.

Putnam, Robert D. 1993. *Making Democracy Work: Civic Traditions in Modern Italy.* Princeton: Princeton University Press.

Ravallion, Martin, Shaohua Chen, and Prem Sangraula. 2007. "New Evidence on the Urbanization of Global Poverty." World Bank Policy Research Working Paper No. 4199 (April 1), available at SSRN: **http://ssrn.com/abstract=980817**.

Razack, Sherene. 2004. *Dark Threats and White Knights: The Somalia Affair, Peacekeeping and the New Imperialism.* Toronto: University of Toronto Press.

Roach, J.L. and J.K. Roach, eds. 1972. *Poverty: Selected Readings.* Harmondsworth: Penguin.

Schultz, Bernd. 2002. "A European Definition of Poverty: The Fight Against Poverty and Social Exclusion in the Member States of the European Union" in Peter Townsend and David Gordon, eds., *World Poverty: New Policies to Defeat an Old Enemy.* Bristol: The Policy Press, 119–145.

Seager, Ashley. 2007. "Gap Between Rich and Poor Widens." *The Guardian,* Wednesday, June 20, 2007, **www.guardian.co.uk/business/2007/jun/20/ globalisation.ukeconomy**.

Sen, Amartya. 1976. "Poverty: An Ordinal Approach to Measurement." *Econometrica,* 44, 2, 291–331.

———. 1981. *Poverty and Famines: An Essay on Entitlement and Deprivation.* Oxford: Clarendon Press.

———. 1983. "Poor Relatively Speaking." *Oxford Economic Papers,* 35, 135–169.

———. 1999. *Development as Freedom.* Oxford: Oxford University Press.

Sen, Binayak. (n.d.) "Poverty in Bangladesh: A Review." Bangladesh Institute of Development Studies. Retrieved on February 13, 2004, from **www.bids-bd.org/za**.

Silver, H. 1994. "Social Exclusion and Social Solidarity: Three Paradigms." *International Labour Review,* 133, 5–6: 531–578.

Singer, P. 1979. *Practical Ethics.* Cambridge: Cambridge University Press.

Smith, Malinda S., ed. 2006. *Beyond the "African Tragedy": Discourses on Development and the Global Economy.* Aldershot: Ashgate.

Taylor, Ian. 2006. "When 'Good Economics' Does Not Make Good Sense" in Malinda S. Smith, ed., *Beyond the "African Tragedy": Discourses on Development and the Global Economy.* Aldershot: Ashgate, 85–104.

Thapa, Ganesh. 2004. "Rural Poverty Reduction Strategy for South Asia." Australian National University, ASARC Working Paper 2004–06 (April 2004), 1–27, **http://ideas.repec.org/p/pas/asarcc/2004-06.html**.

Thompson, Allan, ed. 2007. *The Media and the Rwandan Genocide.* New York: Pluto, and Ottawa: IDRC.

Townsend, Peter. 1985. "A Sociological Approach to the Measurement of Poverty: A Rejoinder to Professor Amartya Sen." *Oxford Economic Papers,* 37, 659–668.

United Nations. 1995a. *The World's Women 1995: Trends and Statistics.* New York: UN.

———. 1995b. *The Copenhagen Declaration and Programme of Action: World Summit for Social Development.* New York: UN.

———. 1999. "Further Initiatives for the Implementation of the Outcome of the World Social Summit for Social Development." Report of the Secretary General, Preparatory Committee for the Special Session of the General Assembly, New York: United Nations, May 17–28, 1999.

UN Department of Economic and Social Affairs (DESA). 2007. "Millennium Development Goals: 2007 Progress Chart." DESA Statistical Division, **http://unstats.un.org/unsd/mdg/MDG_Report_2007_Progress_Chart_en.pdf**.

UNDP. 1995. *Poverty Eradication: A Policy Framework for Country Strategies.* New York: UNDP.

———. 1997. *Human Development Report: Human Development to Eradicate Poverty.* New York: UNDP.

———. 1999. *Human Development Report 1999: Globalisation with a Human Face.* New York: Oxford University Press.

————. 2003. *Millennium Development Goals: A Compact Among Nations to End Human Poverty.* New York: UNDP and Oxford University Press.

————. 2006. *Human Development Report 2006: Beyond Scarcity: Power, Poverty and the Global Water.* New York: UNDP and Oxford University Press.

UNICEF. 2000. *Poverty Reduction Begins with Children.* New York: UNICEF.

————. 2005. *State of the World's Children 2005: Childhood Under Threat.* New York: UNICEF.

————. 2007. *State of the World's Children 2007: Women and Children, The Double Dividend of Gender Equality.* New York: UNICEF.

Walker, A. and C. Walker, eds. 1997. *Britain Divided: The Growth of Social Exclusion in the 1980s and 1990s.* London: Child Poverty Action Group.

Wolfensohn, James D. and Stanley Fischer. 2000. "Building Poverty Reduction Strategies Within a Comprehensive Development Framework." Remarks at the PRSP Launch Promo, Washington, D.C.: World Bank, April 24–26.

Woolcock, M. 1998. "Social Capital and Economic Development: Toward a Theoretical Synthesis and Policy Framework." *Theory and Society,* 27, 2, 151–208.

Woolcock, M. and D. Narayan. 2000. "Social Capital: Implications for Development Theory." *The World Bank Research Observer,* 15, 225–251.

World Bank. 1990. *Assistance Strategies to Reduce Poverty.* Washington, D.C.

————. 2001. *World Development Report 2000/2001: Attacking Poverty.* New York: Oxford University Press.

————. 2004. *World Development Report 2004: Making Services Work for Poor People.* New York: Oxford University Press.

————. 2005. *World Development Report 2005: Improving Investment Climate for Growth and Poverty Reduction.* New York: Oxford University Press.

————. 2007. "List of Economies." World Bank Group, Data-Country Groups, July 1, 2007. **http://go.worldbank.org/D7SN0B8YU0**.

Further Readings

Bush, Ray. 2007. *Poverty and Neoliberalism: Persistence and Reproduction in the Global South.* London: Pluto.

Calderón, José Z. 2007. *Race, Poverty, and Social Justice: Multidisciplinary Perspectives Through Service Learning.* Sterling, VA: Stylus.

Sachs, Jeffrey. 2006. *The End of Poverty: Economic Possibilities for Our Time.* New York: Penguin.

Spicker, Paul, Sonia Alvarez Leguizamón, and David Gordon. 2007. *Poverty: An International Glossary,* 2nd edition. London: Zed Books.

Yunus, Muhammad. 2003. *Banker to the Poor: Micro-Lending and the Battle Against World Poverty.* New York: Public Affairs.

Weblinks

The Development Gap
www.developmentgap.org

Focus on Global South
www.focusweb.org

Poverty Mapping
www.povertymap.net

Southern African Regional Poverty Network (SARPN)
www.sarpn.org.za

World Bank PovertyNet
www.worldbank.org/poverty

Glossary

absolute monarchy A state form resting on the claim that absolute power is vested in the monarch by God.

absolute poverty Measures physical deprivation.

accountability The answerability of government representatives for their actions and inactions. It is a multifaceted concept that usually implies such questions as accountability to whom? for what? and by what means?

accumulation policies Governmental actions designed to ensure that businesses operate as profitably as possible. Examples include low rates of taxation, minimal regulations, and investment in infrastructure, such as roads and telecommunications.

act utilitarianism This moral theory is a common variant of consequentialism. It stresses the utility likely to result from one's action or choice. In its moral context, utility tends to be defined in terms of the increase of pleasure and the decrease of pain.

ad-hoc committee A legislative committee established to investigate particular issues or events that normally disbands at the conclusion of its review.

agency A force, an acting subject, capable of transforming society.

agents of political socialization Institutions that serve to socialize people about the political system and political action. Agents of socialization include the family, educational institutions, the media, and political parties.

ahistorical A theory or approach to politics that discounts the importance of history in explaining political outcomes.

alienated Marx used the term "alienated," or alienation, to describe the separation of the worker from the goods produced and the decisions made by the bourgeoisie under the capitalist mode of production.

alternative service delivery The transfer of responsibility for program and service delivery to private sector providers, nonprofit organizations, or new public sector organizational forms.

alternative voting A variation of a majoritarian electoral system in which the voter ranks the candidates on the ballot in order of preference.

anarcho-syndicalism A form of anarchism that calls for workers to be organized into "management" groups (syndicates) to collectively make decisions and organize production.

anarchy The absence of government at any level. The significance of anarchy at the international level is that it means, in effect, that sovereign states operate in a system in which there is no permanent authority that makes and enforces laws to regulate the behaviour of these states or the behaviour of other actors in world politics.

anthropocentrism A "human-centric" view of nature that devalues other forms of life.

Auditor General An officer of Parliament whose role it is to annually examine the government's financial management and report the findings to Parliament.

austerity A condition facing local governments globally as demands for municipal services grow but own-source revenues remain static (at best) and transfers from senior government levels decline.

authoritarian regime A dictatorial regime based on force, or the threat of force, and obedience to authority among the ruled.

authority Socially approved power and legitimacy. Weber identified three types of authority—traditional, charismatic, and rational-bureaucratic.

autonomy Self-direction; the ability to think, choose, and act solely on one's own, without guidance from another person or group. Individuals are described as autonomous when they are able to give themselves their own moral and intellectual guidelines.

baby boomers The generation born in Western societies between 1944 and 1965.

backbenchers Assembly members in parliamentary systems who are not members of the cabinet. These members sit in the back of the assembly, since the front benches are reserved for cabinet members.

balance of payments A summary of a country's transactions with the rest of the world. It effectively reports receipts earned through export trade of a country's goods and services as well as payments made to other countries for the import of goods and services. The balance of payments also tracks financial flows entering (recorded as gains) and exiting (recorded as losses) the country.

barter A system of exchange that transpires without money.

beggar-thy-neighbour Any policy that aims to increase a country's own competitive edge at the expense of another country's economic performance.

behavioural approach An approach in political analysis, dominant in the United States in the 1960s, that emphasizes the study of observable and quantifiable political attitudes and actions of individuals and the scientific search for enduring laws of politics.

bicameral system A political system in which the legislative assembly consists of two independent chambers.

bilateral An action or agreement taken by two parties, usually states.

biocentric equality The view that rejects anthropocentrism and sees all humans as part of a web of nature, and holds that all species are equally deserving of moral consideration.

biological determinism An assumption that a person's nature and possibilities are determined by biological factors alone.

boosterism A view of city politics in which the role of local government is to support expansion of the community's entrepreneurs at the expense of any and all other objectives.

bourgeois ideology A term associated with Marx that refers to those belief systems that serve to mask the inegalitarian nature of power relations under capitalism and preserve the power of the bourgeoisie.

bourgeoisie A term most often used in Marxist analysis to refer to the social class that owns the means of production, often also referred to as the capitalist class.

brokerage parties Parties that take a non-doctrinal approach to politics and focus on maintaining unity by giving a voice to all groups they perceive as significant.

bureaucracy An organization defined by a hierarchy of offices, by written communications and rules, by a clear division of labour, and by employment based on technical qualifications. Bureaucratic organizations are the norm today.

cadre political party A type of political party, small in membership and focused on winning elections. It is financed by a small number of large donors, usually corporations.

capitalism An economic system organized on the basis of private ownership of the means of production and the employment of wage-labour.

cartel party A new form of party organization funded by the state.

caucus A group of sitting legislators from each party or a meeting in which the group discusses party policy and strategy.

charismatic authority Power and legitimacy accorded to individuals on the basis of their extraordinary personality or other personal qualities.

checks and balances A set of institutional measures adopted in presidential systems, allowing the legislative and executive branches to effectively check the power of the other branch.

citizenship Membership in a nation-state defined by territory and sovereignty. Membership is typically accompanied by various rights and obligations. There are three important aspects of citizenship in liberal democracies—liberty (freedom), equality, and solidarity (feelings of belonging).

city-regions Used as a synonym for census metropolitan areas. In Canada, this refers to an urban core, and its working commutershed, with a population over 100 000. Although one city is usually the focus, the region may contain many other municipal governments containing the larger part of the population.

civic republicanism An approach to community that encourages commitment on the part of individual citizens to the public or community good.

civil rights Citizenship rights that are necessary for the protection of an individual's freedom. Examples include freedom of speech and the right to own property.

civil society All voluntary civic and social organization and institutions that constitute the basis of society and that distinguish from the states structures and institutions.

civil society organizations Nonprofit/voluntary associations of many diverse types—business associations, consumers, criminal syndicates, development groups, environmentalists, farmers, human rights advocates, labour unions, women's networks, among others—that participate in political activity and try to shape the policies of governments and intergovernmental organizations.

clash of civilizations A phrase coined by political scientist Samuel Huntington to describe emerging conflict between peoples and states of different civilizations. Civilizations are wide identities based on fundamentally different religious and cultural world views.

clash of fundamentalisms According to Tariq Ali, the nature of the current global conflict is a clash between two versions of political extremism, a clash between two tiny aggravated minorities who exploit religious/cultural rhetoric for political purposes. This clash can also be characterized as a clash between market fundamentalism and religious fundamentalism.

class analysis An approach to the study of politics and society that assumes that the most important explanatory factor is the division of populations by economic class and that politics is primarily about the necessary antagonisms between the owners of the means of production and non-owners or workers.

class politics A form of national politics, especially party politics, that is organized around citizen/voter identification on the basis of class position (working class, middle class, upper class) instead of on the basis of, for example, religion or ethnicity.

class struggle For Marx, this represents the antagonism between the bourgeoisie and the proletariat. This antagonism is one of the key defining features of the capitalist mode of production and one that will ultimately result in a social revolution led by the proletariat.

Cold War The antagonistic relationship between the United States of America and the Soviet Union approximately between 1946 and 1991. Although these two superpower states (and their allies) frequently clashed, open fighting never occurred directly between them.

collective ministerial responsibility A principle found in parliamentary systems that requires cabinet members to be collectively accountable to the legislature for executive actions.

colonialism A practice of appropriating, dominating, and, in some cases, settling other territories and peoples, usually associated with European expansionism of the fifteenth to twentieth centuries.

colonial division of labour A system of economic and wealth production that divides labour, resources, and benefits unequally between the imperial power and the colony, the colonizer, and the colonized.

common law Judge-made law that is sometimes synonymous with unwritten law.

communitarianism Set of political ideas that emphasize the importance of community ties, or of social relationships, to human happiness and the good life, in opposition to liberal-individualist interpretations of human needs or human nature.

community A group of individuals who identify themselves, or are viewed by others, as having something significant in common.

comparative advantage An economic principle that holds that a country will benefit the most if it specializes in trading the goods and services it can produce with the greatest relative efficiency and at the lowest cost (i.e., relative to other countries).

conditional grant A transfer of funds from one government to support the more local administration of its priorities and programs by another level of government on the condition that the recipient agrees to meet the donor government's terms and conditions.

confidence chamber A legislative chamber in parliamentary systems where the loss of a legislative vote normally requires the resignation of the executive.

consent The notion, beginning with Hobbes, that the people must give their agreement in order to have authority exercised over them.

consequentialism A set of political or moral beliefs that emphasize the moral importance of the consequences of one's actions and decisions. Consequentialist moral theory is contrasted to deontology and virtue ethics.

conservatism An ideology based on the belief that society is an organic (collective) whole. Moreover, conservatives believe that the best form of society is hierarchical—a society in which everyone knows their place, a society where some rule and the rest are ruled. Order and tradition, not freedom and reason, are key political values.

constituency A designated group of citizens who are entitled to elect a public official whose duties are to act for them as their representative. The term is also used in its plural form to refer to a set of electoral districts each containing its own set of constituents.

constitutional convention A non-legal constitutional rule that is not enforceable by the courts.

constitutional interpretation A method by which the judiciary undertake interpretation of written constitutions.

constitutionally entrenched rights Rights that are constitutionally guaranteed and, thus, may only be removed or added to by an amendment to the constitution, rather than by ordinary legislation.

constitutive representation The process of giving meaning to political interest by defining the political identity of those who are being represented.

core A term used in dependency theory to describe the developed capitalist countries (North) which exploit the underdeveloped periphery (South).

corporatism State control and mediation of relations among business, labour, and organized civil society sectors.

cosmopolitanism Rests on the idea that the contemporary world is becoming a single global community with shared values and interests that will require transnational democratic institutions for political action.

crisis From the Greek *kreinen*, which means decision, this word usually refers to a turning point after which things will be different.

Crown corporation A corporation owned by the government that engages in commercial activity often in competition with private firms. In most countries, such firms are called public corporations or government corporations.

cultural capital A term that stems from the work of sociologist Pierre Bourdieu, who argues that success in the educational system is determined by the extent to which individual students have internalized and conformed with the dominant culture.

cultural identity A form of group identification resting on shared cultural characteristics, rather than, for example, shared class position. The term raises a central debate about whether equality in liberal democracies is best achieved by "difference blindness" or by recognizing and valuing "difference."

cultural studies An interdisciplinary (also called anti-disciplinary) approach to understanding power and culture. It draws from Marx and other writers to examine how groups with the least power use culture as a means to express resistance or identity.

culture A shared way of life that is transmitted socially, not biologically.

de facto In reality, despite what may be prescribed in a constitutional document.

de jure That which is prescribed in law.

Debt Crisis When Mexico defaulted on its foreign debt repayments in 1982, this raised the spectre of generalized debt default across the developing world and the collapse of many Western banks. The Debt Crisis was the culmination of growing economic crisis at a global level during the 1970s.

decision-makers Individuals in government who make authoritative policy decisions on behalf of their states, such as presidents, prime ministers, foreign secretaries, secretaries of state, members of Parliament or legislatures, and so on.

deductive method Analytical method that characterizes the normative field of political philosophy. Political philosophers start from an axiom (or principle) and then deduce from this principle.

delegate A representative who votes the way those he or she represents indicate. In practice, the term refers to anyone elected to a party convention regardless of how they approach their representative role.

delegate model of representation A perspective on representation that assumes that the actions of representatives should not be found to be at odds with the expressed wishes of the represented.

democracy (democratic regime) Rule by many, characterized by leadership selection through elections, constitutionalism, and the rule of law. From the Greek *demos* (people) and *kratos* (rule).

democratic deficit A phrase used to describe the lack of trust in politicians and political institutions. Such cynicism is understood to reduce direct public participation in the process of politics because of a perceived inability to influence public policy.

democratic resgime Considered to be "rule by the many." Political decisions are governed by general elections and universal suffrage.

deontology A liberal, individualist approach to ethics and politics that emphasizes the principles upon which one acts or judges. It is strictly a formal, rule-based moral theory because it ignores substantive questions concerning the consequences of one's actions, one's relationship to others, or one's commitment to particular traditions or communities. Deontology is contrasted to virtue ethics and consequentialism.

department A government administrative body over which a Cabinet minister has direct management and control.

dependency theory A theory of development that attempts to explain the gap between living standards in the rich core-industrial countries and the poor peripheral countries of the South. It argues that underdevelopment in the periphery is the result of the exploitation of the countries in that area by core industrial countries, which perpetuates a situation of dependent relations that keeps the countries in the periphery "poor."

deputy minister A non-elected member of the bureaucracy who reports to a Cabinet minister who assumes administrative responsibility for a government department.

deregulation The process of placing matters that had been subject to overseeing by state agencies outside the state's jurisdiction. Deregulation is a governmental practice associated with the neo-liberal state. It is justified on the basis that regulations needlessly impede the profitability of business.

descriptive representation The condition of descriptive representation is met only to the extent that our legislatures are a representative microcosm of the broader society.

developmentalism and modernization theories Central to this set of theories developed in post–World War II is the suggestion that the West is the only society that defends democracy and human rights, while the Rest purportedly lacks or resists such noble modern values. Any resistance to Western values, institutions, and power is the mark of rage, irrationality, and backwardness; thus, the West is justified in advancing its model of progress globally.

devolution A transfer of political authority, usually by law or regulation, from one actor to another.

dialectical relationship A concept that proposes that history progresses through a process of thesis–antithesis that results in synthesis. A dialectical relationship argues that ideas and material circumstances interact to create historical change. Marx traces key outcomes of dialectical relations as the movement in history from slavery to feudalism to capitalism.

diasporas From the Greek, meaning "scattering or sowing of seeds." It is used to refer to many varied groups, who have been forced to leave their homelands and who migrated or whose forbearers migrated from one place to another and are dispersed throughout the world.

dictatorship An authoritarian or semi-authoritarian regime headed by one individual or a very small group.

dictatorship of the proletariat The stage immediately following socialist revolution, according to Marx. The dictatorship represents the empowerment of workers, the public ownership and management of production, and a transition phase to communism.

differentiated citizenship A conceptualization of citizenship that calls for an explicit recognition of group difference to ensure inclusion and full participation. This recognition would entail the public provision of resources and institutional mechanisms for the recognition and representation of disadvantaged groups.

dignity of difference Stands for self-respect and respecting others. It implies self-critique and criticizing others and promotes dialogue among ourselves and others. It requires a careful critique of global and local models. This means that each culture/nation should engage in a critical dialogue with its own traditions and formulate the universal values of democracy and social justice in a local language that can be implemented through local/homegrown institutions.

direct democracy A system of government in which political decisions are made directly by citizens.

direct representation The idea or claim that a person can be represented only by someone whom they directly authorized to do so by voting for that candidate. Those who voted for a losing candidate in an election cannot be and are not represented by the winning candidate.

disciplinary power The ability to produce appropriate behaviours through social definitions of what is normal and expected. Conveys the idea of self-policing and the realization of social interests and goals without resort to force.

distributive justice A principle for guiding the fair distribution of things among people. For Aristotle, this principle entailed distributing more to those who are "good" than to those who are "not good."

discourse An internally coherent story or world view. Popularized in the work of Foucault, it advances the idea that the naming of things and their description through written or spoken language shapes both individuals and the material world around them. Different understandings of truth and reality are contained and find their meaning within discourses.

diversity Describes a multiplicity of socio-cultural peoples.

dividing practices Stigmatizing, controlling, and excluding different groups through the practice of naming as deviant—for example, homosexuals or welfare dependents.

division of labour An economic system's determination of the specific roles and functions performed, and by whom, within production processes.

doctrinal parties Avowedly ideological parties that seek to fit policies into rational value-oriented schemes. Ideological fidelity is more important than winning elections.

doctrine of utility The proposition that the standard by which all human action, public and private, should be judged is the greatest happiness of the greatest number.

domino theory or domino effect The idea that if one state falls to communist domination, other neighbouring states will also fall, either through direct aggression or subversion.

ecological debt A monetary estimate of the debt accumulated by Northern, industrial countries toward Third World countries on account of resource plundering, environmental damages, and the free occupation of environmental space to deposit wastes, such as greenhouse gases, from the industrial countries.

ecological footprint The total area of productive land and water required continuously to produce all the resources consumed and to assimilate all the wastes produced by a specified human population, with the prevailing technology, wherever on Earth that land is located (Wackernagel and Rees 1996).

ecological imperialism The appropriation of the global commons . . . and the carbon absorption capacity of the biosphere, primarily to the benefit of a relatively small number of countries at the centre of the capitalist world economy (Bellamy Foster and Clark 2003, 194).

economic liberalization A process by which the politically imposed barriers to the movement of goods and money are dismantled.

economies of scale Increase in a corporation's efficiency of production as the number of goods being produced increases. Economies of scale lower the average cost per unit since fixed costs are shared over an increased number of produced goods. This is achieved through the reorganization of corporate activities across international borders aimed at taking advantage of better supplies of materials, cheaper workforces, and larger markets—all of which are critical to corporate competitiveness in the contemporary global economy.

egalitarianism A concept that encompasses a belief in the essential equal worth of all persons, and the view that social institutions should ensure equality of opportunity (economic, social, and political) for each individual to realize his or her needs and goals.

electoralist political parties Organizationally thin, with a vague ideology, and characterized primarily by the goals of electoral mobilization and success. This category of political parties includes catch-all political parties.

electoral formulae A rule system to determine the winner of an election.

electoral systems Set the rules that determine how citizens cast their votes, how the votes are counted, and how they are translated into legislative seats.

elite-based political parties Founded around traditional elites or notables. They have a minimal party organization, are not ideological, and aim to distribute benefits to their "clients."

elite theory An approach to politics that assumes that all societies are divided into only two groups—the few who rule, usually in their own self-interest, and the many who are ruled.

embedded liberalism A conception of global economic management, coined by John Ruggie, which describes the vision central to the post-war international economic order negotiated at the Bretton Woods Conference. Embedded liberalism was committed to a cautiously open and liberal world economy but also created space for policies of national economic management and domestic economic stability.

empirical theory An approach to political analysis resting on the belief that knowledge is derived from what is observable, experienced, and/or validated by experimentation. It seeks to generate general explanations for seemingly distinct events through observation and comparison.

empire Michael Hardt and Antonio Negri argue that "Empire is the new world order." It "is the political subject that effectively regulates [the] global exchanges, the sovereign power that governs the world."

end of history A phrase used by political scientist Francis Fukuyama to describe the growing convergence of states and societies with a single, liberal democratic model of governance. The end of history refers to the end of the historic debate about superior systems.

epistemology A branch of philosophy concerned with issues of knowledge, its definition, what it is, how we acquire it, and the relationship between the knower and what is known.

equality A term conveying the idea of equal access to the political sphere, equal access to and benefit of the law, and equal access to social entitlements provided by the state.

essentialism The assumption that, by nature, all members of a group share the same core personal and social qualities. Essentialist thinking, for example, assumes that all women share the capacity to nurture.

ethics The philosophical study of standards of moral conduct and principles of moral judgment. Also called "moral philosophy." In general, a principle, belief, or value about what is morally good, or a system of such principles, beliefs, or values. From the Greek *ethos*, which means the general way of life of a culture or a people.

ethic of responsibility The qualities that Weber ascribed to individuals seeking political leadership. These included passion and a sense of purpose; the ability to calculate consequences of decisions; and a trained relentlessness. Such a leader will defend the state and its people, utilizing violence if necessary.

ethnic cleansing The systematic and forced removal or murder of members of an ethnic group from their geographic communities to change the ethnic composition of a region.

ethnicity Refers to the identity of members of a group who share a sense of people-hood or identity based on descent, language, religion, tradition, and other common experiences.

ethnicity-based political parties Characterized by their desire to work within the system to benefit the members of their own ethnic group.

ethnic groups Cultural communities whose members identify with each other based on a common ancestry and are linked by cultural, linguistic, and religious practices.

ethnocentric Prejudicial attitudes held by one group that feels its own values, customs, or behaviour are superior to any other. The term is also used in relation to political scientists who, often unconsciously, import assumptions or values from their own society into comparative research.

executive committee A part of council, chaired by the mayor and sometimes including the heads of standing committees, intended to coordinate municipal business and to give some limited political direction to council.

exploitation Marx argued that because workers must sell their labour power under the capitalist system, they are vulnerable to the whims and changes in economic fortune that beset the capitalist. This means that the workers' standard of living is constantly in jeopardy and that the worker is in a weaker social position as a result.

export-oriented industrialization An economic development strategy based on maximizing the export of national unprocessed and processed goods.

export processing zones (EPZs) The International Labour Organization (ILO) defines EPZs as "industrial zones with special incentives set up to attract foreign investors, in which imported materials undergo some degree of processing before being re-exported." The concern is that states in need of foreign direct investment will set aside labour and environmental standards in order to attract the foreign corporation while offering preferential tax incentives to these corporations.

faction A division in society based on narrow group loyalty. Factions are seen as being at odds with the idea of the public good.

fairness A principle of distribution that is associated with equality in the modern era. For Marx, this principle involved redistribution, from each according to her ability, to each according to her need.

false consciousness A term, common in Marxist analyses, that conveys the idea that working-class consciousness is influenced by the dominant ideology of the bourgeoisie in ways that are not in the real interest of workers.

fascism A form of repressive authoritarian governance that eliminates democracy and maintains capitalism.

fatalism A belief that our fate is pre-determined by external forces, such as destiny or God.

federal constitution A constitution in which the sovereignty of the state is divided between national and sub-national governments.

federalism A political system in which constitutionally assigned powers are divided among two or more levels of government.

feminism A diverse set of ideas, grounded in the belief that patriarchal societies have oppressed women and united by the goal of claiming full citizenship for all women. Beyond this, feminists disagree about the roots of women's oppression, the appropriate strategies for contesting patriarchy, and about visions for a post-patriarchal society.

feminization of poverty A term describing the predominant gender of the poor.

feudalism An agrarian form of social and economic organization characterized by a strict hierarchy between the property-owning aristocracy and the landless peasants.

fiscal innovation New approaches that are developed to deal with fiscal austerity measures forced upon local governments; success appears to be correlated with growth in the high-tech and service economies, and with municipal co-option of local social movements; it may partly be measured by new participants in the policy process.

formalistic representation The condition of formalistic representation merely requires that legislative bodies are authorized and/or held accountable by regular elections.

Fourth World A political/economic concept to describe very poor nations, which are effectively excluded from the world economy. As such, the term applies to Indigenous peoples living in wealthy nations.

franchise The legal right to vote in the election of some governmental official. Although the term "suffrage" is also used with this meaning, *franchise* specifies a right or privilege that is constitutional or statutory in its origin—that is, a formal legal right to vote in elections held in some jurisdiction.

freedom Traditionally meant the absence of interference and regulation in a person's life. It is coming to have a broader and more social meaning as the ability to live on one's own terms.

free vote A legislative vote that drops the requirement of party discipline normally adhered to in parliamentary assemblies.

fusion of power The integration of the executive and legislative branches in the parliamentary system.

gender A socially, politically, and economically constructed sex-code that prescribes what it means to be male or female in daily life.

gender parity Representation of men and women in proportion roughly equal to their distribution in the general population.

gender-related Development Index Measures the experience of human deprivation and adjusts for the health and knowledge deprivation and overall economic well-being as experienced by girls and women.

genocide Acts committed with the intent to destroy, in whole or in part, a national, ethnic, racial, or religious group. Such acts include the killing of members of the group; causing serious bodily or mental harm to members of the group; deliberately inflicting on the group conditions of life calculated to bring about its physical destruction in whole or in part; imposing measures to prevent births within the group; and/or forcibly transferring children of the group to another group.

global cities Sub-national regional social formations formally described as "dense nodes of human labor and communal life"; post-industrial production sites encompassing international firms providing corporate services and finance, whose overall clout is based on the locational choices of transnational corporations.

global economy Characterized by interconnected production sites all over the world that produce different component parts of a final product.

global governance The mechanisms and processes by which transnational actors—individuals, governments, non-governmental organizations, corporations—make decisions for and about the global community.

global insertion The economic and political location of a country within the global system of states and markets.

global metabolic rift A rift in the "natural metabolism" of the planet.

global South A term used to describe the heterogeneous countries that were once colonized by the West but have since won their independence. The term "global South" has increasingly replaced the terms "the Third World" and "developing countries."

globalism A world view advocating a single system of governance for the planet. Neo-liberalism is often described as neo-liberal globalism because it advocates the worldwide embrace of market-based principles of governance.

globality A term that describes the progressive shaping of the planet as a single political unit. Globality is associated with new communication technologies, the spread of consumerist culture, and population mobility and migration. Political issues and social problems are no longer isolated to one country but, instead, have global impacts and implications.

globalization The intensification of a world-scale reorientation of economic, technological, and cultural processes and activities that transcend state boundaries.

glocal A term used variously to describe "innovative strategies" focused on global issues by empowering local communities for development purposes (social, cultural, economic, and architectural), often in conflict with the traditionally dominant urban interests.

governance The organized exercise of power; the manner in which we organize our common affairs. Also seen as describing the complex relationships among government departments, policy networks, NGOs, and powerful private actors in public policy-making, it has been usurped by neo-liberals to describe the collaborative provision of basic services through the private sector.

government bill A legislative bill introduced by the cabinet in parliamentary systems.

harm principle The principle, classically attributed to John Stuart Mill, that a person's liberty can legitimately be restricted only to prevent direct harm to other persons.

head of government The position that assumes responsibility for the political and effective administration of government.

head of state The symbolic position that is assigned formal and ceremonial powers.

hegemony A term associated with the work of Antonio Gramsci to refer to the bourgeoisie's ideological domination of the working class, which results in the persistence of the capitalist system. Hegemony or *hegemon* is also used to describe the dominant country in the international system.

historical materialism A conception of historical and political development, often associated with Marxism, which relates power to the ownership of economic factors, the "mode of production," and the material organization of society.

human capital Emerged from economic ideas in the 1960s to connote the economic value of skills, knowledge, and good health to firms and corporations.

human development Promoted by the United Nations Development Program (UNDP) as a measurement of well-being that includes more than economic indicators. The UNDP annually publishes these results in a global Human Development Index.

Human Development Index *See* human development. A measure that combines life expectancy, adult literacy, Gross National Product, and education enrolments. It is used by the United Nations Development Program to compare countries with respect to human well-being. Country rankings are published each year in the UNDP Human Development Report.

Human Poverty Index A composite index designed to examine uneven development and poverty in terms that are not exclusively monetary.

human rights Rights that are asserted of all people on the basis that they are human beings.

humanism A philosophical belief system that puts an ideal person at the centre of philosophical reflection. This philosophy suggests that knowledge, happiness, and social and political fulfillment are entirely within human purview; religious or supernatural intervention in human affairs is not considered necessary. Rather than lament human imperfections, early humanists celebrated the human body, the ability to reason, and the capacity to produce beautiful art.

hybrid regimes Regimes that contain characteristics of two or more types.

ideal-type A mental model in the social sciences for categorizing and understanding social events.

identities The tendency of individuals and groups to develop a sense of who they are in relation to their shared cultural, sociological, and political attachments to each other.

identity-based community A group of people who share at least one identifiable characteristic, which members may carry into politics.

ideology A coherent set of ideas that explain and evaluate social conditions, help people understand their place in society, and provide a program for social and political action. Ideology also consists of those beliefs and values that serve to legitimate a certain social order, the so-called dominant ideology, and those values and beliefs that may be said to oppose or challenge the dominant ideology.

imperialism An organization of the international political economy where the globe is divided among great powers into empires; associated with colonialism; for Marxists, the expansion of capital beyond single national markets.

import substitution industrialization A strategy for economic development in which state interventions are used in an attempt to build up a domestic industrial sector so as to reduce reliance on industrial imports.

indirect election A procedure for choosing office-holders in which the members of some group, organization, or governmental body, who are themselves directly elected by the citizens or by the members of their organization, select the persons to hold an office from a set of candidates by voting among themselves.

individual ministerial responsibility Principle in parliamentary systems that requires ministers to assume responsibility before the legislature for the bureaucratic departments they direct.

inductive method An analytical method that aims to build empirically based theory or explanations from the observation of concrete events.

institutionalization A process whereby things that were once random or done with little conscious planning become deliberate, formalized, and expected.

instrumental representation The activity of acting or speaking for the represented.

Integrated Poverty Index Intended to assess poverty as experienced in rural areas.

interest-based community A group formed around concerns that bear directly, but not exclusively, on the members' political interests and that are usually represented in the political arena by organizations or interest groups.

interest party A political party that seeks to represent a particular interest in the electoral process, such as a region or a specific issue of concern. It does not make a full attempt to win power but raises consciousness about its concerns.

intergovernmental organizations (IGOs) International organizations that are composed of state governments, the United Nations being the pre-eminent example.

international community A group of governments, such as the United Nations, or the symbolic expression of the shared sentiments of people in different countries.

international division of labour A way of organizing the international economy wherein the factors of production (materials, labour, finance) are divided among countries.

international political economy A perspective on international relations that emphasizes the close relationship between economic factors, such as trade and investment, and political factors, such as policy settings and issues of distributive justice. IPE approaches generally analyze the interaction of states, markets, modes of production, class, politics, and culture in the international sphere.

internationalization of production The ability of companies to consider the productive resources of the globe as a whole and to decide to locate elements of complex globalized production systems at points that will produce the greatest cost advantage. It is reliant on an environment in which capital, technology, raw materials, and component parts are allowed to cross national jurisdictional boundaries with minimal or no regulation.

internationalization of the state The erosion of state authority in favour of external international forces that are able to exert tremendous influence on domestic agencies and on national policies.

international relations A field of political science concerned with relations among nation-states that engages philosophical, ethical, epistemological, and ontological questions in order to understand relations within the international sphere.

Jihad An Arabic word for "holy war" that is used by political scientist Benjamin Barber to describe the fanaticism of different cultural and national groups. These fanatics are allegedly at war with the growing influence of global consumer capitalism in their particular societies (*see also* McWorld).

judicial review The process whereby the courts judge the legality of political/administrative actions. Judicial review of the constitution refers to when the courts are asked to determine whether political/administrative actions conform to constitutional requirements.

kanikonri:io A Kahniakehaka or Mohawk word, which means "the good mind," the achievement of which requires living in harmony with the other "nations" of the earth, and which constitutes "the path of righteousness and reason into the future" (Arquette et al. 2004, 336–337).

Keynesianism An approach to the management of national economies that was developed by the British economist John Maynard Keynes. This approach was implemented by Western industrialized countries between 1945 and the mid-1970s. The central concern of Keynesianism was to counteract the boom-and-bust tendencies of capitalist economies. In periods of economic downturn, Keynesianism advocated increased public spending and lower levels of taxation to ensure that people would continue to purchase goods in the market. In periods of economic growth, public spending was to decrease and tax rates would rise, thereby curbing excessive growth and restoring balance to the public finances.

laissez-faire **capitalism** A principle espoused by classical economists, such as Adam Smith, that government should minimize intervention in the capitalist market.

legal institutionalism An approach to politics that emphasizes the centrality of formal procedures, constitutions, and institutions.

legal-rational authority Power and legitimacy accorded on the basis of laws, formal rules, and impersonal procedures.

legal-rationalism A way of reasoning that follows the logic of the law.

legal rights Rights that are recognized as law and therefore subject to authoritative adjudication and enforcement.

legitimacy The quality of legal, moral, or social (among others) rightness. Since the beginning of the modern era, an act, decision, public policy, government, or law is most apt to be considered legitimate when it is based on reason. For instance, just as government is considered legitimate if it comes to power as a result of a fair and rational process, so a law shown to be irrational is considered illegitimate and struck down. In the medieval era, in contrast, legitimacy was conferred not by reason but by the authority vested in one of God's representatives, such as a king, priest, or another religious official.

legitimation Justification of the actions of the state to the population at large through policies that contribute to the authority of the state. Public health care, education, and transportation networks are examples of areas of public investment that are broadly supported by citizens and thus provide a rationale for the role of the state in their lives.

less-developed countries A term of relative economic development that is normally used with reference to the poor Third World of Africa, Asia, and Latin America. Least developed countries were defined in 1971 by the United Nations Conference on Trade and Development (UNCTAD) as those with very low per capita incomes ($100 or less at 1968 prices), a share of manufacturing in GDP of under 10 percent, and a literacy rate under 20 percent.

liberal democracy The form of government prevalent in contemporary Western countries. Governments are selected through regular elections in which all citizens of voting age are eligible to participate. Liberal democracies are particularly concerned with protecting the freedom of individual citizens against the arbitrary use of power by the state. Hence, some formal expression of the rights of citizens can be found in the constitutional documents of liberal democracies.

liberal democratic theory A political theory arising out of the Western European liberal revolution of the sixteenth, seventeeth, and eighteenth centuries that emphasizes the importance of freedom, equality, rights, reason, and individualism.

liberal feminism A perspective that sees women's oppression as resulting from unequal treatment of women and men by laws, opinions, and social practices and that regards equal rights and empowerment through gender socialization as the solution.

liberal internationalism A belief that the natural global order has been subverted by non-democratic leaders and by such policies as the balance of power. Adherents believe that contact between people, who are essentially good, will lead to a more pacific world order.

liberalism A political theory and ideology that stresses the primacy of the individual and individual freedom. Freedom, in this instance, refers to the freedom of individuals to do as they wish without interference from others, whether these be governments or private persons. Liberals believe in a limited state where the power of government is restrained by such devices as constitutions. This ideology arose alongside capitalism.

libertarianism A "softer" variant of individualist anarchism that rejects government intervention in the market and social life. Libertarian thought is evident in today's political rhetoric, which promises to "downsize" government.

liberty Freedom from bodily harm, freedom of expression, economic independence.

lobbyist A person who contacts public officials on behalf of a client or an organization that they belong to or are employed by so as to influence public policy in a manner beneficial to their client or organization.

Magna Carta An important written element of Britain's constitution dating from 1215. It limited royal authority and strengthened the political position of the English aristocracy.

majoritarian electoral system An electoral system organized to reflect the principle of majority rule by requiring that candidates or parties obtain an absolute or a relative majority of the total valid vote cast to win control of an elective office.

majority government A situation in which the governing party controls more than half of the seats in the legislative assembly in a parliamentary system.

mal-development Economic growth that devalues the subsistence labour of women and the productivity of nature and instead imposes forms of rationalization, mechanization, and commodification.

maquiladora Foreign-owned business enterprises that have been set up in Mexico in order to exploit cheap labour and low production costs and where local labour is afforded little legal protection. Maquiladora often entail a system in which components are made in the United States, shipped to Mexico for assembling, and reshipped across the American border duty-free.

market Taken broadly, this sphere includes economic transactions related to production, exchange, and distribution. Today, most societies can be characterized as *market societies* in which the social worth of individuals and groups is determined by *market principles*, such as ownership, price, income, costs, and supply and demand.

mass-based political parties Parties with a strong organization, an ongoing ideological political program, and a broad base of active members. Depending on the ideology embraced by the party, this group can be further divided into socialist, nationalist, and religious political parties.

mass party An avowedly democratic political party organization possessing a large membership and active in recruitment. Joining the party involves agreement with principles, and members provide a good deal of financial support. Party conventions decide on policy.

mass politics Political activities citizens can engage in without having to invest large amounts of time, effort, or money. Examples include voting, signing petitions, protesting, writing elected officials, and joining political parties or interest groups. Mass politics must be distinguished from elite political participation, which requires special skills, intense levels of commitment, and particular resources. As well, entrance to elite political roles, such as candidate or officeholder, union leader, or president of an interest group, is partly determined by such factors as public opinion, voting behaviour, and/or by the gate-keeping functions of activists within the organization.

McWorld Derived from the name of the fast food restaurant chain, McDonald's. This term was coined by political scientist Benjamin Barber to describe the negative cultural and political influences of global corporations. These influences include cultural homogenization, the erosion of democratic values, and the provocation of the "intolerant fanatics" around the world (*see also* Jihad).

means of production The physical and human factors of economic production processes (land, technology, infrastructure, capital, labour).

means-tested social programs Social programs available only to those citizens who can demonstrate that they do not have adequate resources to purchase a service in the marketplace. People in this position are required to reveal their level of income and are often required to provide information regarding the conduct of their personal lives.

mercantilism A governing philosophy, common in Europe prior to the Industrial Revolution, that measured a country's wealth by the amount of precious metals it held. It is also associated with colonialism and the division of the world by the Great Powers for exclusive commerce.

military-industrial complex A concept that refers to an interest in high defence spending shared by military professionals and military weapons producers.

ministerial responsibility A principle found in parliamentary systems that requires the Cabinet members to be collectively accountable to legislature for executive actions.

minority government A situation in which the governing party controls less than a majority of seats but more than any other party in the legislature in a parliamentary system.

minority rights Embody two types of rights. First, individual rights as applied to members of racial, ethnic, class, religious, linguistic, or sexual minorities; and collective rights accorded to minority groups characterized by their own ethnic, linguistic, or religious identity and who live within national states where they differ from the majority population.

mixed electoral system A system that combines both majoritarian and proportional representation mechanisms.

mixed-member proportional (MMP) system A type of electoral system that combines a primary tier of seats in a representative assembly assigned to single-member districts with a pool of seats in the assembly assigned to a secondary tier composed either of a single national district or a set of regional districts. A majoritarian electoral system is used to elect the members representing single-member districts, whereas a proportional representation procedure is used to allocate seats in the secondary pool in a compensatory fashion to achieve overall proportionality between the vote shares of parties and the share of seats they won.

mode of production The way that a society organizes its means of production.

modernity A concept historically associated with the Enlightenment and its ideas of reason, progress, emancipation, and universality, as well as with the rise of commercial and industrial capitalism.

modernization A process and endpoint which all societies were assumed, by development theory, to evolve into. Modernization brought rational authority, industrialization, and societies with a complex division of labour.

modernization theory A theory that suggests that all countries progress through a similar series of stages, from traditional agrarian societies to advanced industrial societies.

morality A principle, belief, or value; or the system of principles, beliefs, and values applied to conduct and judgment. Related to the Latin word *mores*, which means the general codes and guides for living that are accepted by a social group.

moral rights Rights that are asserted (1) on the basis that they should be established at law, or (2) where there is a good justification for ascribing both duties and the power to demand that they be performed.

movement political parties Political parties that emerge out of and are based in social movements. They are characterized by fluid organization and represent a challenge to mainstream modern society and political processes.

multiculturalism Refers to a belief or policy that endorses the principle of cultural diversity and supports the right of different ethnic, religious, national, and linguistic groups to retain their distinctive identities and practices.

multilateralism A form of cooperation among states marked by three distinct characteristics. First, that the costs and benefits of cooperation are shared by all participating states. Second, that cooperation is based on certain principles of state conduct that influence the relations among states. Finally, that states are committed to this cooperative behaviour for the long term and do not necessarily expect immediate results.

multinational corporation A company whose operations are located in two or more countries.

mutual fund A collection of bonds or shares that allow investors to spread and diversify their money, which, in turn, reduces levels of risk. Mutual funds are especially useful in international investments where information about foreign companies and markets is not accessible to the average individual investor.

nation A group of individuals who identify with each other (sense of community) based on common history, language, culture, and religion.

national interest A concept referring to the basic irreducible interests of a state (material and ideal) and criteria for action from a realist perspective.

nationalism A belief system that prioritizes or gives special significance to the nation as a focus of loyalty. The nation, in turn, is a particular form of community, with a history, tradition, and identity that it desires to promote and preserve.

nation-state An international legal entity defined by a specific territory, population, and government, possessing sovereignty. Because almost all states comprise diverse ethnic, national, and racial groups, some prefer the term "national state."

natural rights Rights that people are said to possess "by nature" and not as members of particular societies.

negative rights An understanding of rights, entitlements, and liberty associated with classical liberalism. Negative rights entitle individuals to act without any interference from others. They are commonly associated with the freedoms of speech, assembly, religion, and press.

neo-liberalism A modification of nineteenth-century economic and political theory that advocates deregulation of the market, a non-interventionist state, minimal controls on international economic interaction, and individual freedom and responsibility.

neo-liberal structural adjustment A strategy for economic development.

new international division of labour The global economy created through colonialism, characterized by an industrialized "centre" (the early-industrializing, colonial countries) and a "periphery" (the former colonies) producing raw commodities, began to be reorganized in the 1970s. In particular, there was "deindustrialization" in the West as companies relocated labour-intensive manufacturing to cheaper wage zones in the South, and a process of industrialization (either "dependent" or state-led, as in the East Asian countries) in parts of Latin America and Asia.

new localism A term used to explain a variety of both collective (and individual) initiatives in economic development and political action at the level of the community. An analogous 1970s term was "neighbourhood government."

new multilateralism Cooperation among states to protect the security of people, rather than the security of states.

new public management A combination of structures, practices, and processes of public management that were in vogue in liberal democracies in the 1990s. At the heart of new public management is a critical analysis of traditional Weberian bureaucracy and the view that government agencies must be driven by a desire to achieve clearly measurable results.

new social movement theory Seeks to explain the historical meaning of the progressive mass movements that arose in the 1960s, in the context of sociological theories of conflict and change.

non-aligned states A group of states, the majority in the South, that were not aligned with either the Soviet Union or the United States during the Cold War.

non-governmental organization (NGO) An organization that has as its members private citizens or national affiliates of groups composed of private citizens.

non-partisanship The conduct of elections in the absence of political parties. In its pure form, individuals stand for election as independents.

normative Related to the establishing of moral norms or principles. Normative claims, statements, or questions tend to contain such prescriptive words as *should, ought,* or *must.*

normative theory A theory that inquires into ethical questions and considers what is moral, good, and true.

notwithstanding clause A clause in the Canadian constitution that shields an act of the legislature from a judicial declaration of constitutional invalidity.

original inhabitants An alternative term to refer to Indigenous peoples, which makes reference to the immemorial occupancy of their territories.

open regionalism The creation of regions committed with trade creation. Open regions, in contrast, seek to increase the international competitiveness of member states both within and outside the region. It can be distinguished from earlier experiences of international economic cooperation, where member countries increased exchanges among themselves rather than with the rest of the world (trade diversion).

oppression The systematic and systemic subordination of one group to another.

ordinal ballot A ballot form in which the voter is asked to rank the candidates or parties to indicate his or her relative preferences among them. Also known as a *preferential ballot.*

paradigm shift A shift in the intellectual framework that structures thinking about a set of phenomena.

parliamentary system A system of government in which the executive is chosen from and derives its authority from the legislature.

participation Direct action or involvement in processes of decision making.

partisan Having to do with political parties; to demonstrate a particular allegiance to a political party.

party discipline An established principle in parliamentary systems that requires members of a party's legislative caucus to vote collectively on legislation.

party list ballot A ballot form in which each party's candidates for seats in a multi-member constituency are presented as separate lists, and voters must choose among the lists, rather than choosing among the individual candidates appearing on them.

party systems Referring to the total number of political parties present within a political system at any given time. Party systems reflect the level of competition between parties, the numbers of parties present in the system, and the ideological slant of the parties as a whole.

patriarchical family A family form in which the father is the head and primary bread winner and the mother stays at home and takes care of the family.

patriarchy In the anthropological sense, the rule of the father over his wife and offspring (family, kin group, or clan). In the modern sociological sense, the structuring of social relationships and institutions in such a way as to preserve the dominance and privileges of men in relation to women.

paupers Refers to members of a social class in the Middle Ages who met or supplemented their basic needs through the charity of churches or private philanthropy.

peacebuilding Intervention by foreign actors into conflict zones to build governmental institutions, democratic practices, and civil society.

peacekeeping Intervention by foreign actors into conflict zones to maintain peace among warring factions.

periphery A term used in dependency theory to describe the lesser developed regions of the world, which are dependent on and exploited by the developed core.

place-based community A group of people who share geographical, usually local, space and who may also have common interests or feelings of closeness.

plebiscitarian democracy A form of democracy that attempts to replicate the virtues of direct democracy through democratic mechanisms, such as referenda and recall.

pluralist decision rule A form of decision making that favours the option with the most votes, even if it does not constititute a majority.

pluralist theory An approach to politics that assumes that society is composed of individuals who join groups to influence political outcomes. Politics is seen as the competition among groups for preferred policies. It assumes that all citizens can form groups and that no group has a permanent advantage in society.

plurality electoral system An electoral system in which the candidate who gains the most votes wins the office being contested, even though that total may constitute less than a majority of the total valid votes cast. A plurality outcome is also known as a relative majority.

policy community All actors or potential actors who share expertise and interest in a policy area or function and who in varying degrees influence policy.

political culture A term popularized by Gabriel Almond that refers to a particular patterned orientation toward political action. The political culture approach attempts to empirically describe and explain these patterns by measuring the attitudes characteristic of a national population.

political economy The study of the relationship between politics and economics, which emphasizes the intersections between states and markets; power and wealth; and economic and political actors.

political parties Organizations, usually comprised of volunteers and paid staff, that nominate candidates and compete in elections. They provide an important link between citizens, civil society, and government.

political rights Citizenship rights that encompass the exercise of a citizen's democratic rights within the political community. Examples include the right to vote and the right to stand for elected office.

political socialization The process by which people acquire their knowledge of the political system and attitudes toward political action.

political sociology A social-science approach that emphasizes the social and cultural composition of society and its relationship to the state.

political violence The use of physical force to affect power relations.

politics–administration dichotomy A view of democratic politics whereby politicians make policy decisions, which, in turn, are implemented by civil servants. Few observers see the dichotomy as a valid description of reality.

polity Derived from the Greek notion of *polis*, which translates as either "city" or "state." A polity is simply a single political unit that has an organized form of governance.

Poor Laws First introduced in sixteenth-century England, these laws were designed to get the poor off the streets. The underlying premise of these laws is that the poor are responsible for their own plight.

popular sovereignty Also known as *popular rule*. Popular sovereignty exists when the ability to rule or govern is distributed equally among the population of a specific state.

positive rights An understanding of rights, entitlements, and liberty associated with such ideologies as reform liberalism or democratic socialism. Positive rights entitle individuals to the conditions in which they can maximize their chances for full development. They are commonly associated with an interventionist state and specific initiatives, such as public education, social assistance, and affirmative action.

post-development A strand of thought that rejects the notion of development as a profoundly Western-centric concept that has proved inadequate in meeting the needs of the non-Western world.

post-Marxist Approaches that share Marxism's critique of capitalism and its emancipatory objectives, but which reject what they consider to be the economic reductionism of traditional Marxist theory, as well as the scientific and predictive claims of Marx.

post-structuralist Theoretical perspectives associated, in particular, with the French thinkers Jacques Lacan, Michel Foucault, and Jacques Derrida and which have called into question many of the epistemological assumptions underpinning modern political thought (especially regarding the Self [or subject], knowledge, and power).

post-modern feminism A stream in feminist thought that challenges any universalizing or essentializing explanations for women's oppression, arguing that there is no single, unifying women's reality; focuses on exposing the patriarchal ideas inherent in language and discourse.

post-modernism A perspective in the social sciences and humanities that holds that reality is not given; rather, it is constituted by ideas, texts, and discourses (writing, talking). It displays skepticism toward Enlightenment notions of truth, arguing instead that many "truths" can co-exist. Post-modernism holds that modern political ideologies, with their emphasis on reason and a single political identity, silence social differences and impose uniformity and homogeneity on society.

post-sovereign A depiction of the current era, in which the state has lost its capacity to exercise sovereignty within its territorial boundaries.

poverty gap Measures the percentage of the population living below the poverty line within a given state.

poverty line An arbitrary statistical instrument that categorizes a population as being poor or not poor. There are many formulations of the poverty line and ongoing debates about the most appropriate measure.

poverty reduction strategy papers (PRSPs) In the later 1990s, the IMF and the World Bank refashioned their structural adjustment programs into PRSPs, which are intended to cover a wider range of issues, including aspects of good governance.

Poverty Severity Index Measures the intensity of poverty insofar as it focuses on individuals living in conditions of extreme deprivation.

power The capacity of individuals, groups, and political institutions to realize key decisions.

power of the purse A power of review over the expenditure of public moneys.

power over The idea that individuals, groups, or states are unable to realize their interests and goals due to external influences, constraints, and inequalities in resources.

power to The idea that individuals, groups, or states can realize their goals.

pragmatic party A non-doctrinaire party that competes strategically for public office. It is concerned with practicality and with winning elections and gears its campaigns to programs it believes will most likely lead to victory.

precedent Past judicial decisions declaring legal principles that have a bearing on present controversies.

presidential system A system of government in which the executive and legislative branches are independent and assigned distinct powers.

principle of commodification Marxist notion that, under capitalism, items are prized because of their exchange value rather than their use value. This makes all items (including labour) commodities of exchange.

principle of comparative advantage Economic theory that economic growth is best achieved when countries focus production on those things they do best, or that are associated with abundant natural resources.

private The realm of society that has been deemed "natural" and, thus, beyond the possibility of debate or change (often this has included the "market" and the family).

private member bill Legislation introduced by non-cabinet members in parliamentary systems.

privatization A process of shifting public or governmental services and functions performed by the state into the realm of the market and the home.

Privy Council Office An agency of the Government of Canada that provides administrative support to and policy analysis for the cabinet.

productivism A characterization of industrial societies (both capitalist and state-socialist), referring to the priority given to the maximization of production of goods, even when this cannot be shown to enhance quality of life and may even result in its deterioration.

proletariat A term used by Marx for the social class that does not own the means of production but is instead forced to sell its labour-power in exchange for wages.

proportional representation (PR) An electoral system in which the primary aim is to ensure that the percentage of the popular vote that a party receives is translated (as closely as possible) into the proportion of seats that party is allocated in the Parliament.

protectionism A government policy that protects a national industry or sector from foreign competition through subsidies or tariffs.

public bureaucracy The set of institutions and people who form the administrative machinery of government.

public–private dichotomy The gender-based division of personality characteristics, roles, and values. Women are associated with the private sphere of home and family and its accompanying traits, such as passivity, subjugation, and emotion. Men are linked to the public sphere of business and government and its virtues of individualism, rationality, intelligence, and freedom.

purchasing power parity A practice of adjusting currency rates so that the same proportion of income is spent to buy the same item.

quasi-divine A term suggesting that the source of authority is understood to be godly or divine.

race A term that reflects negative tendencies of disassociation and exclusion, where people are falsely grouped based on biological notions of identity. The most widely observed biological features are skin colour, facial features, ancestry, and genetics. Conceptions of race and the specific racial groupings that arise from such conceptions are important because they impact social identity and relations.

racialization The process whereby social groups are assigned racial markings and attributes.

racialization of poverty Reflects the idea that the relationship between race and poverty is under-theorized; that there is effectively a global system of apartheid that sees poverty largely focused according to global racial divisions.

radical feminism A view of women's oppression as resulting from systematic subordination of women to men, especially male control of women's bodies; advocates the eradication of sexual violence and the promotion of bodily autonomy for women.

rational decision making A process whereby important policies are undertaken only after careful delineation of the problem at hand, a thorough analysis of policy options, and a detailed comparison of the costs and benefits of different options. Most public policy making is thought, for many reasons, to fall short of such standards.

rationality A claim to a systematic way of thinking.

realism The dominant international relations theory in Anglo-American academies. It purports to explain the world by holding that the international sphere is dominated by sovereign states, that states act in their own interests, and that international politics is a struggle for power between states.

reason The ability to think, understand, analyze, form judgments, and draw conclusions logically. Reason or rationality is variously considered as (1) a general *capacity* particular to human beings (and perhaps some other animals), (2) an *activity* in which one engages, and (3) a *faculty* of the mind (as one of its components, or hardware).

regime A mode of governance over the organized activity of a social formation within and across four spheres—the state, society, market, and global insertion.

regionalization The process of creation and development of associations of countries, generally in contiguous geographic spaces, mainly for, but not limited to, economic purposes. These associations are generally formalized through legally binding international treaties or intergovernmental agreements, such as free trade agreements.

regulatory agency A government body, enjoying independence from the government of the day, that makes and enforces rules for sectors of the economy.

relative poverty Takes into account the unequal distribution of income within a given society.

representation by population A principle applied in the apportionment of seats in a representative assembly among regions, provinces or states, or electoral districts. It holds that the number of seats assigned to a given region, province, or district should be directly proportional to the share of the population of the nation (or higher regional unit) that resides in that region, province, or district.

representative bureaucracy A view that argues that the civil service should reflect in its composition the major social groups of the society.

representative democracy or indirect democracy A democratic system in which citizens elect representatives, who, in turn, make political decisions on behalf of all citizens.

representative sample A term used in survey research to refer to a sample that is a reflection of the larger population—that is, it has the same profile in terms of gender, age, income levels, and so on of the larger population. It is crucial that a sample is representative if it is to give valid information about the larger population.

republicanism A political belief that holds that we are political animals. Republicans extol the virtues of positive freedom—the freedom of individuals to participate in the affairs of government.

responsible government A convention in parliamentary systems whereby the executive remains in power for so long as it maintains the confidence of the legislative branch.

Rest (the) Countries located in four regions of the global South: Africa, Asia, Latin America, and the Middle East, most having a long history of western colonialism.

revolution The overthrow of a given socio-economic and political order and implementation of a radical transformation.

revolutionary regime A regime where certain elites, groups, and/or the majority have overthrown the given socio-economic and political order and undertaken a radical transformation, usually in the name of a dominated or exploited majority.

rights A legal or moral entitlement.

risk A term used by social scientists to describe personal or social factors that contribute to poverty or personal injury.

rule of law A fundamental principle in liberal democratic political systems. All citizens of a country are governed by a single set of legal rules. These rules are applied equally and impartially to all. No political official is above the law. The rule of law empowers and constrains political behaviour.

self-determination A concept or principle, wherein a people or nation has a human right to freedom from colonial rule and to determine by themselves their destiny.

sentiment-based community A community based on a sentiment that endorses shared values, common interests and goals, participation in public affairs, and ongoing relationships that bind groups of people together.

separation of powers An institutional arrangement reflecting the idea that the liberty of citizens is best secured in those regimes where the executive, legislative, and judicial powers are separated and not fused into one single authority.

sexual division of labour The division of jobs and duties along gender lines.

shock therapy A dramatic response to economic imbalances based on rapid economic liberalization and cut-backs in state expenditure.

simple candidate ballot A ballot on which only the names of the candidates, often with optional identifying information, appear, and voters are simply asked to indicate which one or more of these candidates they prefer.

single member plurality (SMP) An electoral system in which the territory is divided into constituencies and each constituency elects one person (a single member) to the legislature. Individuals representing different political parties compete against each other for the seat and the person who gets the most votes (a plurality) wins. The party that wins the most seats generally goes on to form the government.

single transferable vote A voting procedure employing a preferential (ordinal) ballot in which a person's vote can be transferred from one candidate to another in successive rounds of the counting procedure.

social capital Communal sentiments and actions stemming from these sentiments that add value to society and the political system. Individuals have social capital when they have the education and skills to integrate successfully into society.

social contract The argument by Hobbes and Locke that individuals in a state of nature by mutual consent and agreement form societies and establish governments.

social democracy A democratic regime that uses the state to implement egalitarian redistribution of the wealth produced by a largely capitalist economy.

social exclusion A term used to define those in society that are economically and socially marginalized.

social formation A term applied to a "country" encompassing its given societal, economic, and political systems.

socialism An ideology founded on the recognition of a fundamental division and conflict in capitalist society between social classes. Class divisions are based upon those who own the means of production (the capitalist) and those who do not (the working class or proletariat). The solution to class conflict lies in the public or common ownership of the means of production, a solution to be achieved either through revolution or by working democratically within the existing capitalist system.

socialist feminism A stream of feminist thought that sees women's oppression as fostered and maintained by capitalism and the patriarchal state; the solution lies in challenging the sexual division of labour in the home and the workplace.

socialization of debt A governmental action wherein it takes over the debt incurred by the private sector. In doing so, the burden of responsibility to pay back this converted public debt shifts from private businesses to the average taxpayer. One important consequence of this is the channelling of taxpayers' money toward bringing down the public debt and away from spending in such areas as health, education, and welfare.

social rights Citizenship rights that are necessary for well-being and, thus, for full membership and participation in the political community as defined by the standards and norms prevailing in that community.

social stratification A social hierarchy often based on income or status; division of society.

social welfare liberalism A philosophy of governing resting on the idea that the basic necessities of life should be provided by government for those who are truly in need, for those who are unable to provide for themselves through no fault of their own.

society Refers to the character and composition of one of the four spheres of regimes. Weber argued that the composition of a society would determine the type of state that would evolve: for example, primarily traditional societies would be ruled by monarchies. Marx also studied societies, particularly the way in which class divisions resulted under a capitalist system.

socio-economic growth (development) An ability to produce an adequate and growing supply of goods and services productively and efficiently, to accumulate capital, and to distribute the fruits of production in a relatively equitable manner.

solidarity Membership in the political community, and feelings of belonging associated with acceptance by that community.

sovereignty A legal (*de jure*) and actual (*de facto*) condition whereby states recognize no higher authority either domestically or externally and are thus free to act as they wish. A state's right to manage its affairs internally, without external interference, based on the legal concept of the equality of states.

Speaker of the House A legislative official responsible for overseeing and controlling activity in the legislative assembly.

stakeholders A group of individuals who have identified a common interest in a portion of the more general public interest. They may consider themselves as having a common, sometimes a proprietary, interest in a specific policy area.

Stalinism Refers to the regime of Joseph Stalin, who ruled the Communist Party of the Union of Soviet Socialist Republics (CP-USSR) and the government of the USSR from 1924 to 1953. The regime oversaw the rapid industrialization and increasing military power of the USSR but exercised extreme coercion over citizens, imprisoned, exiled, or "liquidated" suspected dissidents and is widely viewed as having betrayed the democratic, proletarian principles of the international communist movement. Communist parties in the West, which emulated the top-down bureaucratic structure of the CP-USSR and which continued to defend the legacy of Stalinism, were also labelled "Stalinist" by their new left opponents.

standing committee A relatively permanent legislative committee with set responsibilities.

standing orders A set of rules governing activity in the Canadian House of Commons.

state *See* nation-state.

state of nature An imaginary existence without government where all people are equal and free to act as they please.

statute A written law enacted by the legislature.

state sovereignty *See* sovereignty.

sub-culture A different shared way of life within the national cultural setting, characterizing a smaller grouping of people within a country.

subjective Situation in which the observer is part of what is observed or is affected by values and preferences.

surplus value A key relationship of exploitation between capitalists and workers. Surplus value represents the profit that the capitalist gains as a result of selling a product for more than is paid to the worker in wages.

symbolic representation To "symbolize" or be the concrete embodiment of that which was represented.

terrorism An act or repeated acts of violence against arbitrary and/or selectively chosen victims intended to serve political ends by instilling fear in a larger audience.

theory A coherent interpretation or story that orders and makes sense of the world.

Third World A term used to describe the majority of countries in the world or the vast majority of the world's population who live in conditions of poverty, underdevelopment and, often, political instability.

totalitarian An ultra-authoritarian regime that controls virtually all aspects of politics, society, and economy.

trade creation Two regionalized countries together enhancing their overall global trade. The opposite is trade diversion.

trade diversion Two or more member countries of a region increase their exchanges within the region at the expense of the rest of the world. The opposite of trade creation.

traditional authority Power and legitimacy accorded to individuals on the basis of custom or heredity.

traditional society A society characterized by inherited authority and low levels of industrialization, consumption, technology, and diversification.

transnational citizenship Occurs when people identify with more than nationality or nation. Even when people do not have formal citizenship in more than one country, the life of a migrant may be transnational in character through employment and family connections, a diasporic consciousness, and political practices.

transnationalized regime A form of governance carried out by international actors.

Treasury Board Secretariat A central agency of the Government of Canada that has responsibility for overall administrative and management policy.

tribal peoples A legal category used to refer to Indigenous peoples in several countries.

trustee model of representation A perspective on representation that assumes that the first obligation of representatives is to employ their reason and judgment in deliberations regarding governing in the broad national interest.

tyranny of the majority A potentially omnipotent power of the majority. Constitutional guarantees are required so as to curb the majority's potential excesses.

unicameral A regime in which the legislature consists of only one chamber.

unilateral Actions taken by one actor or government.

unipolar moment A condition of global order in which there is a single centre of power.

unitary constitution A constitution in which the sovereignty of the state rests in one government.

universalism A view that laws and policies should treat all citizens the same, irrespective of membership in distinct cultural or identity groups. Universalism collides with demands for recognition and valuing of difference whereby cultural groups are granted distinct rights or treatment in laws and policies.

universal social programs Programs available to all citizens regardless of their income level or their need.

unwritten constitution A constitution where most of a country's key governing principles are not contained in a single document. These principles exist in a combination of written laws and conventions.

urbanization of poverty Anticipated increase in urban (city) poverty levels as one out of every two births is in an urban space.

vanguard A cadre of dedicated revolutionaries. The concept of the vanguard was put forward by Lenin as a means to lead the working class to revolution.

virtue ethics An approach to moral philosophy that emphasizes human flourishing and the uniquely human virtues. Virtue ethicists draw attention to both the consequences of one's decision or act (as in consequentialism) and to the principles guiding the decision or act (as in deontology), but they do so more with a view to judging the individual's moral character than with a view to judging the actions themselves.

vote of no confidence A vote of Parliament that determines whether the executive maintains the support of the legislature.

wage–capital relationship The capital mode of production is defined by the relationship between the proletariat and the bourgeoisie. In this system, workers are forced to sell their labour-power to gain an income to purchase the goods and services they require to live.

war A violent political instrument that continues political intercourse through other means.

Washington Consensus Refers to tacit agreement between the International Monetary Fund, the World Bank, and the United States executive branch over the development policies that the developing countries should follow. The Consensus formed around the key issues of macroeconomic prudence, export-oriented growth, and economic liberalization.

welfare state A form of governance wherein government programs and policies are designed to protect citizens from illness, unemployment, and long-term disability. In modern political debate, a welfare state is said to have a "social safety net."

West (the) Typically refers to countries that have evolved within a liberal and capitalist governing framework.

Western-centred viewpoint An approach that treats the Rest or the global South as a residual category because the character, cultures, traditions, and institutions of the Rest are examined in terms of Western standards, not in terms of its own values. The reference point is the West: the Rest is defined not in terms of what it is but in terms of what it lacks.

world system The idea that the international state system and capitalism have constituted an evolving single global system since the sixteenth century, with a core, periphery, and semi-periphery.

world view A collection of integrated images of the world that serve as a lens through which one interprets the world. It helps the individual to orient to the environment and to organize perceptions as a guide to behaviour, and it acts as a filter for selecting relevant information.

Index